Recovering Lost Footprints

RECOVERING LOST FOOTPRINTS

VOLUME 1

CONTEMPORARY MAYA NARRATIVES

ARTURO ARIAS

Cover image: Láminas 8 y 9 del Códice de Dresden, dibujado por Lacambalam (pages 8 and 9 of the Desden Codex, drawn by Lacambalam). © Lacambalam (Jens Rohark).

Published by State University of New York Press, Albany

Printed in the United States of America

For information, contact State University of New York Press, Albany, NY
www.sunypress.edu

Production, Jenn Bennett
Marketing, Mike Campochiaro

Library of Congress Cataloging-in-Publication Data
Names: Arias, Arturo, 1950– author.
Title: Recovering lost footprints. Volume 1, Contemporary Maya narratives / Arturo Arias.
Other titles: Contemporary Maya narratives
Description: Albany : State University of New York Press, [2017] | Includes bibliographical references and index.
Identifiers: LCCN 2016058082 (print) | LCCN 2017018899 (ebook) | ISBN 9781438467412 (e-book) | ISBN 9781438467399 (alk. paper)
Subjects: LCSH: Maya literature--History and criticism. | Guatemalan literature—History and criticism.
Classification: LCC PM3968 (ebook) | LCC PM3968 .A75 2017 (print) | DDC 897/.42709—dc23
LC record available at https://lccn.loc.gov/2016058082

10 9 8 7 6 5 4 3 2 1

CONTENTS

ACKNOWLEDGMENTS

This book has been a long time in the making. Whereas in-depth research began ten years ago, I can trace its origin to a night in the spring of 1981 in Mexico City. I was living at Avenida Universidad 1900, a large complex of forty towers located a few blocks from UNAM, Mexico's National University. In a close-by tower lived Maya Ixil leader Pablo Ceto, one of the founders of the CUC, Spanish acronym for the Committee for Peasant Unity. CUC was the first-ever grassroots organization in Guatemala to be founded by Mayas and directed exclusively by Mayas. In that famous spring night of 1981, Pablo invited me to dinner in his apartment. In a memorable conversation that evening, he confided me what was then a secret. Though Mayas were supporting various revolutionary organizations struggling against Guatemala's military dictatorship, they were keeping their true goals a secret. Pablo called this "*La conspiración dentro de la conspiración*" ("the conspiracy within the conspiracy"). The conspiracy consisted of trying to move up the revolutionary ladder as far as possible, but not to further the Ladino revolutionaries' goals as a whole; rather, the goal was to further Mayas' own secret goals of agency. I was shocked at his confession and asked him bluntly why had he trusted me with this information. He said he and his then-wife had been watching me for some time, and both had concluded I was not only trustworthy, but someone who could work with Mayas for the rest of his life. I felt as if a lifetime gift had been given to me. Within months, Maya Nobel laureate Rigoberta Menchú—still unknown at the time—was living in my house, after arriving as a refugee in Mexico City. Later came Maya Kaqchikel leader Domingo Hernández Ixcoy to share my home and, towards the end of my stay in Mexico City, Maya K'iche' scholars Francisca Álvarez Medrano and her sister Carmen. I learned from all of them, shared my daily life, my home, and they captured my soul forever.

I also want to thank the many colleagues at the at the University of Texas at Austin with whom we often discussed these topics, debated them, or else, furthered Native American and Indigenous research and shared observations as a team. These include those colleagues who created the Native American and Indigenous Studies Center: Shannon Speed—presently at UCLA—Luis Cárcamo-Huechante, Nora England, Kelly McDonough, Sergio Romero, Pauline Strong, and Luis Urrieta. While at Texas I also enjoyed the support and friendship of David Stuart of the Mesoamerican Center, always generous and willing to share his knowledge. Above all, I want to thank Charles R. Hale, Director of the Lozano Long Institute of Latin American Studies and the Benson Latin American Library, who was always the best of friends, an ethusiastic supporter, and while LLILAS-Benson Director, awarded me research leaves.

Outside of Texas, my network of supporters was enormous, and I risk failing to mention all. I especially want to thank Linda Tuhiwai Smith who organized a Maya-Māori Seminar at the University of Waikato in Aotearoa (New Zealand) in 2013; Kathryn Lehman who invited me as a Hood Fellow to the University of Auckland, thus enabling my contact and exchange with Māori scholars and communities; Elizabeth Monasterios, who facilitated my attendance at Journadas Andinas de Literatura Latinoamericana (JALLA) in La Paz, thus augmenting my knowledge of Aymara culture; Maya K'iche' scholar Emilio del Valle Escalante, who shares our achievements with a wonderful sense of humor; my former graduate students Alicia Ivonne Estrada and Adam Coon, who probably taught me more on Indigenous issues than I had taught them; Maya K'iche' scholar Irma Alicia Velásquez Nimatuj and Maya K'iche' poet Rosa Chávez who read and critiqued the Spanish version of this text; Maya K'iche' leader Domingo Hernández Ixcoy, Director of the Uk'ux B'e Maya Association who always makes a point of keeping me informed on Maya issues in Guatemala; Pablo Ceto, who started me on this path, and is now President of the Ixil University in Nebaj; and Rigoberta Menchú, to whose cause I have rallied during many moments in my life. Old friendships seldom die. And then, all those others who know who they are, but would be impossible to list in such short space.

Finally, but most important of all, I want to thank the greatest love of my life, Jill Robbins, without whom nothing—not this book, not others, not research—would ever have been possible. She has not only been with me through so many changes and struggles that would have tested the toughest of people, but has also led me through a path of joy and discovery that I would never have expected before I met her. There's magic in everything she does, and I welcome some of the glowing powder that enables me to go forward in what is otherwise a bleak world. Thanks, love. I would no longer be around without you.

Introduction

My overall project analyzes Abya Yala's Indigenous literary narratives written from approximately the mid-twentieth century to the present. Abya Yala is the name that Indigenous peoples give to the Latin American continent, a notion to which I return in the last section of this introduction. By "narratives" I mean—from the perspective of literary genres—novels, short stories, and *testimonios*. Going beyond the nature of genres themselves, however, I understand narrativeness as a notion that is opposed to poetry and poetics. Narrativeness privileges storytelling and prose in a more general sense, over poetic genres that are more semiotic, establishing autonomous systems of significance. Though "narrative" has become a contested term, narratives are, in their simplest form, structured discursive practices—which, as we know, can also be multidimensional ones not subordinated to sound—that articulate signifiers for telling or retelling stories, whether recalled or imagined, that, manipulated to a certain degree by the writer/storyteller, ultimately points to larger ontological issues that, in Indigenous cases, often close the divide between nature and culture.

Whereas my analysis is limited to contemporary written Indigenous narratives—and to Guatemalan Maya narratives in this particular volume—there is an obvious connection between written narratives and the heritage of Native American and Indigenous oral traditions as discursive forms intended for live audiences, with varying sets of performativity and performative protocols.[1] In both cases, Indigenous narratives recount cultural histories reenacting aspects of their given epistemologies that Mayas label "cosmovisions," a category to which I also return to in the Indigenous imaginations and alternative modernities section.

Though writing in their native languages, the authors I examine in this book do not live isolated from the West.[2] They interact with non-Indigenous agents and agencies—whether governmental agencies, NGOs, or international foundations—who may train, support, encourage, or finance these literary efforts and movements. Asymmetrical relations of power inevitably materialize in the production of their textualities, in seeing them come out in print, and in activating their circulation and consumption through heterogeneous venues, whether this happens in their home countries or beyond. These factors are analyzed in the four chapters of this book on the emergence of Guatemalan Maya narratives and in subsequent volumes. Accordingly, though most authors discussed here are native speakers, were born in their respective communities, have learned to write their texts in their own native language—if not simultaneously helping to codify their linguistic signs in dictionaries—and consider themselves grassroots activists who belonged organically to their respective communities, they also engage, or have engaged, with many of the aforementioned non-Indigenous agents or agencies in a collaborative and productive relationship. Despite controversial accusations of Westernization, "selling out," or even recolonization in some cases, this process of engagement has begun to yield a significant and valuable corpus of Indigenous-authored fictional narratives throughout the hemisphere.

The explanations behind the emergence of Indigenous narratives are complex. Suffice to state for now that reasons vary from one country to the next. They are linked to the consequences of the 1980s revolutionary crisis, in the case of Guatemala, and to the emergence of Zapatismo in Chiapas, Mexico, in 1994. With the ensuing reaction of the Mexican state to combat the Zapatista insurgency with a wide array of developmentalist models and projects, a greater number of fictional narratives written by Indigenous authors in their own languages emerged in the Mesoamerican region. South America has seen an abundance of poetry written by Indigenous authors emerge during roughly the same period, yet there is considerably less fictional production so far. This may, of course, change in the near future.

These volumes consist not only of explanations of how Indigenous narratives made their appearance in recent decades, cataloging the major texts and authors, and elaborating a discursive critique of these narratives, but primarily seek to evidence the foundational, critical, and political significance of this body of work. In my understanding, these still little-known textualities constitute an epistemic change in the Latin American "lettered city," to borrow Uruguayan critic Angel Rama's conception of the power of written discourse in the historical formation of Latin American societies.

In Rama's argumentation, since colonial times, institutional and legal powers have been administered through a specialized cadre of elite men called "letrados" (men of letters), the producers of symbolic capital. Their autonomy enabled them to feel at home in all kinds of genres, and they covered the terrain presently circumscribed by traditional disciplines. Letrados were, for the most part, *Criollos*, that is, full-blooded Spaniards born in the Latin American colonies. They were the early protagonists of national public spheres during and immediately after independence from Spain. Described by Román de la Campa as intellectuals whose "lust for power" coexisted with "isolated acts of literary transgression" (74), they intervened to legitimize exemplary narratives of national formation and integration in the process of constructing the nation itself as a symbolic entity. As such, they constituted their national imaginaries through discourses, symbols, images, and rites.

Letrados imagined themselves at the vanguard of progress, often playing a role integrating those of military leader, prophet, priest, judge, and person of letters. All of these were linked to an active political career and to political considerations. Nineteenth-century literary production, then, established an ideological hegemony that interpellated individuals and transformed them into subjects who identified with the discursive formation named by the letrado. Following this logic, we can claim that since the 1800s, Latin American thinkers produced a certain kind of knowledge that articulated the collective imaginaries and symbolic codes framed in variously written cultural manifestations with their political, historical, and social context. In its broadest and most general sense, this could be the generally recognized definition of cultural studies as we know it today. Letrados were likewise involved in an intuitive search for a socio-semiotic reorientation of their understanding of themselves and of their national place in the world, while also attempting to define what modernity meant for their young nations. The problematics and methodologies of Latin American cultural studies thus predate the generally recognized field itself. They were centered on issues of colonialism and postcolonialism, although in relation to Latin American identity, and they intuitively configured a new thinking, an event, an encounter, and a response long before the Birmingham model—traditionally credited with the invention of the concept of cultural studies in the 1950s, primarily through the efforts of Stuart Hall and Raymond Williams—or the French school of cultural studies that emerged in the 1960s, whose work emphasized the role of practice and embodiment in social dynamics. However, all these configurations, publications, and the like were always crafted in Castilian[3] (Portuguese, in the Brazilian case), and always within Eurocentric parameters that never questioned hegemonic Western teleology, thus exhibiting a provincial—"colonialized," Peruvian sociologist Aníbal Quijano would say—predisposition to believe that Western European modes of thinking were in fact not only universal but also superior to all others.

Emerging Indigenous textualities disrupt, in consequence, the myth of homogeneous nation-states. They operate in unprivileged peripheral spaces. They aspire to reterritorialize displaced subalternized and racialized identities through their belated, and critical, embrace of the "lettered city," with publications written not in Castilian (or Portuguese) but in their own languages, though all texts are published bilingually so that non-native readers can have access to their transgressive representations. Challenging Western parameters, alternative-knowledge producers have become the purveyors of self-generated cognizance, one that originates in nontraditional and unconventional sites, even if it is expressed in what would appear to be a traditional, even anachronistic, form: the novel. Indigenous narrators thus break the myth that information, social imaginaries, and learning are produced exclusively by cosmopolitan letrados or else through the disciplining of hegemonic academic institutions. In so doing, these narratives provincialize cosmopolitan critics, writers, and academic institutions, challenging the Western-centered knowledge-producing machine. Their imaginaries problematize not only issues such as the confluence of nation, class, ethnicity, and/or constitution of subjectivities but also the tense negotiations of pluricultural and multilingual issues within given nation-states. Indigenous textualities enable racialized and subalternized subjects to reacquire an actualized sense of their world, offering a continuous understanding of alternative codes of ethics and beingness furnished by their respective cosmovisions.

Indigenous political struggles from roughly the 1980s on yielded many forms of decolonial practices among their grassroots intellectuals and artists. The examination of these textual representations enables an analysis of these issues scattered throughout the social imaginaries crafted by Indigenous narratives. Their analysis also grapples with the problems these writers face, not only in converting to written form what had been for the most part oral cultures from the Spanish invasion to the present, but also with the complex implications that this very process invokes.[4] Briefly, this signifies problems of codifying standardized written forms of Indigenous languages, translation processes, and the re-creation of the same representations in both their native language and in Castilian, as is explained later.

Needless to say, Indigenous narratives articulate political and cultural critiques of the never-ending racism, violence, and overall abjection in which their communities have been submerged since the Spanish invasion. Their textualities formulate critiques that inevitably fall within the purview of decolonial perspectives that signal new directions for the future. Yet when examining Native American and Indigenous viewpoints, it is important to uphold Tuck and Yang's recommendation regarding Native American studies that decolonization "is not accountable to settlers, or settler futurity. Decolonization is accountable to Indigenous sovereignty and futurity" (35).[5] We may perhaps be "lucky" in Abya Yala that Mestizo cultures have moved more in the direction of the "*indio permitido*," pointed out by Rivera Cusicanqui and Hale,[6] than in the recolonializing mode where "decoloniality becomes a metaphor," in Tuck and Yang's words. Later in this introduction, I probe the categories "decolonial" and "decoloniality." For now I simply state that I intend to analyze how these textualities mobilize identitary and decolonial issues in their discursivities, to both denounce and gain credibility among their potential readers—be they local or regional, national in some cases, international in a few—but also to position how they may be perceived within their poorer, often illiterate communities, whose members may not be able to read them but are privy to the recognition gained by authors of their same ethnicity living—if only at times—in their midst.

Ultimately, the analysis of these volumes intends to explore the full range of Abya Yala's Indigenous narrative production, starting with the present one on Guatemalan Maya narratives. I remain convinced that the vast complexity of contemporary Indigenous cultural production, hemispherically and globally, will benefit not only their local communities as they move forward in contemporary hostile environments, but also non-Indigenous global citizens seeking political alternatives to the Western conundrum leading the planet in a path to destruction.

This research is inevitably written within the context of what has taken place in US academia in the first decades of the twenty-first century. My text has not been produced in a vacuum or without continuous dialogical and intertextual relations with scholarship produced by a wide array of academics working for the most part—though not exclusively—in the aforementioned institutional spaces, who—be they in the humanities or in the social sciences—have configured their work within vast and complex categories that if only by default, fit under the ample label of "Latin American cultural studies." This heterogeneous group of scholars have all in their own ways elaborated a critique of the symbolic production and everyday living experiences of social reality in the continent, while displaying concerns with issues of subalternization, indigeneities, Afro-descendant issues, racism, and/or coloniality from multiple perspectives. It is a critical reflection that confronts the alleged universality of European modes of thinking, and often—though not always—blends grassroots "knowledges otherwise," as Arturo Escobar named them, with political activism, as explained further along in Note 11.

The inevitable nature of this institutional reality means that the approach chosen in these volumes emerges from within this complex set of ideas, debates, and locations. This introduction is divided into two parts, and these also divide into other sections. The first part is an attempt to position where I see the study of Indigenous literatures emerging. In consequence, this part includes: (1) a summary of what has been labeled "Latin American cultural studies," and (2) a problematization of Marxism's conceptual flaws in its approach to Indigenous issues.[7] The previous critique also enables me to explain (3) the emergence of decoloniality and its questioning of Eurocentrism. After all, this project also aims at dialoguing with, and debating, within, what has been identified generically as US cultural studies, a site where postcolonial studies still dominate over newer trends such as Native American and Indigenous studies, and where Latin American studies remains fairly marginal. Still, US cultural studies has—given this country's role in the world—a degree of global reach, resulting from its presence and influence in many academic institutions in all continents.

The second part explains what these volumes intend to do, both conceptually and methodologically. The second part consists of four sections: (1) a summary of how global indigeneities are presently framed and how they may help advance this particular research; (2) the traits and effects of how these narratives may be understood, by examining the present location of current conceptualizations and their implications; (3) an explanation of Indigenous imaginations and alternative modernities. This section also deals with the problems of bridging Indigenous and theoretical knowledges, the problematics of translation that remains a central issue in any critique, while also naming limitations and potential problems in the usage of Western modes of criticism that nevertheless seem inevitable and justified. Ultimately, I explore work being done by global Indigenous scholars—primarily in the Pacific—who are also wrestling with critical and Indigenous theories and methodologies; (4) a brief explanation of the choice of the name Abya Yala.

PART I

Reconsidering Latin American Cultural Studies in the United States

Latin American cultural studies emerged primarily from within the social sciences in the 1960s, when important thinkers such as Brazilian anthropologist Darcy Ribeiro, Brazilian educator and philosopher Paulo Freire, as well as Mexican sociologists Rodolfo Stavenhagen and Pablo González Casanova, to name just a few emblematic figures, fused what had been the traditional cultural essay form with sociological research to account for the events then taking place on the continent. These systems of thought included dependency theory, theology of liberation, the pedagogy of the oppressed, and the critique of internal colonialism. This new form of critical studies, an offshoot and critique of Marxism, would constitute the economic, social, and political backbone of interdisciplinary cultural studies as they emerged in the late 1970s and 1980s in US academia. Puerto Rican professor Julio Ramos has been cited as arguing that the difference between traditional Latin Americanist thinking up to the 1970s and Latin American cultural studies as it evolved in the United States in the 1980s was rooted in the fact that the former evinced a belief in the integrative capacity of national literatures and art, whereas the latter criticized the concept of a national culture as an apparatus of power (*Paradojas de la letra*, 36). Perhaps it would be better to say that earlier essays, however heterogeneous and irreducible to the autonomous principles they might have been, were framed by a set of epistemological and metaphysical principles aimed at nation building, a phenomenon that presupposed economic modernization, cultural modernism, and democratization, whereas Latin American cultural studies, as we know it now, emerged from the fissures, cracks, and fault lines of the failed process of nation building and its nadir in the late 1980s.

By the end of the 1980s, most academics agreed that the macro-narratives of the 1960s were no longer adequate for explaining the fast changes introduced by emergent globalization (del Sarto, "Introduction," 156). One of the consequences of the collapse of macro-narratives was the idea that literature and all forms of "high culture" had lost their position as the cornerstones of national cultures, that traditional intellectuals had in turn lost their ground as letrados guiding national communities, and that the very idea of nation-states as the only (or at least the privileged) political and cultural synthesis faced serious, perhaps insurmountable challenges. This complex set of ideas led to a revision of the theoretical models of the 1960s. The reformulation of methodologies resulted in the conformation of what would come to be labeled "Latin American cultural studies." Nevertheless, Argentinian scholar Ana del Sarto takes pains to underline that these creative revisions, even when they ventured into new epistemological paths, were done in dialogue with the continent's tradition of critical thinking: in her own words, they were "not the product of epistemological ruptures but instead of concrete historical continuities" (157).

Needless to say, what some people consider a new epistemological path, others consider a rupture.

In the early 1990s the recently constituted Latin American Subaltern Studies Group called into question the role of the academy in reading and representing the subaltern. For these scholars, academic work should focus on making subaltern voices heard in academia (Rodríguez, "Reading Subalterns," [9]). The popularity of Rigoberta Menchú's testimonio provided them with an anti-literary literary genre with which to make their case. However, as Uruguayan scholar Abril Trigo points out, they failed to realize the epistemological fetishization of the text as the ground of unmediated truth and the consequent political fetishization of the poetics of solidarity that enabled the critic's identification with the testimonial subject (Rodríguez, "Reading Subalterns," [78]). The ongoing debate that subalternism generated puts into question the very nature of cultural studies. Nevertheless, by understanding the latter category as a mechanism for problematizing cultural and cross-cultural practices, scholars could work across linguistic, national, ethnic, and cultural borders, not to mention differences along social class. In this transition, the object of study shifted from the formal aspects of given cultural genres, usually within specific national frameworks, to the portrayal of everyday cultural detail, nontraditional or alternative knowledge producers, and the conditions and effects of sedimented linguistic turns. In this sense, Latin American cultural studies allowed for the exploration of imaginary, excentric representations of otherness, underlining both the creative energy of subaltern events and their attempts to create more just and egalitarian societies in the face of globalization.

After peaking in the first half of the 1990s with subaltern studies and its debates on *testimonio*, Latin American cultural studies seemed to enter an epistemological and institutional crisis by the end of the century. It was roughly at this juncture, with important Indigenous mobilizations taking place in the hemisphere, that a critique to move thinking beyond Western and Eurocentric conceptualizations provided a new way of framing the issues of cultural production and agency. Decolonial agendas began to appear in US institutions at around this time. Some tried to derive their principles and/or goals in conjunction or in dialogue with a broad number of Latin American academics. These included Colombian Santiago Castro-Gómez, American-born Catherine Walsh working in Ecuador, and Venezuelan sociologist Edgardo Lander, among others. Briefly, decolonial studies marked the Spanish invasion of the Americas in 1492 as the initial point for the creation of the centrality and superiority of European knowledge. The multiple implications of this latter debate are reviewed and problematized in the following sections of this introduction.

Marxism's Problematic Legacy and Place-based Epistemologies

It would be infantile of any serious thinker not to recognize the significance of Marxist thought in reshaping our understanding of Western modernity and its implications. Most Latin American academics of my generation, myself included, began their careers as Marxists, as did many interlocutors in the United States and Europe. Neither can we deny the Soviet Union's looming presence, without glossing over its systemic flaws. This nation was instrumental in forcing workers' rights and social benefits in Western hegemonic countries during the early decades of the twentieth century, and its armies defeated Nazism. In that sense we have to recognize that globalizing neoliberal policies could rise due only to the Soviet Union's waning power and subsequent disapperance. Yet it would be equally naive to forgo the systemic flaws that made the Soviet Union a model impossible to imitate elsewhere and not admit Marxism's limitations. Paraphrasing Hungarian philosopher Georg Lukács, Marxism is for me the maximum possible consciousness of Eurocentric modern thinking. The description itself makes it evident that this conception has virtually no decolonial implications for three-quarters of humanity.

Marxism, after all, was a system of thought that remained anchored in the European Enlightenment and was logically articulated through all forms of Western modern thinking. It was conceived for the German industrialized state. In practice, more often than not this led to dangerous reductionisms. I do not demonize Marxism. But I do think it is awkward that some leading scholars still consider it contemporary, some fifty years after its "crisis," and twenty-five years after the Berlin Wall's collapse. I acknowledge its critical importance for a Western-centered world, and I owe it an affective debt. Marxism offered me, and many others on the Latin American continent, the basic tools with which to think critically to develop counterhegemonic practices. Because of it, I was able to understand the cultural constraints exemplified within critical questions when, as a young man, I began to interrogate the West's historical formation and the horror it represented for three-quarters of the world's humanity, especially for countries such as the one in which I was born. Precisely for affective—more than ideological—reasons, many scholars emerging from within this trajectory have had a difficult time abandoning it. This attitude oftentimes allows its centripetal force to keep us looking at the imperial center and ignore knowledge production outside of it. We lose sight of the cultural underpinnings keeping us within this "truth." Indigenous and Afro-descendant knowledges are located outside Western forms of knowledge. In consequence, a pro-Marxist bias still prevents scholars from turning their backs to Western-centric ideas and immersing themselves in Indigenous and Afro-descendant knowledges, which still remain elusive, if not invisible, for the great majority of Western Marxist scholars.

In Guatemala, the coded elements imposed by the coloniality of power and displayed by abyssal thinking implied that Indigenous discursivity, as it emerged in the late 1980s and bloomed in the 1990s, violently displaced the political thought of Ladino Marxist cadres who represented the nation's revolutionary leadership from the fall of democracy in 1954 to the signing of the Guatemalan Peace Accords in 1996. (Mestizos are historically known in Guatemala as *Ladinos*; contemporary Mayas make a distinction between both terms. For brevity's sake and succinct understanding: a Ladino is deemed by Mayas as a Eurocentric racist subject who denies his/her mixed blood, whereas a Mestizo is a non-racist subject of mixed Indigenous/European descent who may manifest an alliance with—or a recognition of—Indigenous perspectives).[8] Indigenous discursivity problematized Marxist certainty, transforming it into merely a Eurocentric point of view that privileged class struggle. It thus destabilized and decentered this singular form of modern certainty. It showed Guatemalan Ladino revolutionary leaders that they did not live in a homogeneous and coherent nation. Rather, they were participating in a thoroughly phantasmic one.

As stated in the section on letrados, Western modernity granted the exclusionary monopoly on creating national imaginaries to the lettered and preferentially upper-class, Mestizo, heterosexual men. The exclusionary character of this monopoly is at the core of the modern epistemological disputes between Ladino and Indigenous regimes of truth and knowledge. The traditional Guatemalan Left understood modernity from a Ladino Western-centric perspective, while also enlisting and embracing Mayas for their cause. Mayas, however, were no innocent victims caught between two fires. They clearly understood the historical opportunity offered to them. Revolutionary movements enabled them to undermine the pillars sustaining the system of oppression. From this experience and their exercise of agency, they opened up a new epistemic perspective by showing that allegedly premodern subjects were perfectly capable of grasping all the tools that modernity could afford them. Mayas asserted their difference to transform themselves and reimagine their communities within the framework of a legitimate political conflict. Despite this, Ladino revolutionaries and analysts have systematically refused to account for the incompatibility of Ladino and Maya cultural forms. This systematic neglect also reflected a dearth in the sources documenting Indigenous reports of the Guatemalan civil war. In this logic, it is not surprising that, as of the 1990s, Mayas agreed on their own to rename the nation-state as Iximuleu, which stands for land ("*uleu*") and maize ("*ixim*"). Thus, the "land of maize," in reference to the sacred understanding that human beings, as depicted in the *Popol Wuj*—the heart of the Mesoamerican cultural matrix—could not be created without the germination of maize. As is explained in chapter 2, after harvesting their corn field, the Founding Parents ground the yellow ears of ripe maize nine times, the number of levels of the underworld. They did the same with the white ears of corn. Out of this powder, mixed with water and placed over fire, were created the original human beings, the "men of maize."

Decoloniality and Eurocentric Perspectives

Given this book's attentiveness to contemporary Indigenous narratives and the premise that these opuses articulate decolonial discursivities, we must first take stock of the meaning and impact of "decoloniality" within the United States and Latin America, as indicated in the first section of this introduction.

Immanuel Wallerstein argues that the turning point in perceptions questioning Eurocentric perspectives began with the social movements that peaked globally in 1968.[9] In his understanding, the widespread revolts in the pan-European world, including what used to be the Socialist bloc, as well as elsewhere in what he labeled "the South" (54), all expressed deep skepticism about what had been the traditional Left and called for a new look at strategies. In the United States, the civil rights movement, the feminist movement, the Chicano movement, the Native American movement, the queer movement, and the ecological movement—to name only the better-known ones—shattered the previous paradigm. Most of these tendencies were replicated in Latin America by the 1970s. Subsequent Indigenous revolts in Guatemala, Mexico (Chiapas), Ecuador, Bolivia, Peru, Chile, and other sites led to new, alternative forms of political activity that, confronting the alleged "universality" of Eurocentric thinking, named alternative epistemic spaces. Argentinian scholar Walter Mignolo, professor at Duke University, labeled these perspectives the "geopolitics of knowledge," a notion developed from his seminal book *The Darker Side of the Renaissance* (1995).[10] The Indigenous analyses resulting from their struggles are plural in the sense that they are not systemic and they did not emerge at any one place. They came to light as critical responses to specific political struggles of hemispheric Indigenous populations marked by coloniality. Subsequently, they acquired the status of "knowledges otherwise" as Colombian sociologist Arturo Escobar named them.[11] The appellative conferred upon them by anthropologist Charles R. Hale and the Latin American Studies Association (LASA) in 2005 was *Otros Saberes* ("Other knowledges"), as they promoted deep and sustained collaborations between intellectuals inside and outside the academy to produce knowledge validated by, and useful to both. Indigenous collaborators worked on their own practices from within their singular histories, subjectivities, and cosmovisions.[12] In chapter 2 of *Otros Saberes*, Keisha-Khan Y. Perry and Joanne Rappaport state that North American academics have for the most part overlooked the significant body of critical thought produced by social movements or Indigenous and Afro-descendant communities in Latin America. They understand these communities as simultaneously knowledge producers and political actors, producing, in their words, "a kind of theory-in-action that merges political militancy and cultural renewal" (31). Latin American social researchers are, in turn, politically engaged and often work with grassroots movements as both activists and researchers. Perry and Rappaport conclude that the emergence of organic intellectuals in some Indigenous and Afro-descendant communities led to "a closer working relationship between activists and academics" (46), enabling community researchers to play protagonic roles and to find their own voices. As scholar Catherine Walsh—working at the Universidad Andina Simón Bolívar in Quito, Ecuador—noted as well, the research produced by Indigenous scholars radically challenged and transformed "the historic processes of epistemic and existential subalternization . . . opening up new analytic, critical, post/trans-continental, and decolonial possibilities of knowledge and existence" (16).[13] The analytic foundations of these modes of thinking produced a place-based epistemology that inevitably articulated new theoretical and political logics. It confirmed, to summon Peruvian anthropologist Marisol de la Cadena (2007), that heightening social conflict, new citizens' protagonism, and abandonment of traditional political party practices, could lead to the ontological-political decentering of modern politics. Escobar labeled these processes an alternative modernization with a decolonial project.[14]

Regardless of whether these positionalities were named "coloniality of power" (Mignolo, Quijano), "modernity/coloniality research program"

(Escobar), or "decolonial swerve" (Castro-Gomez, Grosfoguel), all theorists embracing them, whether residing in the United States or in Latin America, agreed that the Spanish invasion in 1492 was the first marker and constitutive element of modernity, a fact ignored by mainstream European and Anglo scholarship that still dated modernity from the Enlightenment. They equally concurred with the point introduced by Quijano in 1991 that this epistemic change not only constituted a pattern of continual production of racialized identities and an unequal hierarchy whereby European identities and knowledge were considered superior to all others in what amounted to a caste system, but also generated mechanisms of social domination that preserved this social classification into the present. In his understanding, the coloniality of power was not in opposition to modernity but constituted its "dark side," as Mignolo added in his 1995 text. Coloniality in this sense was not limited to the colonial period, which ended for most of Latin America in the first quarter of the nineteenth century. Coloniality meant that, despite political independences from Spain or Portugal, the pattern elaborated by Quijano continued to our day, structuring processes of racialization, subalternization, and knowledge production. For this reason Mignolo labeled it a "matrix of power" ("The Logic of Coloniality and the Limits of Poscoloniality," 109).

In this sense, Chilean historian Claudia Zapata Silva, when noting the critical importance of the emergence of Latin American Indigenous intellectuals since the 1970s, has observed that decolonial issues are incorporated in their writings from the very start in a multiplicity of dimensions that appear from the moment when organic Indigenous movements are able to exercise agency and place their own situtation at the center of their demands (349). Yet at the beginning of her introduction, she states that the contribution of these particular intellectual actors to the elaboration of critical discourses remains invisibilized to this day (11).[15] As we can gather from Zapata Silva's abundant evidence, decoloniality is not just a theory. It is primarily a visceral reaction against coloniality leading to concrete, organized, political actions, where the ancestral principles and historic struggles of Afro-descendants and Indigenous peoples begin to disrupt, transgress, and traverse Western thinking. This disruption, transgression, and traversing continuously advance new notions of interculturality and decoloniality.

At the same time, this is not just a phenomenon taking place in Abya Yala. Renowned Māori scholar Linda Tuhiwai Smith skilfully crafts her understanding of this category in the same sense, as I explain in a later section of this introduction. Its relationship to political activism is also popular in the Pacific region, as substantiated by Noenoe Silva (2004), Timote

Vaioleti (2006), J. Kēhaulani Kauanui (2008), Maria Riet Delsing (2009), and Leonie Pihama (2011), to cite a small but significant cluster of thinkers.[16] In the Americas, despite the political protagonism of Indigenous movements since the 1980s and the conceptual articulation of their discursivities more often than not based on their respective cosmovisions and epistemologies, decoloniality remains somewhat ensnared in theoretical debates. This issue is more of a statement about academic power relations in both US academia and in Latin American institutions, as well as on proprietary rights regarding conceptual invention in a shrinking humanistic environment, than it is about scholars' respect for Indigenous agency and about their willingness to collaborate on equal terms with nontraditional knowledge producers.

Consider as example the prologue to Santiago Castro-Gómez and Ramón Grosfoguel's 2007 edited volume, *El giro decolonial: Reflexiones para una diversidad epistémica más allá del capitalismo global*: The decolonial swerve: Reflections for an epistemic diversity beyond global capitalism.[17] This prologue exposes Eurocentric perspectives and teleologies. Yet the authors' explanation remains mired within cosmopolitan theoretical debates, rather than engaged with Indigenous or Afro-descendant knowledge-producers. Their elucidation fits within US academic debates, but colonialized subjects remain invisible. Castro Gómez and Grosfoguel's stance on decoloniality identifies the salient problem from within the realm of critics of Occidentalism located in US academic circles. Decoloniality is seen through inference—but only by inference—as a defense of subalternized and racialized peoples, as a result of the conceptual logic of the prologue's premises. How Indigenous or Afro-descendant peoples view the world is expunged. Given the dialogic intercourses with Eurocentric theorists, readers would be convinced that they were the writers' primary interlocutors. The logical implications would be that Indigenous (and Afro-descendant) subjects were not an integral part of this conversation. As racialized subjects have known for a more than half a millennium, no matter who is debating whom, they will always be the "naturalized" "born" losers.[18]

It is because of academic stances such as those that some South American theorists closely associated to grassroots activist Indigenous scholars, such as Silvia Rivera Cusicanqui, have responded in strong terms to some of these approaches. Rivera Cusicanqui is a Bolivian Aymara sociologist who draws from Quechua and Aymara cosmologies for her work. She is a past director and longtime member of the Taller de Historia Oral Andina (Workshop on Andean Oral History) which she founded and promoted with her Aymara students in 1983. She was also an activist in the Katarista movement, a revolutionary Aymara organization founded in the 1970s of which Bolivia's Vice President Álvaro García Linera formed part. Let us, as illustration, heed Rivera Cusicanqui's words on the matter, while also keeping in mind that some of her harshness has more to due with the internal struggles and contradictions of the Workshop on Andean Oral History than with a genuine debate with US-centered decolonial scholars.

> En 1983, cuando Aníbal Quijano hablaba de los movimientos y levantamientos del campesinado andino como "prepolíticos"—en un texto que oportunamente critiqué—me hallaba escribiendo "Oprimidos pero no vencidos," una lectura radicalmente divergente del significado y pertinencia de las movilizaciones indígenas en los Andes para las luchas del presente. (56)
>
> (In 1983, when Aníbal Quijano was labelling the Andean peasantry's movements and uprisings as "pre-political"—in a text that I appropriately critiqued—I was in the process of writing "Oppressed but Not Defeated," a radically divergent reading of the significance and relevance of Indigenous mobilizations in the Andean region for present struggles; my translation).

Moreover, she adds:

> Los Mignolo y compañía han construído [*sic*] un pequeño imperio dentro del imperio, recuperando estratégicamente los aportes de la escuela de los estudios de la subalternidad de la India y de múltiples vertientes latinoamericanas de reflexión crítica sobre la colonización y la descolonización. (58)
>
> (Mignolo and his followers have built a small empire within the empire, strategically recuperating the contributions of India's subaltern school as well as multiple Latin American perspectives on critical reflection about colonization and decolonization; my translation).

For activists such as Rivera Cusicanqui, one cannot talk of decolonialization nor articulate a theory about it without first implementing its practice in the field with the consent of Indigenous communities. Decoloniality is an everyday living practice, not something learned rhetorically to achieve a finite theoretical goal, as Zapata Silva pointed out. Most Indigenous communities have pre-Hispanic local concepts addressing similar behavioral patterns. For example, Native American scholar Kelly McDonough has signaled how, in the Nahua-speaking region of the Huasteca Veracruzana,[19] the Náhuatl concept addressing this issue is named "ixtlamatini":

> Intellectual, Knowledge, (ix)tlamatini, (ix)tlamatiliztli
>
> My use of the terms "intellectual" and "knowledge producer" requires some elaboration. They stand for individuals who are producers and interpreters of wisdom (broadly defined as cultural, historical, and political knowledges), acquired by experience and/or study, which is then shared in and/or beyond his/her own community. This may not be precisely what is understood by a Western definition of the term for several reasons, namely the nature and the source of knowledge. (6)[20]

The concept evidently implies that no individual can be a teacher or guide by being simply bookish. To be recognized as a teacher/guide, an individual needs experience in the community's affairs. Not having it would presuppose an implicit lack of knowledge of how to grasp the basic but paramount issues that are vital to Indigenous communities. Trust has to be earned *in situ*. An interview, for instance, is not just a means to obtain data from a "native informant." It is a visit in which the interviewer is a guest in someone else's memories and in someone else's mind. A most respectful and ritualized dialogic relationship needs to be forged before such an exchange may even take place. "People" issues are not just in the background. They are an integral part that pushes forth and carries out decolonial changes on a daily basis. If we were to engage decoloniality strictly on careerist grounds, it would lack a moral center.

We could articulate a strong deconstructive critique of Rivera Cusicanqui's vitriolic remarks regarding the US academy. "Visceral," we could call it, to recast Bolivian scholar Javier Sanjinés's conceptualization of Indigenous responses in *Mestizaje Upside Down* (2004). But we should not ignore the source of her displeasure and exasperation. Her speech may be "excitable," as Judith Butler would have it, equivocal, and possibly injurious to Mignolo, Catherine Walsh, Enrique Dussel, and Sanjinés, thus "professionally" damaging her, as it lowers her perceived seriousness and credibility in the eyes of the cosmopolitan academic world. But we should also explore and be receptive to the source of her vexation. Hers is a vulnerability common to Indigenous communities. This is because, for five hundred years and counting, Indigenous peoples of the Americas have been exploited, oppressed, and discriminated against: they have been reduced to social death. Since the end of the nineteenth century, they also have lived a continuous invasion of European and US scholars who have colonized their communities anew, wrestled knowledge from them, and then returned home to gain fame as scholars, without even looking back at those who provided the knowledges that empowered them. Indeed, Jakalteko Maya Víctor Montejo's novel *The Adventures of Mister Puttison among the Maya* (2002), studied in chapter 4 of this volume, deals with this very issue. That being said, Indigenous subjects' level of suspicion is extremely high, bordering, perhaps, on the paranoid but with just and understandable cause.[21]

It is therefore important to grasp the weight of Rivera Cusicanqui's caustic expressions and appraise the affect and emotions behind her discursivity. She is, in guarded fashion, pointing out an ethical trespass. Indigenous communities are being told what to do, yet again, without prior consultation, without a meaningful and lasting dialogue, without respect for difference (even if theoretically respect is enunciated). Many Indigenous subjects feel this as a new affront, and as a lack of respect for the integrity of their cultures that precludes any potential form of collaboration, as Leilani Basham puts it.[22] Rivera Cusicanqui's attitude of defiance is her own positionality—and condition of possibility. Contemporary theorists residing in the United States must be shocked (and rightfully angry) that Rivera Cusicanqui attacked them. Yet they have to realize that not only fiery "diatribes" also constitute "the possibility of agency in speech" (Butler, 41), but that their interlocutors conflate speech with conduct. Paternalistic behavioral patterns tinted with heteronormativity and perceived as "white entitlement" when attempting to dialogize with Indigenous subjects—and most especially with female Indigenous subjects—are not separated from epistemic notions that de facto continue telling them how to run their lives. Subjective value is relational. As US scholar Lisa Marie Cacho states, "Contemporary progressive politics must rely . . . also on the 'value practices' that will make social statuses recognizable" (31). Scholars working in the United States are often perceived by subalternized and racialized subjects living elsewhere as "Western-centric"—and thus, white by inference, even if they are Latin American or Latina/o scholars. They need to be especially sensitive to, and patient with, the subjects they are working with, weaving a social fabric that provides continuity to their political and epistemological searches, while accepting non-academic counterparts as equals. This attitude enriches their research dialogue. Revising scholars' old-fashioned, heteropatriarchal attitudes is also critical for Indigenous and Afro-descendant communities trapped in the Eurocentric project of modernity, who need to enforce agency when they are neither accepted nor acknowledged. As Cherokee scholar Jace Weaver reminds us, work concerned with Indigenous subjects is, more often than not, about community (xiv). His vision is reflected by his coining of the concept of "communitism," a fusion of "community"-cum-"activism" (xiii). Rightly or wrongly, Abya Yala's Indigenous intellectuals, as Weaver would state it, are being put "constantly in the position . . . of answering Whites and thus allowing them to continue to set the agenda of discourse" (xii).

A good deal of Rivera Cusicanqui's disapproval concentrates on Mignolo. This is in part due to Mignolo's salient role in framing the conceptual apparatus to analyze the modern/colonial world system to understand the continent's historical formation and ethno-racial configuration. In US academic settings we owe to Mignolo, to be sure, the widespread articulation of Quijano's coloniality of power, paired with his other corollaries: colonial semiosis, border gnosis, geopolitics of knowledge, and post-Occidentalism. These insights sometimes operate as epistemic metaphors deployed to move thinking beyond Western and Eurocentric modes. The coloniality of power provided a new way of framing issues of cultural production and agency. In Rivera Cusicanqui's perception, though, his concerns, and those of the M/C network as a whole, were US-centered research agendas that pretended to be anchored in Abya Yala's Indigenous debates, enunciated by scholars who—with the marked exception of Sanjinés and Walsh—had never done much research in Indigenous communities. Besides, the popularity of these concepts is due to the reemergence of Indigenous issues in the Americas and to globalized Indigenous or native issues elsewhere in the world: from Aotearoa, Hawai'i, and Rapa Nui to Sápmi, Nunavut, and other native or "First Peoples" territories.[23]

When we turn to Indigenous writers and intellectuals, Western referents disappear altogether. Náhuatl poet Natalio Hernández names his writing *in xochitl in cuicatl* (41), the flower and the song, and draws a subtle evocation of Netzahualcoyotl (1402–72), the Acolhua *tlatoani* (literally, "speaker" in Náhuatl, but in actuality the ruler of an *altepetl*, a pre-Hispanic state) of the city-state of Texcoco, to whom poems in classical Náhuatl have been attributed in *El despertar de nuestras lenguas/Queman tlaqchixque totlahtolhuan* (2002). McDonough informs us that "Nahua (Guerrero/Morelos) poet and activist Gustavo Zapoteco Sideño has called himself a 'tlacuilo' (writer/painter), a 'xochitlacuilo' (flower-writer/poet), and a 'cuicajpike' ('hacedor de cantos' or a song/chant/poem-creator)."[24] Maya Q'anjob'al novelist Gaspar Pedro González—to whose work chapter 3 of this book is dedicated—speaks of *K'otz'ib'*, implying "our" literature in his language. He is careful, however, to qualify his words.

> Kotz'ib' abarca las distintas maneas de expresar el pensamiento mediante signos, símbolos, colores, tejidos y líneas. La literatura maya como producto cultural de una sociedad, que tiene un particular punto de vista filosófico sobre el mundo y la vida, no siempre debe ser sometida al análisis bajo los cánones de la cultura occidental. Pues los ojos y los sentimientos de sus autores, se enmarcan dentro de esa cosmovisión que les permite la cultura. (7)
>
> (*Kotz'ib'* covers the different ways of expressing knowledge through signs, symbols, colors, weavings, and lines. Maya literature, as a cultural product of a society and with a particular philosophical point of view about the world and about life, should not always be subjected to analysis according to the norms of Western culture. This is because the eyes and the feelings of their authors are framed within the worldview of their own culture; my translation).

González's appeal immediately invokes a conceptual problem. Is it possible not to apply Western-centered "norms" in a globalized world hegemonized by the West? Let me recognize the virtue of enacting the critic's situatedness—his authorial positionality—and take stock of his privileged relation with his object of study. González restates goals that may also be viewed as a claim and a demand to interpret Maya literature qua Maya literature. His vantage point stands in relation to the Maya languages and their linguistic traditions, to Mayas' cosmovision and other ontological positionings, with the goal of articulating a new cultural genealogy going against the grain of the West that serves the interests of Maya subjectivity.

In the US Native American world, we hear echoes in González's definition of what Creek scholar Craig S. Womack claims in *Red on Red* (1999), that

> native artistry is not pure aesthetics, or art for art's sake: as often as not Indian writers are trying to *invoke* as much as *evoke*. The idea behind ceremonial chant is that language, spoken in the appropriate ritual contexts, will actually cause a change in the physical universe. This element exists in contemporary Native writing and must be

> continuously explored in building up a national body of literature and criticism—language as invocation that will upset the balance of power, even to the point, as Zebolsky argues, where stories will be preeminent factors in land redress. (16–17, emphasis original)[25]

Red on Red is a call for Native American writers' self-determination. Womack sees both literary and critical production as part of "sovereignty: Indian people exercising the right to present images of themselves and to discuss those images" (14). This forges a step toward nationhood because it constitutes "a people's idea of themselves, their imaginings of who they are," contributing to "keeping sovereignty alive" and giving it meaning "that is defined within the tribe rather than by external sources" (14). He adds that "even postcolonial approaches . . . miss an incredibly important point: how do Indians view Indians? Literature departments have done little to answer this question, and this area of history we must dig up ourselves" (13). Finally, Womack claims for Creek culture what I also see in Mesoamerican cultures: namely, that his nation's ceremonies form the kind of communal ritual knowledge that in Mesoamerica is named "cosmovision." This concept names the articulation of ontological knowledge in relation to stellar patterns and celestial phenomena, by way of numeracy, the recording of time, and the keeping of calendrical records, resulting from early cosmic observations and emerging predictive capabilities, which succeeded in establishing a subsequent social and cosmic order. Yet given the different lived experiences of heterogeneous inhabitants of Abya Yala, located in dissimilar expansions and contractions of multifaceted ecospaces while coexisting with variable topographic features generating dissimilar relationships to their biotic environment, not all its native inhabitants use that name.[26]

Critic Luz María Lepe Lira explains in a Mexican context that many Indigenous writers still disagree on how to label their literary production (76). Lepe Lira cites Yukateko Maya playwright Feliciano Sánchez Chan, who thinks that genres and critical categories should be named in their own language and within categories created from within Indigenous knowledge (76). Lepe Lira advances Binnizá poet Víctor de la Cruz's adjustments to Zapotecan literature that would submit genres such as *libana* (a sort of sermon given by elders), *diidxagola* (a proverb or refrain meaning the "ancient word"), *riuunda'* or *liuunda'* (a mixture of poetry and song accompanied by instruments), and *diidxaguca'–diidxaxhiihui'* (in literal terms, a "composition with exaggerated words" that references short stories with a strong communal content [79–80]). Lepe Lira's outline underlines the difficulty involved in elaborating a taxonomy encompassing Indigenous literatures written in hundreds of languages located in more than a dozen modern nation-states.

How to craft tools from within Indigenous perspectives that analyze their literary production? The issue, of course, is that we are dealing—in Abya Yala alone and counting only those communities whose works are represented here—with dozens of ontologies. Many of them are similar, as in the Mesoamerican case. Yet they are never identical. We are well past the reductionist age to ignore even the slightest variants. If, as Kichwa cultural critic Armando Muyolema argues, Indigenous literatures from Abya Yala represent a point of enunciation from which Indigenous subjects utter their languages and politics—and if this is analogous to what Aymara scholar Fausto Reinaga proposed when he called for an "Indian Revolution"—we cannot fall back on obsolete universalist notions of literary criticism for lack of conceptual resources to critique these narrative textualities.[27]

PART II

Global Indigeneities and "Our" Fields

Chilean historian Florencia Mallon's explanation in her edited book *Decolonizing Native Histories* (2012), emphasizes "recognizing relationships of domination and inequality that arose historically in different parts of the world with the expansion of Europe" (1). Working from within a theoretical terrain that is Indigenous initiated, Indigenous defined, and, preferably, if at all possible, Indigenous controlled, her introduction immediately plunges into native interests, stating that

> they involve the conquest and expropriation of territories; massive loss of life through war, forced labor, and disease; erasure of or marginalization of culture and languages; and the redefinition of a process of violent conquest as "inevitable" because of supposed differences in levels of "civilization." (1)

Mallon argues that the aforementioned process led to "the racial construction of white privilege," adding that "decolonization, therefore, involves the questioning of the racial and evolutionary bases of colonial power, and how these have tended to underlie the construction of knowledge" (2). She punctuates that native peoples have "generated their own intellectuals, who have taken center stage in debates over cultural interpretation and translation."

Mallon thus propels scholars to place native peoples' intellectual agency at the center of their inquiries and forces nonnative scholars "to rethink the ethical, methodological, and conceptual frameworks within which we locate our work on questions of Native histories and cultures" (2). Mallon develops five points from the affirmation that "traditional academic narratives about Indigenous peoples are still embedded in a colonial framework, both epistemologically and politically" (3). First, there is the scholarly need to nurture collaborative relationships that respect native communities and recognize them as knowledge producers. This implies enabling Indigenous scholars to choose topics of study and the language in which it will take place. Second is the exploration of the relation of language to power and to empowerment. This is linked to recognizing Indigenous intellectuals and alternative-knowledge producers in academia irrespective of the language in which they work. Third is the problematic relationship between orality and textuality. This involves respect for orality, our role as scholars in guaranteeing the continuity of both, yet of not superseding orality to textuality, as well as the need to implement a decolonization of language so as to turn it into an empowering tool. Fourth is the importance of storytelling traditions as a "form of cultural preservation . . . memory and empowerment, legitimacy and autonomy" (4). Finally, Mallon stresses the challenges of autonomy, especially intraregional Indigenous movements and the role of academics participating in these debates. Mallon quotes Brian Klopotek on Louisiana's Choctaws, stating that "we aim both to decolonize the methodologies used in research and writing and to elaborate methodologies that decolonize the relationship between researchers and subjects" (6). Mallon's project is qualitatively different from previous US academic efforts. It is much closer to the Aotearoan perspectives of Linda Tuhiwai Smith. "Aotearoa" means the "Land of the Long White Cloud," renamed "New Zealand" by its Pākehā (European) settlers.

While engaging with the figures already quoted in US academia, and recognizing Ngũgĩ wa Thiong'o's epochal study on writing in native subjects' languages (*Decolonising the Mind: The Politics of Language in African Literature* [1986]), the work of Linda Tuhiwai Smith may possibly be the greatest contribution to clarifying native viewpoints. Her seminal *Decolonizing Methodologies: Research and Indigenous Peoples* (1999) is not just a foundational marker on how to work from an Indigenous perspective. It is also a blueprint of the research she has implemented since becoming provost of Waikato University in 2006, an institution with a majority of Māori students.[28] The text's wide acceptance has led to a second edition in 2012 with two new chapters added, and to a translation in Spanish. In a Derridian move, she stresses the need for researchers to choose "the margins" (202). But Tuhiwai Smith is fully aware of the implications, including the need to preserve research ethics (207), while acknowledging that researchers who opt to work in the margins "are at risk of becoming marginalized themselves in their careers" (213). Tuhiwai Smith problematizes the "relationship between activism and research" (217) and calls for the need to bring together "the Agenda for Indigenous Research and Indigenous Activism" (218). She reminds us that "research exists within a system of power" (226), insisting that researchers need to get the story "right" to tell the story well. Her article "On Tricky Ground: Researching the Native in the Age of Uncertainty" proffers a significant glimpse of Tuhiwai Smith's contribution to a generative definition of global indigeneity. She writes:

> Indigenous peoples can be defined as the assembly of those who have witnessed, been excluded from, and have survived modernity and imperialism. They are peoples who have experienced the imperialism and colonialism of the modern historical period beginning with the Enlightenment. They remain culturally distinct, some with their native languages and belief systems still alive. They are minorities in territories and states over which they once held sovereignty. Some Indigenous peoples do hold sovereignty, but of such small states that they wield little power over their own lives because they are subject to the whims and anxieties of large and powerful states. Some Indigenous communities survive outside their traditional lands because they were forcibly removed from their lands and connections. They carry many names and labels, being referred to as natives, Indigenous, autochthonous, tribal peoples, or ethnic minorities. (86)

Tuhiwai Smith illuminates a will to articulate a comprehensive focus of global indigeneities.

My one divergence from Smith's statement is found in the leftovers of a certain Anglocentric bias, a critical annotation explainable in the cultural context of her native Aotearoa. This background leads her to claim that the experience of imperialism and colonialism began with the Enlightenment. With regard to the Americas, this interpretation is evidently problematic for Indigenous peoples, as they first suffered this pounding and battering during the first half of the sixteenth century—in effect, two hundred years before the Enlightenment took place.

Quijano, Mignolo, and Dussel have convincingly argued that colonization, imperialism, and coloniality, alongside the racialization of peoples of the Americas, all date from the sixteenth century.[29] This is of course the foundational moment of Spain's and Portugal's imperialist deployments. Indigenous peoples in the Americas, as academics such as US writer and critic Frank Wilderson have pointed out, have a spatial positioning within their nation's foundational narratives. European invaders could not question Indigenous legitimacy, even when overcoming the Indigenous militarily, destroying their nations, and imposing a brutal regime of exploitation, discrimination, and oppression. However emblematic the role of the Mexicas (known as Aztecs), Mayas, or the *Tawantinsuyu* (Inca empire, though the name means "four regions") might be—to cite just those classic examples—they play a significant role in configuring the point of departure of their nations' ethos and values.[30] By their very presence, other subjectivities such as Criollos and Mestizos become destabilized, as we know in contemporary experiences such as those in Chiapas, Guatemala, or Bolivia. Despite the wide separation between symbol and reality, Indigenous peoples form the ruling episteme that grounds the dynamics of naming and valuation in countries where they constitute significant, though subalternized and racialized, majorities of the population.

It is hard to define global indigeneity better than Tuhiwai Smith has. Her task as a Māori woman and knowledge producer was to devise the instruments necessary to generate a first generation of Māori scholars to work in their native land in decolonial efforts. Tuhiwai Smith states that the history of research from Indigenous perspectives is "deeply embedded in colonization" (87) to such a degree that, more often than not, it has been regarded more as a tool of colonization than as "a potential tool for self-determination and development." She nuances her positionality when she comments:

> Chow (1993) refers to the "fascination" with the native as "a labor with endangered authenticities." The identity of "the native" is regarded as complicated, ambiguous, and therefore troubling even for those who live the realities and contradictions of being native and of being a member of a colonized or minority community that still remembers other ways of being, of knowing, and of relating to the world. What is troubling to the dominant cultural group about the definition of "native" is not what necessarily troubles the "native" community. The desire for "pure," uncontaminated definitions of the native by the settler is often a desire to continue

> to define the "Other," whereas the desire by the native to be self-defining and self-naming can be read as a desire to be free, to escape definition, to be complicated, to develop and change, and to be regarded as fully human. In between such desires are multiple and shifting identities and hybridities with much more nuanced positions about what constitutes native identities, native communities, and native knowledge, in anti/postcolonial times. (86)

The complexity is self-evident. Tuhiwai Smith's effort to articulate positionings that facilitate a critical analysis from within multiple perspectives adds significantly to the debate on global indigeneities with critical implications for many nations of Abya Yala.

Conceptualizing Narrativities

To analyze narrative textualities of whatever kind, we cannot skip over a certain degree of theorizing their nature. Certainly, there are a few specifically literary issues that may also be highly problematic when applied to Indigenous cultures. On the one hand, we are talking about narratives—novels and short stories—and there is a certain specificity to what these narrative forms comprise. On the other, we are talking about the elaboration of a critique of these same forms. These are different positionalities. Both involve the articulation of language for rhetorical purposes, yet with different ends in sight. Literature, as Gabriele Schwab has it, "is an 'experimental system' that uses language to explore, shape, and generate emergent forms of subjectivity, culture, and life in processes of dialogical exchange with its readers" (2). I do not disagree with this definition. Schwab inevitably needs to explain what she understands by "experimental systems." They constitute, she tells us, the ability "to generate emergent forms of language, subjectivity, culture, and life" (3). Prior to doing so, she had already outlined the provenance of the category: it was conceived by German science historian Hans-Jörg Rheinberger, who, in turn, took from Derrida's *Of Grammatology* the notion that the single most important source for emergence is writing itself. Rheinberger implies that new systems of meaning will emerge from writing. Schwab, a first-rate critic, is obliged to qualify once more her secondary delineation, adding how "emergence is facilitated not only by the anticipatory potential of writing but also by a reader's intuitive grasp of something that is experienced before it is understood" (3).

If I call attention to the rhetorical gestures it is not to disrespect Schwab. I do so instead to signal the inevitable inscription of meaning in signifiers such as "experimental" and "system," with their Western-centered connotations and a genealogy that traces their epistemic predetermination to Enlightenment thinking.

From an Indigenous perspective, that is our conundrum. Unlike literary rhetoricity, which is by nature free to be in whatever language it pleases, regardless of whether it is read or simply ignored, critical language is loaded with Western-centric conceptual thinking. How do we elaborate a critique, conceptual or not, of literatures not written in Western languages by authors who are trying to decolonialize their own societies and systems of thought from Western colonial intrusion? At stake in this analytic tension lies this consideration: that such purposeful critiques cannot renormatize non-Western languages and interlocutors through Western parameters and common usage of Eurocentric conceptual thinking.

Eurocentrism is a fact. We—myself included, along with every scholar I know—have been trained in Eurocentric theories and methodologies, naturalizing the logocentric gestures later critiqued by Derrida. Still, can we articulate a conceptual criticism of Indigenous literatures whose epistemic forms of knowledge are antithetical to Western-centered conceptual abstraction, and do so in translations to Castilian, the colonizing language? Such is our conundrum, our disciplinary dilemma. Research is not only about satisfying a need to know or extending the boundaries of existing knowledge. It also entails being part of, with all the contradictions this implies, a decolonial process reasserting Indigenous aspirations and cultural practices.

It is no accident that Yukateko Maya writer Javier Gómez Navarrete inserts the following excerpt in his novel *Cecilio Chi'*:

> Yes, peons begin the workday as phantoms in the morning fog. By noon the sun's anger is toasting them, but they do not interrupt the cutting of the pencas with their curved machete. After taking the thorns off, they throw them to complete the bundle of fifty leaves, that they then carry to the edge of the road. Their rags are sweat and dust, they are bleeding on their feet, hands, and back; sometimes, they lift a calabash gourd to drink their bitterness.[31]

There is nonetheless a significant mistake in the way I transcribed Gómez Navarrete's passage. Were it to stand as it appears, the quotation would seem as if the original had been written in English, conforming to US academic writing protocols. The Castilian version, however, is also a translation. Not mine. The fragment was written by Gómez Navarrete from his *original* text in Maya Yukateko. There's the rub. Literary rhetoricity encodes—embodies—epistemic knowledge. Give prudent attention to these classical Maya glyphs:

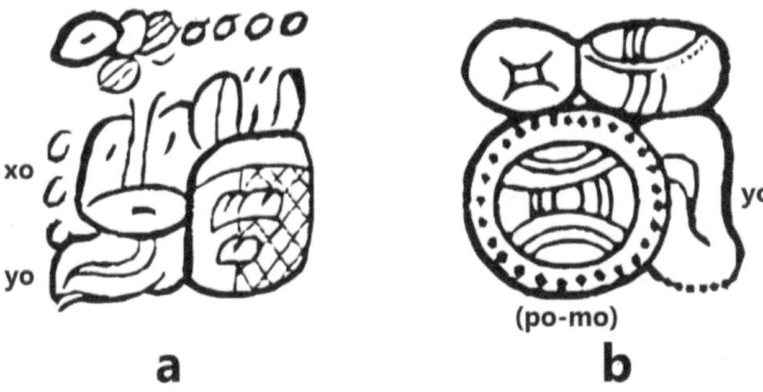

David Stuart briefs us with regard to them, stating that this is a "*yo* sign . . . a prevocalic possessive pronoun. (a) yo-OTOOT-ti, y-otoot, 'his/her house,' (b) yo-OHL-la, y-ohl, 'his/her/its heart/center.'"[32] He details that the "most familiar uses of the **yo** syllable are as a sign prefix, to indicate the pre-vocalic third-person pronoun *y-* before a word beginning in *o-*. Thus **yo-OTOOT** for *y-otoot*, 'his/her dwelling,' or **yo-OHL-la** for *y-ohl*, 'his/her heart.' On rarer occasions the **yo** sign is used in non-initial position as part of spellings of certain roots."[33] In its original form, Gómez Navarrete's notation evinces rhetoric forms embodying non-Western epistemic knowledge.

It is productive to move back to Schwab at this point. After further theorizing her position, Schwab reaches a new way of framing literature:

> We could describe the literary text as a "language object" that performs a speech act that, in turn, becomes the generative matrix for the reading process by anticipating a knowledge that is not yet available discursively. . . . This "language object" embodies what one does not yet know. (4)

I highly regard this exegesis, because it expresses how I conceive literary texts as working. Yet I also find some excisions within it. Only a Western reader of an Indigenous novel could say that a narrative textuality anticipates a "knowledge that is not yet available discursively" or that it embodies "what one does not yet know." "One" in this case would be the Western subject reading Indigenous narratives. But all Indigenous texts embody knowledge that is already available discursively to the community, by orally and performatively tapping their traditions and cosmologies. They embody what just about every member of the community already knows (or should know within the parameters of how the traditional community was originally constituted, and the degree of colonial destruction and deterritorialization that has taken place, as well as the degree of preservation of ontologies). Indigenous novels make explicit claims about the validity, sophistication, and legitimacy of the Indigenous languages embodied in their signs and symbols. The only subject not to recognize those symbols and what they stand for is the individualized Western reader, who does not know these narrative textualities' original language.[34] This is because Indigenous literatures are, for the most part, a rediscovery of learning as spirituality and nurture. If these knowledges are discursively unavailable, it is only because Western genocidal practices erased them in the first place. Contemporary Indigenous communities are presently reconfiguring them in contemporary terms, rediscovering those lost footprints that nevertheless remain, haunting them in dreams, an idea for which we could use the notion of hauntology. Hauntology is Derrida's neologism, a pun on "ontology" that refers to the present as it exists only with respect to the past. After the collapse of Eurocentric thinking, Derrida cues us, these societies will begin to orient themselves toward ethical principles that Eurocentric modernity appraised as archaic, primitive, or discarded. Put another way, it is the direction of those "ghosts" of the past that Indigenous cosmovisions perennially rearticulate, for Indigenous peoples are reinscribed within modernity. Thus, the double gaze of Indigenous narratives, forever in the pre-Hispanic past and in the modern present, exploring those material effects of the "ghostly," of that which is excluded from conscious recollection and the historical record and yet has effects precisely in virtue of its absence, as sociologist Avery Gordon reminds us in *Ghostly Matters*. Gordon stresses the ways in which "questions of narrative structuring, constructedness, analytic standpoint, and historical provisionality of claims to knowledge" (11) problematize sociological truth-claims and reveal "stories" to be "fictions of the real"—that is, complex negotiations of the fictional, the theoretical, and the factual. This is much like de la Cadena's interaction of human beings with Earth beings as a conceptual practice for the Quechua, for whom Earth beings are a seething presence, the epistemic translations of their "ghosts." To write stories concerning exclusions and invisibilities, according to Gordon, would be to write Indigenous narratives, because for her, "the ghost is . . . a social figure, and investigating it can lead to that dense site where history and subjectivity make social life" (8). Derrida's and Gordon's categories both echo the Andean concept of *pachakuti*, a Quechua and Aymara word addressing the universe's disruption. *Pacha* is "time-space," and *kuti* means "turn" or "revolution." As with many Andean concepts, *pachakuti* can take on different shades of meaning, whether "catastrophe" or "renovation."

This contradiction/opposition between Derrida's, Gordon's, and Andean terminologies—or, even more, epistemological naming—is emblematic of the problem of dealing critically with Indigenous narratives. However, there is also an issue with language itself, with how it is configured, with what it achieves, and with how it names and frames things. For example, Maya Kaqchikel culture does not have a word for "art" or "artist." Instead, they say *patän samaj*, which can be translated as an ensemble of feelings, emotions, intuitions, thoughts, purposes, and responsibilities immersed in any kind of a job.[35] In the second case, Elizabeth Monasterios informs us that in Aymara there is no such concept as "poem" or "poetry." Thus, a poem is defined more as "beautifying thought."[36] Within reason, this may be analogous to Foucault's statement in the introduction to his *The History of Sexuality* that whereas the West's discourse of sex is a *scientia sexualis* aimed at concealing the truth by way of a rationalizing scientificist discourse, other non-Western cultures produced instead an *ars erotica* where sexuality was valued as a reward for attaining that kind of knowledge. The West treated this matter as something outside of human experience, unlike *ars erotica*, which is not a "rational understanding," but values and preserves those affective practices that bring about pleasure as part of a path to wisdom. In other words, Western thinking separates ontology from metaphysics. Indigenous conceptions fuse them.

Add to these preoccupations a shift to the plural when we are talking about languages. This is another problematic factor for scholars such as myself. We are dealing with hundreds of languages that we—cultural critics trained by Western notions of epistemological knowledge in Western-centered institutions where we also work, and whose positionings become inevitably our lookout into the world—are, to a significant degree, incapable of understanding or speaking. At most, some speak a handful of these languages, perhaps a dozen, in a best-case scenario, most of these scholars being anthropological linguists. This lack inevitably produces a call for accountability, a need to recognize our own implications in the violent subordination that has led to Indigenous absences in modern literary histories. Witness, as illustration, the original quotation from Gómez Navarrete's *Cecilio Chi'*:

> Beyistako', le paalitsilo'ob ku káajs ku meyjul bey áak'ab kulenkulo'ob ich u y-e'eb píik sáastal. Chúumuk k'iin ku k'éelkubáao'ob tio'su lep'óol Yuum k'iin, yéetel u loch máaskabi' mu p'áatko'ob u cháak u le'ob kij. Je' ka' ku luk'so'ob u k'i'xo'ob ku puulko'ob tak ka u chukbeso'ob u k'aax lajun ti' óox k'áal le'ob, laktúun biin u kúuchko'ob tak tu jáal beej. Yéetel u xexéet'al nook'o'ob ch'u'ula'an yéetel k'iilkab i'ix ma'ay lu'um, kex táan u chooj u k'i'ik'el tu yooko'ob, tu k'abo'ob yéetu pu'ucho'ob ku chan líikso'ob u chúujo' utia'al u yuk'o'b u ok'om oólal u kuxtalil. (78–79).

More will be said about translation. Allow me for now to move in what may appear to be a different direction, one geared toward issues of visibility and Indigenous epistemic thoughts.

The point that propelled me to elaborate a critique of contemporary Indigenous narratives, is to make Indigenous strength visible. Strength seeps from the printed lines of Indigenous texts. It is imbued in the smell of ink and paper that still marks their narratives. These texts configure complex societies with a sophisticated understanding of cosmology and spirituality, with epistemologies that impress readers with their breadth, refinement, and finesse, in addition to the composure and elegance of the words in which they are written.

Indigenous peoples cannot forget what they have experienced since approximately 1519, when Hernán Cortés landed in Chalchihuecan, present-day Veracruz.[37] What has transpired since, what they have continued to live through every day and every night until our present moment, would be unbearable for most human beings. The contents of Indigenous novels are a chorus of powerful voices screaming out myriad details about atrocities committed against them. In the case of this volume, we go from Maya Kaqchikel Luis de Lión's pioneering abject representation of the deep pain and traumatic sexuality resulting from the Maya/Ladino split identity traversing both text and society, which destroys the individual subject as well as his hometown and the entire community. We find this in *El tiempo principia en Xibalbá* (1985; *Time Commences in Xibalbá*, 2012) analyzed in chapter 2. Then we go chapter 3 to Gaspar Pedro González's characterization, in *La otra cara* (1992; *A Mayan Life*, 1995), in his Q'anjob'al language, of the social death generated by the lack of value, the impossibility of living in meaningful ways, and the lack of agency suffered by Mayas working in sugarcane plantations in Guatemala's southern coast. We then move on to Víctor Montejo's ironic portrayal in his native Popb'al Ti of the tragic consequences of the 1930s arrival of US anthropologists to an isolated village in *Las aventuras de Mister Puttison entre los mayas* (1998; *The Adventures of Mr. Puttison among the Maya*, 2002).

These narrative textualities articulate a countermodernity to the West's teleology of progress and ethos of "natural" superiority. They insert themselves simultaneously within Guatemalan modernity—however contradictory this may appear to be—and within sophisticated cosmovisions and epistemologies devised millennia ago, anchored in complex elucidations of the cosmos and the planetary role of Indigenous spirituality and beingness. These publications thus frame the murky waters of the lingering inheritance of subalternity and racialization. All the texts mediate among the national, the personal, and the cosmological, without ever renouncing their cultures, or the specifics of the characters' identities, transparently crafted in the stories told by de Lión, González, and Montejo, whether in novels, testimonios, fables, or short stories.

In a situation where violence is constantly perpetrated against racialized subjects by Westerners convinced of their superiority, it is significantly difficult to become an ethical subject. This is why the idea of a persistent epistemological enterprise equips us with the capacity to learn from the cognitive damage inflicted in a subalternized and racialized context. Epistemic change cannot be made when it is presupposed that what needs to be done is already known, that one already has predetermined answers. In this context, I thus argue that embedded in the Guatemalan Maya narrative textualities studied, we find rich and intricate linguistic discursive practices gaining scriptural visibility, alternative forms of knowledge and epistemic understanding of the world, relational ways of positioning subjects connected both to our planet and the cosmos (i.e., cosmovisions, by way of metaphors and other tropes), and motivational articulations of affect that become not only transformative enunciations for both resistance and change, but also manifestations of alternative codes of ethics.

Indigenous Imaginations, Alternative Modernities

Contemporary Mayas continue to use the term *cosmovision* to define Mesoamerican Indigenous ways of framing knowledge. This term specifically names a cyclical interpretation of time, the expression of the *k'atunic* prophecies—a *k'atun* being a period of twenty years in the Maya calendar, as is explained further—, and the presence of the myth of the return of

Kukulkán, or Quetzalcóatl in Nahuatl, as a liberator figure. Cosmovision names the articulation of ontological knowledges in relation to stellar patterns and celestial phenomena, by way of numeracy, the recording of time, and the keeping of calendrical records, resulting from early cosmic observations and emerging predictive capabilities, which succeeded in establishing a subsequent social and cosmic order.[38]

The Mesoamerican calendar is a system used in pre-Columbian Mesoamerica. At least sixty variants have been recorded. It dates back to at least the fifth century BCE. It shares aspects with calendars employed by other Mesoamerican cultures, such as the Binnizá and Bene Xon (Zapotec, in Nahuatl), and Olmec, as well as later ones such as the Mixtecs and Mexicas (Aztecs). We do not know if the Mesoamerican calendar originated with the Mayas, but their subsequent extensions and refinements were the most sophisticated. Along with the Mexicas', the Maya calendars are the best documented and most completely understood.

In the Maya calendars, there were thirteen *k'atuns*, a period of 260 years. They repeated themselves in cyclical fashion. A prophecy was attached to each of them. For example, *K'atun Eight Ajaw* was supposed to be one where great tragedies would befall Mesoamerican civilizations. As it was, both great Postclassic Yucatecan cities of Chich'en Itza and Mayapan were destroyed during this *k'atun*. As for Kukulkán, he represents the feathered serpent deity. This image has been worshiped by many different ethnopolitical groups in Mesoamerican history. The existence of such worship can be seen through studies of the iconography of most Mesoamerican cultures, from the oldest of them all, Olmec Stela nineteen at La Venta, in the Mexican state of Tabasco. On the basis of the different symbolic systems used in depictions of the feathered serpent deity in the many cultures that extended themselves throughout Mesoamerica until the Spanish invasion, scholars have interpreted the religious and symbolic meaning of the deity in Mesoamerican cultures.

For all these cultures, the center of the cosmos, the axis mundi, was the Tree of Life, emblematic of the central cosmic axis of a galaxy symbolized by thirteen layers of the overworld, with the feathered serpent at the highest layer, enveloping the Tree of Life. Mesoamericans saw the circling Dippers as the pole of this galactic tree, pointing to the celestial center, the axis of the four directions and their four trees, bringing the cosmos into a coherent vertical hierarchy. This Mesoamerican Indigenous worldview has been recorded since at least two thousand years ago in surviving Mesoamerican written documents and reconfigured in others collected since the Spanish invasion. Thus, "cosmo-knowledge" became the foundation and legitimization of Mesoamerican rulers. In this logic, we should also echo historian Nancy M. Farriss's words:

> The key . . . to the Mesoamericans' conception of time and to their entire cosmology is their preoccupation with . . . cosmic order. . . . For the Maya and the rest of Mesoamerica, time is cosmic order, its cyclical patterning the counterforce to the randomness of evil. (574)

These ideational aspects of Mesoamerican culture and worldview are what contemporary Mesoamerican Indigenous peoples understand to this day as "cosmovision." It is used by contemporary Mesoamerican Indigenous thinkers, and even tweaked by some, such as Leopoldo Méndez, a Maya Kaqchikel *ajq'ij* or spiritual guide (shaman), and a leading intellectual of the Uk'ux B'e Maya Association, who plays with the term, labeling it *cosmocimiento*; that is, cosmo-knowledge, in Spanish. He has argued how observing celestial phenomena culminated in a complex set of calendrical principles and associated mytho-ritual practices, producing an interrelation of time, calendrics, and the cosmos. Those same factors enable anthropologist Prudence M. Rice to propose that the *Popol Wuj* myth of cosmogenesis and human origins is an allegory of the history of calendrical developments. She argues that "calendrical advances . . . were being noted by the end of the third millennium B.C." (191). For Rice, the creation of the Mesoamerican calendars demanded focused intellectual effort in at least six areas: observing seasonal and celestial phenomena; developing a counting and tallying system; inventing the 260-day calendar; refining the solar calendar to 365 days; coordinating the two calendars (the Calendar Round); and innovating a system of signs.

The narratives written by the authors examined in this volume—Kaqchikel Luis de Lión, Q'anjob'al Gaspar Pedro González, and Jakaltek Víctor Montejo—all articulate their respective cosmovisions in their narratives. We should not forget that they operate in those liminal spaces between Westernness and Otherness to configure alternative modernities. This project explores ways to bridge Latin American Indigenous narrative imaginations and their knowledge production with Western cultural critical thinking. This is a dialogical decolonial gesture that contributes to broader innovative thinking and Indigenous empowerment.[39]

In the wake of the Spanish invasion of the Americas, native peoples confronting the erasure of their identities were forced, if they could, or if it was legal, to gain knowledge of Castilian to obtain minimum rights and articulate basic claims. Native peoples had no choice but to accommodate themselves, or to otherwise resist these processes, choosing "to remain *outside* the state and history" (italics in original) as Mexican colonialist José Rabasa has claimed.[40] Now, these roles have been reversed. It is hegemonic Western-centric populations that are forced to keep up with Maya mobilizations and multiple exercises of agency in a continual entanglement of the Maya and Ladino worlds. Maya religious practices are legal, Ladino subjects frequently request *limpias* (spiritual cleansings) from Maya *ajk'ijab'* (spiritual guides), and the ceremonies of the *Oxlajuj B'aktun* (literally, the thirteenth cycle of 394.26 years) celebrated on December 21, 2012, were broadcast live on Guatemalan TV, while the country's president attended the largest one of them in the classic Maya site of Tikal.

Unfortunately, these modernizing trends have also been accompanied by a loss of Maya languages at an alarming rate. Mayas have migrated in massive numbers to both Guatemala City, and the United States. Both migratory patterns were the result of the 1980s genocidal campaign launched against them by Guatemala's military, followed by the implementation of neoliberalist economic policies during the 1990s that bankrupted small growers, and the lack of a substantive international aid to rebuild the war-ravaged country after peace was signed. The actual effect of post-war neoliberalism was one of little economic growth, massive unemployment (officially recorded at 50 percent, in Guatemala but most likely higher, especially among Mayas), and the gradual emergence of a nonregulated parallel power to the state produced by criminal gangs and drug cartels. These last two factors brutally impacted the country after 9/11.

Mayas have lost their language in Guatemala City, where they speak and write only in Castilian, or in the United States, where the 1.5 generation is already fluent in English, partially so in Castilian, but has already lost its first language. Linguist Nora England states that whereas Maya languages are among the most vigorous of Indigenous languages in the Americas, language shift and loss among Mayas is growing at an alarming rate (99). This logic impacts Indigenous writers. They are fully cognizant that the percentage of readers in their own languages is small. Most authors recognize that the bulk of their readership will experience their texts more as a perplexing element. Indigenous narratives are discerned semiotically rather than linguistically by nonspeakers, or by those who were never literate in their own language. These readers perform at most a surface reading in the original.[41] Only few readers with a legible access to their given language could separate surface from depth. The majority of readers will navigate a dialogic process that consists of an effort to understand the original language's few words or conventions, while plunging into the translated material to grasp its meaning.

As scholars, we always equate reading with interpretation—that is, assigning meanings to texts. But how valid can this practice be when the original text is inaccessible? Translation articulates readers' partial understanding of the comprehension process (many texts are rewritten in Castilian, rather than translated in a literal sense; many others "hide" their true meaning in the original), and their equally imperfect understanding of the historical contexts (social, cultural, political, and so on) in which the material narrated operates or reconfigures meanings. Their reading in translation thus becomes a sort of "transpositioning" (thought up by Julia Kristeva as an alternative to intertextuality) referring to a "redistribution of semiotic functions" that articulate the text's meaning. The translation can also be interpreted as a transcreation: that is, as two different compositions of the same topic in two different languages.[42] Transposition from one language to another occurs in a primary mediation, given the author's role in the translation process. At the same time, Indigenous creative writers are familiar with the auratic role that originary texts play for the non-Indigenous reader. The preferred articulation of a text in the original language, even if no one could potentially read it, garners authority and confirms the veracity of the author's identity and heritage. This guarantees a perceived authenticity or empirical "truth" to his or her belonging within the community he or she claims to represent, in analogous fashion to the 1990s debate on testimonio. These terms, we well know, often overlook or repress elements. Articulating them is, of course, a display of decolonial affirmation.

That said, it is worth revisiting the notion of "Rigoberta's Secrets" that Doris Sommer framed in the mid-1990s as an ethico-aesthetic resistance on the part of Indigenous speakers to keep hegemonic Eurocentric comprehension of their intimate world at bay.[43] While no secrets are for the most part intended to be hidden in the original languages of these narratives, Indigenous languages do encode meanings that are not easily transcribable to a European one, even when the author chooses to convey as clear a translation as possible rather than hide information. Forms of discourse, whether oral or written, are produced and received in the context of a genre or tradition (see Bakhtin [1986] and Foucault [1977]) and are bound to their medium. We cannot forget Bakhtin's claim that "language is heteroglot from top to bottom: it represents the co-existence of socio-ideological contradictions between the present and the past, between differing epochs of the past, between different socio-ideological groups in the present" (Bakhtin, 291).

This could not be truer for Maya languages, oscillating between a pre-Hispanic glyphic past, and a contemporary alphabetic present where occasionally, Castilian terms—for which there is no meaning in the original language—jump out grotesquely in the middle of the carefully woven texture of a Maya phrase.

There are minimally two discursive forces and contexts interacting in the shaping of Maya narratives: the two languages involved and the particularities of the genres in which these texts are written. Since no scholar, no matter how fluent he or she may be in a given language, can master all the ones in which literatures are written, the question about the nature of Indigenous semiosis in literature will forever accompany critical reflections on this particular scriptural practice.[44] Whatever we may think, it expands the definition of both writing and literature. Still, in Luis Cárcamo-Huechante's words, they will unvaryingly represent "the will of native intellectuals to translate the principle of self-determination into the field of knowledge production, and thus become agents in the formulation of concepts, approaches and narratives in the linguistic, cultural, political, and historical terrains" (5).

These languages, condemned as secondary and as being worthy only of "oral literatures" by many Eurocentric thinkers, are happily beginning to prosper in written form. Their study, even in translations that deprive us of their jouissance, validates their textualities and the subjectivities whose discourses they represent, notwithstanding readers who are deprived of their signifiers' epistemological sedimentation. But, as critic Gayatri Spivak has argued, in their inevitable translation "lies the disappeared history of distinctions" (18) that would have enabled readers to more richly decipher the staging of the rhetoric of their respective collectivities. When problematizing Indigenous literatures through the Eurocentric lens of Castilian, the goal becomes to translate oneself into the imagined horizon of the racialized other.

Translation can of course be an instrument for disfiguring texts. Certain rhetorical elements, such as figures in fiction, are not susceptible to hermeneutic or analytic procedures, rendering something utterly comprehensible. Tropes cannot be conclusively and exhaustively revealed for what they may indeed be. Figures cannot be pinned down to any definitive substance or specific content. They are pure signifiers, rather than signifieds. We have to recognize the impossible and therefore provisional character of this type of undertaking. Just as a reading or a translation is never conclusive or even the end of the story, we also have to recognize these texts' alterity. When techniques of cultural knowledge production (such as comparison) predicate the recognition of difference on the ability to systematize otherness within codes of Western intelligibility that are not subject to interrogation, knowledge of "the other" serves an ideological function. It reinforces the inevitability and stability of the center: Eurocentrism. Reading the other should unsettle the agency of reading. It should problematize reading as a social site building both an-other identity and an-other alterity. The obsession with taxonomy and classification is a positivist reaction and an attempt at universalism that, because of its presumption to generality, can end up being perceived as a variant of imperialism, however harsh this accusation may sound. Not to classify also means a relinquishing of the rational center and a possible abandonment of intelligibility as a methodological ideal. Favoring the inevitable aporias and un-knownness of alterity, I have opted for exploring the dimensions of incongruity that exist in the texts studied that we may casually label as "literature."

There will always be discrepancy in all analytical processes; translation is necessarily incomplete. This involves more than mere methodology. It necessitates an ethics of alterity that conceptualizes the visibility of the other as the founding gesture of a responsive and responsible cultural studies. With the transformation of the old disciplines, the acknowledgement of "the other" as producer of knowledge has to be turned against "us," the Western producers of knowledge.

In a different sense, Joanne Rappaport and Abelardo Ramos Pacho, working with Nasa scholars in "Collaboration and Historical Writing: Challenges for the Indigenous—Academic Dialogue," conceive of translation as a significant part of Indigenous theorizing. It becomes for them a form of "appropriation, rethinking, and reconfiguration of language and concepts from Indigenous perspectives" (8). Rappaport and Pacho state that Indigenous languages "improves the original Spanish term, injects it with a new . . . significance that liberates it from its original limitations" (125).[45] They are, however, thinking of the conceptual translation to Indigenous languages, rather than reading Indigenous literatures in a translated language—namely, Castilian. Indigenous languages become texts through a dualistic process of decontextualization and recontextualization, and hence "multiple translations" (9), in the words of Frank Salomon.[46] Though reading from Castilian positionings, given the limitations of accessing multiple Indigenous languages, readers and critics still emphasize the importance of storytelling, representation, language, and empowerment.

While recognizing the complex set of logics outlined, I remain convinced that academics can, and should, work with Indigenous communities, not in the old paternalistic approach already mocked by Montejo in *The Adventures of Mr. Puttison among the Mayas* (1998), but in a genuine exchange that engages both as equal partners that jointly unmask the corporate nature of a model of research still engaged in coloniality, paired with a decolonial effort linked to Indigenous agency and sovereignty. To draw from Tuhiwai Smith:

> Research is not just a highly moral and civilized search for knowledge; it is a set of very human activities that reproduce particular social relations of power. Decolonizing research, then, is not simply about challenging or making refinements to qualitative research. It is a much broader but still purposeful agenda for transforming the deep, underlying structures and taken-for-granted ways of organizing, conducting, and disseminating research and knowledge. . . . It is the corporate institution of research, as well as the epistemological foundations from which it springs, that needs to be decolonized. (88)

Researching Indigenous literatures should be transformative experiences that benefit Indigenous subjects and their communities by recognizing their subjectivity and agency as well as by making space for and with Indigenous knowledge. These aims pursue social and institutional changes to Western-centered structures of all sorts. Liminal spaces should not be limited to the articulation of indigeneities within Western forms such as the novel but should also include the liminality of the research process.

It may be because of the different historical conditions of the Pacific's colonization that today we see more advances being made by Indigenous scholars from this region than in the Americas. Tonga scholar Timote Vaioleti, for example, has developed what he dubs Talanoa as a methodology in this part of the world. More pointedly, Vaioleti is concerned with how Western scholars will perceive

> issues pertaining to knowledge and ways of being that originated from the *nga wairua* (spirits) and *whenua* of Samoa, Tonga, Fiji, Tuvalu or the other Pacific nations. Research methodologies that were designed to identify issues in a dominant culture and provide solutions are not necessarily suitable in searching for solutions for Pacific peoples, whose knowledge and ways of being have unique epistemologies. (22)

Talanoa comes from "*Tala*, to inform, tell, relate and command, as well as to ask and apply. *Noa* means of any kind, ordinary, nothing in particular, purely imaginary, or void" (23). Its meaning can range from talking about heterogeneous aspects of tradition and culture to interacting without any rigid network. It is an "ancient practice of multi-level and multi-layered critical discussions and free conversations" (24) and a traditional way of collecting information from villages, leaders, and various agencies, governmental or not, to formulate policy proposals. Talanoa "requires researchers to partake deeply in the research experience rather than stand back and analyse . . . and is resistant to rigid, institutional, hegemonic control" (24).

One of the advantages of Pacific peoples is linguistic approximation and similarities. Despite the vastness of the Pacific Ocean, they have to contend with only three cultural zones (Micronesia, Melanesia, and Polynesia), and strong similarities exist among their languages' linguistic characteristics. This enables them to basically comprehend each other from Hawai'i to Aotearoa. These rather unique linguistic conditions and characteristics are attributable to the region's migrations over a long period of time, together with contacts and linguistic merging. The Latin American Indigenous case differs, with nearly five hundred languages, for the most part incomprehensible from one to another.

I do not renounce using Western theories and methodologies when I find them capable of both deconstructing Western ontologies and articulating an ethical research agenda. This is not to say, as Māori scholar Leonie Pihama has firmly pointed out (49), that Indigenous peoples have not analyzed critically or interpreted knowledge in complex ways for thousands of years. Still, there is no pan-Indigenous theories encompassing the many varieties and positionalities of Abya Yala's heterogeneous Indigenous groups. In consequence, we are presently seeing a creative fusion of Indigenous knowledges. Scholars borrow elements of a Western theoretical corpus as long as it does not recolonize Indigenous knowledges but contributes to furthering the transition away from hegemonically sealed Western-centered teleologies. This may be done, as Pihama makes known, "as long as we borrow them from our own place; as long as we use them from our own place" (50).

Latin America or Abya Yala?

Finally there is also the choice of a way to name the Latin American continent in these volumes: Abya Yala. The phrase, from the Kuna language, represents the Latin American continent from an Indigenous perspective. Abya stands for "blood." Blood, we must remember in this definition, signified life among Mesoamerican peoples. Yala stands for "mountain." The pre-Hispanic expression is understood as meaning "land in its full maturity," or "land of vital blood." This affirmation, which imparts authority and recognition to Indigenous knowledges and cosmovisions, is traced in more recent times to Bolivian Aymara leader Takir Mamani, (legal name, Constantino Lima Chávez), one of the founders of the Tupaj Katari Movement in Bolivia in 1978. In a jointly published article, my colleague Luis Cárcamo-Huechante makes précis of Mamani's powerful recovery, captured in this statement: "Llamar con un nombre extranjero nuestras ciudades, pueblos y continentes equivale a someter nuestra identidad a la voluntad de nuestros invasores y a la de sus herederos" ("To name our cities, villages, and continents using a foreign name is the equivalent of subjugating our identity to the will of our invaders and that of their descendants").[47] The name was ratified at the "Declaración de Kito" (Kito Declaration) of the II Cumbre Continental de los Pueblos y Nacionaliades Indígenas de Abya Yala (Second Continental Summit of the Indigenous Peoples and Nationalities of Abya Yala) held in Ecuador's capital on July 21–25, 2004. Kichwa cultural critic Armando Muyolema claims the name was used by the Panamanian Kuna people for the continent. Abya Yala, for the Kuna, was a resource well before Columbus accidentally ran aground in the Bahama islands on that fateful evening in October 1492, whereupon he scarred forever the well-being of Abya Yala's indigeneities. Not unlike Mamani, Muyolema casts light on this process of continental restoration, giving prominance to how, from the closing decades of the twentieth century onward, "recuperamos para nuestro continente el nombre de Abya Yala, nombre asumido por las organizaciones indígenas de varios países desde la década de los 80 . . ." (329; "we recuperate for our continent the name of Abya Yala, a name adopted by Indigenous organizations from various countries since the 1980s"). The name implies a different kind of ethical relation. Abya Yala is a call of conscience, an ethical decision, one of justice and responsibility, that discloses an Indigenous will to power. It marks the impossible possibility of reclaiming for oneself (meaning, Indigenous subjects) "that" self which should have always belonged to oneself, but that was forcefully and violently taken away.

There, to be sure, are risks involved in naming. Naming raises questions of identity and legitimacy. It confers an identity that punctures the heterogeneity of the alleged communities that are named, considering that most of their members never chose the designation in question. Giving a name is an ontological foundation that risks, in José Rabasa's words, mythifying even more that which is being demythified.[48] It may be an initiation into a secret or secretive society, but it may also be an offering, a second gift of life. The latter would doubtlessly echo in many Indigenous minds. Names, after all, make memory possible: with them, communities otherwise condemned to oblivion can leave traces of their knowledges and cultures. The end of names would also mean the end of cultural memory. Let us, then, accept and admit the Abya Yala name and proceed from here, recognizing, all the while, our own departure's fragility, the temporariness of this project's chosen name, its provisional nature, its interim notions: in effect, those floating signifiers yearning for more permanence.

1

A Brief History of Guatemalan Maya Literature's Emergence

THE SILENT BEGINNINGS

Contemporary Maya Indigenous literature came into existence before we even knew it as Maya—or literature, for that matter—long before it was written in a Maya language. But it was Maya, and it was literature, just the same. It consisted of a solitary, obscure effort by two friends in the early to mid-1960s, Luis de Lión and Francisco Morales Santos. They were teenagers from the town of San Juan del Obispo, a few miles from Antigua, Guatemala, the colonial capital of Central America. Francisco Marroquín (1499–1563), Guatemala's first Catholic bishop and Antigua's founder, selected San Juan del Obispo, which literally translates as "St. John of the Bishop," for his personal residence. De Lión and Morales Santos knew this. The old bishop's palace remains the main tourist attraction, hence the preposition's significance in the town's official name, "of the Bishop." The site was abandoned subsequently, as earthquakes chased the Spanish colonial administration away from the Valley of Panchoy, where Antigua is located. Those who built the bishop's palace or worked as his servants set up residence around the palatial edifice, establishing a new Indigenous town without a pre-Hispanic presence. Not unlike de Lión and Morales Santos, most Indigenous peoples in this part of the country are Kaqchikel Maya. Spaniards forced them to transplant to this site against their will during the sixteenth century to build for them and to serve them. The Kaqchikels are the second-largest Maya group after the K'iche's, vying for hegemony with them since the 1400s. Given San Juan del Obispo's artificiality, coupled with its lack of a pre-Hispanic existence and absence of an established lineage of Indigenous leadership as well as traditional sites of worship and a priestly caste, this community was inevitably a candidate for "Ladinization." Ladinization brings about a gradual and subtle transformation from an Indigenous to a Mestizo village. Residents lose their language and culture, thereby becoming monolingual Castilian speakers over time and practically abandoning all remnants of their originary Kaqchikel culture.[1] Or so it seemed.

De Lión was born José Luis de León on August 19, 1939, and Morales Santos was born on October 4, 1940. What binds the two bibliophages from the beginning follows: they were both carrying literary books as they spotted each other in the town's main square and soon developed a rapport. Their animated exchange centered on literature. Other pressing topics related to ideas of permanent and universal expression included the need to migrate to the capital, Guatemala City, to pursue further studies and, mostly, to improve their writing skills and to learn to write literature. They were precocious poets who had participated in local contests and readings as young students. Neither spoke Kaqchikel at the time, but they were heavily marked by their Indigenous ancestry, for they were the embodiment of indigeneity. De Lión and Morales Santos felt the stigma of racism and discrimination because of their phenotype, a factor that was rarely explored by 1950s social scientists. This was the beginning of a camaraderie that would last a lifetime. While de Lión wrote militant poetry later in his life, most of it awaits publication. He was primarily a short-story writer and a novelist, whereas Morales Santos remained mainly a poet, though he has written children's literature too.

A few biographical notes mark the tensions in educational processes with an impulse toward Ladinization: first, de Lión's father was a policeman. This occupation enabled him to provide Luis with elementary and high-school education. This was extremely unusual among Mayas in the 1940s and 1950s, given the marked socioeconomic, cultural, and racial discrimination that placed them in a precarious condition of misery and exploitation. De Lión was able to go to Guatemala City, managing to formally complete his *escuela normal* in the city's poor public school system (exclusively Castilian-based in language and Eurocentric in culture), which granted him a high-school diploma and a teacher's certificate. He became an elementary-school educator, first working in the Indigenous countryside and later in Guatemala City. He was a prolific writer, producing several poems and short stories on a daily basis—most of which have been lost—in his literary language: Castilian. In 1960s Guatemala there was no Kaqchikel in existence, and de Lión knew of no Indigenous scholars working in Kaqchikel.[2]

Morales Santos's biographical sketch runs along these lines: he studied in a Jesuit Catholic seminary from 1957 to 1959. He realized he had no vocation for the priesthood, but this experience helped him get an initial education in the European literary classics. Still, after dropping out of the seminary, he had to redo his entire secondary-school curriculum to have his education validated. The Ministry of Education did not recognize the seminary's schooling, even though it was far more rigorous and thorough than what was available in the country's deficient public-school system.

Morales Santos demonstrates the various stages of becoming an officially recognized educated subject and illuminates a nascent trajectory of articulating an Indigenous identity in Castilian. Sample his take on Indigenous subject formation and literary creation:

> Yo estaba consciente de mi ascendencia indígena, pero no compenetrado de ella. En primer lugar porque aunque unas tías por el lado paterno hablaban cakchiquel, por alguna razón que nunca entendí dejaban de hablarlo cuando yo estaba cerca. De mi padre no podía esperarlo porque muy joven comenzó a trabajar de mozo de finca, donde el administrador y el caporal sólo se comunicaban en español. Con Luis nunca hablamos de esto, quizá porque teníamos claro nuestro origen. Nuestras preocupaciones iban más por lo social y por la literatura. A veces pienso que por estar inmerso en el mundo indígena, que era común verme rodeado de tías que vestían corte y huipil no me preocupaba si era indígena o no.[3]
>
> (I was conscious of my Indigenous ancestry, but did not fully understand its implications. First, because although some aunts from my paternal side spoke Kaqchikel, for some reason I never understood they would stop speaking it when they were near me. I could not expect to hear it from my father, because ever since he was very young he began to work as a farmhand in a hacienda, where both the administrator and the foreman only spoke Castilian. With Luis we never spoke about this, perhaps because we both had clarity about our origins. Our concerns were more about social issues and about literature. Sometimes I think that because I was immersed in the Indigenous world, and it was common to be surrounded by

> aunts dressed in a corte and a huipil, I was never concerned about whether I was Indigenous or not.)

With these lines Morales Santos gives primacy to social affairs and literary matters, tracing his preoccupations to a different kind of urban literary planning in Guatemala City, so to speak. And so he headed for the capital, paradoxically at a time when de Lión got a job as a rural teacher and left Guatemala City. Morales Santos, as an urban dweller, soon won a position at the Dirección General de Bellas Artes.[4] While working there, he met Delia Quiñónez, a poet about his age. Quiñónez was then running the Department of Literature in the Dirección General and introduced Morales Santos to Julio Fausto Aguilera, another young poet. In 1968 this cohort formed the literary group Nuevo Signo (New Sign), which Morales Santos describes as follows:

> Prácticamente el surgimiento de Nuevo Signo se da en Bellas Artes. Un día veo el mimeógrafo de la institución y se me ocurre comprar esténciles y pedirle a la secretaria que transcriba unos poemas míos, agrupados bajo el título *Nimayá*: un intento de afianzarme en mis raíces. Solo un intento. Al final con el permiso de la dirección se hace una impresión de cien copias, se les pone una funda y los pongo a circular. El entusiasmo prende en Delia y luego en los otros poetas. Con el tiempo empezamos a reunirnos, "sin estatutos ni formalismos", como escribió José Mejía. Después vinieron las lecturas en algunas sedes sindicales, escuelas secundarias públicas, al interior fuimos a Quetzaltenango, San Marcos y Chiquimula.[5]
>
> (Basically, the Nuevo Signo group happened at the Fine Arts institution. One day I saw the institution's mimeograph, and I got the idea to buy stencils and ask the secretary to transcribe some of my poems, grouped under the title *Nimayá*, an attempt to affirm my roots. It was only a first try. In the end, with the director's support, we printed an edition of one hundred copies, we added a dust jacket, and I began distributing them. Delia was rapt with enthusiasm and then the other poets were too. We began to meet soon thereafter, "without writing any statutes or any other formal aspect to our meetings," as José Mejía wrote. Poetry readings at some labor union headquarters and public secondary schools followed, as did trips to the interior, when we went to Quetzaltenango, San Marcos and Chiquimula.)

The collective met at Homero & Compañía, a bookstore owned by literary critic José Mejía and poet Antonio Brañas, also a Nuevo Signo member, located in front of the old law school in downtown Guatemala City. In addition to the previously mentioned figures, Nuevo Signo also included among its cognoscenti Roberto Obregón, Julio Fausto Aguilera, Luis Alfredo Arango, and José Luis Villatoro. They all came from elsewhere in the country—meaning, in less elegant terms, that they were collectively regarded as "provincial" inhabitants of the capital—and they were of very modest means. It bears mentioning that Morales Santos was Nuevo Signo's only Indigenous poet.[6] But just as important is this detail: Morales Santos was not a marginal member. He was sufficiently bold to take the first steps to publish small poetry booklets by the group's members, one of which was entitled *La gran flauta* (The great flute, a picaresque pun on a common Guatemalan epithet). He vigorously promoted literary readings, until, that is, Roberto Obregón was "disappeared" by the Guatemalan army on March 28, 1970, as he crossed the Salvadoran border. This traumatic event brought the group's activities to a halt. Obregón's disappearance was a foundational marker that radicalized many writers such as de Lión, who enlisted in antigovernment militant organizations.

While de Lión and Morales Santos continued to see each other periodically, de Lión was never a part of Nuevo Signo. Instead, he began to spend time with Ladino poet and novelist Marco Antonio Flores, a controversial figure in Guatemalan letters. Flores and the abovementioned José Mejía were the coeditors of the national university's journal *Alero*. Flores was breaking new literary ground, and de Lión joined his group, which included another young writer with traits similar to those of Flores, Mario Roberto Morales, who would become a close friend of de Lión. Perhaps more than by grounding de Lión to literature, Flores contributed to his life by helping him publish in a literary magazine, *La semana*, and encouraging him to take courses at Guatemala's San Carlos University. De Lión studied literature and philosophy there and published in *La semana* the first-ever article on ethnic identity, "El indio por un indio" ("The Indian as seen by an Indian"). At the university, he teamed up with his old friend Morales Santos and formed a Saturday study group, where they read and discussed works by major literary figures such as Jorge Luis Borges and Octavio Paz.[7] The early personal history of de Lión and Morales Santos must be framed and grasped within the context of Spanish imperialism in the Americas and its legacy of conquest, racialism and racism, violent displacement, colonialism, and coloniality. In Guatemala's case, this is an abject history of terror, brutality, and dehumanization.

As we progress with this first chapter, I wish to underscore that this plotting of Maya literature's inception requires attention to dates and details that are particular to national political alliances and ideologies and their impact on subaltern subjects and literary praxis. The events narrated here allow for intricate openings concerning the cultural role by motley Maya generations who have struggled to voice and preserve Indigenous languages and literary production. A critical question that grows out of these historical annotations and that the reader should take cognizance of is what conditions have given rise to creative imaginations from Indigenous perspectives? The consideration that follows strives to map how the divergent and unequal experiences in the place where "we" live have placed and displaced certain groups.

THE BURDEN OF HISTORY

In general terms, Spain's Eurocentric colonialism created in Guatemala what Xinka-Pipil scholar Egla Martínez Salazar, presently living in Canada, labels "heteropatriarchies" (3). This is one of the many possible outcomes of Peruvian sociologist Aníbal Quijano's concept of the coloniality of power, as expounded in this book's introduction. The coloniality of power incorporates domination and racialization to the known factor of colonialism as a critical dimension of modernity. Patterns of social discrimination outlive formal colonialism and become integrated in postindependence and postcolonial social orders. Quijano's idea speaks to how colonized peoples were effectively subalternized during the centuries of colonization and forever after as well. Not only was it the result of racializing their subjectivities, knowledges, and cultures, but also of the imposition of social hierarchical orders that disenfranchised them. A caste system was implemented: Spaniards were originally ranked at the top, and those they had conquered at the bottom due to different phenotypic traits and a culture presumed to be inferior.[8] Inevitably, the aforementioned categorization resulted in a permanently racist discourse that was reflected in the colony's social and economic structure. It then continued to make its way in modern and contemporary social fabrics, wherein all descendants of white European immigrants with a clearly defined Western outlook now occupy the privileged site originally designed for Spaniards during colonialism. It is a system that effectively denies Indigenous peoples their own "worlding." Argentine philosopher María Lugones has touched upon the imposition of values and expectations on gender aspects from within this contour, a scrutiny later amplified specifically for Guatemalan contexts by Martínez Salazar.

These conceptual aspects in Guatemala have translated into an originary exploitation and enslavement of Indigenous labor within a hacienda arrangement that evolved into what came to be known in the nineteenth century as a "latifundia-minifundia system" of land tenure. Under this configuration, large plantations owned by a minuscule economic elite, all descendants of Spanish criollos or European migrants, coexisted with subsistence-oriented tiny plots of land parceled out to Indigenous populations. Indigenous peoples could not feed themselves and their families from their exiguous yields and were forced to submit themselves as seasonal sharecroppers at the mammoth coffee (and later sugarcane) plantations for miserly wages, while obtaining no social or health benefits whatsoever. Indigenous peoples obviously resisted the system from the start. Their resistance ranged from secretly preserving their religious and cultural practices, which had been officially outlawed by Spaniards since the advent of colonialism, and continuing them through underground practices by recording their culture and beliefs for posterity as in the *Popol Wuj*—a textual construct explained further down—to launching periodic insurrections. In the twentieth century they organized peasant leagues and other communal organizations, ultimately leading to their participation in 1970s guerrilla rebellions. Despite the trauma of the civil war, attempts at reconciliation after the signing of the peace treaty in 1996, and superficial bids to recognize indigeneity by some government administrations, Guatemalan Ladinos continue to see Mayas as fragmented nonorganic bodies coexisting and intermingling with modernity. Mayas remain non-subjects excluded from conventional discourse. They are considered deliria of the secret threads of coloniality, what Boaventura de Sousa Santos has called a "sociology of absences."[9] This term alludes to an attitude that, under the guise of rationality, ruling elites condemn subjects they label as "the ignorant, the residual, the inferior, the local, and the nonproductive" ("The World Social Forum," 17) to social forms of nonexistence. De Sousa Santos fleshes this out:

> They are [considered] social forms of nonexistence because the realities to which they give shape are present only as obstacles vis-à-vis the realities deemed relevant, be they scientific, advanced, superior, global, or productive realities.

It is no accident that contemporary Guatemalan Maya leaders such as Pablo Ceto still connect current events to their defeat by the Spanish in

1524.[10] Through this lens, coloniality is the hidden face of modernity, as Walter Mignolo has noted, although Javier Sanjinés warns that we should not locate it "'before' modernity and the nation-building process" (*Mestizaje Upside Down*, 4). Coloniality is constitutive of modernity and hovers as a tangible presence in our day.

Even if Guatemalan Mayas were subalternized as they seemingly acquiesced to an externally imposed Eurocentric worldview, their contemporary identity has been reconfigured. This should not, and cannot, be confused with an unproblematized, ideal Indigenous identity with essentializing traits that would continue an unmodified trajectory since the sixteenth century, despite the community's strong ideological ties to the classical Maya order. Guatemalan Maya identity, as I have examined elsewhere, is a fluid notion. It cannot be more than a symbolic expression to determine agency, as Kay Warren has cued us. Its construction is an activity whose effects are never firmly fixed: it is never present, but always re-presented and reiterated in the slippage of its own production. There are lines of flight within it. It is an assemblage of a multiplicity of perceptions without a center or verifiable data other than the actual process of its own reiteration as a "truth effect" and, evidently, their unbending will to, as emphasized above, wield agency. Its repetition—a sort of never-ending dress rehearsal—produces and sustains the power of the truth effect and the discursive regime that has constructed it and that operates in the production of racialized and ethnicized bodies. The need for anchoring one's beingness within a valued identitary horizon that spelled "roots" of some sort—the idealized Maya world in this case—and the necessity to articulate the community's self-worth and gain recognition in a society where success matters above all else, and the Ladino subject is situated in asymmetrical relations of power, is real.

Crucial to this order is, of course, the *Popol Wuj*, the heart of the Mesoamerican cultural matrix. The *Popol Wuj* constitutes a positive counterpoint to the "Mongolian spot," another colonialized antecedent operating as an epistemic metaphor of the trace of indigeneity in Mestizos. For them, it is an apparently visible sign of their equally colonialized inferiority complex in relation to "genuine European whiteness." These twin emblems are key for problematizing Ladino literature's representation of Maya subjects and for explaining the present-day flourishing of Guatemalan Maya literature. They make up a way of thinking beyond that which fits easily within what Mignolo has labeled "macro-narratives from the perspective of coloniality."[11]

Under this premise, culture moves faster in one direction, and it is true that the force with which Maya cultures entered and modified Europe's was notably much less significant than the reverse. At the local level, however, the impact of Indigenous cultures has been more marked, considering the Guatemalan Mayas' numerical advantage in relation to European settlers and their visceral resistance to the colonizers' cultural onslaught and domination.[12] If Mayas' identity became hybridized and/or transcultural (meaning that after the Spanish invasion it was vulnerable to Western deployment of power), Ladino identity, also a result of miscegenation between Spaniards and Mayas, cannot be described as European either. Ladino identity, after all, is impacted by Maya culture on a quotidian basis. Since a good deal of this epistemic struggle took place in the discursive arena, we must turn to discourse to better detect and explain this cultural hybridity. For Mesoamerica that discourse is embedded, to some degree, within an Indigenous cosmological source, the *Popol Wuj*. This is a worldview that outlines acts of protest, the creative energy of subaltern events, and processes leading to a more just and equal society. The same holds for texts that might employ traits of Christian cosmology or a secular view of Western civilization. For this reason, contemporary symbolic figurations in Mesoamerican and Central American imaginaries differ in significant ways from traditional Western parameters, and their repeated, often subtle, allusion to that foundational discourse renders many of their signs "illegible" outside the region in question. This "invisible matrix" is problematic for critics who are unfamiliar with it, or who want to "translate" all literary production originating in the "marginality of marginality" into urban or metropolitan signs of Westernness that are, in turn, presented as the macro-narrative of Latin America's literary modernity.

The *Popol Wuj* tells the story of creation in a fashion that conflates the origins of all Mesoamerican peoples in one foundational discourse. During the Spanish invasion, Indigenous peoples endured the destruction of their cities and their cultures, the rape of their women and the enslavement of their men. In the fifty years following the event, they lost approximately 86 percent of their total population. Those who survived were forced to accommodate their perception of the world to new cultural and social realities. But the *Popol Wuj* became a foundational manifesto of resistance in the Guatemalan highlands. It was originally written around 1550–55 in K'iche' Maya but using a Latin alphabet. After the Holocaust of the Spanish invasion, surviving Maya K'iche' leaders/priests of the Kaweq lineage or *chinamital* sensed their imminent extermination and/or the loss of practicing their spirituality, except in deep secrecy. The need to both leave a trace of their peoples' experience and a record of their beliefs became urgent. Much as their classic ancestors had done by carving glyphs on stelae to record their deeds and history with astronomical associations, they chose to secretly write a narrative that explained their origins, their spiritual practices, and their culture. The *Popol Wuj* offers an account of the world's creation, the fashioning from maize of the first humans, signaling the emanation of the K'iche' people, followed by the history of their rulers up until the Spaniards' arrival. The *Popol Wuj* empowered those rulers to make claims while under Spanish rule. Most importantly, K'iche' leaders declared that they received the insignia and gifts of Quetzalcoatl/Kukulkán, the feathered serpent, the highest deity in the cosmos, god of arts and culture. In other words, the *Popol Wuj* claims that the K'iche' were the chosen ones, and the Spaniards were simply the barbarians who won the war. As a caveat to this statement, we should recall that, as we know it, this text is already born in a colonial semiosis, where the written letter, the Latin alphabet, is employed for the first time both to name a non-Western referent, K'iche' Maya significations, and to occlude the vaporous condition of the original, an oral text performed before audiences for thousands of years. We have to nuance the quasi-celebratory mantle placed over this seemingly ur-text, emerging from a zone where the aura of the other, and of otherness, has been smothered.[13] Still now, however, contemporary Maya organic intellectuals reimagine it as an interstitial text, interpreting it to create meaning in the present. More is said about the *Popol Wuj* in chapter 2, prior to discussing Luis de Lión's seminal novel, *Time Commences in Xibalbá*.

Emblematic Ladino figures such as Guatemala's Nobel laureate Miguel Ángel Asturias—bestowed the 1967 Nobel Prize—used the *Popol Wuj* as a model for a contemporary masterpiece; in his case, *Hombres de maíz* (1949; *Men of Maize*, 1993).[14] However, this Ladino author has also been named by Maya intellectuals for silencing Indigenous voices even as he created the illusion of speaking from an Indigenous perspective, as is developed further on in this same chapter. In this logic, Asturias mythified the allegedly hybrid quality of *mestizaje* as a harmonious synthesis of Western and Guatemalan Maya values in the aforementioned novel. In so doing, Asturias was equally guilty of relegating Mayaness to a subaltern role within Ladino identity. Maya culture provided symbolic icons for his romanticized, liberal conception of nationality, an adequate stand for late 1940s Ladino culture. The outcome was that the subaltern voice was expressed exclusively by the Ladino letrados and exclusively in Castilian. Since the acquisition of agency implies control of one's enunciations, Asturias's attitude wrested agency from Guatemala's Mayas. The Nobel laureate may have indeed named the Maya community, spoken for it, and defended it. But he did not speak *with* it. In this chain of representational circumstances, Mayas did not speak. Asturias's discursivity stripped identity from the Maya and symbolically attacked them. *Men of Maize* underscored the limits of the representation of subalternity when the subaltern's own enunciation is suppressed. If *Men of Maize* is the maximum possible consciousness to which a Ladino letrado could aspire in his immersion with modernizing parameters, wherein the subliminal and discontinuous emergence of the subaltern subject is traced, we can clearly witness the difficulty of representing alternative expressions of a complex heterogeneity in literary discursivity. But, again, it was Asturias who defended Maya culture and who bequeathed the Nobel Prize money to his son Rodrigo, so that he could create a guerrilla organization that fought for Indigenous rights. Rodrigo Asturias took Gaspar Ilom as a nom de guerre, honoring his father's heroic Indigenous leader of resistance in *Men of Maize*. This is doubtlessly the complex inheritance of conquest, coloniality, and its vast corollaries, including rebellion and mestizaje.

THE REVOLUTIONARY WAR: A LONG INTERLUDE BETWEEN CULTURALIST SOLUTIONS

Between the publications of Asturias's major works and the actualization of a new Maya literature came thirty-seven years of civil war in Guatemala. The latter part of that conflict exposed a spontaneous insurrection in the Maya highlands from 1979 to 1982. The army counteroffensive, begun in the summer of 1982, was brutal. The UN Truth Commission has stated that the army wiped out well over six hundred Maya villages. More than one hundred thousand people were killed—primarily older people, women, and children—and over a quarter of a million were driven into exile. In the spring of 2013, General Efraín Ríos Montt was tried and convicted of genocide because of these activities, but a higher court ordered a retrial. The horror notwithstanding, this genocide led to a Maya cultural revival as well.

The war originally had little to do with Mayas. It was a consequence of the June 1954 coup d'état that overthrew democratically elected president Jacobo Arbenz Guzmán, elected in 1950 and due to finish his term in 1956. Resistance to the coup turned into armed struggle after a failed countercoup on November 13, 1960. That date became emblematic of the civil war's beginning. Two trends were implemented in the country along the lines of *desarrollismo* (developmentalism) in the volatile 1960s: to improve economic conditions and to attempt to reduce discontent and prevent the dispossessed from joining guerrillas. These approaches impacted Guatemalan Maya communities and were ultimately responsible for their radicalization. These directives fostered a commercialization that gave rise to new crops for export and new levels of technology and modernization. Observe:

> These processes contributed to major social and economic diversification in the Guatemalan countryside, processes with particular impact on Indigenous communities. In the highlands, textile industries began to appear, finding markets outside the local and regional environment, making incursions to the capital city and even in the international market. The growth in demand for artisan products stimulated production on a large scale and commercialization on a national and international scale. (Ja C'Amabal I'b [6])

Maya communities grew in unprecedented fashion. Mass communications entered many of these communities for the first time. Reading and writing in Castilian were introduced as well, and, given the market growth, even monolingual speakers were forced to learn Castilian. Ideas and knowledge seeped in from multiple sources, primarily via radio: "People could buy radios, and radio stations sprang up which spoke to them of their problems and linked them to a larger world" (Ja C'Amabal I'b [7]). Perspectives and worldviews thus began to change. The latter had economic and social consequences. As the agricultural land base in Maya communities decreased and as the externally driven commercial activity increased, those Mayas involved in the commercial sector consolidated power, and in many instances they ran counter to religious and political stances from their town's *principales*.[15] Mayas linked to this newly powerful commercial sector often joined Acción Católica (Catholic Action; AC) and began to implement new organizational modes learned from AC catechists, such as cooperatives.[16] Despite their moderate developmentalist orientation, the growth of cooperatives brought about serious conflicts with entrenched local Ladino power. This accelerated the radicalization of AC members and their mentors. The Guatemalan military dictatorship, as a result, came into conflict with the church. Peasant leagues were formed by AC organizers to defend Maya rights from Ladinos and their authorities. The government reacted by claiming this was a guerrilla front and responded accordingly. The extension of capital into the rural economy led to the minifundio's incorporation into the money economy through the production of agricultural commodities and the acquisition of consumer goods and fertilizers, a key aspect of the "Green Revolution."[17] Mayas' traditional isolation was broken, and a new generation of activists with access to education was engendered.

Prior to the mid-1960s, Mayas had not been on the Guatemalan Left's radar. The pre-1968 belief among Guatemala's communists was that Mayas were feudal leftovers and, by extension, a human reserve for reactionary landlords. This logic was evident in communist cadres' embrace of the classical tenets of Mexican *mestizaje* and *indigenismo* (as is explained later in this chapter), thereby justifying *mestizaje* and forced acculturation.[18] Such thinking ultimately rewove the threads of coloniality and racism into the seemingly radical communist narrative regarding the nation.

As previously outlined, the state tried to fulfill the role of agent for development while still repressing the population to keep those modernizing features from bringing about changes in the Ladino power structure. Those attempts at modernization instituted expectations among Mayas, who were excited by the initial promise of the Green Revolution. This, in turn, unsettled the traditional order by generating rapid changes, paired with a combustible mix through the work of Catholic missionaries practicing liberation theology in line with Guatemala's Indigenous poor.[19]

Ricardo Ramírez, future commander-in-chief of the Guerrilla Army of the Poor (EGP) made an evaluation, under the pseudonym Rolando Morán, of the state of guerrilla warfare after the Rebel Armed Forces (FAR) were defeated in the mid-1960s. He argued in a document titled *Documento de marzo 1967* (March 1967 Document) that one of the main reasons for their defeat was FAR's incapacity to mobilize the Maya population. Morán launched a foundational critique of the revolutionary/Indigenous paradigm by pointing to a deeper, qualitatively superior second stage in Guatemala's civil war. He proposed a political-military structure in which Mayas would be incorporated as the base of support for a guerrilla column that centralized political and military decision-making.

These issues sparked a full-fledged academic debate at the University of San Carlos in the early 1970s, in which major Guatemalan academic figures such as Carlos Guzmán Böckler, Mario Solórzano Foppa, and Severo Martínez, among others, participated. They produced an initial theorization about ethnicity on the part of Ladino intellectuals, the first to ever emerge in the country. This theorization, however limited and partial, was also the first to configure Maya subjectivity from a Ladino point of view. It thus became a foundational source for two political-military organizations launched in the early 1970s, the EGP and the Organization of People in Arms (ORPA).[20]

In 1972, AC launched a literacy campaign in Guatemala's western highlands—Maya country—that lasted approximately four years. The linguistic fluency campaign included teaching reading and writing in Castilian to monolingual Maya speakers. Following Paulo Freire's method, literacy became a way of discussing local problems and of raising the students' awareness and problematizing issues such as racism, identity, and analogous topics. Many organizations soon burgeoned, enabling members to develop self-reliance, explore self-government, and master leadership skills. Seminars began to be held in Quetzaltenango, whose K'iche' name is Xelajuj Noj', Guatemala's second-largest city, to capacitate many of these organizations' leaders, who were popping up like mushrooms all over the western highlands.[21] Around the same time, in 1973, development fever led to bust as the Arab oil embargo drove up the prize of fertilizers, undercutting developmentalist paradigms and closing off the expectations generated since the 1960s. Thousands of Maya peasants went bankrupt. Lands were mortgaged and frustration rose, leading to rebellious outbreaks in some areas. Combined with the February 4, 1976, earthquake that killed roughly twenty thousand people and left more than one million homeless, this shook free of ancient conservatism significant sectors of Guatemala's rural Mayas, especially the younger generations, who were already seeking political leadership within the various organizations providing guidance. Most of the victims of the collapse of the Green Revolution and the earthquake were Mayas. These events radicalized significant numbers of young Mayas, inducing their subsequent incorporation into late-1970s revolutionary battles. The armed conflict truly took off when the army occupied the Ixil town of Nebaj for the first time, on March 1, 1976, less than a month after the earthquake. Repression began barely two weeks later.[22] Events then cascaded, from contacts with labor unions in early 1977 to seek protection and participation in the May 1 demonstration as a display of numbers and force, to support of the Ixtahuacan miners' march in November 1977, which crossed the entire western highlands to achieve political change. Mayas spontaneously joined this groundbreaking march, and approximately 150,000 of them accompanied the miners into Guatemala City. By 1978 Mayas were ready to take the next step and align themselves with the guerrillas.

And yet the traditional Ladino-led revolutionary leftists considered themselves the revolution's intellectual architects. Within the scope of what Uruguayan cultural critic Ángel Rama defined as "the lettered city,"[23] these Ladinos monopolized leadership posts and power/knowledge relations. Mayas were conceptualized as providing most of the cannon fodder and logistical support. Mayas, of course, saw it differently. They kept their ethnic goals a secret. As stated in the acknowledgments of this same volume, they called this *la conspiración dentro de la conspiración* (the conspiracy within the conspiracy). As told to me by Maya Ixil leader Pablo Ceto in 1981,[24] it consisted of trying to move up the revolutionary ladder as far as possible but not to further the revolutionaries' objectives as a whole. Rather, they sought to further Mayas' secret goals of agency. Because of their grassroots organizing, they called themselves "*maya populares*." Other Maya cadres agreed on agency and empowerment but disagreed on the need to violently confront the Ladino state. Many of these other cadres were primarily urban Mayas. Their rivals later labeled them as "*maya culturales*." The Ladino-led revolutionary process became, from a Maya point of view, a mere vehicle for the defense of Maya identity, for gaining agency, and for the future configuration of their enfranchisement, regardless of whether they were members of one tendency or the other. Ladino members of the revolutionary Left, however, were blind to this outcome. The EGP garnered the highest numbers of Mayas. But their political conception remained rooted in the pre-1968 *foco*-theory, as developed by Che Guevara in the Cuban Revolution's aftermath.[25] Morán remained faithful to this viewpoint until late 1978, when the rapid mass incorporation of followers of Catholic Action forced him to reconsider his strategy and further develop the "ethnic-national" question. He asked second-in-command Mario Payeras to write both.[26] At the time their ideas about ethnicity were not any more developed than those espoused by Joseph Stalin, as commissar of nationalities in 1917, when granting the right of self-determination to the various nationalities within Russia.[27]

According to the Ladino history of the Guatemalan civil war, a spontaneous insurrection in the Maya highlands surfaced from 1979 to 1982, and broader revolutionary plans began in 1974 when the EGP was founded. The Ladino revolutionary organizations were unable to bring the "undisciplined" masses under their centralized control. The revolutionary movement, as a whole, was neutralized politically by 1982 and defeated militarily the following year. After lingering in the jungle for more than a dozen years as a power factor, the movement signed a peace treaty in December 1996 that enabled them to become a legal political party. In this narrative of events, it is clear that the revolutionaries lost the war.

It was a recounting that I embraced in the past, but I recognize now that it contains significant errors. For one, it soft-pedals the guerrillas' paternalistic behavior and neglects to problematize and critique authoritarian manipulations and the inevitable militaristic normativity weighing down political-revolutionary organizations from their very beginnings. This retelling does not address either the guerrillas' exercise of violence when forcing people to join them in liberated areas or war zones or their attempt to hegemonize the heterogeneous and fractured leftist movement. It especially failed regarding Mayas. The categorical separation between *maya populares* as peasants and *maya culturales*, labeled as bourgeois or elite, cannot pass the litmus test of history, given the two groups' similar goals. In the official history of the Guatemalan Left, the liberation theology–espousing priests and the organized Left considered themselves to be the engine of history. The Maya population remained primarily a reactive object of history, and their struggle for agency was ignored.

Rethinking the Maya narrative from the Maya perspective, we observe decentralized sites of struggle where subjugated peoples contest hegemony and recover local voices. We discover, as well, alternative struggles for agency and self-empowerment. This is as it should be: Mayas remain, in statistical terms, the war's greatest victims. Among the quarter of a million war dead and the hundreds of thousands of refugees, most were Mayas, and the army was officially accused (in *Guatemala: Memory of Silence* [Commission for Historical Clarification, 1999]) of wiping out more than six hundred Maya villages. But the apparently absolute division between the group favored by Ladino leftist ideology, the *maya populares*, and their supposed rivals or class oppressors, the *maya culturales*, is greatly attenuated if we read the story from the Maya viewpoint. In general, maya populares were poorer, illiterate, rural Mayas, such as Nobel laureate Rigoberta Menchú and her family. Maya culturales were, by contrast, mostly urban dwellers. Some, but not all, were members of Maya elites, with high school diplomas or higher levels of education, hailing from the towns of Quetzaltenango or Santa Cruz del Quiché. Many of the maya culturales enrolled at the University of San Carlos. Some members of the Maya elite, such as the Álvarez family of Santa Cruz del Quiché, joined the EGP, while many of the sons and daughters of the so-called Maya bourgeoisie in Quetzaltenango joined ORPA. Class is not the central issue in this division, which is more conceptual and cultural—one of means, not ends.

In this struggle's earlier part, from the 1979 semi-insurrection to the summer of 1983, maya populares that were linked to revolutionary organizations had more visibility. But this was so only because they accepted a subservient role within the ranks of Ladino-led revolutionary organizations. This self-disciplining process generally implied a renunciation of their demands. When the revolutionary war stalled, and new political organizations were created vis-à-vis the 1985 constitution and the democratic elections that followed, maya culturales poured their energy into reviving their cultural heritage through peaceful and institutional means.

During the years leading to the peace signing in 1996, the hegemony of the Maya movement as a whole flip-flopped between maya culturales and maya populares as both groups struggled to gain the upper hand. This was most evident in October 1991, when the latter tried to keep the former from participating, or having any say, in the celebration of the Second Continental Meeting of Indigenous Peoples commemorating five hundred years of Indigenous resistance to Spanish/Western colonialism.[28] At this juncture the maya populares, having lost their base of support, which now lay scattered either in refugee camps in Mexico or in the jungle, had become virtual intellectual prisoners of the Unidad Revolucionaria Nacional de Guatemala, the Guatemalan National Revolutionary Unity (URNG), formed of the four revolutionary organizations: EGP, ORPA, FAR, and the Partido Guatemalteco del Trabajo, PGT (Guatemalan Workers Party, of Communist orientation), which kept a tight party discipline in typical Leninist vertical fashion. Maya culturales complained that they were either not allowed to participate in the event or were placed in marginal positions within it, so that maya populares and Menchú could play a preferential role, since she was already a candidate for the Nobel Peace Prize at that time. Despite the tension, this was the first time that the two groups participated jointly in an event. Within a year Menchú won the Nobel Peace Prize. Her initial gesture was to break with the URNG and build a bridge to the maya culturales, in the hope of forming a single and unified Maya movement free from any Ladino/revolutionary/Marxist-Leninist tutorial role. The Maya movement as such emerged as the one distinctive, rising social movement during the peace accords. Consider:

> Mayan organizations in the ASC fought vigorously for the Accord on Indigenous Rights and Identity (AIDPI), and grew in strength and stature during the negotiations. Forming COPMAGUA, the largest umbrella group of Mayan organizations, was considered a crucial step for Maya unity. The peace accords recognized COPMAGUA as an official counterpart of the government in peace implementation. These developments made many feel that the time of the Maya had finally arrived.[29]

The problem with the Coordinadora de los Pueblos Mayas de Guatemala (COPMAGUA; Coordinating Body of the Maya Peoples of Guatemala) was that it was still controlled by the URNG, which, rather than allowing free-flowing horizontal relations among Indigenous groups, imposed a verticalist discipline. Maya culturales negotiated bilaterally with Menchú, who had become a third force and a bridge between maya culturales and maya populares. Politically, though, COPMAGUA's verticalism prevented the realization of a genuinely autonomous cultural citizenship. This lack meant that public processes to generate support for Maya issues in the public arena never took place. It sufficed that military officers and guerrilla commanders negotiating the peace process behind closed doors agreed. The result was that, whereas the peace accords of 1996 established bilingual education for Mayas, and other rights—such as a land fund, a right to judge and be judged in their own language, and even the implementation of Maya law at the local level—alongside recognition of their subjectivity, Maya organizations still were absent from the national scene. Very few believed in COPMAGUA because it was perceived as a front for the URNG, even if this was only partially true. Even though it appeared in 1966 that Mayas were ultimately this war's victors—despite the huge cost they had paid in terms of the dead, the disappeared, and the immeasurable psychological trauma for hundreds of thousands—once the euphoria of the peace signing faded, most social trends returned to business as usual.

The verticalist imposition of Maya rights by maya populares acting on behalf of the URNG was thus a Pyrrhic victory. At a time when Mayas could have induced a movement similar to the one that led to Evo Morales's 2006 presidency in Bolivia, the URNG's traditional understanding of politics as an agreement exercised exclusively among top leaders behind closed doors caused this moment to dissipate. Instead, Guatemala slid into an era that Charles R. Hale has labeled as that of the *indio permitido*, an age controlled by Ladino forces across the political spectrum (298).[30] "It is more accurate to view the COPMAGUA debacle," Hale informs us, "as a punctuating episode in the long-term cycle of alliance-estrangement between Mayas and the ladino-controlled left" (296).

The split between maya populares and maya culturales was part of the heritage of shifting conceptions of global politics, sharing the emblematic date stamped on it by world-systems theorists or the World Social Forum: "1968."[31] This date is characteristic of the differing political views for which 1968 stands as a divide. In Guatemala's case, maya populares, though providing the backbone of revolutionary resistance and insurrection in the late 1970s and early 1980s, were tied to a pre-1968 vision of politics. Theirs was a modern, verticalist, and ultimately Eurocentric vision. Mayas were the masses behind an avant-garde political party of Marxist-Leninist inclination that thought and decided in their name but that also instrumentalized them as subjects, deploying ethnic animosity as a driving force behind class-based revolutionary violence. This is to say, then, that the political-military structure of guerrilla organizations politicized ethnicity without ever reflecting on the implications of the colonial nature of power within their organizations. We could go so far as to claim that the manipulation of Maya populations by political-military organizations could very well have had a basis in the heritage of colonial attitudes and practices.

Maya culturales, on the other hand, who originally were nonbelligerent in their approach, slid more comfortably into the spaces of the local and into the articulation of Indigenous identity as a site of contestation, even as they participated in the process that would conform the *indio permitido* era, in Hale's terms. Through the affirmation of Maya rights and identity in the context of a Maya cultural struggle, maya culturales had a better basis for redefining their terms of engagement with the state and with Ladino political forces. Without ever conceptualizing themselves as a post-1968 model of multicentric networks, maya culturales de facto ended up behaving like such a network, a loose affiliation of the type that has emerged in the context of the World Social Forum (2007). By returning to the local to reanchor the legitimacy and the self-worth of the community, they became better equipped to reposition their locality within those newer global designs that have emerged since 1968. In Latin America today, indigeneity, from Zapatistas to Mapuches, "is a historical formation characterized by its eloquent embrace of modern and non-modern institutions," as Marisol de la Cadena argues.[32] According to this logic, an Indigenous neo-developmentalism could point the way toward a new Left, one very different from the outdated and verticalist authoritarian model inherited from the Jacobins. Some Guatemalan Maya thinkers, such as the Uk' ux B'e Maya Association—working primarily with K'iche', Tz'utujil, and Kaqchikel populations on educational and linguistic issues—embrace positions such as this, but as a part of long-term goals. These objectives are stated as "sustentados en la cosmovisión y cultura maya contribuimos en la formación intergeneracional del liderazgo maya para la reivindicación y el ejercicio de los derechos históricos del Mayab' Tinamit" (sustained by Maya cosmovision and culture, we contribute to the intergenerational formation of Maya leadership for the recognition and the exertion of the historical rights of the Mayab' Tinamit).[33] Uk' ux B'e forms linkages with the grassroots principles they embody and are beginning to theorize this, albeit in a tentative way.[34] What these communities might be producing is *un modo de futuro* (a type of future) as Raquel Gutiérrez and Luis Gómez labeled this critical disposition, using Morales's first presidential election as an emblematic example of what took place in Bolivia.[35] We can, of course, wonder if the communal system can achieve a stable expansion of their noncapitalist practices and nonstate forms of power, and many more analogous issues. Can these practices of economic, ecological, and cultural difference be institutionalized in some fashion without falling back into dominant modernist forms? One may further ask: Can communitarian models ever be the basis for an alternative and effective institutionalization of the social? Can the new worlds envisioned by organizations as disparate as the Zapatistas, the World Social Forum, and many other analogous social movements be reached through the construction of nonstatist, postcapitalist, and postliberal local and regional autonomies? And can these alternatives find a way to coexist in mutual respect and tolerance with what until now have been dominant, and allegedly universal, modern forms of life? The main issue, more than the remnants of utopian thinking that may permeate them, is that this myriad of endeavors is emerging in noncentralized fashion through an equally numerous array of grassroots organizations, behind which stand Guatemalan Mayas who are exercising their agency without kowtowing to anybody else's priorities, needs, or interests. This alone reassures the nature of these enterprises, whatever the obstacles ahead may be.

HOW THE *CULTURALES* WON THE WAR AND PROPELLED THE EMERGENCE OF GUATEMALAN MAYA LITERATURE

After 1970 the paths of de Lión and Morales Santos diverged. Perhaps more audacious and impulsive in his political behavior—more visceral, in Sanjinés's sense—de Lión secretly joined the communist PGT. He invested the bulk of his energies in organizing political cells that would lead to Guatemalan peoples' insurrection. De Lión published his first book of short stories, *Los zopilotes* (*The Buzzards*), in 1966. His second one, *Su segunda muerte* (*His Second Death*), appeared in 1970. Both were written in Castilian, but their stories articulate a laboratory for representing racialized subalternity in various forms and fashions, while also evidencing a very distinct hybrid form of Castilian that undermined monolingualism by reconfiguring within it fragments of what could only be labeled "Kaqchilelian Spanish" in a delightful mongrelization that echoes the social, cultural, and political world of Maya subjects living on the abyssal line that decenters urban spaces from the perspective of racialized subjects. These stories constitute a sort of dress rehearsal for the novelistic project already lurking in the back of his head at the time of their writing. Still, his work was ignored entirely at that time. Even writers close to him, such as Flores and Morales, mocked him for his looks and Indigenous "comportment." They tried to convince him to write in an entirely different fashion. Only Morales Santos encouraged him to continue working in his chosen sensibilities and direction. De Lión also wrote numerous poems, but most were not published until the 1990s. He began working again on his masterpiece, *Time Commences in Xibalba,* which both Flores and Morales dismissed as a failure, during the closing decade of his truncated life. Finished in 1972, *Time Commences in Xibalba* technically won Guatemala's most prestigious literary award, the Juegos Florales de Quezaltenango.[36] To explain: the jury declared that no manuscript had won the first prize, but *Time Commences in Xibalba* was awarded second place. We can only speculate on the racist issues that influenced this controversial decision on the jury's part. It never happened before or after, though this award's prestige dwindled dramatically post-1970s. De Lión's novel was never published in his lifetime, as I discuss in the next chapter. His energy, from this point on, was consumed by political work, though he took time to write militant poetry (unpublished up to this time), study Kaqchikel, and encourage his young daughter, Mayarí, to join the revolution. As a clandestine member of his party, he continued to live, badly, in San José Las Rosas, near the town of Mixco, originally a Poqomam village that now has become part of Guatemala City's metropolitan area.

A polar opposite in personality, Morales Santos was more timid, cautious, and prudent, keeping a quieter life away from the public spotlight, even though he secretly shared many of de Lión's ideas. He made a career working for the Dirección General de Bellas Artes, which was absorbed into the Ministry of Culture when it was founded in 1986. Morales Santos continues there to this day and now runs the Department of Literature. He has remained a prolific poet throughout his life, while making incursions into children's literature. Morales Santos was also an active organizer of literary contests, poetic anthologies, and cultural pages in Guatemala City's dailies. He was even a film censor at one point. In subtle fashion, though, Morales Santos helped shape those conditions that would enable the gradual emergence of literature written in Maya languages. Similar to de Lión, he never recuperated his Kaqchikel language, and Morales Santos's oeuvre is in Castilian. His greatest poems, of which perhaps "Madre, nosotros también somos historia" (1988; "Mother, we are also history") stands out, represent the voices of racialized subalternity and constitute an emancipatory decolonial project. In this masterpiece, "Mother" stands for his mother, the motherland, Maya mothers, Maya motherhood as a symbolic notion, and last but not least for all the nation's poor mothers. Emilio del Valle Escalante explores the poetic voice's journey back to his Maya origins in this poem, stating that this journey expresses a critique of modernity and its hegemonic narratives, particularly an official historiography that justified the plundering of Indigenous lands and culture in the name of modernity.[37] Del Valle Escalante sees Morales Santos's poem as articulating a mental and political process of de-alienation for readers of Maya origin, who, like the poet, had fled from their personal identities and roots but belatedly attempt to recover them. "Mother" was translated into K'iche' by Maya- K'iche' poet Humberto Ak'abal in 2001 and published in a bilingual Castilian/ K'iche' edition.[38] Morales Santos imparted some insights regarding the last months he shared with de Lión. They meshed writerly preoccupations, a distinctive peer workshopping of their compositions, politics, and a cautious judgment on guerrilla involvement as a topic of mere conversation. Take note:

> Meses antes de que lo secuestraran, [de Lión] venía a nuestra casa, leíamos los escritos de ambos y hacíamos crítica de los mismos. En esos días él escribía cuentos para niños, daba clases en la Escuela Primaria José Clemente Chavarría, donde convirtió en taller la clase de lenguaje, y también impartía cátedra en la Escuela de Psicología, mérito ganado a pulso pues no hizo estudios universitarios. Para mí fue enriquecedor y con el tiempo saludable escuchar sus comentarios sobre la necesidad de hacer una literatura para niños que fuera lúdica en lugar de infantilista, fantasiosa y didactista.
>
> Por otra parte, hablábamos de la situación del país, compartíamos preocupaciones, pero fue muy discreto hasta el final al no hablar de su participación en el PGT.
>
> (Months before he was kidnapped, he would come to our house and we'd read our writings to each other and critique our work. In those days he was writing children's stories, since he was teaching at the José Clemente Chavarría elementary school, where he turned the language class into a writing workshop. He also taught at the School of Psychology [at the University of San Carlos], a merit he earned by sheer hard work, as he never received a university degree. For me it was enriching and, as time went by, healthy to

> hear his comments about the need to produce a children's literature that would be ludic, instead of childish—in the embarrassing sense of the word—phony, and didactic.
>
> On the other hand, we talked about the conditions of the country, we shared concerns, but he was very discreet to the end and never talked of his involvement in the PGT.)[39]

As the war began to wane and as constitutional and safety conditions improved, cultural initiatives began to vigorously enter the country's public space.

Starting in 1985, well-known Maya public intellectual Demetrio Cojtí Cuxil, virtually a Maya statesman who has invested his life in struggling for Guatemala's Mayas to be recognized as a nation, began to publish articles on the need to expand the use of Maya languages.[40] Cojtí's articles came to light as a result of his leading the Seminar in Education and Literacy in 1978 and the Second National Linguistic Congress in 1984. The latter occasion was held thirty-five years after the first and only conference had been organized in 1949, as I elaborate later. Cojtí's writings and seminar occurred at the right time. The army had strategically defeated the guerrillas' insurgence. The remaining armed units were cornered in the jungle, coexisting with the Communities of Population in Resistance (CPR). The Guatemalan state, in turn, moved toward the celebration of a constitutional congress that redrafted the nation's new political charter. The newly formulated document recognized Maya individual and communal rights to their own customs and languages for the first time (article 58), promised to protect the ethnic groups' cultures (article 66), and authorized Indigenous languages as the nation's patrimony (article 143).[41] Elections were also held in 1986, formally ending military dictatorship. There was, however, already a background behind Cojtí's pursuits.

The catalyst in the linguistic efforts was the Proyecto Lingüístico Francisco Marroquín (PLFM), an independent NGO aided and housed in Antigua by the Centro de Investigaciones Regionales Mesoamericanas (CIRMA) after 1978 but originally founded in 1969 by Benedictine monks.[42] Edward F. Fischer adds that Jo Froman, Robert P. Gersony, and Anthony M. Jackson assumed the direction of the PLFM in 1971 and reinforced the role of language as the core of Maya cultural activism (93). Funded by the Peace Corps, the Ford Foundation, and OXFAM, PLFM began training Maya linguists for the first time, as well as codifying and documenting Maya languages.[43] The production of Maya lexical materials was pioneered through teams organized and conducted by linguist Terrence Kaufman and other North American linguists, many of whom produced their doctoral theses as a result of the experience in the 1970s.[44] PLFM went on to publish numerous dictionaries and grammatical sketches and to train countless speakers in lexical documentation and grammatical analysis.[45]

CIRMA is an independent think tank founded in 1978 by American scholars Christopher H. Lutz and William Swezey to create a library capable of housing a compendium of the Central American social sciences. For this purpose, it obtained donations from major scholars with personal links to its two founders to launch the Central American Library of the Social Sciences, which presently has over seventy thousand volumes.[46] The PLFM became the model for the governmental Academia de las Lenguas Mayas de Guatemala (ALMG; Academy of Maya Languages of Guatemala), created in October 1986.

After the 1984 Second National Linguistic Congress, all groups working on Maya linguistics came together.[47] This is what led to ALMG's founding. This institution systematized the writing of all surviving Maya languages and published dictionaries of each. This accomplishment was critical for literature written once again in the original Maya languages. A linguistic objective such as this had never truly happened before, considering that Guatemalan Maya languages had been forcibly condemned to a state of orality. This oral "nature," of course, was a consequence of the cultural devastation imposed by the Spanish Conquest and by colonial laws that prevented Indigenous peoples from gaining literacy in any language. Virtually nothing had been written in Maya languages since the immediate postconquest classics: the *Popol Wuj* in the middle of the sixteenth century and *El Título de Totonicapán* and *Anales de los Kaqchikeles* from later during that same century—the first two in K'iche', the last one in Kaqchikel—as well as the theatrical piece *Rabinal Achí*, written in Achi' and dated to the seventeenth century, though most likely of pre-Hispanic origin. On top of these, according to Guatemalan Mayanist Adrián Recinos, there are sixty-eight so-called "títulos" in the nation's archives. Literally "title," or "deed," these were documents written in Maya languages, yet using already the Latin alphabet, by surviving Maya elites. They were configured as land titles to demand legal recognition of their possessions from Spanish authorities. To justify their claims, they often narrated the story of how their people came to be in these lands in the first place, thus providing histories, mythologies, religious practices, names of clans, and other miscellaneous yet rich documentary sources. Some were written in poetic form, evocative of pre-Hispanic glyphic writing.[48]

Edward F. Fischer posits that the modern relation among language, culture, and politics began in the 1940s (90). He attributes the foundational credit to Maya K'iche' academic Adrián Inés Chávez (1904–1987), who, at a 1945 meeting of the First Convention of Indigenous Teachers of Guatemala in Cobán, exposed a new alphabet for writing in the K'iche' language (90). Up to that point, no guidelines or programs had been implemented previously by any institution, whether governmental, private, or international, to codify Maya languages' lexical syntax. The 1944–1954 democratic period heralded the governmental creation of the Instituto Indigenista Nacional (Indigenist National Institute [INI]), with the caveat that it was closely modeled on its Mexican counterpart in both structure and ideology. Like its original example, INI also celebrated a traditional conceptualization of mestizaje configured by Mexican anthropology, a notion attributed in the early 1940s to anthropologist Gonzalo Aguirre Beltrán, who was then director of Mexico's National Indigenous Institute. Aguirre Beltrán, as the assistant secretary for popular culture and extracurricular education, was primarily responsible for forming policy toward Indigenous populations.[49] His work encouraged a gradual assimilation of Mexico's Indigenous cultures into a Western perspective. This process was systematically implemented in that nation until it was violently denounced in the publication *De eso que llaman antropología mexicana* (1970; of so-called Mexican anthropology), coauthored by eight young anthropologists, an issue on which I dwell further in the second volume of this series.[50] Aguirre Beltrán presents mestizaje as a congruent representation of what is evidently incongruous and antagonistic—namely, the fusion of Indigenous and Western cultural patterns. Those smooth visions were deliberately designed to visibly emphasize Latin America's modern, urban aspects that were strictly derived from European roots, as the continent became more citified and cosmopolitan in the 1940s boom decade. This ideological position hid and degraded its "shameful" Indigenous/African aspects. Greatly overlooked was that mestizaje's representational components portrayed an asymmetrical fusion. Implicitly, the Western face prevailed, since it was believed to be the only one capable of signaling a "civilized state" for—and the civilized public face of—the Americas. Indigenous aspects were presented only as a sort of embellished adornment on a cosmic body with a rational, Western head.

And yet Guatemala's INI copied the Mexican model with fewer resources, as their blueprint led to the celebration of the 1949 First National Linguistic Congress. Adrián Inés Chávez tirelessly promoted this meeting (Fischer, 91; a second would not take place until 1984, as indicated previously) where graphemes for writing Maya languages were first chosen. This initiative led the Ministry of Education to formalize written alphabets for the four languages with the greatest number of speakers: K'iche', Kaqchikel, Q'eqchi', and Mam.[51] Ever the forerunner, Chávez valiantly ventured to found the Maya K'iche' Language Academy in Quetzaltenango in 1962, but the times were not then ripe for this association to truly prosper. PLFM's independent emergence was critical for advancing the country's linguistic developments. American linguist Nora C. England, who collaborated with PLFM and then was a founder of the Oxlajuuj Keej Mayab' Ajtz'iib' (OKMA) to systematize K'iche', Kaqchikel, Poqoman, and Q'anjob'al, working in this NGO from 1990–2006,[52] states what was happening in the 1980s:

> Maya are concerned with language maintenance in the face of increasing signs of language shift, they are concerned with expanding the domains of usage of Mayan languages, especially written language, and they are concerned with achieving a balance between languages as a marker of local identity. (Fischer and McKenna Brown, 178)

This sentiment was radically new. OKMA, financed largely by the Norwegian embassy in Guatemala, helped prepare young Maya people from multiple linguistic communities to collect, analyze, and publish linguistic data.[53] OKMA trained Maya investigators in preparing dictionaries in various Maya languages. They invited specialists on the subject to counsel them.[54] The systematization of Maya languages and the education of Maya children in those languages created a new generation of "lettered" Indigenous peoples. We speak here, of course, of a tiny segment of Maya society that had access to not only primary or secondary school but also university studies. The publication of foundational Maya texts, which were also incorporated within the state educational system, gave recognition and value to Maya culture. The establishment of presses dedicated to the publication of texts in Maya languages created an outlet for new writing and a market for new writers.

It was in this context that Maya-K'iche' poet Humberto Ak'abal (born in Momostenango in 1952), possibly the best Guatemalan Maya poet to date, appeared in the literary arena. Ak'abal left his town for Guatemala City in the late 1970s, after the army killed two of his best friends.[55] He worked as a laborer in the city, while reading and writing on the side, until he met poet Luis Alfredo Arango, who was from Totonicapán, a town very close to Momostenango. Arango became a lifelong friend. He helped Ak'abal get published in newspapers in the second half of the 1980s, prior to the 1990 publication of his first book.[56] Francisco Morales Santos was also instrumental in launching Ak'abal's initial writings,[57] the first being *Ajyuq'/ El animalero* (1990). But his sophomore book, *Chajil tzaqibal ja'/Guardián de la caída de agua* (1993), was what truly put him on the map as a poet. After this publication Ak'abal was invited for the first time to the United States, then traveled to Mexico, where he met Guatemalan novelist Mario Monteforte Toledo (1911–2003) and his daughter Morena.[58] Monteforte had lived in Mexico City after being jailed in Guatemala in 1954, but he returned to his home country in 1986 at the invitation of the first democratically elected president since 1950, Vinicio Cerezo Arévalo, who instituted the peace plan to end the civil wars in Central America in the Guatemalan town of Esquipulas on May 24 and 25 of that same year. Morena Monteforte was half Tz'utujil, the daughter of a Maya woman Monteforte married in the 1940s. Morena immediately fell in love with Ak'abal's poetry and, at her death, requested that *Chajil tzaqibal ja'/Guardián de la caída de agua* be incinerated with her.[59] Monteforte had been the only Ladino public figure to marry a Maya woman prior to the 1980s. Once permanently living in Guatemala, he became one of Ak'abal's champions as well. Ak'abal went on to publish many more books, obtain significant international literary prizes, and become Guatemala's best-known Maya poet in international literary circles. Fruitful and internationally renowned, he penned, among other works, the well-known *Ajkem tzij/Tejedor de palabras*, his masterful anthology originally published in 1996 but reprinted in many countries; *Kamoyoyik/Oscureciendo* (2002); *Raqon chi'aj/Grito* (2004); *Uxojowem labaj/La danza del espanto* (2009); and, most recently, *Are jampa ri abaj kech'awik/Cuando las piedras hablan* (2012), the first-ever bilingual book published in Spain and where the imperial Castilian language shares equal space with an Indigenous one.

In a parallel course, Q'anjob'al Maya novelist Gaspar Pedro González had been very quiet while the war raged on. He worked as a bureaucrat assigned to the western highlands, where he was exposed to the armed conflict. González's office was attacked at least once, but since the late 1970s he had been working on a novel written in his native language, *Sb'eyb'al jun naq maya' q'anjob'al/La otra cara* (1992; *A Mayan Life*, 1995). This fictional exercise required that he single-handedly invent a good portion of written Q'anjob'al. Meanwhile, a Jak'alteko Maya named Víctor Montejo had begun to write in Popti', the language of the Jak'alteko Maya, in the United States. His trajectory to the North transpired after he had been miraculously released from a Huehuetenango army garrison. Montejo had been kept as a prisoner there and was tortured after the army occupied his village. Fleeing to a refugee camp in Chiapas, Mexico, where he was rescued by an American mission and taken to the United States, Montejo began anthropological studies. He published an initial testimonio translated to English in 1987, *Testimony: Death of a Guatemalan Village.*

Along similar lines, Kaqchikel Maya poet Calixta Gabriel Xiquín (born in Aldea Hacienda Vieja, Chimaltenango in 1956), also fled as a refugee to California in the 1980s but returned to Guatemala in 1988. She began affirming a Maya female presence on the literary horizon with her poetry. Xiquín had been writing since the mid-1970s, when she was a student of Guatemalan Ladino novelist Méndez Vides (born in Antigua in 1956) at the Instituto Indígena Nuestra Señora del Socorro in Antigua.[60] Méndez Vides, then still a young man, was a critical mentor in helping Xiquín improve her writing in Castilian and in Kaqchikel. Her first publication, scarcely known to a wider audience because of its expensive limited edition, was *Hueso de la tierra* (1996), a trilingual book in Kaqchikel, Castilian, and English. It was followed by *Tejiendo los sucesos en el tiempo/ Weaving Events in Time* (2002), with an English translation by Susan G. Rascón and Suzanne M. Strugalla. Published by the Yax te' Foundation, its first printing sold out in Guatemala.

Q'eqchi' poet Maya Cu Choc did likewise. Born in Guatemala City in 1968, she began experimenting with poetry in the 1990s. Her family had left Cobán, their place of origin, after the coup against Arbenz that ended the democratic period in 1954, and they settled on Guatemala City's outskirts.[61] Because of racism, her parents, both Q'eqchi' speakers, opted not to teach the language to their daughters, thinking that this would help them integrate more easily to the urban Ladino world. Growing up in the city, Cu Choc underwent a period of political radicalization during her high-school years, prior to thinking through identitary issues, an experience she undertook in the early 1990s while at the university.[62] Writing in Castilian with a poetry decisively immersed in Maya cosmovision, Cu Choc first published in the anthology *Novísimos* (1997), where her initial short collection of poems, *Poemaya*, appeared. Her first solo book was *La rueda* (2002), followed by *Recorrido* (2005). A 2011compilation, *conVersos*, includes Cu Choc's "Ix Tzib," a masterful poem about the female Maya scribe.

These separate Maya writerly commitments began to converge, or at least appear on the horizon of cultural and progressive social sectors, in the closing decade of the twentieth century. Their visibility transpired around the same time that Menchú's testimonio first reached a Guatemalan audience. Menchú's narrative—and the Nobel Peace Prize she was awarded in 1992—contributed to validating Maya voices that articulated their singular understanding of recent Guatemalan history and enunciated genocidal practices for the first time in that nation.[63] Barely noticed was that, here and there, she motioned toward small concrete examples of Maya cosmological vision. Menchú's pointing to Maya prayers (*The Rigoberta Menchú Controversy*, 57) is one instance where she, like Gaspar Pedro González, gives rise to a textual interplay between the Maya classical past and the present. A common nod among defenders of Maya religion, it denotes a desire to underscore the uninterrupted continuity of Maya culture and community for more than fifteen hundred years.[64] This concept of time erases traditional Ladino periodicity and creates a foundational act to nurture that imaginary continuity of Maya history from the classical past to the present. In this sense it parallels more explicitly Maya cultural texts, such as González's *La otra cara*.

The 1990s was also the decade of Maya NGOs. A number of independent NGOs appeared between the late 1980s and the early 1990s, such as the Asociación de Escritores Mayenses de Guatemala (1987; Association of Guatemalan Maya Writers), Coordinadora Nacional de Viudas de Guatemala (CONAVIGUA, 1988; National Committee of Guatemala's Widows), Consejo de Desplazados (1989; National Council of Displaced Peoples), Consejo de Organizaciones Mayas de Guatemala (1990; Council of Maya Organizations in Guatemala), Centro de Documentación e Investigación Maya (1992; Center for Maya Documentation and Research), and Consejo Nacional de Educación Maya (1993; National Council of Maya Education), among others. They became very public and active in the years leading to the signing of the peace treaty in 1996. This decade was perhaps the most promising era for Guatemalan Mayas. As Montejo observed, it began under the right auspices:

> The visibility of Maya leaders at a national level rose when they opposed the celebration of the quincentenary of the "discovery" of America (1492–1992). This was a period when the popular left organized international gatherings. . . . Among the Maya cultural participants, primarily academics, some wrote poems, essays, and even letters to the king of Spain, denouncing the continuous destruction of the Maya people in Guatemala. (xvi)

The letter Montejo cites is one of the cleverest testimonios ever written. Titled *Brevísima relación testimonial de la* continua *destrucción del mayab'(Guatemala)*, co-written in Castilian with Q'anil Akab' and published in the United States, this remains a masterpiece of the genre. It is one of the best testimonios ever written, very much on the borderline of a creative piece, even if its circulation was unfortunately limited. Montejo became one of the scholars/writers pushing for Maya visibility as celebratory tributes of Columbus's quincentenary and the "discovery" of America approached. His second testimonio was a part of this concerted quest. Montejo poignantly reminds us that "the quincentenary of the 'discovery' was described by (K'iche' Maya scholar Luis Enrique) Sam Colop in 1991 as the *500 años de encubrimiento* (500 Years of Cover-Up)" (xviii). It was around this period that Mayas renamed Guatemala as Iximuleu, a name explained in the introduction to this same volume.

As the American Anthropological Association conference was being held in Chicago in 1990, some scholars led by Montejo performed a religious ritual at the city's Newberry Library, where the original manuscript of the *Popol Wuj* is housed. Taking a photocopy of the original with them, their call was to "bring it back" to its original community.[65] Maya clothing became a source of critical creativity around this time and a means for mobilizing widows and Maya women around the concept of their identity, thereby transforming their dress into an issue of "beingness" (Fischer and McKenna Brown, 154). That same year K'iche' Maya academic Sam Colop (1955–2011) also finished his groundbreaking dissertation on Maya poetics at State University of New York (SUNY–Buffalo). For the first time Maya literature written in the original Maya language began to appear, and mostly in bilingual editions, because readership in Maya languages was significantly small, if not nonexistent. This materialization also set in motion a Maya cultural influence over Ladinos, as the 1990 creation of Iximuleu's only Maya publishing house, Cholsamaj, attests. This press, first established as Maya' Nimajay Cholsamaj (Cholsamaj Educational and Cultural Maya Center), became a foundation in 2003.[66] Cholsamaj is a Kaqchikel neologism, from "chol" (future order) and "samaj" (work). The name refers to planning and systematizing—in other words, knowledge management. Cholsamaj has been instrumental in the production, circulation, and marketing of bilingual literary texts, dictionaries, and academic enterprises written by Maya or non-Maya authors. Cholsamaj's range of authors includes Maya-centered Guatemalans writing in Castilian, such as novelist Mario Payeras and sociologist Marta Casaús Arzú. The press has published classical Western texts in Maya languages, including Homer's *Odyssey* and Franz Kafka's *Metamorphosis*.[67] Norway's government, US AID, and other European agencies or foundations have funded Cholsamaj, shedding light on linguistics and political issues affecting Iximuleu's Mayas.[68]

In the late 1980s a retired Chicano professor, Fernando Peñalosa, used his own funds to found an editorial house, Yax Te' Press, to explicitly publish books by and about contemporary Mayas. Early in his literary life, Peñalosa was a very bubbly, colorful character, a sort of latter-day Renaissance man. The author of *Introduction to the Sociology of Language* (1981), he had also worked at Tsiterboym Books, publishers of Yiddish theater. Peñalosa studied at the University of Southern California, wrote about Yosemite National Park, and went on to teach sociology, linguistics, and Chicano studies at California State University–Long Beach. Yax Te' Press was founded after his retirement from CSU–Long Beach in the late 1980s, as he became greatly interested in the community of Mayas then fleeing Guatemala's war and settling in Southern California. Maya Q'anjob'als constituted the majority of Maya migrants in the greater Los Angeles area, and Peñalosa took note of demographic transformations and interpersonal communication.[69] Peñalosa worked for the next twelve years with Mayas in Guatemala and in the Los Angeles area, assiduously studying their languages and oral literature. When he founded Yax Te' Press in his residence in Rancho Palos Verdes, California, he invested all but his entire retirement fund in publishing bilingual Maya texts, in Maya languages, Castilian, or English translation, academic assignments he often performed on his own. Peñalosa compiled and published *Tales and Legends of the Q'anjob'al Maya* (1995) and *The Mayan Folktale: An Introduction* (1996). He has this to say about Yax Te' Press publications, which provocatively render Los Angeles as a meaningful Maya point of communication:

> I collected these tales from my friend don Pedro Miguel Say, a Q'anjob'al Maya from Guatemala, who presently resides in Los Angeles. You might say he's an elder, although we are the same age, seventy. Young people simply do not know the stories, or at least are not able to tell them. I translated the tales from Q'anjob'al Maya into Castilian and English.
>
> A trilingual edition of the tales was first published by the Mayan self-help organization IXIM in Los Angeles, but this volume has long been out of print. I am now planning to get out a bilingual (Q'anjob'al–Castilian) edition for distribution primarily in Guatemala and in the refugee camps in Mexico, and have several other such collections in the works.[70]

Peñalosa traveled everywhere he could to promote his published books. His goals for bilingual publications articulate a linguistic affirmation, in oral and written forms, that encourages sustained engagement with Maya writing. It proves constructive to consult Peñalosa's concise recapitulation in *Istmo*:

> 1. Demostrar que se pueden escribir estos idiomas. Y hacer hincapié en el hecho de que son idiomas, no son solamente dialectos, como erróneamente piensan algunas personas: "Nosotros, los civilizados, de caras blancas, hablamos idiomas; esas personas no civilizadas con caras oscuras que viven en el tercer mundo hablan dialectos."
>
> Con la edición de libros escritos completa o parcialmente en un idioma maya se demuestra que tiene su ortografía estandarizada, su gramática, su diccionario. (Algunos mayas en Los Angeles nos han comprado diccionarios de sus idiomas para enseñárselos a sus amigos mexicanos para convencerles que tienen su propio idioma, que se escribe como cualquier otro.)
>
> 2. Fomentar el uso del idioma maya escrito. Antes de poder escribir, hay que saber leer. Hasta muchos mayas se maravillan la primera vez que ven su idioma escrito. Empiezan a leer, al principio con mucha dificultad, porque están acostumbrados a leer en español, pero luego sonríen al reconocer las palabras de su idioma materno, el idioma que recibieron simultáneamente con la leche materna. Al ver su idioma escrito, empiezan a pensar que tal vez ellos también pueden ser autores.
>
> 3. Las ediciones bilingües utilizan el español para facilitar la lectura del texto en idioma maya, hasta para los hablantes nativos. Es cierto que en algunas escuelas, primero les enseñan a los niños a leer su idioma, pero es solamente para facilitar la transición a la lectura del español.
>
> [1. To prove that these languages can be written. And emphasize the fact that they are languages, not just dialects, as some people think erroneously. "We, the civilized peoples with white faces, speak languages. Those non-civilized beings with dark faces that live in the Third World, speak dialects."

> With the edition of books written totally or partially in a Maya language one proves that it has a standardized orthography, a grammar, a dictionary. (Some Mayas in Los Angeles have bought from us dictionaries in their languages to show their Mexican friends and convince them that they have their own language, which is written like any other one.)
>
> 2. Foment the use of written Maya languages. Before you can write, you have to know how to read. Even many Mayas marvel when they first see their language in written form. They start reading, at first with great difficulty, because they are used to reading in Spanish, but they then smile when they recognize the words of their mother tongue, the language they first received together with their mother's milk. When they see their written language, they start thinking that maybe they can become writers as well.
>
> 3. Bilingual editions use Spanish to facilitate the reading comprehension of the text in the Maya language, even for native speakers. It is true that in some schools children are first taught to read their own language, but this happens only to ease the transition to the reading of Spanish.][71]

By February 1997, Peñalosa's Yax Te' Press was reorganized as a 501(c) 3 tax-exempt nonprofit organization, becoming the Yax Te' Foundation. The foundation's operations were transferred, in March 2003, to the K'inal Winik Cultural Center at Cleveland State University.

The quincentenary arrived in the midst of this cultural effervescence that transformed Guatemala into Iximuleu. González, mentioned earlier, appropriately timed a 1992 publication for his novel *La otra cara*. Indigenous literary responses to this monumental event generated international interest in Ak'abal's poetry as well. Human rights activist Rigoberta Menchú was awarded the 1992 Nobel Peace Prize. Kay Warren has argued that Maya "cultural" leaders at this juncture wanted "to stabilize and standardize core elements of Mayaness that . . . survived Spanish colonization and the birth of the modern state" (32). They opposed all manifestations of what we would now label as coloniality, wherein racism is located at its core. Mayas created "a cross-class movement—a new sort of Maya solidarity—that would include middle-class professionals and businesspeople as well as cultivators, students, teachers, development workers, and rural shopkeepers" (49). This configuration of contemporary Maya identity, as Warren has it, was a process in flux, where appropriating, discarding, and hybridizing elements continually reconfigure a position tantamount to the maya culturales' exercising of agency in a transformational process that also hauls with it coloniality's racism and genocidal violence that would make such exercise nearly impossible.

Menchú's Nobel Peace Prize tilted the balance of power in the country. She pushed for and approved the UN proclamation of the decade of Indigenous peoples beginning in 1994, advocating for congressional approval of the International Labor Organization (ILO) Convention 169 on Indigenous rights. She created the Rigoberta Menchú Tum Foundation in 1995, the same year of the Accord on Identity and the Rights of Indigenous Peoples, which became a part of the peace accords signed a year later between government representatives and the URNG. That same year, the XEL-HUH coalition won the mayoral election in Quetzaltenango for its candidate, Maya K'iche' Rigoberto K'emé Chay. He was subsequently reelected in 2000, the first-ever Maya presidential candidate in the 2003 elections.

At the first conference on Maya studies in Guatemala City, previously mentioned K'iche' scholar Sam Colop—a poet, public intellectual, and newspaper columnist who debated politics in the national press and whose greatest contribution to Maya scholarship was his brilliant translation of the *Popol Wuj* from K'iche' to Castilian—accused the country's most celebrated Ladino writer, Nobel laureate Miguel Ángel Asturias, of racism. This charge was based on ideas Asturias expressed in his 1923 undergraduate thesis, *El problema social del indio*. When Ladino writer Mario Roberto Morales attempted to defend Asturias, Mayas in the audience heckled him and agreed with Colop's arguments. Colop's support was emblematic of a radical position, typical of the times, regarding identity among Mayas. But it was also a testament to the leading role he had played since 1991, when he began to expose Iximuleu's historical roots and the perniciousness of racism.[72] Colop attacked an obscure work written by the Nobel laureate in his formative years as a college student, before Asturias had published anything remotely literary or had left for Europe, where he gained his insights on Maya culture. His remarks were part of a strategy that challenged those who have presumed to speak for Mayas. Colop's intervention created a public controversy in the Guatemalan press because, as Warren pointed out, his attitude generalized essentialist constructions to all non-Mayas, suggesting that non-Mayas were universally racist (21). Colop's asseverations won the day for a while, becoming an unquestionable dogmatic referent for all pan-Maya stances. This would come back to haunt Ak'abal, as we see later, when he was awarded the Premio Nacional de Literatura Miguel Ángel Asturias.

Expanding on key 1990s highlights, we come across González's publication of the first book of Maya literary criticism, *Kotz'ib': Nuestra literatura maya* (1997). González defended Mayas' conceptual space, arguing that their oral tradition had by that point become a written expression. This allowed Mayas to constitute an alternative identity within the country (125). He added:

> *Kotz'ib'* abarca las distintas maneras de expresar el pensamiento mediante signos, símbolos, colores, tejidos y líneas. La literatura maya como producto cultural de una sociedad, que tiene un particular punto de vista filosófico sobre el mundo y la vida, no siempre debe ser sometida al análisis bajo los cánones de la cultura occidental. Pues los ojos y los sentimientos de sus autores, se enmarcan dentro de esa cosmovisión que les permite la cultura.
>
> (*Kotz'ib'* covers the different ways of expressing knowledge through signs, symbols, colors, weavings, and lines. Maya literature, as a cultural product of a society, and with a particular philosophical point of view about the world and about life, should not always be subjected to analysis according to Western cultural norms. This is because authors' eyes and feelings are framed within their culture's worldview.)

As I have stated elsewhere, we cannot ignore this argument's conceptual problems.[73] It has the virtue of responding to the Maya critic's position and to the privileged relation she or he articulates with her or his object of study. González restates the problematics of interpretation in relation to Maya languages as well as their philosophical worldview, with the goal of reinventing a new literary history that stands, in the logic of the 1990s, at the service of emerging Maya subjectivity. He adds: "Metodológicamente, se presenta el trabajo en tres momentos históricos: período prehispánico, período colonial y período contemporáneo." (Methodologically, the present work is organized around three historical periods: pre-Hispanic, colonial, and contemporary.) By conflating dissimilar historical periods in relation to Maya beingness and oppression, González generates a foundational discourse for Maya subjectivity, with the obvious risks involved whenever a thinker articulates such a metanarrative process, an issue discussed in US academic circles since at least the 1970s.

More than that, González theorized the concept of cosmovision (*cosmovisión*) as opposed to merely a worldview, a will to become constituted as subjects through an agency process permeated by the community's cultural values framed by their understanding of their position in the cosmos in much the same way Mayas read their lunar and solar calendar. In so doing, he posited a notion different from those of transculturation and heterogeneity. What mattered to González was neither the transposition of cultural values from one culture to the other nor the emergence of an alternative mestizaje that creates a new modality of heterogeneous cultural traits. Rather, the crux of the matter is who exercises the power/knowledge relations in this given process. Under González's grid, Mayas have no problem with being mestizo or Western, as long as these shifts transpire organically from their resources and agency process mindful of an intrinsic revaluation of their own cultures and languages.

The governmental apparatus reflected the transformations taking place. During the period leading to the peace process in 1996, various institutions were established inside and outside bureaucratic structures that facilitated Maya agency. A cabinet-level position was created, the Secretariat for the Maya Woman, which was occupied for the first time in 1986 by a Christian Democrat Maya leader, Gloria Tujab. Alfredo Tay was appointed minister of education in 1993, the country's first Maya cabinet member. In 2000, Otilia Lux de Cotí was named minister of culture, and she altered the name to the plural, "Cultures." Since then, it virtually became a tradition that Maya subjects claimed, for all practical purposes, the Ministry of Cultures as their own, until General Otto Pérez Molina—one of the artificers of the genocide in Nebaj, Ixil Country, was elected in 2012 (he was arrested for corruption in August 2015). A negative aspect of this trend was that Ladino governments assumed that it sufficed to name a Maya individual as minister of culture in paternalistic fashion, to assuage the colonial and racist sentiment that had built up during five centuries, barely ten years after a brutal genocidal campaign. Guatemalan governments subsequently became more Ladino-centered as the twenty-first century advanced, until they reached virtually the same place they had been when the civil war started with the government of General Otto Pérez Molina.

The first Maya minister of culture, Otilia Lux de Cotí, appointed Gaspar Pedro González as the literature director of the ministry, with the objective of pushing bilingual editions, a task supervised up to then by poet Francisco Morales Santos. Kaqchikel scholar Demetrio Cojtí was named viceminister for education, pushing for bilingual education during his years in service (2000–2003). The bilingual program failed, however, to get off the ground, and Cojtí left his post virtually in disgrace. Del Valle Escalante has put forth that this program did not try to "divide the country and the State but accomplish a new social pact that takes into account Guatemala's diverse realities [and] recognizes and respects their expressions, rights, and necessities, without the mediation of violence and polarizing confrontations."[74] He claimed, moreover, that "interculturality in the educational discourse should confront the coloniality of power" and urged that Mayas, "instead of spreading the idea of a biological cultural identity should emphasize Mayaness as a political positioning that implies, more than a geographic place or a specific language or how one dresses or acts, a historical experience and an affective and political cultural relationship from which we think and act." At the same time, Professor of Politics and International Affairs Deborah Yashar assessed that while Maya visibility in governmental ranks rose since the signing of the peace accords, basic material needs for the same population had been abandoned by these same governments that brought Maya faces to their cabinets. Not only this, but neoliberal agendas were imposed, neglecting any social concern for the country's dispossessed, of which the Maya population continued to be emblematic, and even more so after the trauma of war.[75]

Maya organizations gradually faded from the national scene after 2001, the dawning of the twenty-first century. This social dimming was due in large part to the economic crisis that defunded many NGOs, a global shift toward terrorism in the wake of the September 11, 2001, attacks on the World Trade Center and the Pentagon, and a global turn toward conservatism that ultimately led to the 2008 global economic crisis. Hale keys into where Maya rights stood at this millennial moment:

> With the rise of neoliberal multiculturalism in the 1990s, an inversion of racial ideologies in the making since the 1960s came into view. Before, most ladino power holders vehemently defended the separate and un-equal ideology, while the state weakly evinced a discourse of universal equality. Today the state weakly promotes the notion of differentiated citizenship in the name of multiculturalism, while provincial ladinos express ambivalence: wanting to respect Maya cultural rights, but preferring the comfort of assimilationist politics that keep their own racial privilege firmly intact. (*Más Que Un Indio,* 80)

Neoliberal governance implied that Maya subjects were tolerated, but only if they did not cross the threshold that would transform them into national subjects. Those crossing it were Mayas who asserted a form of will to power, questioned their subaltern positioning within the national social pyramid, or asserted agency challenging Ladino hegemony. This Maya agency claimed ancestral rights, autonomy, or control of natural resources, a situation that ultimately reaffirmed institutional oppression, as articulated by racially constructed and structurally predictable privileges inscribed within the long legacy of coloniality.

Guatemala, in this globalized context, wanted to prove to the world that it had changed its racist attitudes toward Mayas. Critical situations, however—such as the ongoing crises linked to the occupation of Maya lands to develop mines and build hydroelectric plants, combined with the first massacre since the end of the war, which took place in Totonicapán in October 2012, when all eyes were focusing on the country because of the upcoming celebration of the Oxlajuj B'aq'tun—revealed that this was nothing more than superficial public relations. An exemplary case in this respect was the awarding of the 2003 Premio Nacional de Literatura Miguel Ángel Asturias (Miguel Ángel Asturias National Literary Lifetime Achievement Award) to Ak'abal. This prize, created in 1988 as part of the nation's new democratic face, quickly became the most important literary distinction. When it was offered to Ak'abal, the first and only time the accolade has gone to a Maya writer to date, he declined the honor, to the amazement of most Ladino Guatemalans. Ak'abal gave what had become the standard pan-Maya position—namely, Colop's argument: that it honored an author with racist inclinations against Indigenous peoples, as punctuated in Asturias's undergraduate thesis, *El problema social del indio* (1922; the social problem that Indians represent; my translation).[76] His decision ignited a major rumpus among Guatemala's established Ladino writers and even among a sector of Maya intellectuals. The laurel, after all, had been bestowed upon him by the country's first Maya Minister of Cultures, Otilia Lux de Cotí, a member of Ak'abal's same ethnic group, though of a different social and professional class, who defended the prize's name and spirit. The other figure supporting Ak'abal's homage was Francisco Morales Santos. The public heard as well from Montejo, who disagreed and postulated that the Nobel laureate was an extraordinary writer even if he lacked a solid academic formation. He added that while Asturias did not understand Indigenous themes, he did use Indigenous traditions in his corpus.[77] Montejo mentioned that Asturias's thesis should have never been published, but he still thought that it was an important historical document, for it is evidence of how Indigenous peoples were seen by elite Ladinos in those times. Mario Roberto Morales, by contrast, who loved to polemicize with Mayas and to put them down, claimed that Ak'abal's position was "infantile" for believing that Asturias was racist. The poet's reaction, Morales suggested, demonstrated that he had not read Asturias's thesis, which demanded to be understood in its historical context.[78] Ak'abal's declining of the award turned him into persona non grata in Ladino circles. Their underlying racism burst out to the surface with a vengeance. Ak'abal received threatening phone calls blatantly insulting him for his stand. He was pointed at in the city streets for being the "uppity Indian" who dared to tarnish Guatemala's greatest writer (whom, incidentally, most Ladinos had never read and had lambasted in the past, accusing him of being a communist).[79] The situation became untenable, and Ak'abal opted for leaving the country shortly afterward. To the present day, Ak'abal spends most of his time in Fribourg, Switzerland, with his Swiss wife and son.[80] Most Ladino writers still manifest hostility against him. Ultimately, Colop's stance launched a process of resemantization that destabilized racial hierarchies, implicitly disqualifying Asturias's creative attempts to portray Guatemalan identity as ethnically hybrid.[81] Ironically, though, the extreme manifestations of this literary tumult ended up validating an essentialist position on Mayaness that became the photographic negative of Ladinos' own pernicious racism against Mayas. We undoubtedly landed in the murky territories of reverse racism.

The 2004 award was subsequently offered to outstanding Ladino novelist Rodrigo Rey Rosa. He accepted it but donated the money to create a Maya literary award, named B'atz'. The name made reference to the thread of time in the Maya Cholq'ij 260-day calendar. (Mayas also have a 365-day calendar named Haab').[82] Rey Rosa collaborated with Aporte para la Descentralización Cultural (ADESCA, Contribution to Cultural Decentralization), an NGO directed by Elsa Son Chonay, who later became vice-minister of culture.[83] The B'atz' prize was awarded to Maya K'iche' poet Leoncio Pablo García Talé for *B'ixonik tzij ke uk'ulaj kaminaqib/Canto palabra de una pareja de muertos* (Word song for a dead couple) and Maya Kaqchikel short-story writer Miguel Ángel Oxlaj Cúmez for his short story "Ru Taqkil Ri Sarima'/El Sarimá" (The Sarima) on August 8, 2007. F&G Editores, the rising mainstream Guatemalan publishing house in the twenty-first century, agreed to publish the material. Unfortunately, there has been no continuity with this award, the only one ever conceived for Maya literature in Guatemala.[84]

In his blog "Las páginas vulgares," noted Ladino writer Maurice Echeverría quoted Rey Rosa as stating that he not only believed in Maya literature but also thought that it was more likely that Maya literature existed than Guatemalan literature.[85] Echeverría also cited Mario Roberto

Morales's remarks that it made no sense to talk about Maya literature, feminine literature, gay literature, or Mexican American literature. These categories, he contended, only served to compartmentalize literary criticism. But Morales recognized Mayas' right to name themselves as such if they so choose and to label their literary production as Maya literature.[86] Echeverría summarized Montejo's position about a Maya renaissance in Guatemala, adding the differences between Ak'abal and Colop regarding written versus oral literature. For Ak'abal, they were two different things, whereas for Colop, they formed part of the same body of literary production. We can add to the growing constellation of Maya literature, González's book on the approaching end of the 5,200-year Maya cycle, the Oxlajuj B'aq'tun. And yet in this time span not many younger Guatemalan Maya novelists have appeared, although a young K'iche'-Kaqchikel Maya poet Rosa Chávez has established herself as the best-known young poet in both the national and international scene.

By introducing into the literary/symbolic process new linguistic and representational challenges, Iximuleu's Maya literary works managed to provincialize Castilian as an organic vehicle in the constitution of the nation's imaginaries. They especially succeeded in problematizing the colonial nature of the nation-state. These foundational writers allowed young Mayas to forge a cultural memory articulating their history, cosmovision, political views, and basic demands. They laid the groundwork for contemporary young activists and those cultural actors who took the lead in the April 2012 Maya peasants' march from Alta Verapaz to the capital; who denounced the October 2012 massacre of Totonicapán; who celebrated the Oxlajuj B'aq'tun and injected into it clear political demands and later mobilized around the judicial condemnation of genocide against the Ixil peoples, and against the fraudulent cancelation of General Ríos Montt's trial and the absurd and surreal National Congress vote that there had never been a genocide in Guatemala.

Numerous young Maya creative subjects have moved away from literature, as is the case globally. Many are presently engaged in video, film, theater, electronic music, and a wide array of multiple electronic and technological creative expressions, leaving the literary scene seemingly in a state of abandonment. There is even online Maya television now. And yet none of this would have happened had Maya literature not emerged in the first place to consolidate a creative channel for Iximuleu's Maya subjectivities. Maya literature has freed younger subjects to express their artistic articulations in whatever direction that may take them. They do not have to feel any further obligations to assert political positions, marginalize themselves from mainstream Ladino society, or simply migrate elsewhere, without abandoning their singular Mayaness or their maternal language. They may also integrate English, Mandarin, or whatever expressions may better fit their desires. However, things are far from rosy for Iximuleu's Mayas in 2015: the Oxlajuj B'aq'tun celebration—that is, the beginning of a new calendric cycle on December 21, 2012—came in the midst of grave political tensions associated with multiple issues. These included global corporations attempting to dispossess Mayas of their lands for mining or hydroelectric purposes. The latter provoked turmoil in corners of the nation as dissimilar as Barillas in the west, Santa Rosa in the south, and San Felipe Chenlá in the north-central area. This tension led to the first postwar massacre in Totonicapán in October of that same year, barely two months before the celebration, as well as to a new national social polarization, when dictator General Ríos Montt was put on trial on charges of genocide against Maya Ixils in 2013. Despite these ill winds, we can most certainly assert that young Maya creators have freed themselves, to a large extent, of the mental constraints, self-hatred, and inferiority complex that often imprisoned subaltern subjects' creative passions in the recent past, an integral part of the vicious circle that coloniality imposed upon Iximuleu's Mayas. This alone is worth celebrating.

This chapter summarizes the historical, political, and cultural conditions that enabled the emergence of a body of literature written by Iximuleu's Mayas from the mid-1960s to the present. Maya literature was contextualized mostly (though not exclusively) as published in their native languages and bilingually in Castilian with translations elaborated by Maya writers, regardless of the chosen genre. The three chapters that follow investigate the novelistic output of its three salient figures, Luis de Lión, Gaspar Pedro González, and Víctor Montejo.

2

Luis de Lión: The Tragic Pioneer

The early life of Luis de Lión is introduced in chapter 1, while tracing those cultural conditions that enabled the emergence of Maya literariness in Guatemala. In this chapter I search for de Lión's Indigenous strategies, interrogating primarily those manifestations of racism and subalternization that point in the direction of a pioneer decolonial effort—if visceral and instinctive—in his foundational novel *El tiempo principia en Xibalbá* (1985; *Time Commences in Xibalbá*, 2012).

Luis de Lión's origins in San Juan del Obispo and his Kaqchikel Maya roots have already been juxtaposed with those of his friend and fellow writer Francisco Morales Santos; I claim that both shared an Indigenous sense of knowledge, despite not speaking or writing Kaqchikel Maya. In the present chapter, I begin by examining the complete stories of his two books originally titled *Los zopilotes* (1966; *The Buzzards*) and *Su segunda muerte* (1970; *His Second Death*), which have recently been reissued by Guatemala's Ministry of Culture in a single volume titled *La puerta del cielo* (2011; *The Door to Heaven*). This title is taken from his most famous story, also analyzed in this chapter. It is my contention that the short stories preceding de Lión's groundbreaking novel are much more than personal remembrance, as early works by most major writers often are. Rather, together they are a laboratory for representing racialized subalternity in various forms and fashions. They constitute a sort of dress rehearsal for the novelistic project already lurking in the back of the author's head at the time of their writing. It is my premise, therefore, that at the earlier stage during which de Lión wrote his stories, he still had not configured exactly how racialized subalternity could become an emancipatory decolonial project. He would stage this only in *Time Commences in Xibalbá* (1985), which I analyze in the second part of this chapter. Nonetheless, having embodied indigeneity, which predetermined a subalternizing sense of selfhood that positioned him and others in a caste-like social system impeding upward mobility by virtue of their racial determinants, de Lión had already affectively suffered, and then apprehended, what racialization meant, and how it impacted Indigenous subjectivities.[1] He was thus staging it in various ways and forms in his earlier stories, in experimental fashion. We can see, in consequence, an anticipation of future theoretical turns in many of them.

By "racialized subalternity" I mean, as explained in the introduction to this volume, those implications of ethnic/racialized classifications of the populations subjugated by the Spaniards in the 1500s, as explained by Peruvian sociologist Anibal Quijano in his theorization of the "coloniality of power."[2] That de Lión could stage this in the 1960s, twenty-five years before Quijano configured the category, and at such an early age—even if it was only by way of his artistic instinct—given his erratic schooling in a country with such low-quality public education as Guatemala, can attest only to his brilliance and sensitivity. But it is also the result of his personal embodiment of Mayaness in the process of constituting himself as a racialized subject, as an active self. As Guatemalan scholar Rita Palacios points out in her dissertation, poet Ana María Rodas wrote that de Lión was known among his Ladino friends as "el indio" (86). This may possibly have been so in those times, and Rodas certainly meant it to be articulated as an affectionate sobriquet when writing about it; but for a Maya subject, this sort of daily denigration of his beingness, one in which he may have collaborated as a survival mechanism to show before his Ladino literary circle his capacity to laugh at himself, nonetheless denotes an interiorization of rage, one we see further along exploding in his manifestations of Ladino hatred displayed by the character named Pascual Baeza in *Time Commences in Xibalbá*. It certainly must have affected his psyche and generated a degree of trauma, which would also explain his obsession with confronting relations of class and ethnicity. In this respect, his son Ixbalanqué stated that in 1979 his father notified him that he had decided to learn Kaqchikel, because it was the mother tongue of his ethnic group.[3] At about the same time, de Lión wrote in a private notebook:

> No puedo participar del llamado mestizaje precisamente porque lo hispano es la negación de mi lengua, de mi cultura. El lenguaje cackchiquel [sic] sí podría prestarme recursos más íntimamente poéticos. La realidad guatemalteca actual no es grito, es dolor, profundo dolor.[4]
>
> (I cannot participate in what is called mestizaje precisely because the Hispanic elements are the negation of my language, my culture. Cackchiquel [sic] language could indeed lend me more intimate poetic resources. The present Guatemalan reality is not a scream; it's pain, deep pain.)

We must remember here Foucault's analysis that the potential for the exercise of agency from within different discursive fields is always already present, and this has significant repercussions for the development of alternative subjectivities and for countering the various "truths" generated by dominant social imaginaries. He states:

> Let us not therefore ask why certain people want to dominate what they seek, what is their overall strategy. Let us ask, instead, how things work at the level of ongoing subjugation, at the level of those continuous and uninterrupted processes which subject our bodies, govern our gestures, dictate our behaviours, etc. In other words we should try to discover how it is that subjects are gradually, progressively, really and materially constituted through a multiplicity of organisms, forces, energies, materials, desires, thoughts, etc. . . . We should try to grasp subjection in its material instance as constitution of subjects. (*Power/Knowledge*, 97)

Indeed, the presence of notions of racialized subalternity in de Lión's early short stories may appear striking but only because they denote a high degree of lucidity, even when this particular topic does not appear as the central theme of many of the stories. The resentment for embodying Mayaness would have been present in virtually every member of the Maya population at the time. But none had the capacity to articulate this affect in words, in literature, as de Lión had. His aesthetic project indeed reassesses the internalized inferiority felt by provincial Maya youth as a result of racialized subalternity. De Lión struggles to transform these traits into a viable and legitimate cultural identity, one capable of generating agency and configuring an emancipatory movement at a future date. However, specific imagings and figurations of racialized subalternity appear in all of them. His consciousness of what he was trying to achieve also leaks out of Mario Roberto Morales's newspaper column, when the Ladino novelist recognizes:

> Yo había publicado ya *La debacle* y también varios relatos en un periódico que se llamó *La Nación* y que desapareció del medio, en los que trataba de captar elementos del mundo indígena mediante el manoseado recurso del realismo mágico. Cuando Luis los leyó me dijo riéndose: "Mejor ocupate de tus ladinos y dejame los indios a mí."
>
> (I had already published *La debacle* [The debacle] and also some stories in a newspaper that was called *La Nación* [The nation] and that later disappeared from public view, in which I was trying to capture elements of the Indigenous world by way of the overused technique of magical realism. When Luis read them, he laughed and told me: "You better take care of your Ladinos and leave the Indians to me.")[5]

Palacios has already signaled that for de Lión it indeed mattered a great deal that he become the artificer of a notion of Indigenousness (91), though this should be understood as an exercise of agency in decolonial fashion. Racialization was undoubtedly the central issue tormenting his existence, and it is also in this light that we should understand his comment regarding the fact that Nobel laureate Miguel Ángel Asturias ought to be "killed." As Morales Santos has claimed, and as Palacios summarizes, de Lión's statement was not meant in a literal way. Rather, it was a symbolic articulation of his thinking, whereby he believed that Asturias indeed was a master craftsman of words and ought to be studied and understood as a writer but certainly not as a spokesperson for Indigenous causes, since, in de Lión's—and most Mayas'—understanding, Asturias had no political sense whatsoever of what being ethnicized, racialized, and subalternized subjects was all about. For Asturias, Mayaness was simply the topic, the representation, the basic material from which he constructed his cathedrals of words. Unlike Gaspar Pedro González, de Lión admired Asturias as a writer, but he abhorred his political stance. It is because of this that Emilio del Valle Escalante argues that de Lión's text suggests that Pascual

Baeza's actions in the novel generate a decolonizing Indigenous mobilization that becomes an expression of Maya nationalism.[6] However, my inclination is to disagree with his statement. While I do see de Lión as a self-configuring intellectual who single-handedly reached conclusions pointing in the direction of racialized subalternity and could creatively process them into an emancipatory project, I do not see his literature as inscribed within the parameters of political mobilization per se (though I do see his own militancy in the PGT working in that direction). Rather, I visualize it more as decentered experimentations whose plurality of voices, rhythms, and other innovative textual strategies correspond to alternative forms of knowledge inscribed more within affect (and literary knowledge) than ideology. As we know, those primary sensations, feelings, or intuitions that constitute literary works can be discovered, conceptualized, or processed by just about any creative subject, which is why artists on the so-called periphery often appear to prefigure theoretical writings later conceptualized with their full pomp and regalia of philosophical trappings in the European "center," as was the case of de Lión with racialized subalternity. In this same logic, though, I do think that Palacios's observation that the novel denotes "absolute violence" (102) in Fanonian terms is correct. This manifestation closely corresponds both to Bolivian scholar Javier Sanjinés's category of "viscerality" and to Puerto Rican philosopher Nelson Maldonado-Torres's depiction of the logical consequences of what he labels the *ego conquiro*. Palacios reminds us how Fanon argued that "absolute violence" was necessary to interpellate and vanquish colonial forces subjugating colonialized subjects (103).[7] Viscerality is for Sanjinés an analogous force, apparently anarchic or unexpected, "that helps explain how Indigenous subalternity has resisted giving up its identity to rationalist Western discourse" (5), as explained in note 12 of chapter 1. Maldonado-Torres, on the other hand, argues that machismo is the consequence of the *ego conquiro*, a will to conquer and enslave, which he associates with masculine sexuality as a source of aggression, as is explained later in this chapter. Coloniality, more often than not, places subjects of color under a murderous gaze that inevitably elicits an equally forceful reaction. It is in this sense that del Valle Escalante could ultimately be right. De Lión's fiction does not stage a process leading in the direction of an emancipatory revolution. But it certainly represents the chaos and violence encompassing colonialized beings, and there is evidence that it would seem nearly impossible to eliminate these constraints other than through violence of one form or another.

RACIALIZED SUBALTERNITY IN THE SHORT STORIES OF LUIS DE LIÓN

I begin my analysis by looking at the first story in the volume I am presently examining, "El inventor" ("The Inventor"). In this text the categorical phrase that begins the narrative by stating, "This is the town of Juans" (23), positions readers at the entrance to a world that has internalized its own racialization.[8] The act of naming everyone the same, "Juan," generalizes the objectifying gaze of Ladino racism (i.e., a mixed European and Indigenous identity with a Western-centric worldview).[9] Ladinos often call all male Indigenous subjects "Juan" or "José" (and all women "María"), because they objectivize Indigenous peoples as racialized nonbeings. In the racist's gaze, they are not subjects. They are simply objects. Nonetheless, de Lión plays with this uniquely unpleasant gesture and turns it upside down by articulating the incongruity of irony as a rhetorical device. His discursive use of irony enables him to reappropriate Maya subjectivity as a mechanism for agency:

> Juan Caca, el del mismo olor de su nombre, pero que, sin embargo, siempre es invitado de honor en todas las reuniones. Y Juan Hueso, el casi sin carne y sin sangre y que, para su suerte, vive junto al cementerio. Y Juan Burro, el viejo medio baboso que, además, es dueño de un animalito orejón que da las horas más puntual que los mejores relojes. Y Juan Poste, el insensible en su cuerpo, el quieto toda la vida, el firme cuando camina. (23)

> (Juan Crap, the man who smells like his name, but who, nonetheless, is always the guest of honor at all of the gatherings. And Juan Bone, the man who's got no meat on him, no blood and who, lucky him, lives next to the cemetery. And Juan Burro, the old, half-dumb man who is also the owner of a long-eared little animal that is more punctual in keeping time than the best clocks. And Juan Post, numb in body, quiet his whole life, solid when walking.)

Mocking begins with his capacity to make fun of Indigenous peoples by representing them as provincial ("pueblerinos") and, on top of that, Indigenous. The narrative voice introduces this element to contrast the subjects named with the original meaning of the words defining them (crap, bone, donkey, post) and their surnames, an obviously artificial notation. This generates an incongruity between what is said and what is meant. The rhetorical wordplay absorbs the humor of the characters' naming, a discordance deliberately created that depicts a situational irony, one in which Ladinos mocked Indigenous peoples with these insulting nicknames, yet the Indigenous writer appropriates them in turn to mock Ladinos by making incongruous the outcome of the offensive epithets. At the same time, the descriptive expressions that accompany the "Juans" also individualize each of the characters, thereby transforming them into subjects. They are no longer interchangeable Juans; rather, they have become specific Juans with differentiating characteristics. This rhetorical gesture humanizes them. The sarcastic play thus becomes a simulacrum of the Ladino racialized model, reminding Ladino readers of their own racialized behavior. We can consider what Baudrillard wrote more than thirty years ago—the simulacrum does not hide the truth, but rather the truth hides a lack of substance. According to him, when it comes to simulation and simulacra, it is "no longer a question of imitation, nor duplication, nor even parody. It is a question of substituting the signs of the real for the real" (2), thus pointing to the loss of our ability to make sense of the distinction between nature and artifice.[10] In this double play, by mocking the reification of Maya subjects, de Lión ends up mocking the lack of substance in Ladino racialization.

Of course, in this particular story the parody centers on Juan Father (Tata), whose representation transforms itself into a burlesque reversal of the colonizing process and, in turn, humanizes the representation of the Catholic Christ figure:

> Este Juan, sin embargo, no es de este cielo; es de más allá de estas montañas y aun de la mar; nació en la otra cara del mundo y de allí se vino cuando lo mandó a llamar un obispo que había dispuesto fundar aquí su encomienda. (23)
>
> (This Juan, however, isn't from this heaven; he's from beyond these mountains and even beyond the sea; he was born on the other side of the world, and that's where he came from when a bishop who had decided to establish his *encomienda* [land grant][11] here called for him.)

The parodic play previously stated is complicated by the details that Juan arrived with his goat, "sweating, struggling, and holding himself up with his wooden staff" (23). The text tells us that he arrived half naked, "only a few pieces of leather covered his private parts" (23), and was surprised when they grabbed him, asked to name the town after him, ushered him into a procession, put him in a palace "of stone and brick, with stairs leading up to it and bell towers,"[12] and:

> lo metieron a puro huevo hasta adentro de su casa, lo colocaron en el centro del altar principal acompañado de su chivo, le dijeron que contara su historia, que inmediatamente pintaron en grandes cuadros en ese mismo altar para que nadie olvidara quien era él, y lo dejaron allí para siempre. (24)
>
> (they forced him violently into his house, they put him in the middle of the main altar accompanied by his goat, they told him to tell his story, which they immediately painted in huge portraits around the altar so nobody would forget who he was, and they left him there forever.)

As such, the easiness of the story transforms itself into a counterdiscourse of colonization. Underneath the parody of the Jesus figure, there is a problematization of the local population's Catholic beliefs and a critique of dominant models of exegesis about Jesus's life. A little while later, a character named Juan Without History appears before Juan Father. The narrative voice changes at this point from the third to the first person. This narrative "I" is the Indigenous subject: Juan Without History, "a man who had nothing between heaven and earth, because not even the little piece of my today in which my feet found themselves was mine, much less the time that my shadow occupied" (25–26).[13] Once again, the ironic sarcasm articulates the centrality of the peripheral subject: the marginal Maya subjects lacking interpretive history due to their exclusion from official history. Official history, in turn, exposed as an imposture in this rendering, recognizes only a Criollo-Ladino teleology to justify the occupation of the geopolitical space, a literary chronotope in the Bakhtinian sense, which Ladinos name "Guatemala," and Mayas call "Iximuleu."[14]

The sarcasm that turns to irony evidences the textual tension existing between the uses of signifiers indicating playfulness and the scathing denunciation articulated by Maya subjectivity. It displays the black holes hidden within Ladino rhetoric, which Ladinos violently attempt to impose as Reason itself. The writing process is thus a struggle to create an alternative truth and to validate it above and beyond the racist "official" Ladino discursivity. The stories are written in Castilian. However, behind the specter of this imperialist language, one can subtly, metalinguistically, perceive the hidden presence of the author's incantation of his native Kaqchikel. De Lión is proposing to make himself understood from within the perspectives of this basic conflict: the existing tension and dispute between written Castilian and a Kaqchikel voice lurking behind those utterances like a forked tongue that creolizes and deliberately mixes signifiers to confuse, exploiting turns that are unacceptable to the Spanish academy. This positionality enables a discussion about the Eurocentric nature of the concept of "literature" and the problems implied when oral practices defying attempts at translation are included within the framework of what is labeled "literature." It also opens up a debate regarding the Eurocentric nature of literariness as the recognized form of constituting social imaginaries in illiterate countries such as Guatemala, flooded by subalternized and racialized positionalities, which nowadays include even black indigeneities claiming belongingness after living for centuries in the Caribbean coast.

Let us return to the analysis. In "Los hijos del padre" ("The Sons of the Father") de Lión rearticulates parody by way of two Holy Week processions—one for the "rich" and one for the "poor." Yet underneath this class antagonism lies, once again, the specter of racialism. It is known that the processions on which this story is based are those of the Escuela de Cristo (Christ's School) Church, for upper-class Ladinos from both Guatemala City and Antigua who have a criollo worldview, while the "poor people's" procession is that of San Felipe, a suburb of Antigua, where the penitents are primarily Indigenous. The race between the processions to be the first to cross an intersection in the town of Antigua is, thus also about "race," broadening the presuppositions of this signifier. Inevitably, it leads to a confrontation of the two groups of *cucuruchos*. A *cucurucho* is a conical pointy hat. In Guatemala, however, cucurucho has become the name for the male penitents who carry over their shoulders the processional floats with images of Christ and the Virgin, regardless of whether they wear such pointy hats. A crucial line in this story reads, "[I]t had been a long time since our little father enjoyed his processional carpet; a long time now that the other one left ours only the discarded bits and pieces of it" (30).[15] Here de Lión is describing the carpets that are made mostly of dyed sawdust, flowers, seeds, fruits, and bread, by residents, friends, and families, and that are presented along processional routes. They are offered up as a sacrifice in anticipation of the procession that will ruin them. The cucuruchos carry the floats over these carpets, inevitably destroying them with their feet as they walk. Thus, a procession that passes over any given carpet after the first has gone over them gets only "the discarded bits and pieces of it," the phrase in de Lión's story. The tropes in this phrase synthesize the unfortunate consequences of five centuries of colonial oppression. Indigenous subjects get only leftovers, bits and pieces of the country they once owned, in metonymic fashion. The trace of coloniality, hidden behind this chain of significations, problematizes Ladinist rhetoric, if colloquially, and inevitably generates the irreducible energy of those others who see themselves as humiliated, forgotten, marginalized, and racialized. We have here an echo of Derrida's words that "play is the disruption of presence. The presence of an element is always a signifying and substitutive reference inscribed in a system of differences and the movement of a chain. Play is always play of absence and presence" (*Writing and Difference,* 292).

When the poor procession's cucuruchos literally fight those participating in the rich one so as to get there first, for once, their reaction stages the struggle for decoloniality; that is, the poor cucuruchos embody the energy of those subalternized subjects who, without knowing coloniality's logic, react viscerally against the conventionalist rhetoric of a racist and exclusionary modernity. The phantasmic shadow of injured Mayaness seeking payback emerges from under the cucurucho's hood. We know that "my mother, my father, and my dog went down to Antigua to be with our own for a while" (28).[16] This sentence clearly delineates an Indigenous family that transports itself not only geographically but also conceptually from the Maya village to the Ladino colonial city, and its positioning is clearly racialized:

> Ambos (cristos yacentes) son hermanos. Si son hijos del mismo Padre.
>
> Pero el de la ciudad es el que les hace los milagros a los Ladinos . . .
>
> Y el de la aldea es el que nos hace los trabajitos a nosotros, la indiada, la pobrería de los pueblos. (28)
>
> (Both [recumbent Christs] are brothers. They are children of the same Father after all.
>
> But the one from the city works miracles for the Ladinos . . .
>
> And the one from the village does little jobs for us, the mass of Indians, the poor townsfolk.)

The quotation reveals the point of articulation between the illusion of a world that considers itself and constructs itself as the only possible one (that is, the logic of Ladino modernity) and the underlying consequences behind the axiomatic imposition of such arbitrary rhetoric (the logic of coloniality weighing on Maya culture). The short story clearly captures all existing binary oppositions—rich/poor, city/village, Ladino/Indigenous—in a few lines, and articulates the colonial wound inflicted, in this case, on the Maya population. Additionally, the story further underlines its irony by referring to both social groups through the same ritual figure and religious practice—namely, the recumbent Christs of Good Friday, in the Catholic Holy Week.

A different way of presenting similar issues occurs in "La puerta del cielo" ("The Gate to Heaven"), the featured story in this volume. Ethnicity affirms itself in a regional locale marked as a *topos*, a geographically delineated identitarian space associated in turn with the perspective of childhood:

> Yo no he salido más allá de los ixcos de Guatemala, pero a todos aquéllos que traen en sus pestañas el color de otras tierras, que traen su corazón bailando con otras músicas distintas de la música de la marimba, que traen en sus zapatos miles de capas de polvo de otros caminos—tanto que ya nos parecen más altos—les he preguntado si en alguna otra parte donde no hay guardabarrancas ni cenzontles ni quetzales ni xaras ni chipes, sino otra clase de pájaros, hay alguna puerta del cielo. Me han dicho que no. (31)
>
> (I haven't ventured beyond the *ixcos*[17] of Guatemala, but of all those who carry in their eyelashes the color of other lands, whose hearts dance to music that is different than the marimba, who carry on their shoes thousands of layers of dust from other roads—so many that they seem taller to us—I have asked if in different places where there are other kinds of birds, where there are no *guardabarrancas, cenzontles, quetzals, xaras,* or *chipes,* if there is a door to heaven. They've told me there is not.)

Ixcos, music, the color of the land, and birds are the topographical factors configuring identity in a specific "habitus" in the sense of Bourdieu, one that generates what Abril Trigo labels an "emotional memory," without which we cannot conceptualize social imaginaries.[18] When the local children discover the door to heaven, "we were a mass of barefoot, flea-ridden kids with broken Spanish" (32).[19] De Lión adds the element of childhood to consolidate the reliability of a nonreal trope (a door leading to heaven) but ratifies the topographical trait laden with Maya beingness. The children are positioned in a precise place and geographical environment, as are their economic conditions:

> de lunes a sábado íbamos la mitá del día a la escuela y la otra mitá a trabajar duro en el monte y casi todo el domingo lo ocupábamos en ayudar en otras cositas a nuestros tatas . . . acarrear agua, ir a conseguir leña . . . cortar frutas para que nuestra nana las vendiera en el mercado, y solo en la tarde . . . cuando el sol se vuelve el pan de que se alimenta el volcán de Fuego, nos juntábamos . . . a jugar fútbol con una pelota de trapo. (32)
>
> (From Monday to Saturday we spent half the day in school and the other half working hard in the fields, and almost all day Sunday we spent helping our folks out with other little things . . . getting water, finding firewood, . . . gathering fruit so our moms could sell it in the market, and only in the evenings . . . when the sun becomes the bread that feeds the Fuego volcano, we would get together . . . to play soccer with a ball made out of rags.)

The description names Maya subalternization without enunciating it. The rest of the plot unfolds from the perspective of Chabello, a child who sees what adults cannot, because they are not positioned in the same cultural and imaginative perspective, in the same locus of meaning. They constitute different ways of thinking and feeling culture. The story brings both codes together, but de Lión does not let them interact. The adult man who "was not from around here" is incapable of observing what the children see. Parodic enunciations manifest themselves in the description of this man, which clearly marks him as an alien figure within the tightly knit community:

> Su cara era colorada y llena de rayitas de lo chupada; tenía unas cejas grandes, como si fueran de paja . . . y unos ojos que . . . buscaban a saber qué; su nariz era larga, puntiaguda, afilada como machete, de gruesos pelos en las ventanas, y debajo de la nariz le nacían unos bigotes que se alargaban y luego se enrollaban como patas de mesa colonial. Era alto y seco . . . Tenía una voz vieja, reguardada, podrida, que antes de que le saliera por la boca, le hervía primero en el pecho. (34)

> (His face was red and full of those lines that skeleton-thin people have; he had some big eyebrows that looked like they were made out of straw . . . and eyes that searched around for who knows what; his nose was long, pointy, sharp like a machete, with thick hairs in his nostrils, and under his nose whiskers grew out and curled up at the ends like the legs of a colonial-style table. He was tall and skinny. . . . He had an old, guarded, rotten voice that, before it came out of his mouth, first boiled up in his chest.)

"Parody," from the Greek *paroidia*, meaning "burlesque poem or song," is both a symptom and a weapon; it disfigures canonical presuppositions, but, fundamentally, it is a critical act of revalorization. Certainly the "literariness" of the work is marked by the presence of the parodic element. In the background, however, stand contingent discursivities of Ladino teleology, against which de Lión's figures and signifiers are measured as if they were catachreses. Parody thus inverts the racialized subject's sense of nonexistence, the dehumanization and inferiorization felt, and the structural and institutional racialization and subalternization that continue to position Maya subjects, their knowledges, logics, and life systems below those of a Eurocentric perspective. Once de Lión describes Ladinos and foreigners, they can never again be seen as "normal." De Lión's parody unsettles the traditional ordering of knowledge, which has placed Eurocentric discourses over Indigenous ones throughout modernity. Humor thus unsettles alternative insights, while placing the exceptional nature of Western-centric hubris. De Lión's signs efface their credibility; they are left as if preread and deconstructed. Instead of eliciting "truth," Eurocentric discourses have been transformed into objects of mockery. Additionally, de Lión's parody is an acclimatizing gesture. When he mocks the subject residing in a "place above"—here, the rich foreigner who came to the village to construct a mansion on a mountaintop—the narrative voice makes the reader familiar with the Maya cosmovision from within, which the child operates. It forces the reader to work to locate himself/herself within Chabello's perspective. Readers thus unknowingly enter into a Maya cosmovision, which makes seeing the entrance to heaven possible. The latter is a trope acting as a metonymy of a secretive culture.[20] This figure of speech plays into Mayas' knowledge of the cosmos. The "gate to heaven" stands textually as an ecstatic signifier that intends to activate a nonrational understanding of the human spirit, if we are to understand "nonrational" here within strict Western parameters that dismiss affect. Because of this, parody is the principal, formal means of constructing the text. Derision becomes a symbolic means of articulating a sense of the subject's integrity with his/her cosmic environment. Furthermore, the contrast between parody and the cosmic symbol accomplishes a hermeneutic function by articulating a reading that specifies the cultural space from which the act of reading itself should be practiced. It forces the reader to configure his or her subjectivity as a reader—to feel Maya in the act of reading.

Parody is one of the principal means of self-reflexivity. De Lión seems to suggest that all fiction is a grimace copied from reality, in the sense of both informing the reader of events that could have happened and articulating an effort to convince him/her of their veracity. By configuring a texture of affective interactions in the contact zones of racialization, his corrosive mockery dissolves the pompous, querulous Ladinoness that would like to inscribe itself within Eurocentric patterns of power. Ladinos do exercise race as a system of domination and subordination of Mayas, precisely because they are insecure about their own identitary configuration. Ladinos continue to flee from the Mongolian stain that would seal their belonging to an Indigenous world.[21]

According to this logic, "the gate to heaven" becomes the untangling of a textual strategy that articulates the superior discernment and clairvoyance of the Mayas vis-à-vis Eurocentric subjects (whether this is confirmed or not) and its violation by the latter. De Lión's critical vision as articulated in various grammatical and semantic variations is a performative force that wants to engage with Eurocentric racism from within its own rhetorical system as an event of resistance. He launches humorous provocations with excess, so as to then unchain an alternative subjectivity—Maya subjectivity—that opposes as well as complements Ladino discursivity. De Lión's occurrences' humor nonetheless frames his understanding of what it means to be caught in the webs of coloniality's rapacious stretch. The categorical ending of the story—that is, the affirmation that the gate to heaven is closed "forever"—anticipates Anibal Quijano's theorization in the 1990s of the problem of racialism as the mainstay of the coloniality of power. The ending symbolically configures the world as one marked by social stratification based on racialization. This is what has blocked Mayas' entry to "heaven," a trope of their aspiration to a qualitatively superior existence, one which would be possible only if racialized subalternization were to disappear. In other words, it could happen only prior to 1492, before those men with "red faces" (as that of the adult man who "was not from around here," which is also an ironic play on "redskins," the racialized labeling of Native Americans by Anglo subjects) first appeared on the mountains, or—perhaps implicitly or hypothetically—after a revolution liberates Maya ecospaces from the trace of colonization. Without a doubt, this is one of the most complete stories of the collection.

In contrast to "The Gate to Heaven," parody functions in a different way in the story "Tarzan de los monos" ("Tarzan of the Apes"). The textual appropriation of the popular early twentieth-century British series complicates the plausibility that a reader could accept a disempowered Maya subject named Benigno Julián as playing the role of Tarzan, and that his girlfriend, "Jane," could be played by Angelina Chonay, a woman who also happens to be Maya. Therefore, the parodic play is here the reverse of the previous story. This time around, mockery strikes the Maya actants of the text.[22] The caricature is somewhat ameliorated once again by the fact that the protagonist is a child. The story articulates the fantasy of this boy (Benigno) who, believing he is Tarzan, falls in platonic love with another child he calls "Jane." She is older than he is. When she falls in love with somebody else, Angelina abandons "her" Tarzan. The story is also a proposition for settling accounts with the Anglo-Saxon imaginary that permeates popular culture, pushing it to its limit, while stripping away the coded white illusion of reigning over subjects of color and unmasking its preposterousness.[23] "Tarzan of the Apes" thus offers a new model for processing the transference and reorganization of the Eurocentric legacy and archive for populations that happen not to be of that accursed cultural origin. The children "meet" Tarzan in the Díaz Theater in Antigua, a provincial town that is not even the capital of this country located at the margins of social visibility and presentability. The child "realizes" that he is Tarzan, and he projects that imaginary onto his surroundings:

> Desde que anunciaron que yo iba a aparecer en historietas, me puse a ahorrar para comprarme. Centavo que me daba mi mamá, centavo que guardaba. Cuando apareció el primer número, inmediatamente me compré. Me gustó un poco, pero no tanto. Allí aparecía yo hablando bien el español, y eso no era cierto. Con cada número me desilusionaba más, pues siempre se me exageraba. A veces aparecía manejando un avión, yo que solo los veía pasar en el cielo. Un tal Lex Barrer era el que me imitaba. A pesar de eso, siempre me compraba. (42–43)

> (After they announced that I was going to be in a comic strip, I started saving to buy it for myself. Every coin my mother gave me was a coin I saved. When the first issue came out, I immediately

> bought it. I liked it OK, but not that much. It showed me speaking Spanish well, and that wasn't the truth. With every issue, I was more disappointed, since they were always overdoing me. Sometimes I'd be flying a plane—me, who'd only seen them go by in the sky. Some guy named Lex Barrer played me. Regardless, I always bought them.)

The parodic form of double identity plays with the tension created by the historical awareness of the gap between the fantasies articulated by the Eurocentric dominant world-view and those of its other, operating outside of the privileges of the former. In the imaginative world of Tarzan, an English lord turns into the "noble savage" whose empire consists of animals from the African jungle. In the imaginative world of Benigno, he is Tarzan. He does not know how to swim, because there is no river in his community, and this humorous description marks those traits that imply the conditions of underdevelopment under which Benigno lives:

> Si apenas había agua en las pilas. Antes si había un pequeño riachuelo que venía del nacimiento de las Minas en el pico del cerro de Cucurucho. Pero como África estaba en una finca, el dueño lo desvió para sus regadíos y nos dejó sin río. (41)
>
> (There was hardly any water in the water tank. Before, there was a little river that came down from the Minas spring up on top of the Cucurucho Mountain. But because Africa was on a plantation, the owner rerouted it to water his fields and he left us with no river.)

Similarly, while it might have been fun being Tarzan on Sunday, he stopped being Tarzan on Monday, when he had to

> agarrar su azadón y su machete e ir a trabajar a su minifundio, luego regresar al mediodía, cargando de leña y sin waziris que me ayudaran y de ahí agarrar para la Antigua, a la escuela, a pie y no en los lomos de Tantor, mi elefante, y regresar ya casi de noche. (41)
>
> (get his hoe and machete and go work on their little plot of land, then come home at noon carrying wood with no Waziris to help me, and from there, be on my way to Antigua, to school, on foot and not on the back of Tantor, my elephant, and then return home late in the afternoon.)

The subalternized reality of this mode of Third World contrasts with the idealized Africa found in comic books, which themselves elude the racial tragedy of the so-called Black Continent, a colonial epithet originating in the European nineteenth century. The story thus transforms itself into an allegory of the exploitation of subalternized innocence that also names the African racialization embodied in the Tarzan narratives so as to project a sense of global coloniality, while continuing to demand sovereignty for Mayas' cultural patrimony. The parody in the story reveals the crisis of inequality marking the relationship between the imperial subject and the colonized subject. The story becomes circular, one in which a Maya Tarzan denotes the historical impossibility of a subalternized subject becoming a superhero. At the same time, the elliptical displacement of his irony-laced rhetoric points at the historical possibility of a need to combat global racism:

> Muchá, nos quitaron África y África es nuestra—les decía a mis amigos.
>
> A ellos les daba risa. . . .
>
> —¿Y qué querés que hagamos?
>
> —Luchemos, muchá. Ya no para nosotros. Para nuestros hijos. (44)
>
> ("Guys, they took Africa away from us, and it is ours," I would say to my friends.
>
> They would just laugh. . . .
>
> "And what do you want us to do about it?"
>
> "Let's fight for it, guys. Not for us. For our children.")

In other words, the story evidently questions Eurocentric premises of a coherent and uninterrupted universality of significations rooted in a world closed off to racialized subjects of the planet, while deferring explicit political solutions in the name of humor. De Lión's parody openly challenges the universality of those imaginaries articulated from within the positionality of hegemonic centers of cultural decision making that uniformly reduce nonwhites to mere signifiers of exoticism in a simplistic, homogeneous form.

Parody also appears in the story "El simio" ("The Monkey"), one of the most overtly political stories of the collection. However, it avoids creating simplistic binaries, as the narrator announces at the start of the story that he had always believed that the comparison of Latin American dictators to apes was over the top, "until one day. . . ." Then the narrator, a schoolteacher, tells us the story of Juan Bonito, a Maya faith healer (*curandero*), and his little monkey. "El mico era el alma de don Juan, y don Juan decía lo mismo. Y andaba con él pararriba y parabajo" (The monkey was Juan's soul mate, and even Juan said so. They went everywhere together [47]). In this instance, de Lión plays with the cartoonish stereotype of a dictator. Instead of representing him as an ape, as is often done in political lampooning, he represents the dictator consulting with a monkey to avoid political coups. The gesture of ridiculous imitation, a typical trait of political satire, becomes an inversion in the story's structure. The challenge posed by de Lión is that of regulating the caricature so as to transform it into ironic difference. At the same time, he adds a carnivalesque element to his description to induce easy laughter. For example, the cathedral, referred to at the beginning of the story, is not an important religious temple; rather, it is a shack behind the school where Juan Bonito lives with his monkey. The dictator is described as follows:

> Era gordo y mantecoso como un cerdo y llevaba una cachucha, una estrellita al hombro, un montón de babosaditas en el pecho y una 45 en la cintura. Caminaba tieso, bien macho, rodeado de su ministro de la defensa, de su plana mayor y de sus asesinos, todos con lentes oscuros. (45)
>
> (He was fat and greasy like a pig, and he wore a military hat, a little star on his arm, a bunch of stupid little pins on his chest and a .45 at his belt. He walked tall, a real macho man, surrounded by his minister of defense, his staff officers and his assassins, all of them wearing dark sunglasses.)

But the parody goes beyond these mocking quips. Rather, it is located within the power of the Maya ritual. As a healer, Juan makes the dictator, "who had at his disposal a stream of psychologists instilling terror" (49),[24] repeat the monkey's prayer and drink contaminated water "that Juan kept on his altar and gave to everybody who consulted him" (49).[25] The healer makes a fool of the dictator, something he will do again later in the story when his monkey dies from alcohol poisoning. The dictator orders a dignified funeral for the monkey and sends a coffin lined with white silk for the burial. The corrosive irony appears in the narrative voice when the teacher recalls, "[W]hen I saw it, I thought about the child who days earlier had his wake at the train station and who had been wrapped up and buried in some newspapers" (51).[26]

This perspective highlights a reconsideration of the norms and expectations with which this dictator articulates his power. It is not merely a shameless abundance of superstition and idiocy taken beyond imaginable limits. The transgression primarily points to the latency of the invisible and infinite fear perpetually gripping the dictator, which the Maya healer is capable of conjuring up. For that reason, parody lies in the transference of fear from the population living under the dictator's rule to the dictator himself, which thus frees the population from the dictator. The dictator's behavior turns laughable, something ridiculous that strips him of his authority and power. If what is called normalcy is preserved by repressing perversion, in this story Juan Bonito succeeds in making the dictator incite it and reveal it in turn, thereby breaking the unstable and precarious balance of the "order of things" and guaranteeing its failure. This loss of fear turns into rage when the dictator's agents insist that the monkey be buried in the cemetery. They insist, despite the municipal mayor's objections that the animal is not human and should not be buried there. The dictator's agents mandate that the burial take place:

> Y fue enterrado en el cementerio, entre una lluvia rala de rezos y cantos y una lluvia espesa de flores que habían sido llevadas en un jeep. Don Juan le puso una cruz, una bonita cruz de cedro oloroso que también había sido donada por el Dictador. (53)
>
> (And he was buried in the cemetery, in a light rain of prayers and chants, and a heavy rain of flowers that had been brought in a jeep. Juan placed a cross on his grave, a beautiful cross of fragrant cedar that had also been donated by the Dictator.)

The transgressive act of the funeral impacts the dictator as expected, a closure of presence, so to speak. He indeed falls victim to a coup d'état. The power play articulated by de Lión is subtle. For the imaginary society represented in the text, the monkey's burial on sacred land represents a transgression. It is unacceptable. But this image is generated by the linguistic function of the utterances. As artifacts, they are the ones defining the anthropological function that conjoins the complexities of absolute power to the absolute fear felt by the dictator himself.

The dictator's lack of moderation is translated into ethical terms. The transgressive function—the burial—generates an invisible element within the text. Between the lines, in the blank spaces devoid of signifiers, we, as readers, can imagine popular opposition cracking the power structure and hastening the fall of the tyrant. Once this happens, the cycle repeats itself. The new dictator gives Juan Bonito a new monkey as a gift so that he can foresee potential coups. As the story comes to a close, we see that the real power lies with Juan Bonito. The fact that he is a healer points in the direction of a Maya cosmovision. Without naming it, the story highlights the superiority of Maya cosmovision, while simultaneously demonstrating how humor is capable of corroding fear of dictatorships. Maya cosmovision, though never named, becomes the place where new power/knowledge relationships favoring subalternized and racialized subjects can be built, overcoming traditional "Indigenous/Ladino" dichotomies. Additionally, the story reveals the antihumanism of dictatorships without falling into the trodden paths of the social literature of the 1930s. This story is emblematic of the collection in that it questions those prejudices localized underneath the racialized assumptions of the Ladino nation and the apparatus it has built to exercise a tyrannical, yet fragile, domination.

"La miss" ("The Beauty Queen") is closer to "La puerta del cielo" in the sense of articulating the imaginaries of the marginal Maya subject in the context of Eurocentric modernity. Again narrated in the first person, but this time by the protagonist, the story features José Raxón, who is obsessed with the image of a woman from a faraway city. From the story's title and the referential signs pointing to the image of a desired "miss," the readers assume that we are dealing with a foreign woman whom the narrator saw in a magazine photo at some point:

> De la revista pasó a mis ojos y se quedó en mis pupilas. Para no perderla, me esforcé en soñar todas las noches. Pero mantener la cabeza habitada por una mujer es terrible. Mis ojos amanecían con bolsas debajo de los párpados y mi boca se abría cada instante para emitir bostezos. ¿Escribirle? No. En la revista solo estaba el nombre de la ciudad. No había otro camino que viajar y buscarla. O mi cabeza estallaría. (55)
>
> (She went from the magazine to my eyes and she remained in my pupils. So as not to lose her, I tried to dream about her every night. But having a woman inhabit your head is terrible. My eyes would wake up with bags under the lids and my mouth opened all the

> time to emit yawns. Write to her? No. Only the name of the city was in the magazine. There was nothing to do but travel and look for her. Or my head would blow up.)

The narrator's obsession with the image of this woman encodes a movement from a rational and ordered state to an irrational and disordered one. In this transition we find the transgression in the story. The transvalued image seen in the foreign magazine names a trope of a mirage of the developed world that draws toward itself subalternized subjects of colonialized countries in a nonanalytic fashion, while simultaneously articulating the image of that desired world into a fetishistic desire. But crossing to irrationality goes further. It implies transforming the main character's will to power into a cruel joke, an abyssal shadow game. The narrator is so determined to meet the fetishized image that he saves money his whole life to be able to travel and do so. He starves himself, sells his parents' property when they pass away, and obtains a passport. Although supposedly articulating his desire to meet this mysterious foreign woman through a series of scenes that also give evidence of his low self-esteem, they in fact contain a veiled attack on the moral, social, and legal borders that define the Guatemalan state. It is here that the story's transgression is located. This display constitutes an astonishing articulation of the theories of excess originally enunciated by French philosopher George Bataille, which evoke the limits imposed on the subject.[27] We should remember here how, according to Bataille's theory of consumption, the accursed share is constituted by that excessive, nonrefundable part of any economy destined for social expenditure. This excess must either be spent luxuriously and knowingly without gain in the arts—in nonprocreative sexuality, in spectacles and sumptuous monuments—or be destined for outrageous and catastrophic disbursements such as wars.

The ending of the story reveals once again a humorous irony. The narrator travels to New York, and the reader discovers that the object of his affection is the Statue of Liberty. However, lacking a visa, he is deported back to Guatemala. The protagonist then returns to Aura, his childhood girlfriend who has had a child with her cousin during his long absence, because she has dimples similar to those of the Statue of Liberty. The latter, humorous as a "silly" object of affection, nonetheless remains standing as a trope of liberty in evoking Emma Lazarus's lines ("Give me your tired, your poor, / Your huddled masses yearning to breathe free"), in contrast to living under Guatemala's perpetual dictatorships.[28] This gesture thus reveals an ambiguity about the neocolonial role of the United States from a subaltern, racialized perspective and a double bind for subjects who cannot enjoy this freedom in either country. Ultimately, though, the narrator remains mired in his world and perspective, with Aura's dimples standing as scant trace of the freedom and modernity that remain out of reach for racialized Indigenous subjects.

"El perro" ("The Dog") reduces the care and generosity one may have toward animals to a problem of power. Once again we have two contrasts. On the one hand, there is Teodoro, nicknamed "el Teniente" ("the Lieutenant"), who names his dog "Fuhrer." The Lieutenant, despite being a Ladino, is proud of his German heritage, even though it is essentially limited to his last name. Nonetheless, his character reflects the attraction that subjects originating in "underdeveloped" societies often have for the developed world's authoritarian models of power:

> Y Mi Teniente cerraba los ojos por un momento y se veía, con quepi y uniforme, parando en una tribuna, firme como un poste del alumbrado público, mientras abajo desfilaban cientos de soldados. Pero abría los ojos y se veía nuevamente tal cual era, un oficinista de la Municipalidad capitalina recibiendo órdenes de unos jefes civiles que le decían Mi general, en broma.
>
> Todos los domingos, sin embargo, Mi teniente se realizaba a medias. Todos los domingos, sin preocuparse de su mujer y sus hijos, salía rumbo al campo de Marte a patear y putear a las fuerzas de reserva del ejército. Era instructor. (66–67)
>
> (And my Lieutenant would close his eyes for a moment and imagine himself with his kepi and uniform, standing on a platform, solid as a lamppost, with hundreds of soldiers parading by below him. But he would open his eyes and see himself once again exactly as he really was—an office worker in the city hall taking orders from civilian bosses who would call him "my General" as a joke.
>
> Every Sunday, however, my Lieutenant halfway became what he imagined. Every Sunday, unconcerned for his wife and children, he would set out for Camp Marte to hassle and kick around the Army Reserve soldiers. He was an instructor.)

Teodoro Flhor actually was a volunteer instructor. He was not paid for his work. However, as a result of his aforementioned German last name, his

Germanophile obsession ("'remember that in this country of Indians you have German blood—it doesn't matter that it is just a few drops,' his father used to tell him," [68])[29] leads him to desire the transformation of his subjectivity. He projects himself into a psychologically torturous imaginary:

> Cuando era adolescente, siempre se miró en el espejo y esperó el momento en que dejaría de ser lo que era para pasar a ser un teutón. Y amó a las rubias, pero ninguna de ellas se fijó en el moreno que era él. Pasaron los años y, como a pesar del uniforme que por un tiempo había usado como caballero cadete, no pudo conseguirse una novia de color de cerveza, tuvo que casarse con una muchacha de segunda, con Lámpara. (68)
>
> (When he was a teenager, he always looked at himself in the mirror, wishing for the moment in which he would cease being who he was and become a German. And he loved blondes, but none of them noticed a brown guy like him. The years went by and, despite the cadet's uniform he wore for a while, he couldn't get a lager-colored girlfriend, so he had to marry a second-rate girl, Lámpara.)

The irony, of course, is present in both his self-inflicted social repression as well as in his own limitations. Teodoro could not be an army officer because he could not pass mathematics. He placed his hopes in having a blond boy, but instead he had three dark-haired girls. Thus, the phantasmatic projection of his anxieties about being a brown Ladino is transferred to the dog. He orders his family members that the dog never be tied, so he can roam freely in the house without any boundaries. This is another transgressive gesture, but one that reverses the one articulated in the previous story. Here, the Lieutenant transgresses the limits of the family's social interactions by destabilizing himself as a subject. His behavior is neither stable nor rational.

The contrast to Teodoro (who aspires to be a dictator) and his dog, Fuhrer, is represented by "Pulgoso" ("Fleabag"), a "lumpenproletariat" dog rescued by a poor family in the neighborhood. In contrast to Fuhrer, Pulgoso has a happy upbringing. He receives all the love and affection that Fuhrer does not get. The story will move forward for Pulgoso, but in this story there will not be any winners. The dogs, and what happens between them, become metonymies of the armed conflict of the 1980s. The subject of the narration disappears. Nothing remains. In Fuhrer's last escapades, the scenes slip from one to the next with no point of reference to place them. The metaphoricity of dizzying destructive movements lacking sense evokes the disturbing atmosphere of the systemic violence of the 1980s, in which all of civil society's moral truths were threatened.

It goes without saying that, for the most part, the richness and complexity of de Lión's stories are found in their resistance to being cut down to a single interpretation or a simplistic binary meaning. The author wills a continuous and consistent articulation of otherness that weaves into language and tone an ethical narrative, which forces an environment of parody, irony, and other rhetorical mechanisms at his disposal and is capable of generating humor, to stitch in the reader's consciousness the phantasmatic memory of Indigenous will to power. This humor is thus not an end in itself. It is deployed to disarticulate the referential horizons framing Guatemalan Ladinoness. Ethics emerge from within language itself by his foregrounding the false rationalist frame that traditionally would denote meaning and lay it open to the judgment of others. De Lión never loses faith in the transgressive capabilities of literature. He flirts with cartoonish stereotypes, but he always flips them upside down to extract ethical meaning from them.

The self-reflection in the structures of de Lión's stories provides a new model of artistic processing of knowledge. He demystifies the fetishization of the Indigenous subject, previously represented by the various *indigenismos* as sullen, opaque, long-suffering, hieratical, or hermetical figures, but always, by extension, as dehumanized subjects; or else depicted as comical drunkards who could magically transform themselves into their naguales at their whim and will.[30] In contrast to these dated, racialized images, de Lión articulates parody to seek the reader's complicity. Once this has been obtained, he mocks the conditions that subalternize both himself and Mayas as a whole, by enunciating a bitter, acidic, corrosive laughter. This type of discourse ultimately emphasizes those fissures marking his social formation. The irony and humor enable de Lión to position them at the interstices of his racialized environment so they may ultimately be interrogated by his readers. De Lión displays a textual strategy in which the obsession with cultural memories and the tyrannical weight of oppression are reversed through self-irony. In each of these stories, his capacity for ironizing the conditions of subjection affecting Indigenous characters provides the elements that articulate their emancipatory potential. This representational achievement destroys the Ladino world.

We can conclude by arguing that whereas de Lión wrote his stories in the mid- and late 1960s, when most decolonial theories were nonexistent and Marxism still reigned in Latin America, his artistry and his own embodiment of racialization enabled him to anticipate them by way of his creative work, one articulating an embedded conception of agency. His work proves, once again, that Latin American writers do not need to follow paths previously opened by conceptual theories, nor does any writer need theoretical orientation to generate meaningful creative acts. De Lión's fictions place the corporeal body within the realm of race perception, and he plays around with the idea of the body as a signifier clearly denoting racialization and subalternity. As previously stated, in the realm of ideas there is no such thing as a linear, progressive history moving from the center to its periphery.[31] Ideas and creative gestures can indeed be rediscovered, reconceptualized, or reprocessed by just about anyone, which is why subalternized, Indigenous writers living on the "fringes" of the so-called modern (Western-centric) world can, and do indeed, prefigure notions that will appear only much later in theoretical writings emerging from the "center." Far from imitating, de Lión anticipates many of the theoretical tendencies that would come in vogue in the late 1990s and the early twenty-first century. It is now time, therefore, to give a master his due. It is fitting that de Lión should be credited with initiating ideas linked to racialization and decoloniality that constitute to date the most epistemologically significant instruments for freeing racialized subjects from the Eurocentric subjection that the coloniality of power imposed upon them. His ideas continue to stand as a revolt both against the heritage of the Spanish invasion and against the global imposition of Enlightenment's "order of things."

RACIALIZED SUBALTERNITY AS EMANCIPATORY DECOLONIAL PROJECT: *TIME COMMENCES IN XIBALBÁ*

As stated in the previous chapter, *Time Commences in Xibalbá* was finished in 1972. At that time the novel technically won Guatemala's most prestigious literary award, the Juegos Florales de Quezaltenango. By "technically," I meant that the jury declared that no manuscript had won the first prize, but *Time Commences in Xibalbá* was awarded second place.

Despite the controversial award, the novel was never published until 1985, a year after de Lión's disappearance. There are various explanations for this, which are hinted at but not developed in the previous chapter. On the one hand, the award offered neither financial benefits nor promised publication of the winning manuscripts. At the time, all Guatemalan authors had to pay for their own publishing out of pocket, a tradition that persisted well to the end of the 1980s. As an elementary schoolteacher with a meager salary, de Lión was in no position to finance his own book. Also, the quality of his text was questioned by both Marco Antonio Flores and José Mejía.[32] Given the brutally racist nature of Guatemala City, perhaps the equivalent of Birmingham or Atlanta circa the early 1960s, de Lión's insecurities as an Indigenous subject kicked in, combined with the fact that he trusted Flores's aesthetic judgment. He then began to rework the manuscript. As the years went by, and the political situation in the country deteriorated rapidly, he prioritized his militant political work over the text. By the late 1970s, civil war seemed inevitable to all concerned. De Lión was also a leader of the teachers union that launched major strikes in the early 1970s, and a clandestine member of Guatemala's Workers Party (PGT). After his disappearance on May 15, 1984, his widow, Tula, gave the manuscript to his old friend Francisco Morales Santos, also described in the first chapter of this volume. His daughter Mayarí and Morales Santos prepared the manuscript for its first printing. To their surprise, they discovered that various versions of the text existed. As Emilio del Valle Escalante has explained (204), after de Lión's disappearance, nothing was known about his fate until 1999, when the Peace Accords Commission made public a Guatemalan army document listing 183 people captured in the early 1980s by military units. The name of Luis de Lión was number 135. In typewritten form the document indicated that he had been captured on the date previously indicated, May 15, 1984, at 5 p.m. in downtown Guatemala City. Added in pencil below was "05-06-84 300," a code indicating that he was executed on June 5, three weeks after he was captured.

As *Time Commences in Xibalbá* derives its title, its topic, and its symbolism from the *Popol Wuj*, in this section I will first explain the importance of this classical Maya book, expanding further on the brief elucidation already remarked upon on chapter 1, prior to shifting to a textual analysis of the novel. Finally, I will place it within a decolonial perspective, one deployed, as the introduction to this volume indicates, to move thinking beyond limiting Western and Eurocentric conceptualizations. As indicated, this approach provides a new way of framing the issues of Indigenous cultural production and agency, transcending subalternized identities originally associated with specific Latin American nation-states in a creative reframing of the implications of racialized classifications of the populations subjugated by the Spaniards in the 1500s.

Spanish invaders created the myth that Indigenous cultures were illiterate societies. This was not true: Maya cultures prior to the invasion were literate. Maya epigraphers Stephen Houston, Oswaldo Chinchilla Mazariegos, and David Stuart argue in *The Decipherment of Ancient Maya*

Writing (2001) that literacy in Mesoamerica can be traced to the Middle and Late Formative periods; that is, within a range going from 1,000 to 400 BCE (16). They add that Maya Itzas living in *Tah Itza* ("place of the Itza"), known by the Spaniards as Tayasal, a city on the edge of Lake Petén Itzá in Guatemala, continued to write in hieroglyphs until the end of the seventeenth century (21). In Mexico some codices, texts painted on folding books of bark paper, are still extant. These were presumed to have existed in Iximuleu at the time of the Spanish invasion, but none survived, as Carmack indicates in *Quichean Civilization* (12–13). In this respect, we should also remember *Writing Without Words* (1995), edited by Elizabeth Hill Boone and Walter Mignolo. In the introduction to this volume, Boone defines writing as encompassing a large spectrum of encoded marks, icons, and other visual forms that do not have to be associated with spoken utterances. She then proceeds to explain how Pre-Columbian peoples employed both semasiographic and glottographic systems (15). The first of these used independent graphic languages not tied to any one spoken language, whereas the second one deployed visible marks to represent elements of a specific spoken language. Mignolo understands this process as defying logocentrism.

During the early colonial period the Latin alphabet was employed for the first time to name non-Western referents. In Mesoamerica, the salient text of this kind is the *Popol Wuj*. It was briefly stated in the previous chapter that the *Popol Wuj* was written in K'iche' in 1550–1555. To this day it constitutes the heart of the Mesoamerican cultural matrix. All Maya groups, whether in Mexico or Guatemala, make references to its creation stories, even if every community changes some names or details and ignore the K'iche' genealogies. The *Popol Wuj* lingers even at the center of Ladino literariness as an epistemic metaphor of the trace of indigeneity among mestizo *letrados*, as also argued in chapter one. It remains a visible sign of their inferiority complex in relation to "whiteness."[33]

The *Popol Wuj* creates an alternative macro-narrative to the Western Bible, by telling the story of creation in a fashion that conflates the origins of all Mesoamerican peoples in a monological foundational discourse. Mythogenesic representations of this text have been traced to the late Preclassic period, from about 300 BCE to 300 CE, though most surviving evidence dates from the Classic period (300 to 900 CE). Most of the figures associated with the *Popol Wuj* first appear in polychrome ceramic vases from this era. Archaeologist Michael D. Coe has related this imagery to Xib'alb'a.[34] The imagery in question shows some of the main characters, such as the hero twins, Junajpu and Xb'alamke (explained in the following pages), as well as the howler monkey gods. Certain scenes have been associated with the shooting of Vucub-Caquix and the restoration of the twins' dead father as the emblematic representation of maize.

Carlos M. López argues that the *Popol Wuj* is not a single text but a compilation of various texts of different ages and origins within the Mayab' (Maya region), leading him to use the term *Wuj* in the plural: *Wujs*, or books. *Popol* in turn stands for "weaving," itself a metaphor for "social fabric." He claims that those books or texts relate both to the origins of the Mayas and to "Xib'alb'a" (explained in the next few pages) date from the Preclassic period; the ones dealing with the hero twins, Junajpu and Xb'alamke (associated with the sun and the moon), to the Classic period; and finally, the ones dealing with K'iche' genealogies (which include many Kaqchikel experiences, as the latter were originally a K'iche' lineage or *chinamit* that broke away from the former in a struggle for power), to the Postclassic.[35] The books included a register of their religion, what López called the *popol cabauil* (deities belonging to the social fabric), a device for day keeping, a task closely associated to religious practices, given that the Maya calendar associates specific rites and meaning to every day of the year; an esoteric ritual register, one of the founding of cities and towns; and a list of the K'iche' dynastic rulers.[36]

More recently, Dutch scholar Ruud van Akkeren has argued that the myth of Xib'alb'a has a Cho'ol origin. In his understanding, the cult begun by the lowland Mayas in present-day Yucatan pushed south at the end of the so-called Classic period (ninth to tenth centuries CE) prior to arriving to the Guatemalan Western highlands. Van Akkeren believes the cult may even have originated much earlier in Teotihuacan, the great Classic city in the central valley of Mexico.[37]

The creation story itself, present in the first three books, is one of a series of successful and failed creations, one where "Xib'alb'a" plays a prominent role. First, the cosmic deities, who include Tepew (Sovereign), Q'uk'umatz (Quetzal Serpent), and three other deities collectively named Heart Sky, succeed in creating the Earth. Feeling lonely, they decided to create beings that would worship them. They manufactured beings made of mud, but those creations could neither move nor speak. After destroying the mud beings with a flood, they tried again, by creating wooden creatures that could speak, but those beings lacked a soul and blood, and they soon forgot about their makers. Angered by the flaws in their wooden creations, the cosmic deities destroyed them with fire.

The creation stories are then interrupted, and the books shift to the story of the hero twins, Junajpu (Blowgun) and Xb'alamke (Hidden Sun).

This is not a gratuitous interruption. It enables readers (and also ancient audiences, since the *Popol Wuj* was performed at public occasions, as Tedlock has argued[38]) to understand the emergence of maize as the substance of life. The hero twins' dual fathers, Jun Junajpu (One Blowgun) and Wuqub Junajpu (Seven Blowgun), are summoned to the underworld, Xib'alb'a, for playing their ball game too noisily (Xib'alb'a is located under the field where the boys played ball). They are given a series of trials. When they fail them, Jun Junajpu and Wuqub Junajpu are killed. Jun Junajpu's head is placed in a calabash tree. His skull later impregnates Ixkik' (Young Blood Moon), daughter of a Xib'alb'a lord, by spitting into her hand. She flees the lords and goes to live with Ixmucane, mother of Jun Junajpu and Wuqub Junajpu, where she gives birth to the hero twins, Junajpu and Xb'alamke. When these two become adolescents, they discover the father's ball-playing equipment suspended from the ceiling of their house, and they start playing as well. Once more, their noise leads in turn to their being summoned to Xib'alb'a for making too much noise while playing. Like their fathers, they are given a series of tests. Unlike their fathers, however, the twins outwit the lords of Xib'alb'a and destroy them. Afterward, they rescue the head of their father, Jun Junajpu, and transform him into a head of maize. They then ascend to the night sky as the sun and the moon. Note that Xb'alamke (Hidden Sun), is the one who becomes the moon. Though described in the episode as a boy, the name begins with the prefix "X" denoting a feminine name. By becoming the moon, Xb'alamke also emblematizes the feminine force complementing Junajpu, who represents the male one in the male/female principle of complementary forces.

At this point we understand the point of the interruption. Human beings could not be created without the germination of maize. With the sun and the moon in the sky, there is water and sunlight to enable the maize plant to grow. Once the cornfield is harvested, the founding parents grind the yellow ears of ripe maize nine times. They do the same with the white ears of corn. Out of this powder, mixed with water and placed over fire, were created the original human beings, the "men of maize." Throughout these fascinating stories there is a constant play of the sun and the moon, associated with fire and water, respectively. The symbology not only is present in the names of many of the characters (i.e., Young Blood Moon, Hidden Sun) but is supposed to represent a cosmological order as well.

In this logic, Xib'alb'a in K'iche', meaning "place of fear." It is generically associated with the underworld, one ruled by deities of disease and death. Xib'alb'a was described in the *Popol Wuj* as either a city or a realm below the surface of the earth, ruled by twelve gods or powerful rulers known as the Lords of Xib'alb'a. Some Christian commentators have associated Xib'alb'a to the Christian hell. However, unlike the latter, Xib'alb'a is more a passage through which all the dead have to go, regardless of good or bad behavior. It is more like another dimension, one associated with suffering and disease, which all beings have to traverse. Symbolically, Mayas associated it to those times when the sun was invisible (the night), or when the moon was invisible (the day). Nonbeingness in the visible world seems to imply being in Xib'alb'a. But, since everything is cyclical for the Maya, all beings that cross through Xib'alb'a have the potential to return, as do the sun and moon every day, after completing their cycle. Though there is the cautionary tale of Jun Junajpu and Wuqub Junajpu, who technically did not return by virtue of their getting killed, in reality they symbolized corn seeds. As such, they germinated, bloomed, were harvested (had their heads cut off), and died, only to repeat the cycle as their own seeds (Junajpu and Xb'alamke) succeeded in replacing them on the surface of the earth. Thus, Xib'alb'a is simultaneously the place of death and the space underground where life germinates when there is enough water and sunlight. It is the space under the ground where seeds have to be planted, and where they transform themselves in order to germinate, ultimately emerging as new corn seedlings in the outside world.

The version that has come down to us was originally written around 1550–1555 in K'iche' Maya, as previously indicated. It is thought that it was copied from either an oral recitation or a hieroglyphic manuscript that has since been lost. K'iche' scholar Sam Colop argues that the second K'iche' generation of leaders made a pilgrimage to Nakxit, near, or in, Chich'en Itza, Yucatán. In Sam Colop's understanding, here they received the original copy of the classical versions of the *Popol Wuj* (17). Ruud van Akkeren disagrees in *Xib'alb'a y el nacimiento del nuevo sol* about the location of Nakxit (94), which he places on the edge of the Chixoy River in the lower Petén. He agrees that the myths and rituals displayed in the *Popol Wuj* came down from Chich'en Itza, but he sees this happening by way of an Itza migration to the south in the tenth century CE (20–21). Whatever the true history may have been, the text we know was written after the first missionaries arrived in the 1530s. For Sam Colop, it is assumed to have been written before 1558 by prominent members or rulers of the Kaweq, Nija'ib, and Ajaw K'iche' lineages (17). For Ruud van Akkeren, exclusively by the Kaweq *chinamit* (222). The K'iche' manuscript was shown in the town of Chuwila (present-day Chichicastenango) to Dominican priest Francisco Ximénez in 1703. He translated it to Castilian, as well as copying the original K'iche' version. After independence from Spain, this manuscript was kept in a neglected corner of the Universidad de San Carlos library in Guatemala City until Brasseur de Bourbourg and Carl Scherzer discovered it in 1854. However, the original Chichicastenango manuscript has disappeared from history.[39] Brasseur and Scherzer published French and Castilian translations a few years later. Brasseur found another copy of the Chichicastenango manuscript in Rabinal, Guatemala, also made in the early eighteenth century. He stole it and took it to Paris. Following his death, it was sold, finding its way to the Chicago Newberry Library. Since Brasseur's and Scherzer's first translations, the *Popol Wuj* has been translated into English and other languages.

I have explained in detail the *Popol Wuj*, because Luis de Lión's novel *Time Commences in Xibalbá* deliberately establishes a dialogical relation with it. De Lión was an avid reader of the *Popol Wuj*. He was also convinced that his own effort was the first narrative written by a Maya subject since the *Popol Wuj*, which he evokes in the title of his novel. Unlike Asturias, he did not want to create a modern reproduction of the *Popol Wuj*. Rather, he wanted to evoke it, while also borrowing some elements of it, such as the image of the twins, which are multiplied in the novel. It may also be a sort of "untranslation," yet one providing a Mesoamerican continuity to the spirit of the *Popol Wuj*. As a writer, he intuited how the differences in language would indicate significant differences in understanding the cosmovision represented in the *Popol Wuj*. He sensed the unique ways in which the play of signifiers in a modern Western context and pre-Hispanic non-Western contexts could be bridged only by an act of the imagination. Besides, as previously indicated, de Lión could not read Maya languages. He was thus a prisoner of Castilian monolingualism.

Time Commences in Xibalbá is without any doubt the pioneer Maya novel of the movement outlined in the first chapter of this book. Having already explained much of its cultural history, I here add Mario Roberto Morales's claim that in 1970 he and de Lión decided to implement a literary experiment, whereby they would both write a circular novel, thus explaining in this fashion the genesis of de Lión's text.[40] Rita M. Palacios also quotes another document by Francisco Morales Santos, where the latter claims that de Lión, having arrived in the city from the countryside, would definitely not write for a country audience; rather, he would do so for those who actually read him, middle-class individuals linked to the literary world in Guatemala City.[41]

Written in Castilian, this experimental text destroys all possible attempts at any linear chronology. It almost feels as if it were rebelling against the temporal, linear explanation of history offered by Western philosophy as a means of decolonizing the Maya eco-space. The text is built exclusively through flash-forwards and flashbacks with iterative phrases and images to the degree that the prologue is the last part of the book, and its last line connects with the first one. If to Western eyes this may seem to complete a *Finnegans Wake* type of circularity, the vision behind its conception is the Mayas' cyclical notion of time, the *k'atun*, which is already present in the earliest forms of the Maya calendar, dating back three thousand years.[42] *Time Commences in Xibalbá* is clearly one of the most complex novels ever written in Central America. Kaqchikel/Castilian linguistic fusion is indicated either by words that function as tropes or by popular sayings associated with village-style life (*naguas*, or *canillas chorriadas*, archaic Hispanisms closely associated with "Maya Castilian" meaning "skirts" and "grimy legs"), often articulated in the characters' dialogues ("*—Allá, muchá. —¿Donde, vos?*" similar to the above, meaning —There, guys. —Where, *vos*?), what Laura Martin calls "the conventional forms of high style expressive rhetoric still found in Mayan languages today" (59). Indeed, in her article she elaborates a rhetorical comparison of the styles of the *Popol Wuj* and *Time Commences in Xibalbá* (53–57), pointing out how grammatical markers are gradually reduced, while highlighting semantic relationships and spatial associations, to conclude that

> [t]he manipulation of internal structures, the ambiguity of interpretive association, and the overlapping referencing that are exhibited here are among the factors that make the highly constrained parallel Mayan discourse forms so entertaining and appealing. (58)

The *Popol Wuj* is, of course, invoked in the title by the term *Xib'alb'a*. Early on in the text, it is further addressed as "that strange book," a coded *mise en abyme* of temporal elements appearing in the larger context of the work itself.

Those are not the only connections to the classic text. De Lión also borrows the duality of the twins, as indicated previously. The two main characters are named Pascual Baeza and Juan Caca. As we see later, they are not exactly hero twins, nor are they actually true twins. They resemble more the hero twins' dual fathers, Jun Junajpu and Wuqub Junajpu, who were defeated and killed by the Lords of Xib'alb'a. The heroine is Concha, who, despite being Maya, looks identical to the Catholic statue of the Ladina Our Lady of the Immaculate Conception in the church (they are even the same height), except for the fact that Concha is brown. She marries Juan and sleeps with all the men in the unnamed town.[43] Because of her looks, local men confuse her with Our Lady of the Immaculate Conception.[44] However, Concha is also portrayed as a twin of Pascual Baeza, yet the two of them are also not true twins in the novel. More than twins, all these characters are truly problematic dualities representing different tensions: man and woman, gay and straight, army and church. The text in this multiplicity of problematizations becomes more like a broken mirror of the *Popol Wuj* than its spiritual reenactment. This is why, in his "Translator's Introduction" to the English version, Nathan C. Henne states in his subsection appropriately titled "Paired Couplets" that

> the very first mention of Concha takes the form of an impossible pair of terms, terms that in fact appear to negate each other. "The Virgen de Concepción was a whore." If we remove the linking verb, we are left with the term *virginwhore*. The poetics of the uncertain imply Concha is both and neither at the same time. . . . But *the* meaning of the apparent oxymoron can never coalesce, though this *seems* to be a primary challenge the novel puts before the reader as a driving force behind the narrative. (xiii-xiv)

The narrative indeed goes beyond a brilliant display of stylistics, form, and Maya symbology. Henne goes on to point out that *nawalismo* (a person's "animal spirit") addresses the identity crisis undermining any possibility of consolidating a foundation for what would be another oxymoronic trope: a Guatemalan nation-state (xx). Emilio del Valle Escalante argues that it is "also an attempt to articulate Maya nationalism as a political alternative in the struggle against racism and colonialism" (205), while adding that it stages "an epistemological challenge to the discourse of *indigenismo*" (210) and, in particular, to Asturias's own *Men of Maize*, "which promotes the vindication of the Indigenous world through cultural *Mestizaje* (hybridity)" (210).[45]

The novel is divided into five parts, if we include the epitaph among them, with a "prologue" at the end of the text. Each part is in turn divided into various sections. The first part, titled "First There Was the Wind," begins with an allusion to the strong wind hitting the town.[46] Afterward, the town's dogs and coyotes howl. The narrative voice represents all the villagers as a nonindividualized collective. Laura Martin has argued that the use of a plural, unspecified voice is a key element in traditional Maya narrative (46). In her understanding, the "most cursory reading of the Hero Twins' exploits, introduced by the collective 'we the K'iche,' illustrates all of them" (46).

A cold wave then ensues, followed by silence. The sound of a cart is heard as it advances noisily from the cemetery to the main square. In the cart is a skeleton. It laughs, plays marimba music on its ribs, and begins to dance. Then it moves on, stopping in front of all the houses to dance in front of each. Finally, it steps into the last house and disappears. The narrative voice then addresses the reader, stating that if you opened the gate of this "plastered and whitewashed adobe house with a tile roof" and then went into the small room where all the saints were housed, you would see a table where there are pictures depicting Christ, saints, and Our Lady of the Immaculate Conception. The scene is described almost as if a movie camera were traveling from a medium shot of the house to a close-up of the pictures on the table. This initial sequence finally unveils an unknown "I" behind the narrative voice: "So . . . if, from there, you walked ten paces to the left—and it was exactly ten paces; I know, because I counted them many times. . . ." (6). We still, however, have no clue as to who is talking, nor do we understand entirely why he is describing those items in the house.

All of a sudden, this voice makes an unexpected and shocking claim: "The Virgen de Concepción was a whore. I never met her. But I remember her" (8). The shock passes when we find out that the narrative voice is describing a real, fifteen-year-old woman:

> someone first noticed she looked like the image of the Virgen de Concepción there in the church from which she got her nickname: she had the same hair, the same face, the same eyes, the same eyelashes, the same eyebrows, the same nose, the same mouth and she was even the same size; the only difference was that she was dark, that she had tits, that she was flesh and bone and, what's more, that she was a whore. (8)

Having thus introduced Concha, the narrative voice proceeds to describe her wedding night. When her unnamed husband mounts her, he describes her vagina as "the entrance to hell" (9). She feels insulted. Nevertheless, he desires her. But "her body kept filling up with more and more birds" (10), an allusion to her sexual voracity in desiring more and more orgasms, until her husband "wasted away to pure skin and bones from a real good case of tuberculosis" and died.

Sexuality is thus introduced in the text. Karen Poe argues that the novel is structured around masculine impotence or fear of it (87). She adds that we are confronting characters who masturbate alone, who are always waiting for someone else who never arrives, and who fail to obtain pleasure from sex. The only exception is Concha. Amy Olen sees her husband's insult as an aural "rape" that launches Concha's self-awareness of her status as a subalternized woman of color and initiates her as a transgressive, counterhegemonic force by means of her sexuality (8–9). However, the sexual language of Concha's body, denoting a budding transgressive, feminist position, defeats her husband's injurious masculinist discourse, vindicating her sexuality as a powerful, transgressive force ("Hacia una lectura decolonial," 10). In Olen's understanding, then, Concha redefines the biopolitics controlling feminine Indigenous sexuality.

An aggressive, desiring woman, Concha returns to her parents' house and has sex with all the men in town. Males complain that she only uses them but never falls for anyone in particular. When rumors about her spread and the local priest curses her, her parents kick her out of the house. She then moves to a little hut down the road and keeps having sex. Her father chases her farther away; "she ended up at the last little thatched hut on the last street. And from there she didn't budge" (11).

The priest visits her to expel her from the town but ends up sleeping with her as well. The same is true of the local authorities. At this point she feels "at the very height of her powers" (12), and "she'd start feeling like crying from pure joy" (12). However, the narrative voice then informs us that men enjoyed their sex as well because they fantasized that they were "actually on top of the real Virgen de Concepción" (12). This utterance is followed by a racialized epithet: "Once a fucking Indian, always a fucking Indian!" (12). It is at this juncture that the reader discovers the racialized element of the novel. Coloniality always makes reference to race, as we see in the last section of this chapter. Indigenous men, victims of opprobrious discrimination, fantasize about having sex with the image of the Virgin, not out of sacrilege but because she is the only Ladina woman in town. Since Guatemalan Ladinos think of themselves as white, this would be the equivalent of having sex with a white woman. Here we stumble upon what María Lugones labels the "colonial/modern gender system," one in which "men who have been racialized as inferior" (1) inflict symbolic or real violence on women of color as coloniality militates against masculinist beingness. Lugones claims that "colonized females got the inferior status of gendering as women, without any of the privileges accompanying that status for white bourgeois women" (13). Nelson Maldonado-Torres also associates the crisis of masculinist sexuality with coloniality. He argues that machismo is the consequence of what he labels the *ego conquiro*, a will to conquer and enslave, which he associates with masculine sexuality as source of aggression. For him, this syndrome includes the feminization of the enemy (in the novel, Maya males) as an expression of symbolic domination, and dependency on exploiting female labor and their bodies.[47] Concha is not seen as a subject by masculinist desire. She's a stand-in for Indigenous males' racialized desire, thus denying her the agency she has struggled so hard to achieve. As Henne also mentions, she never conceded her agency as a woman (xiv).

After the aforementioned incident, Concha moves with Juan Caca to the plastered and whitewashed adobe house with a tile roof described at the beginning of the text, but this is not at first enunciated by the discursive voice. Men continue to visit her, and, significantly, the narrative voices claim that they "all felt white" (13). Surprisingly, one day Juan Caca and Concha show up in church in the middle of mass and tell the priest that they want to get married. The priest acquiesces. However, they never have children. The text informs us that in her first marriage, she gave birth to a stillborn baby. She hated the pain of childbirth and loved intercourse, so she determined never to have a child again and took measures to avoid getting pregnant.[48]

In the section that follows, Concha confirms that all the men in the town indeed have had sex with her, leaving "their armies of Indian spermatozoids on her mountain" (19), another racialized reference marking her power over Indigenous masculinities. Suddenly she recalls that there is another man in town. She sneaks out at midnight and visits him. She remembers that her parents told her she was born at the same time as this man. Consequently, they had always desired each other.[49] She thinks this is not true, because "it didn't matter to her when he went off to the army" (21). Those reading the text for the second time know at this point that "army" is a giveaway reference to Pascual, who will indeed serve in the armed forces, but he remains unnamed in the passage. Concha tries to seduce him, but he turns her down, claiming that he is waiting for another woman, without naming his fantasy: the Ladina Virgin of Concepción.[50] He tells her to run along. The narrative voice adds:

> Yes, he's waiting for the other one. For this one that's here, only if she dies, then if she comes back years later, if her dust pulls itself back together, if that dust forms her bones again, if, with those bones, she walks. (22)

Here we can also see the association of Concha with Wuqub Junajpu (who, despite being represented as male in the *Popol Wuj*, is a feminine force; he/she becomes the moon, the emblematic symbol of womanhood, fertility, weaving, and sexuality for the Mayas); not only was she born at the same time as Pascual, thus being a symbolic twin with him, but she will die and turn to dust, and then her dust will return to reconfigure her bones, as happens to Jun Junajpu and Wuqub Junajpu.

Concha returns home and tries to seduce her husband. She jumps on top of him, but he resists, uttering another injurious speech to her: "Concha, don't be such a whore" (23). She claims that he is not a man. He flees, then returns with machete in hand to defend himself from her, but she ignores him. She goes to the kitchen, "picks up the piece of firewood with the reddest embers" (24), returns to the bedroom, lies down on the floor, and, opening her legs wide, "wields the glowing piece of firewood, and, little by little, as though it were a member, she slowly puts it up inside herself" (24). The smell of charred flesh spreads all over the town.

Gruesome as this scene is, Olen claims that it raises Concha's consciousness regarding the racial and sexual nature of coloniality. She reads Concha's self-mutilation as a gesture of empowerment, an alternate means to efface her sexual being so as to rearticulate herself as a subject ("Hacia una lectura," 14), by eliminating gender domination in closing down her vagina for good, in response to the town's efforts to discipline her by controlling her sex. Poe in turn sees here a female flagellation, paired with a similar masculinist gesture when Pascual, later in the text, engages in violent sex with the wooden statue of the Ladina Virgin (88).

In the ensuing section the narrative voice interpellates Pascual: "And it was to this town that you came back" (26). We learn that he has returned to die and be buried next to his mother, but he has spent time in "that hated world, that Ladino world, where you were the target of discrimination" (26). Nonetheless, he is dying of boredom, drowning himself in alcohol, and continually masturbating. He goes to the church just to watch women go by but is disappointed to see only "common, run-of-the-mill [women], with long hair, bare feet: Indians" (27). He decides to leave; but, before he moves, he sees the object of his desire: "it was her; he felt it. It was her he had been waiting for with love-hate" (27). The first part of the book closes without revealing the mystery of his desire. However, Pascual makes evident the intermeshing of the racialization and gendering process that violently inferiorized colonialized women of color, thus contributing to the disintegration of communal relations that will take place near the end of the text.

The second part, "The Other Half of the Night They Didn't Sleep" (29), begins with a short interlude about how all the townspeople are in the dark, cold and starving to death, waiting for the sun to rise. Convinced that they may be dead and possibly merely souls living in darkness, they try to determine whether they are indeed dead or alive. The brief section, reenacting the mythic move from darkness to dawn in the *Popol Wuj*, ends with the lapidary phrase, "And so, in order not to go on suffering, they decided to invent the day, just in their heads . . ." (30). In the *Popol Wuj*, however, daylight means the beginning of life and a cyclical transition from the darkness and cold of the night. In de Lión's text, people seem mired in darkness and incapable of actually experiencing the arrival of the sun, in a reversal of the classic text, as Martin's work has already pointed out (46). A good deal of the meaning of the entire novel could very well be traced to this short episode illuminating, oxymoronically, its greater signification.

The text then shifts to Juan, again without naming him. He is described as an unfeeling person who did not care for his parents, but he valued the land he inherited, never worked it himself with his own hands but rather was a "little village plantation boss" (31). Immediately following, the narrative voice provides the description of Pascual's return to the town. We learn that his mother was named Piedad Baeza. She was ugly, marrying an old man who barely had time to procreate before he died. Pascual was born small and sickly on November 2, the Day of the Dead. Unable to name him "Deceased," the calendar name for that date, she names him Pascual, "which is the same as calling him deceased, except that it's a saint's name, so it means alive" (34). We then follow his growing-up process. He is skinny but strong. As he grows he becomes a ruffian, beating up other kids and developing a cruel streak. His mother protects him at any cost. His meanness increases. He attacks other kids with a slingshot and later learns to handle the machete better than anyone else. At age thirteen he begins molesting women and girls. One day he cuts a finger off the hand of another kid, and the town finally reacts against him.[51] His mother offers to do time for him. Pascual hides at first and then tries to obtain food from the townspeople, but everyone rebuffs him. In desperation he decides to enroll in the army. Everyone assumes he will rise in the ranks because of his evilness, but soon "a warrant for the arrest of one Pascual Baeza was delivered to the town on account of his having deserted from the army" (39).

In the following section Pascual returns to his village to drown himself in alcohol:

> When Pascual came back to town he brought with him . . . strange words, unknown, like a man who has learned other languages; on his feet he had shoes in place of the sandals made from strips of discarded rubber tires; on his head he had a hat made of vicuña leather in place of the simple grace of the woven straw hat; and on

> his body clothes that were different from those that people wore in the village. He wasn't from here anymore. (39)

Nobody recognizes him. The narrative voice offers a key element for understanding his return. Pascual "had lived with a prostitute who never bore him a child because she didn't want it to be an Indian like its father, but whom he loved anyway because of her color" (41). This telling information explains how Pascual was traumatized by the racism experienced in the Ladino world but also, as Olen points out ("Hacia una lectura," 6), how he has interiorized coloniality himself to the point that a man who has been racialized as inferior loves a Ladina prostitute simply because of the color of her skin, thus signaling the abjection of racialism. In Lugones's words, it makes "visible the instrumentality of the colonial/modern gender system" in subjecting "both women and men of color—in all domains of existence" (1).

Pascual, carrying a big wad of bills in his pocket, heads to a cantina and starts drinking nonstop until he collapses from drunkenness. He repeats the same scene day after day until he runs out of money. He then tells Señora María to charge his bill to Juan Caca. She is surprised but goes to the white house and tells "Mister Juanito" what the drunken man had said. Juan Caca then gives her "the money for the bill—plus some extra money as an advance on the man's next bender" (43).

Following that section, Juan visits Pascual. However, Juan is called Gallina (Hen) by the narrative voice, and Pascual is addressed as Coyote. It becomes obvious that they know each other, but both are gendered in this episode. Pascual is male (coyote). Juan is female (hen), and, for that matter, a hen admiring his gaze, his way of walking, his arms, his whole body, one wishing to be his female coyote (*coyota* in the original Castilian). Hen says that s/he thought Coyote would never return. Coyote then says:

> . . . even if your town hates you, you won't find anything like the warmth of your own little thatched hut anywhere else. Yeah, in other places, they'll open their doors to you, but when they see your skin color, your face, your hair, they think that you're not a man, but just a poor imitation of one, that you're more like an animal, that your natural condition is to be below them. (44)

Afterward, Pascual repeats the story about the prostitute:

> And then you get together with some woman—any woman as long as her skin is a different color than yours—and that woman gives

> you everything a woman can give a man, except a child; because she doesn't want that child to be like you. (45)

Hen then gives him a sack full of white corn and another one full of black beans. Coyote "felt like crying for the first time in his life" (46).

Once more, the text stresses here the abjection of racialism, giving evidence as to how coloniality permeates all aspects of social existence, controlling sex, subjectivity, and self-worth, while naturalizing subalternization. Behind it is the colonialized presupposition that all Indigenous peoples are naturally inferior. Coloniality places subjects of color under the murderous gaze of the vigilant Eurocentric *ego conquiro* of Maldonado-Torres, thus debasing their very subjectivities by making them collude with the inferiorization of racialized females. Pascual and Juan are debased twins in this narrative. Only when this condition is overcome will "dawn"—that is, a new order of things in which coloniality is no longer present, and, presumably, neither is gendered sexism—arrive. Still, Pascual and Juan, both racialized, colonialized males, discover each other as their equal and establish a relation of solidarity between themselves.

The third part is titled "And, in Fact, They Were Alive" (48). The text returns to the townspeople as a group looking at each other as if they were dead, because "they had slid down and suddenly fallen among the coals of the other side of the world" (49). At this point they begin to relive history backward "until they bumped into the last memory that they no longer remembered" (50). Then they begin to walk forward, while crashing into everything they wished for. Xib'alb'a is here the damnation of non-European racialized subjects lost in the darkness of perpetual serfdom marked by continuous violation of their bodies, be that through rape, hunger, slavery, or any other means depriving them of agency and subjectivity.

In the following section Pascual visits the church, stealing and then raping the wooden statue of the Virgin of Concepción, in a gesture brimming with ethnic hatred. The Virgin is referred to elsewhere as "la Ladina" and "the only Ladina in the village." Despite the evident machista attitude implied in this abject gesture, de Lión here reverses its ethnic signification. The rape of Indigenous women by Spanish/Criollo/Ladino men has been common since the Spanish invasion. To this day the rape and murder of women continues to be one of Iximuleu's most entrenched crimes. In social terms, the act symbolizes the ways in which the Guatemalan army—an extension of the state—formed and deformed Pascual's subjectivity, making of him a brutal, macho destroyer of his own culture. As

Foucault might say, the state makes bodies what they are and who they are. There is ample evidence of how the army made rape an instrument of destruction and "re-education," employing it as a punitive counterinsurgency measure throughout the late 1970s and 1980s, along with the murder of Maya children.[52] The racial resentment became confounded with machismo in the dreams of revenge, an untidy and grotesque affirmation of violence offering a problematic masculinist expression of agency. Through Pascual's experience, the entire (male) community acquires consciousness of Ladino racism in an unresolved misogynist gesture. In "Maya Nationalism and Political Decolonization in Guatemala: Luis de Lión and *El tiempo principia en Xibalbá*" (2006), del Valle Escalante argues that "the rape . . . is a radical transgression, an act that will culminate in a collective move to destroy a symbol of domination" (206). The implied "deconstruction" of the image's power functions in the text in a way akin to sacrifice. De Lión invites the reader to imagine a rite that violates received notions of colonialist acceptance. Whereas I agree with del Valle Escalante that the Virgin is "a symbol of power that spreads a colonialist Western ideology" (207) as he claims in the same article, in my reading, instead of seeing rape as "symbolically representing the spiritual and political decolonization of the community" (207), the act becomes a destructive sign eliminating the possibility for transformation. Masculinist misogyny could never be a space for a constructive decolonial process. It is hard to visualize sexuality as a sort of conscious manifesto when, as Karen Poe reminds us, it is mostly "the space of dissolution of subjective identity, of the loss of the self, of the failure of the exercise of power" (87). She adds that sexually, the Virgin's ardor defeated Pascual (88). Besides, there is no rebirth after this experience. The protagonists, once again, are more like the hero twins' dual fathers in the *Popol Wuj*—defeated and mutilated by the lords of the underworld—than the hero twins themselves, who emerge victorious at the end of their trek through Xib'alb'a. Where del Valle Escalante sees "a new national project" (208) in his quoted article, I see a chaotic, failed spontaneous insurrection that, nevertheless, is transgressive in its anarchic, carnivalesque way. This action may represent a promise of further changes to come that will permanently challenge coloniality. After all, we both agree that Xib'alb'a is "where the conflicts between death and regeneration are played out" (208) as del Valle Escalante states, and that, indeed, as he adds in the same page, "the challenge is to defy the gods of the underworld" (208), to finally efface the legacy of coloniality, in the text as well as in contemporary Iximuleu.

After raping the wooden image, Pascual falls asleep. The narrative voice informs us that the incident was not without precedent. One of the town's leaders once kissed her during the procession. Despite the priest's intervention, all the men realized that they "wanted her, hungered for her, desired her," and that they all had "kissed her on the mouth vicariously through the mouth of the cofradía leader" (54).[53] As a consequence, their women realize that their men did not love them. They had

> only used them to release their sexual tension, to have their children, to cook their food; . . . the men had of course always known that their women weren't white; that they didn't have blond, flowing hair . . . that they didn't have thin bodies; and that they certainly were not Ladinas like her; now these differences seemed to weigh on them, hurt them. (54)

When Concha and Juan hear the news, Concha walks out of the house.

In the fourth part, titled "And the Day Came" (63), we return to the townspeople. When they find out that the couple is not dead, they begin to rebuild the town. Suddenly, all the men realize at once that Concha is in the streets. They run to the church, force it open, throw out the old wooden Ladina Virgin guilty of sleeping with Pascual, spit on her, strip her of her clothes and crown while calling her a "whore," dress Concha with her attire, place her on the procession carrier, and take her out in a procession. The women try to rescue their husbands and sons, but the men

> grabbed them by their braids, dragged them to the ground, ripped their dresses; they struck them with machetes and with pieces of firewood and slapped them in the face, on the breasts, in the sex, on the ass, on the legs, on the arms, until they left them lying there facedown or face-up in the streets, bleeding; and then, marching right over their bodies . . . they continued the procession through the streets of the town. (65–66)

When the procession returns to the town square, Concha asks to be taken to the *pila* (water fountain) in front of the town hall. She jumps from the procession carrier and runs to it. Taking her clothes off, while all the men see her naked, staring at her black vagina, she jumps into the *pila* while the men rush at her and kill each other in the ensuing struggle (66–67).

Olen argues that this scene transforms Concha into a redeemer, akin to Ixkik', the mother of the hero twins ("Hacia una lectura," 22). In her reading, Concha first introduced fire into herself when burning her vagina, then plunged into the water of the *pila*, thus combining the two sacred elements, fire and water, both needed for the birth of maize. She also succeeds in destroying the town, as the hero twins did with the lords of Xib'alb'a. Unlike Ixkik', however, she is not pregnant with twins but with the understanding of the nature of coloniality and gender oppression. Olen goes on to argue that Concha is the sole character in the novel that not only undergoes a transformation but also reappears at the end in a positive light, feeding grains of maize to a rooster, a clear symbol of fecundity.

In the short section immediately following, Concha explains to Juan that all the men in the town feel nothing for the Virgin but "a pure desire to fuck her" (68). Juan protests, but Concha argues that "she's not our mother. She's just another fucking ladina; except that she was put here to show us up; you know, a town ladina" (68). She then adds that "when the men from here are in the city, they look for the face of the Virgen in the faces of the ladinas; but when they're here in the village, they look for the face of the ladinas in the face of the Virgen" (68). We also find out that Juan acquired "his unmanly mannerisms" (69) in the seminary, where he had studied for the priesthood. Concha finally states that she does not love him because he never gets his hands dirty "with shit" (68) and because he is "a hollow-ass faggot" (69), and then she leaves.

In a surrealist situation that could very well be a dream, a remembrance, or just Juan talking to himself, a woman enters his bed and forces him to have sex. Unlike in previous situations, he succeeds in achieving an erection and ejaculates. The situation is written in such a fashion, though, that the reader does not know if it happened or not, and if he had sex with Concha, with the Ladina Virgin, or with his own mother. The notable thing, as Poe points out, is not so much whom Juan had sex with, but the fact that the woman is the active agent, transforming the male into a passive receptacle of sex, one implying the dispossession of the only power he had left as a colonialized male of color (89).

When Juan wakes up, he discovers he actually did have sex, and he can smell the woman's scent. He goes out to look for the woman and runs into the procession where all the town's men are carrying Concha, and the only missing men are Pascual and himself. But then he discovers, or hallucinates, that the person being carried in the procession is his mother. She tells him that she is going to die and adds that he should get a woman to make him food, to wash his clothes, and to close his eyes when he dies. He promises his dying mother he will do this. The reader then discovers that after agreeing with his mother's will to get married, Juan decided to find out who was the woman that all the men visited, and "one morning, when he was able to get a look at her, he realized that she looked like the one he loved in secret. Except that she was dark and Indian" (77). Like Pascual, Juan was in love with the wooden Ladina Virgin to start with, thus confirming his state as Pascual's symbolic twin.

In the epitaph that follows, after a surreal psychic turn, the reader further confirms that Pascual and Juan are, in reality, symbolic twins:

> to console himself, he looked for his other. . . . He went to the mirror. . . . He wanted at least the other to keep him company. . . . When he thought that the whole him from the other side was there, he let his eyes cross the dividing line between them, to greet him, so that the other would greet him, so that he would tell him not to worry about it, that He would keep Him company. (81)

In my reading, this split personality is both a trope of Jun Junajpu and Wuqub Junajpu and, at the same time, an epistemic metaphor of the Maya/Ladino split identity traversing both text and society, which destroys the individual as well as the town and the entire community. Henne sees them as each other's schizophrenic voice (xxi). The split protagonist(s) represents two faces of the excruciating difficulties confronted by Westernized Indigenous subjects after becoming Ladinoized, as symbolized by Maya men who stood as racialized beings within the two pillars of power configuring the colonial order: Pascual with the army, Juan with the church. This is why all the townspeople are dead, waiting for the dawn of a new order, and why both Pascual's and Juan's mirror images are "only bones . . . with a few chunks of flesh still on it, but not many, just a few rotten remnants" (81). In Henne's reading, both have failed to negotiate the Ladino world (xxi).

The text ends with the prologue, where "the sugar apple trees . . . were populated with . . . heads of children" (83). The trees finally let go of their fruits, but they fall "not little by little as the fruit matured, but all at once, like rain" (83). The land then becomes dust, a wasteland. Everything rots, and the rooster in Juan Caca's house begins acting as a hen and seeks a nest to warm her eggs. The text ends with the phrase "Then, that night, first there was the wind . . ." (84), the same one as the opening phrase in the text, thus completing the circular textual spin, analogous to the Maya calendar wheel.

COLONIALITY AND DECOLONIZATION

The local histories of Latin American nations with subalternized and racialized populations appear to be both systemic and intrinsic to broader relations ensnared in a racial, caste hierarchy and identity formation of Eurocentric origin that Peruvian sociologist Anibal Quijano labeled "the coloniality of power" in his seminal article "Colonialidad y Modernidad/Racionalidad" (1991). Quijano pointed out that we cannot conceive of Latin American nation-states without a definitional framework enabling a comprehensive understanding of the position of non-European colonialized peoples. Simultaneously, he articulated a need to problematize racialized subjective formations grounded on the social classification of the world's population around the idea of race and/or caste and the memories of violence that these invoke when they articulate their discursive production.[54]

From the point when Quijano launched his concept, many newer theoretical developments have emerged, providing a solid foundation to ground studies done by, or else to benefit, global Indigenous communities, as already indicated in the introduction. At present, as Boaventura de Sousa Santos has pointed out, these alternative knowledges have taken the lead in valuing those systems of thought of populations historically exploited and racialized by the various colonialisms, their sequels, and the dire consequences of Eurocentric socioeconomic models.

Coloniality would coincide with what Boaventura de Sousa Santos labels "abyssal thinking," in his article "Beyond Abyssal Thinking: From Global Lines to Ecologies of Knowledges" (2006), in which subalternized peoples become nonexistent in the eyes of Westerners exercising hegemony. As Arif Dirlik claims, "Nationalism of the ethnoculturalist kind has always presented a predicament of easy slippage to racism" (1368), one in which Mayas always end up essentialized as premodern, inferior beings lacking reasoning. We cannot lose sight of the power dynamics of this labeling, or of the coherence it lends to racial thinking across Iximuleu. To the Guatemalan state, Mayas have always been condemned to social forms of nonexistence. Starting with *Time Commences in Xibalbá*, however, we begin to witness the rebirth of a process that testifies to the knowledge, skill, value, experience, and authority of modern Maya subjects employing fascinating rhetorical devices to engage coloniality and rearticulate their subjectivities within a decolonial framework. The overall Maya textual archive in process of constitution is already a rhetorical monument to this effort, a counterdiscursive strategy of the first order for the rearticulation of alternative social imaginaries within their scope, and a promise of people's abilities to reclaim their knowledges within the Eurocentric world, to then deploy across borders, disciplines, ethnicities, epistemes or temporalities, creative frameworks to engage and confront centuries of subalternization and colonialized oppression. In the following chapters we continue to explore how these manifestations concretized themselves in the literary production of two other narrative authors from Iximuleu: Gaspar Pedro González and Víctor Montejo.

3

Gaspar Pedro González: A Maya "Best Seller"

In the previous chapter I analyze Luis de Lión's short stories and his foundational novel, *Time Commences at Xibalbá*. In the present one I locate the defining characteristics of the two novels published by Maya Q'anjob'al novelist Gaspar Pedro González (1945), *Sb'eyb'al jun naq maya' q'anjob'al/ La otra cara* (1992; *A Mayan Life*, 1995) and *El retorno de los mayas* (1998; Return of the Maya, 1998). It is my contention that both texts, though leaning on the side of the melodramatic as formal novels, do so to manifest affect and grieving as calls to knowledge and as means to grapple with the brutal racism and genocide experienced by Iximuleu's Mayas during the last three decades of the twentieth century.

Gaspar Pedro González was born in 1945 in the Q'anjob'al Maya village of San Pedro Soloma in the western department of Huehuetenango, on a day called Ox Tz'ikin in the Maya calendar, meaning "three birds" and implying creativity and initiative.[1] He has stated that as a child, growing up in his village, he had no idea that he was Maya. A few years later, González won a Catholic scholarship to study in the town of Huehuetenango, the capital of his department. When he entered school there, González was told that he was an "indio," that most insulting of epithets in Guatemala, one where bodies are reconfigured as dispensable objects, and he began to experience daily discrimination both at school and in the streets of the town. Needless to say, González survived, even if marked by the racist traumas that accompany all Indigenous subjects in the country. While there, he was also offered a scholarship to enter a Catholic seminary. González did not think he had a priestly vocation, but he did want to benefit from the possibility of further study. So he accepted the scholarship and was sent to Quetzaltenango, Guatemala's second-largest city, known to Iximuleu's Mayas as Xelajuj Noj. There he completed secondary school in 1968. After leaving the seminary, González went to Mexico City to attend the School of Fine Arts, spending three years in this institution. He went on to graduate from the Universidad Mariano Gálvez in Guatemala City, where González currently teaches Maya literature and linguistics. He also became a longtime functionary of the Ministry of Culture of Guatemala. In addition, González founded and served as president of Sb'eyb'al, a leading Maya cultural organization, which organized the First and Second Congresses of Indigenous Literature of the Americas in Guatemala City in 1998 and 1999.[2]

González began working on *La otra cara* in the 1970s.[3] Originally it was not a novel but a diary of sorts, an attempt to tap the dark recesses of his memory so as to reconfigure his fragmented subject, to heal the trauma of racism by recodifying his childhood and origins in affective terms. It was certainly an exercise of willpower and a desire to come to terms with the fact that, as an Indigenous subject, he did not fit the narrow and stringent specifications of "normality" in his country. The normalizing "truth" constructed through power relations to race and caste had unintended visceral consequences in Iximuleu in the 1970s, as outlined in the first chapter. It often led to radical actions resulting in revolutionary engagement. This was not, however, the case for Gaspar Pedro González. He sought to flee this world instead, first to the capital, and then within himself—to explain it to himself. He immediately ran into a basic problem, however: his childhood world expressed itself in Q'anjob'al, and he did not know how to write in that language. So González began to experiment, to invent, to study linguistics, so as to come to terms with it. He knew instinctively that this "diary" had to be written in his mother tongue, as it was the definer of that specific ambience that he needed to recapture. Only Q'anjob'al could be entrusted to set the affective criteria for constituting a sense of his own subjectivity, for conceiving his body as an inherently existing, thinking, feeling, political being, without this implying a need to rush to armed conflict. It made possible for González to contextualize his childhood experience. Writing enabled him to externalize himself, to challenge Ladino techniques of power, resurrecting his subjugated knowledge that enabled González to generate a self-embracing story. Again, this was not political action implying the will to transform society through violent means, as was then fashionable. Rather, an internal process; almost a subliminal mode of healing himself, which ultimately challenged the subjugation of racialized beings from Ladinos exercising a will to power configured by Spaniards in colonial times. It took him a number of years to finish the manuscript. Over time, he did decide to transform his diary into a novel, though he did not expect that it could be published anywhere. That belief depressed him considerably. When the civil war exploded in late 1979, González stowed away the manuscript. It stayed hidden throughout most of the 1980s. In this sense, the text's history is analogous to *Time Commences in Xibalbá*—finished in 1972 but unpublished for thirteen years.[4] Given all the existing obstacles Indigenous peoples have confronted since 1492, this is not surprising. Innovative or transgressive knowledges favoring subalternized and racialized subjects always take much longer to emerge. This seems inevitable when we consider the enormity of challenges faced.

Finally, in the early 1990s, the author felt it was time to bring the manuscript out and get it published. Not knowing where to seek help, he turned to Steve Elliott, then director of CIRMA in Antigua, the NGO explained in chapter 1. Elliott helped González transcribe the material, and his wife, Elaine, translated it to English for its subsequent publication with Yax Te' Press.[5] Eventually, the bilingual Q'anjob'al/Castilian version was published by the Guatemalan Ministry of Culture.[6] As Rita Palacios has already indicated, the author stated, "La escribí en q'anjob'al. Pensé la novela en q'anjob'al. Pero la iba traduciendo, capítulo por capítulo, al español. El q'anjob'al fue lo último que se metió en la computadora porque la mayor posibilidad de publicar la novela era en español." (I wrote it in Q'anjob'al. I thought the novel in Q'anjob'al. But I translated it at the same time, chapter by chapter, to Spanish. Q'anjob'al was the last thing that went into the computer, because there was a greater possibility of publishing the novel in Spanish [87]).[7] The book was presented to the public on the exact date of the quincentenary, October 12, 1992, in Antigua.[8] At this point in his life, González had the good luck of meeting Fernando Peñalosa, of whom many things are said in the first chapter of this book. Peñalosa's support, his personal visits with him in Guatemala, and his many invitations to the greater Los Angeles area to read in front of Q'anjob'al Maya émigrés consolidated his standing as a novelist. It also enabled the author to attend an Indigenous writers' conference in 1992.

This novel can thus claim the historical role of being the first-ever Iximuleu Maya novel to be written first in a Maya language. It is also the first novel to become a best seller among its people, if by "best seller" we are to understand Guatemala's terms, in which selling five hundred copies in a single year constitutes a record of sorts. Nonetheless, the appearance of this novel, and the year of its appearance, can certainly be read as both emblematic and auspicious. In its English translation in 1995, *A Mayan Life* became a best seller for Yax Te' Press.[9] Its editor, Fernando Peñalosa, however, has this to say regarding the Q'anjob'al edition:

> Conozco un solo caso en que el autor escribió una versión de la obra completamente independientemente de la otra. Se trata de *La otra cara* en español y la versión en Q'anjob'al que se titula *Sb'eyb'al jun naq maya' q'anjob'al*, escritas por el Lic. González. La Fundación Yax Te' publicó la edición bilingüe de esta novela, y tanto para el autor como para el editor y el pueblo maya q'anjob'al ha sido un logro cultural significativo, y un motivo de orgullo para todos. Pero ha sido un fracaso económico. Hemos obsequiado bastantes, pero hemos vendido pocos. ¿Por qué? Porque pocos q'anjob'ales leen su idioma. Es motivo de alegría para ellos saber que se ha editado una novela en su idioma, aunque muchos no pueden leerla. No nos arrepentimos de haber invertido nuestros recursos en este libro, que nos ha dado mucho prestigio pero pocos quetzales.
>
> (I know of only one case in which the author wrote a version of his work in a totally independent way from the other. It is *La otra cara* in Castilian and the Q'anjob'al version titled *Sb'eyb'al jun naq maya' q'anjob'al*, written by Lic. González. The Yax Te' Foundation published the bilingual edition of this novel, and for both the author and the editor, and for the Q'anjob'al people, it has been a significant cultural achievement, and a reason for all to feel proud. But it has been an economic failure. We have given away many, but we have sold very few. Why? Because very few Q'anjob'als read in their own language. It is joyful for them to know that a novel has been published in their own language, even if most cannot read it. We do not regret having invested our resources in this book, which has given us much prestige but very few dollars.)[10]

Indeed, in the mid-1990s, Peñalosa estimated that there were four thousand Q'anjob'als in Southern California; according to professor Nancy J. Wellmeier, around that time there were approximately one hundred thousand Mayas in the United States.[11] Unfortunately, the English translation of the novel not only eliminated critical representations that added Maya symbolic meaning, as I explain later in the chapter, but it also eliminated Q'anjob'al words. These do appear in the Castilian version to underline the significance of Maya concepts in a modern context, and to highlight a hybrid use of language that resignifies the validity of Maya conceptual knowledge. The English version of the novel unfortunately anglicized it to facilitate consumerism, thus stealing from its transgressive core and transforming it into a sort of complacent story of exotic subalternized subjects making good.

Rita M. Palacios argues that Maya writers have to "perform the ethnicity in order to successfully participate in Guatemala's cultural establishment" (82). Whereas this performativity may indeed gather international attention, I disagree that it helps Maya writers within the country itself. Given the nature of racism, it is a detriment, rather, as de Lión discovered early on in his life. In this sense, Gaspar Pedro González may "perform" his ethnicity when giving readings in Los Angeles in front of his own community, or elsewhere in the United States, and abroad. But he never does so within Guatemala, keeping a very low profile, while dressing and behaving like any middle-class Ladino subject. The writing, however, is powerfully decolonial.

Regarding the narrative itself, the author claimed that some notions, such as love, God, and other metaphysical matters, were hard to transpose from Q'anjob'al to Castilian, not because those experiences do not exist in the Maya world but, rather, because they are not spelled out as in Western languages.[12] He states:

> En las lenguas mayas las cosas se llaman por su nombre material. El amor, por ejemplo, no tiene traducción en idioma q'anjob'al. Pero no es que no existen esas experiencias. Se viven. . . . Por eso, cuando escribí la parte de la novela en que Luín y Malín se enamoran, me di cuenta de lo que significa el amor. . . . Pero para los mayas es sentir, experimentar y vivir. No se dicen palabras. . . . Esa noche cuando ellos bailan por primera vez, ellos no se dicen palabras. No hay discurso y palabras muy bonitas. Más bien son sentimientos que se experimentan.
>
> (In Maya languages, things are named by their material name. Love, for example, cannot be translated as a word to the Q'anjob'al language. But this does not mean these experiences don't exist. They are just lived. . . . That's why, when I wrote the part in the novel when Lwin and Malin fall in love, I realized what love meant. . . . But for Mayas this is feeling, experiencing the sensations and living. One does not utter any words. . . . That night, when they danced for the first time, they did not say any words. There was no

> discourse or pretty words. Rather, it was feelings that were being experienced.)[13]

The problem enunciated here reappears in many Indigenous novels. It certainly brings forth, however empirically this sense may appear at first, different modes of experiencing the world. If Westernness is ultimately the legacy of the European Enlightenment, with its enthronement of rationality over the senses, as Kant put it, then many Indigenous literatures offer evidence of non-Enlightenment alternatives of experiencing life not as reflective rationality about the self but as a series of affective states that may include mourning the pre-Hispanic past, and the melancholia of feeling stranded in the racialized present. This is another example of the epistemic violence suffered by racialized subjects. Implicit in this positioning is the notion that if "your" culture has no words to "name" experiences, it must be inferior. Yet this naming and alleged introspection is a direct legacy of Eurocentric rationality and Freudian psychoanalytic legacies, which cannot possibly impinge upon cultures that deliberately have been excluded from the basic tenets of Westernness and have thus developed alternative ways for exercising agency. It also evidences that not all colonialized populations underwent a process of what Spivak calls "worlding" at the same degree, if we are to understand that as "the process through which the local population was persuaded to accept the European version of reality for its modes of understanding and structuring its social world," as Pramod K. Nayar has explained (192). The matter also proves that that there existed multiple forms of colonizing, and the latter category should not be conflated to a single axiomatic model. Perhaps we should follow here Charles Altieri's initiative to rescue our understanding of the affects from philosophical theories that subordinate them to cognitive control and ethical judgment.[14]

I state in another article that Gaspar Pedro González's *La otra cara* is more traditional in form and structure than *Time Commences in Xibalbá*.[15] In the same article, I also claim that this novel operates much like a traditional bildungsroman or "novel of formation." This non-nuanced statement may have given the impression that the use of a Eurocentric literary subgenre of nineteenth-century German origin was not apparently contradictory when critiquing a text problematizing the legacy of Eurocentrism. In this regard, I want to turn to Tobias Boes, who argues:

> The rise of feminist, post-colonial and minority studies during the 1980s and 90s led to an expansion of the traditional *Bildungsroman*

> definition; the genre was broadened to include coming-of-age narratives that bear only cursory resemblance to nineteenth-century European models. (231)[16]

Boes goes on to state that "post-colonial critics have rightfully asked themselves whether the very notion of *Bildung* does not serve to reify hegemonic ideology" (239). He adds a reflection from Maria Helena Lima whereby she questions the form for its presumably humanist goals but also includes Claudine Raynaud's observation that subaltern coming-of-age narratives often imply the discovery of racism (240), and Mark Stein's statement that these texts can have a dual function: on the one hand, they are about the formation of the protagonist, but on the other, they address the need to transform racist societies and cultural institutions. Boes adds, "Whereas traditional novels of formation figure society as a normative construct, the novel of transformation portrays a dialogical process. The hero no longer merely changes with the world; instead, the world also changes with and through him" (240). Ultimately, Boes cites his own opinion on Conrad to argue, in that particular case, for "an 'inclusive exclusion,' a speech act that divides at the same time in which it unites" (241). Whereas this attitude may ultimately prove to be only a sort of "symbolic locus" of belated modernity in the racialized discursivities of marginalized sites such as Iximuleu, it is nevertheless useful, and I therefore include it in the analysis of this text.

THE STRUCTURE OF THE TEXT

The novel's plot appears to trace the lives of Lwin, his father, Mekel, and his mother, Lotax. Lwin, the main character, is born in Jolomk'u ("head of the sun"), the present-day village of San Pedro Soloma, in the Cuchumatán Mountains of Iximuleu.[17] His life is emblematic of the racist violence connected to never-ending governmental abuses and everyday discrimination by Ladinos in all walks of life. The text traces the arc of his life from birth to death. Initially, Lwin grows up immersed in his community's traditions. He then leaves his village to be educated in a Ladino school, where he suffers brutal discrimination from teacher and students. Paradoxically, this leads to his being seen as a suspicious character in his own community, since he is no longer "one of them," by virtue of his acquisition of Ladino cultural traits. Nonetheless, he gradually develops a Maya consciousness. In the end, he succeeds in transforming this into a full-blown ethical conscience based on his ability to reimmerse himself in his ancestral roots. Ultimately, this leads to Lwin becoming capable of exercising agency as a community leader by way of concrete political action.

Underneath this development, a more complex structure emerges. The novel is divided into thirteen chapters, and this is not incidental. The author explicitly wants to relate this numerical factor to the first and last words enunciated in the text itself, given the calendric connotation of the Oxlajuj Ajaw (literally, Thirteen Lord), the most important deity, according to Q'anjob'als, in the Maya calendar. Lwin, the main character, is born on the Oxlajuj Ajaw day and dies on that same day at the end of the novel. Each chapter thus is a calendric stage, one of the thirteen months that the calendric deities have to traverse in the Cholq'ij, or Moon calendar, which is known as "the distribution of the days." Each day is numbered from one to thirteen, and then repeated. The day is also given a name (glyph) from a sequence of twenty day names. The calendar repeats itself after each cycle.[18]

Throughout the narrative flow, there are numerous discontinuous moments that place into question a "natural" understanding of the world, events, and people. For example, the realist prose is often interrupted by mythological language from the *Popol Wuj*. These contrasting styles also allude to different moments and concepts of time: the everyday life of Lwin and his family is framed within the mythic time of the classic Maya text, creating a complex heterodiegetic space, layered with symbolism. The repetitive mention of classical Maya motifs gives rise to a textual interplay between the classical past and the present; it is a desire to underscore the uninterrupted continuity of Maya culture and community for more than fifteen hundred years. This concept of time not only erases traditional Ladino periodicity; it also creates within the text a foundational act to nurture that imaginary continuity of Maya history.

In an as yet unpublished monograph, scholar Gloria Chacón labels this double gaze as *Kabawil*. Represented as a double-headed eagle called *k'ot*, meaning "one head looking at the sky and the other looking at the earth," among some contemporary K'iche' communities, it is presumed to symbolize the classical god Kabawil, meaning "double-sighted deity," and implying two faces, two forms, two opposing energies. The motif originated as the ancient Maya sky saurian representing the ecliptic (the path of the sun and planets through the sky) and the midday sun at the "Heart of Sky" portal. Although the design recalls the European Hapsburg royal symbol, the diamond in the eagle's breast affirms its ancient origin as a celestial icon. Kabawil stands for Chacón—and for some contemporary Maya thinkers in Iximuleu such as Maya Mam scholar Sergio Mendizábal, whom Chacón cites—as the capacity to see reality on a permanent double dimensionality.

This meaning is then narrowed down to a specific process whereby contemporary Mayas see, understand, and problematize the present, without ever losing sight of the pre-Hispanic classical Maya civilization. If I raise this critical contribution made by Chacón here it is because *La otra cara* seems to me to be the most emblematic text I have ever found of this very category.

In this logic, even in the "realistic" part of the narrative, it becomes evident that the plot is not truly centered on Lwin's life. He is not the only protagonist of the story being told. Lwin is featured only in chapters 1 (when and where he is born), 7 (when he goes to school), and 13 (when he is already an old and recognized community leader). His father is the prominent character in an equal number of chapters, and there are some in which none of the family members are mentioned. In those chapters the community as a whole is the protagonist. Indeed, the true central character of the novel is the community of Jolomk'u, and the plot is about their collective path to wisdom. The individualization of the family members becomes necessary only to generate affect in the reading process. But, from beginning to end, there is an ethical understanding that the only meaning possible for any individual is within his or her community. As ethical subjects, individuals are validated only to the degree that they respect and embrace the community's tradition, while observing the symbolic rites and practices that mark a clan-like membership within the community, operating as a *chinamit*. It is this belonging to the community that guarantees the permanence and fulfillment of its individual members while performing mundane tasks of survival. In the text, the village is experiencing horrible misery because of the effects of coloniality, which imply in this context Ladino domination, exploitation, and racism. To this plight, members of the community have responded as separate families, have lost their way. An adult Lwin will point out to them that all they have done to respond to colonialized oppression up to that point is

> Llorar, embriagarnos, desesperarnos, conformarnos con nuestra mala suerte, sentarnos a esperar la muerte; tender las manos a los transeúntes para pedir y recibir lo que les sobra; arrodillarnos ante los que tienen, suplicar, seguir a falsos líderes que nos conducen al abismo y a la muerte. (238)

> (Cry, get drunk, give up hope, accept our fate, sit down to wait for death, stretch out our hands to passersby to ask them for leftovers, grovel in front of those who have something, beg, follow false leaders who take us over the precipice and to death. [219])

The process of regaining Maya local knowledge from within their originary Western-centered frames of reference is what the community needs. Lwin then emerges as the condition of possibility for this new form of agency in the novel and becomes a respected leader, though his concrete political actions are never described in the text. Without naming a guerrilla affiliation, González represents Lwin as a successful grassroots organizer, similar to many activists of the late 1970s, particularly members of the CUC (Committee for Peasant Unity), to which Nobel Peace Prize laureate Rigoberta Menchú and her father belonged.[19] However, unlike its historical emblematic model, in the text the entire initiative comes from Lwin, the Indigenous subject. He realizes this while meditating on the importance of their Maya heritage as a source of strength. Lwin then begins educating community members on this matter. These meetings are represented in the text. Because what matters is the intrinsic nature of Maya culture as constituent of communal cohesion, and as an emotionally charged symbol of strength, Lwin cannot follow the leadership either of radicalized priests of European or Ladino origin, or that of veteran Ladino organizers and activists, contrary to the way most Ladino revolutionary groups recount the "official story" of the Guatemalan revolution, as indicated in chapter 1 of this volume.[20] Finally, as del Valle Escalante points out, there is no textual representation of the effects of the civil war on Jolomk'u itself, even though mention is indeed made to war in chapter 12. Yet the only dead person from the village described textually is Nikol, Lwin's younger brother, who was forcibly drafted into the army and died in its ranks far away from the village.[21] Let us look at this claim in greater detail.

Chapter 1 is dedicated to the birth of Lwin. The text opens with the calendric allusion previously indicated: "Todo comenzó cuando los dioses esculpían en las estelas del tiempo, el gran signo: Trece Ajaw" (1; "It all began when the gods inscribed their great signs on the stelae of time. It was on the day Thirteen Ajaw," [5]). Immediately afterward the narrative voice informs the reader that we are located in a town named Jolomk'u. However, the text emphasizes the name: "Jolomk'u se llamaba desde tiempos remotos, desde los cuentos de los abuelos" (1; "Jolomk'u, according to the stories of the grandparents, was the name of a village," [5]).[22] The emphasis on the real name of what is now San Pedro Soloma is analogous to what happens with Lwin's name in chapter 2, as I explain later. The issue becomes one of naming. Mayas name places and people one way; Ladinos, on the other hand, accept unquestioningly the renaming process imposed by Spaniards in colonial times and stand by them. Indeed, the actual name of the town as officially recognized in the Republic of Guatemala (Iximuleu, for Mayas),

San Pedro Soloma, is never mentioned in the text at all. This issue is further underscored, as the text insists that this is "una noche de mil katunes de historia" (1; "a night of a thousand centuries of history," [5]). The English translation, needless to say, fails to convey the contestatory nature of the text by choosing the signifier "centuries," a Western notion of time counting, over *k'atunes*, a Maya measurement in all Mesoamerican calendars denoting 7,200 solar days, or approximately twenty solar years as understood in Western counting.[23] In that initial descriptive section, reference is also made to *nawales*, in order to further the reader's notion that we are in a different reality from that of the West. It is an alternative belief system engaging subjects in socio-ecologically specific and developmentally patterned ways. It is in this context that we have a description of Lwin's birth, sufficiently detailed to, once again, enable the reader to perceive the contrast between a Western birthing and a Maya one. Mekel has to go find the midwife, Ewul, in a distant village. He is wearing "sandals with their soles made of tire treads" (6), a machete, and his *kapixhay* jacket. The midwife's birthing preparations include "artemisia and *pericón* herbs, chicken fat, and a bottle of liquor" (7); the liquor, in reality, is *kuxha*, clandestinely made Maya liquor, as the Castilian version states on page 3. Meanwhile, Lotaxh—Lwin's mother—has prepared a straw mat for birthing. She also worries about whether the howls of a mountain cat (3; translated as a fox in the English version, for some unknown reason) are a bad omen. The reader finds out that the hut lacks electricity when a reference is made to the *candil* (3; a lamp with a candle in it), and about the nature of the hut itself with the signifier *bajareque* expanding the meaning of "wall" (3; a wall made of a mixture of mud and hay supported by a wooden frame, the reference to which is omitted in the English version). By the time Lwin is born, we cannot have any doubt that we are witnessing a different reality, one in which Maya signs themselves woven by the author into the narrative—*nawales, kuxha, tapexhkos, kapixhay*—serve as linguistic markers to rhetorically emphasize the otherness of this world. It is indeed the presence of the past in the present, a way of having been socialized, and a social practice that has become entirely natural by virtue of springing forth from experiences in early childhood as the text depicts it, yet one performed generation after generation, a rhetorical insistence throughout the text. This accumulation of tropes aims to keep a Western reader at bay; he or she can peek inside but not enter. Here we have a reader discovering his or her irreducible secondarity in relation to the text, because meaning is already eluded on the basis of the Maya rhetoricity serving the function of fence posts; they limit the entrance to meaning.[24] Again, here we have an echo of Sommer's classical warning about Menchú's secrets, already referenced in the introduction to this book, about the ethico-aesthetic resistance on the part of Indigenous speakers to keep hegemonic Eurocentric comprehension of their intimate world at bay. It manifests itself differently here, yet it is there. But the Derrida reference is also the sense of an original theft causing a fundamental alienation; in this instance, the thief would be the Eurocentric reader/commentator not abiding by the racialized subject's will to establish limits to his or her accessibility, but the logic would otherwise be analogous:

> *stolen* by a possible commentator who would acknowledge speech in order to place it in an order, an order of essential truth or of real structure, psychological or other. The first commentator, here, is the reader or the listener, the receiver. . . . Artaud knew that all speech fallen from the body, offering itself to understanding or reception, offering itself as a spectacle, immediately becomes stolen speech. Becomes a signification which I do not possess because it is a signification. Theft is always the theft of speech or text, of a trace. (175)

In this logic, Derrida also implies that "theft" points in the direction "*inspired* by an *other* voice that itself reads a text older than the text of my body or than the theater of my gestures" (*Writing and Difference*, 176). The latter notion would also apply here, to the degree that Maya writers clearly evoke foundational articulations anteceding the West's invasion and occupation of the Mayab' Tinamit, as explain in chapter 1. The organizational field of contemporary Maya fiction in this sense becomes a rhetoricity evoking this founding anteriority that Maya terms invoke not only with their anti-Latin roots' abundance of consonants but also with their phantasmatic recollection of existing first as glyphs—a non-Western hybrid pictographic and phonetic system of writing. It is indeed Gloria Chacón's double gaze, *Kab'awil.*[25] *La otra cara* evokes this in its English and Q'anjob'al versions, as well as in the second edition in Castilian, whose cover is decorated by the Thirteen Ajaw glyph. It is this writing protocol that enables the constitution of the Maya subject in the text. The quest for authenticity is articulated and performed by his or her positioning within self-perceived Mayaness. For Maya subjects, this automatically means that they are different from Western-oriented Ladinos. Thus, the last details surrounding the birth of Lwin—a woolen *kapixhay* to make the baby cry with its stiff hairs, because "he was a Maya, so he needed to become accustomed to discomfort right from the start" (9), the midwife symbolically shaping him as if he were being shaped from clay, the red cap on the head, and then blowing in the baby's mouth three times as the Makers and Founders of human beings do in the *Popol Wuj* when creating the men of maize, a gesture that marks the breath "of the Mayas of all ages, drawn from the root of time like a symbol of the life and the inheritance of the ancestors" (9)—all contribute to articulate the function of Mayaness in the text. These linguistic signs incorporate attributes of agency and intentionality from the start. The text informs us that the space where Lwin is born is blessed with incense and the smoke of a corn-husk cigar. Symbolically, so is the text, with this cumulus of tropes envisioned as possessing knowledge of socially strategic information that, having unlimited perceptual access to socially maligned behaviors that occur in private and therefore outside the perceptual boundaries of everyday humans, operate textually as cleansing agents.

In chapter 2 the Ladino and Maya worlds begin to collide. The narrative voice, having previously organized Maya words as symbolic objects serving as actualizers of the foundational principle of Maya continuity, enables readers to position themselves within the perspective of Lwin. This gesture allows the readers to discover "the other face" of the title (the title of the novel in Castilian, lost in its English translation). In this fashion, not only are Ladino readers forced to recognize Lwin as a dignified subject, as a validated other, but they also squirm when racism raises its ugly head. This is the chapter where Mekel and the *ajtz'ib'* (Maya priest) go to the main town to get a birth certificate for Lwin. Unfortunately, they do not know that it is Columbus Day, ironically a date celebrating the "encounter" of races in the Americas. Maya subjects, however, are unfamiliar with this holiday, which pertains only to Ladinos as a means of justifying their belongingness within the structuring dispositions of the ecospace of the Mayab'. Mekel and the *ajtz'ib'* are thus forced to walk the distance between town and village one more time to perform their legal duty. On the way back, the two comment on the implication of these events. The *ajtz'ib'* states that Mayas are foreigners in their own land, a fragment omitted in the English version. Days later they succeed, after paying a bribe, to finally register Lwin. However, his name is changed to Castilian. After all, names and naming imply an exercise of power. Historically, Ladinos have assumed this power since independence, continuing the colonial tradition of transforming Maya names into Castilian ones as a racialist policy:

> The secretary read in a Spanish that limped into Mekel's ears, the paper with the name of Lwin Mekel, changed to Pedro Miguel for the Ladinos, planted like his umbilical cord. It was one more link in the line of Lwins and Mekels from Jolomk'u. (16)

This text, by marking the names Lwin and Mekel as the true given ones, the signs that give continuity to the clan's lineage, the chinamital, inscribes a different genealogy than the one represented in the official documents belonging to what Mayas consider a foreign state occupying them: Guatemala—an attitude marking the provisionality of those very same documents. The narrative voice conscripts the reader into recognizing Lwin's true name as well as valuing him as an ethical subject and an equal participant in any future community to be constructed as a validated ontological category. This is further reaffirmed in the remaining part of this chapter, where the Oxq'in celebration takes place. Whereas the description may appear somewhat anthropological in nature, it is represented primarily through affective means that clearly avoid the normative rationality informing Western-centered social and political orderings that describes ceremonies such as this one as tolerated events of exotic otherness. The textual episode offers, in turn, a nonrational or nonepistemic awareness of the racialized self located within a world she or he does not control. The emotional identification provided by the narrative voice enables the emphasis on the *ajtz'ib*'s spirited speech about Ladinos' negation of Mayas' existence and their daily proto-genocidal practices (24 in the Castilian version; 25, and abridged, in English). Violating Ladino ontological categories, this speech-act operates textually as a counterintuitive code that reframes the communal yearning within an affective will. At the same time, it signals the commitment to share this belief. The breadth of this episode encompassing the second half of the chapter thus focuses on the principles of an alternative Maya knowledge, from which an appeal for their validation as a people may be articulated. An oratorical accusation is also launched in this last part to explicitly name the fundamental loss and theft experienced under Ladino domination.

In chapter 3 the couple consults their *ajtz'ib'* regarding the convenience of Mekel going to work in a plantation to make extra money. The *ajtz'ib'* studies the vibrations of the veins in his leg and the *tz'ite'* beans before informing them that the trip will be safe. At the same time, he also insists that they perform a series of rites to guarantee this outcome. The text thus represents agency operating in consistently patterned and behaviorally significant ways. Immediately afterward the narrative voice describes the departure of all those heading south to work on the unhealthy southern coast plantations. A young girl's loss becomes metonymic of the entire situation. Her family arrives late through one of the many paths emerging seemingly out of nowhere (38, 39). The father is carrying an enormous box in a *mecapal* ("tumpline," [39]), waving to the truck with his hat so they will wait for them. The wife "came out of the underbrush" (39) carrying another heavy load as well as a baby. She's running with only one sandal on, as the other is broken, and she holds it in her hand. Finally, the daughter, "despeinada y llorosa con la cara sucia" (39; "with uncombed hair and a dirty tear-stained face" [39]) is struggling to pull her little dog, who refuses to go any farther. The truck takes off. They barely make it and jump into the moving truck with the help of others. In this struggle, the dog escapes the girl's grasp and falls out. The narrative voice informs the reader that the dog "cayó en el camino entre piedras y aullidos" (fell on the road amidst rocks and moans). Then the narrative voice presents the key element in this overall description:

> Se fue haciendo cada vez más pequeño ante los ojos de su dueña *que gritaba* pegada a las rendijas de los corrales del camión en marcha. Era su única pertenencia aquel infeliz perro. (39; my emphasis)
>
> (It grew smaller and smaller in the tearful eye of its owner, glued to the railing as the truck pulled away. That unfortunate dog was her sole possession. [39])

The English version eliminates the phrase "que gritaba," implying that the owner is not just tearful but actively and desperately screaming as she watches the dog become smaller by the second. The semantic value of this visually striking image represents two orders of reality. It packages the unnamed girl's emotions that she herself could never had articulated in words, within the emotional farewell taking place between Mekel and Lotaxh. As readers, we never "see" Mekel's and Lotaxh's farewell. It is kept out of the reader's gaze and purview. But we can transpose it to the girl's feelings of being torn apart, being destroyed, dispossessed, having lost her sole affective support. This short scene thus contributes to the forging of a new body of feeling that later constitutes Lwin's subjectivity. It becomes the possibility of a new *event* that takes place later in the plot, in chapters 12 and 13. In this sense the lexemes have a syntactic function much like a sort of *mise en abyme* of the Maya situation. They will justify Lwin's ultimate response in the end, on top of mirroring Mekel's and Lotaxh's feelings. The lexemes multiply depths of affective meaning and generate a plurality of emotional layers that advance the plot towards its resolution.

This intensity continues in the representation of the trip inside the truck carrying Mekel and all the other Mayas going to the Pacific coast as if they were cattle. It is not unlike descriptions of cargo trains full of political prisoners in many World War II films and was also narrated by Menchú's testimonio. Like the latter, we have here a portrayal of suffering corporeal creatures imbued with subliminal affective intensities and resonances that decisively influence or condition their political beliefs; yet, as subjects, they are experiencing a torturous nonlinguistic, bodily "intensity" (442), as Ruth Leys would express it.[26] Thus, the affect is conveyed linguistically by the narrative voice, trying to condition the reader's response by means of empathy. There is clearly intentionalism on the part of the narrative voice. None is manifested by the subjects represented in the text. Leys argues that "affect is independent of signification and meaning" (443). Yet scenes such as this one evidence that in literary representation the autonomic responses occur in the bodily realm of the subjects represented, while there is indeed intention of meaning or cognition as far as the narrative voice is concerned. Leys argues that

> there is a gap between the subject's affects and its cognition or appraisal of the affective situation or object, such that cognition or thinking comes "too late" for reasons, beliefs, intentions, and meanings to play the role in action and behavior usually accorded to them. The result is that action and behavior are held to be determined by affective dispositions that are independent of consciousness and the mind's control. (443)

She is indeed right, as far as the represented subjects are concerned, yet not in the literary reading process in which the narrative voice displays the chosen representation precisely to generate a specific form of cognition, if also through empathetic affect (indignation, anger, etc.).

The remaining part of this chapter narrates Mekel's experience at a cotton plantation on the Pacific coast, in scenes described not only by Menchú, but also by 1930s Ladino "*criollista*" literature, as well as Monteforte Toledo's *Entre la piedra y la cruz* (1949; *Between the Stone and the Cross*).[27] Where it differs is in the point of view, which addresses also distinct reference points in place and time. The narrative may be heterodiegetic—the narrator does not take part in the plot—yet this part of the story is told through the eyes and mouth of Mekel, a Maya subject, again with the primacy of the affective marking the representation and attempting to condition the reader's empathetic response by way of the narrative voice's rhetorical selection of lexemes. This narrative continuity basically remains operative throughout the ensuing chapters.[28]

When Lwin is eight years old, he is told that he will be sent to school (chapter 6, 102–103; 97–98). The trauma of attending a Ladino school is described in the following pages. It is at this point in the text that Lwin—as opposed to his father—actually becomes the protagonist. This transition is marked by the child's turn in the direction of Western education, acquisition of Castilian and literacy. It will also unfold into a clash of values between Maya and Ladino ways while he is at school. In a temporal diegetic rupture that becomes a prolepsis or flash-forward, the reader is told by the narrative voice that years after this happened (though in the same chapter, before he actually does go to school), Lwin is conversing with a friend who also went with him to school and then dropped out. The friend states,

> Me acompañaba permanentemente—decía uno de ellos,—una zozobra al hablar, pensar y actuar ante mis educadores extraños; porque no sabía si era lo correcto o no, eso fue estrangulando mi propia libertad, hasta convencerme de que había una clase de hombres superiores a mí, y que yo no podía aspirar a ser como ellos. (109)

> ("I always felt anxious with teachers who were strangers among us," one of them said, "when I had to speak, think or act, because I didn't know if I was doing the right thing or not. This strangled my freedom until I was finally convinced that these people were superior to me and that I couldn't aspire to be like them." [103])

Lwin, instead, lives this experience as a sort of schizophrenia, whereby he has a happy lifestyle at home on weekends, followed by a "personalidad postiza y unas costumbres artificiales" (109; "a false personality and artificial customs" [103]) at school. Another interlocutor uses the image of tying a rattle to a cat's tail and letting the cat then flee, unable to get rid of the rattle, to explain how he felt (109; 104). Back to diegetic time, the totality of chapter 7 is dedicated to describing the misery of school. Maya kids were hit by the teacher with a big yardstick (110–11), and were also tortured by having to kneel over a handful of corn grains or stand in the patio under the sun or rain with their hands up until they fainted. Whereas these corporeal punishments were an actual possibility for all students, the narrative voice informs the reader that they were, for the most part, imposed upon Maya pupils, given the teacher's overt racism, celebrated in turn by Ladino classmates who then took advantage of the teacher's attitude to add to the provocations and/or torture itself. The text makes it clear that for both Lwin and his other Q'anjob'al classmates, the educational experience was a phenomenon that overwhelmed all of them, made their adaptation to society infinitely harder, and, on occasions, generated threats to bodily integrity and severe emotional scars, a sort of betrayal trauma in the sense defined by Jennifer J. Freyd as the kind that occurs when the people or institutions on which a person depends for survival significantly violate that person's trust or well-being (1996). During the ordeal, they all experienced psychological numbing or shutting down of normal emotional responses, which most theorists associate with trauma.[29] They never forget this experience, nor do they want to. As Suleiman states, their experience is "not only a drama of a past event, but also, even primarily, a drama of survival" (280). In this case, Lwin has to live with the implied guilt—implied since it is never stated outright in the text itself—that he survived the experience, while his friends did not; they dropped out. For Lwin, though, it becomes a positive experience despite the trauma, though it takes him years to realize this fact. It is ultimately a powerful impetus for responsibility, pushing him into the leadership role that he eventually plays in the community. At this point it is convenient to remember that the inherent Eurocentric orientation of trauma theory has already been stated, as Irene Visser has pointed out, because the Freudian model "sits uneasily with postcolonialism's eponymous focus on historical, political and socio-economic factors in processes of colonization and decolonization" (273).[30] She also cites Dominick LaCapra's warning about indiscriminate generalization regarding trauma studies. I agree that trauma theory has to be not only enlarged but also reformulated historically and gnoseologically to "enable interrogations of the complex workings of trauma during colonization as well as in processes of self-construction under decolonization processes" (276), because, among other things, the emphasis is on the debilitating effects. I point out alternatives in an article where I address the concept of *Txitzi'n*:

> *Txitzi'n* is analogous to trauma, but with a difference. Whereas trauma implies suffering fear or helplessness as a result of an event . . . the Maya women's response has not included those effects. This is because for them, *txitzi'n* is also a mystical or inner experience. . . . *Txitzi'n* encompasses both aspects: trauma and healing. (116–17)[31]

After all, decolonial struggles are not an impairing disease or melancholic paralysis. Rather, they are a visceral effort of cultural recuperation and the initiation of a process of healing that subverts the traumatic experience.

Another important break in the text's diegetic flow happens in chapter 8, which describes the arrival of the green revolution in the area. The narrative point of view breaks away here from either Mekel or Lwin—the only chapter in the entire text where it does so—as a foreign technician arrives to explain the usage of chemical fertilizers. He has to be fed by the locals at their cost, and the fertilizer has to be purchased from the village town hall, a private business that the mayor runs on the side (122–24). The promised new seeds arrive too late to be planted, and then they do not germinate, because they are too old (124). Those who plant in the traditional way do better than those who embrace the new methods, with the added burden that the latter have to borrow to purchase the fertilizers. The rupture in the point of view is significant, given its uncanny deviation. It seems to mark an experience that, in appearance, is secondary to the travails of Lwin and Mekel; it is unclear whether it concerns them, yet is central to the narrative of victimization of the community through Western meddling that impinges on collective, prolonged, and cumulative experiences of traumatization as well. The seeds' incident reinforces the idea that the true central character of the novel is the community of Jolomk'u. The scene in question echoes the same narrative voice's intention in this regard, previously pointed out when discussing chapter 3. The fact that in most of this chapter the action takes place away from the emblematic family that represents Jolomk'u, yet the narrative voice's tone flows without any apparent change, is a narratological trace of this doubling. The addressivity remains unchanged, expressed by lexical, morphological, and syntactical elements similar to those crafted when the family is staged in the text. In this chapter we have access to the narrated content without Mekel's or Lwin's affective responses. If the fictional narrative normally possesses a specific property that enables readers to distinguish it from the narrative of real facts, historical or autobiographical, this trait breaks down in this chapter, evidencing the rigorous identification of the author and the narrative voice, as these two dispense with the alleged main characters and with any trace of free indirect discourse, but not with the narrative itself. The supposed dissociation between the author and the narrator has broken down as the former uses the narrative function to constitute a historical world with equally historical events, and in this instance chooses not to delegate the narrative to his fictive characters. This apparent error is in fact evidence of the decolonial will on the part of the novel's author. It is a specter, a different relationship of existence to colonialized negativity. The spectral operates here as a form akin to the undead—that is, as a tangible preoccupation of a death that is never assured to actually manifest itself precisely because it is more like a presencing that may have already passed the point at which it could indeed appear. It works much like in the section waiting for the light to emerge in de Lión's novel, as I explain in the previous chapter. The green revolution plays this role in the present text.

Chapter 9 initiates the marriage sequence between Lwin and Malin that is included also in the following two chapters. In the beginning of this concatenation, the community helps build new houses for young adults (143), an action that also points out the continuity between generations in the community. In this task Lwin meets Malin, the sixteen-year-old girl he falls in love with (144). Stressing the collective factor, he sees her again at the communal celebration that takes place after the task is completed, when he desperately searches all over for Malin and finally discovers her helping in the kitchen (162). He then asks her mother's permission to dance with Malin (164). The narrative voice informs us that the experience they were living could not be translated to spoken language but had to be lived in silence (164). Silence here performs a positive, importantly affirming gesture, even when understood in the context that the author explained it, as noted at the beginning of this chapter. It is certainly not a reluctance to communicate. Rather, it is a display of an ethnicized naivete on the part of the characters, which the narrative voice does not share. But it is also a will to break with the Eurocentric regulative idea that imposes speaking to manifest agency on the part of the subject, a notion more associated with Enlightenment thinking. In this scene, affects dominate instead.

In chapter 10 the previous sequence continues. Now the action takes place at the town's fair. Lotaxh informs Mekel that Lwin plans to ask Malin to marry him, but he has no money (170). They therefore decide to sell their two pigs to buy new clothes. On the patron saint's day, there is a parade in town (177). Lwin repeats the thought, previously addressed by the narrative voice, that what is called "love" in the Western world had no verbal expression in his language (181). We return here to the blind faith in the purity of silence that the narrative voice displays, ignoring the inherent disquiet of the Western reader. Lwin finds Malin with her family just when her father has paid to have her fortune read. The next day is the public dance. Lwin's family meets Malin's, and the couple dances together (188). But cuteness and goodness cannot survive long in a racialized world. The army inopportunely raids the village to kidnap young men and enroll them forcibly into military service (190).[32] Everyone flees, destroying the stands and the little fortune-telling birds (191). Lwin manages to escape, but one of his brothers is caught (193). This is a gesture that does not seem to fit with the illusory romanticism of the moment.

The soldiers' noise flattens the naive silence of the young couple, destroying their implicit wish for a culturally clean slate. If the couple's silence expressed a mythic project of illusionary freedom, even if it articulated ways of thinking that most Westerners do not know, the sense of symbolic rape injected by the soldiers' presence dispels this possibility once and for all, leaving the characters—and readers—with the sense of urgency that will be appeased only with decisive resistance to the abject behavior of Ladino domination.

In chapter 11 Lwin's parents consult the *ajtz'ib'*, who believes that Lwin and Malin are made for each other, even if he also predicts that war will come to their homeland (201). The couple's union also expresses here a transformation of the previous silence into a restless need to launch a discursive field through which Lwin articulates the mechanisms of political organization that will lead the community in the direction of a political struggle. Since the latter is rooted in ancestral knowledge and principles, we have, prior to this transcendental event, the representation of a narrative justification for the inherited meanings of their culture by describing the process of the "*pedida*," Lwin's request of Malin's hand in marriage (202–09), followed by the wedding preparations (210–14) and the actual wedding (215–16). This apparent contradictory juxtaposition has led some critics, such as Michael T. Millar, to see "no suggestion of undermining the authority of state structures nor the system within which they function" (75). As explained in the first chapter of this book though, maya culturales did not believe in the outright political confrontation of the Ladino state, unlike maya populares, but favored a subtle infiltration of Maya principles and values to articulate a seemingly invisible resistance. We see these manifestations in the concluding chapters of *La otra cara*, though, admittedly, with some apparent logical contradictions from a Western perspective that give the impression of, well, imprecision, in connecting the Maya world with Indigenous modernity. I do, however, see this phenomenon working as an undercurrent within the text itself.

In chapter 12 the civil war begins (202). At this point the time of narration becomes more elongated; the duration of the story now covers wide tracts of time in relatively few pages. Lwin's brother Nikol is killed while fighting for the army (203). Time passes. Mekel dies (206). Lwin is forced to emigrate to the jungle to feed his family. Years later he is sued by a Ladino for a loan Lwin had contracted with him (209). When he goes to court, he discovers that the papers have been forged and the sum of monies owed altered. He immediately protests but is arrested. After spending time in jail, Lwin is released, and he feels he has reached rock bottom. He then hikes up the mountain where he had gone with his grandfather, to meditate about what to do next (230). The text states:

> Luín era hombre que no había nacido para perder. . . . Quería luchar por su familia y su comunidad y buscaba encontrar el camino más adecuado.
>
> En su fuero interno surgían las alternativas a seguir y las analizaba cada una. Así pasaron horas de meditación y al atardecer bajó de la montaña reconfortado para buscar el calor de los suyos. (230)
>
> (Lwin was not a man who had been born to lose. . . . He wanted to fight on for his family and his community and was looking for the most appropriate way.
>
> Various possibilities rose to consciousness, and he analyzed them one by one. Thus he passed hours in meditation. As evening fell he came down from the mountain, finding comfort in the warmth of his own people. [212])

This is the transcendental moment in the narrative, the instance when Lwin is finally grounded and able to access his inner strength and stability. He faces the most stressful and challenging circumstances in his life up to that point. Yet, by way of a shamanic use of trance, Lwin is capable of visualizing ancestral wisdom. While in this state of flow, he gains information on pre-Hispanic classical Maya civilization and its continuity into the present and future by understanding the Mayas' cyclical notion of time (the *k'atun,* previously explained). The comprehension of the circularity will enable Lwin to live in total integrity with himself and resolve the community's social and political conflicts. Let me add that the shamanic trance and what Lwin visualized is not described in the text. It is all implied. As readers, we know only what was previously quoted—namely, that he spent hours in meditation on top of the mountain, and that many possibilities "rose to consciousness" (212). Yet from those signifiers, readers familiar with Maya spirituality can deduce the transcendental act. One where the top of the mountain becomes the cosmos, aligned by a vertical imaginary line with the axis mundi, pointing to the Tree of Life at the center of the galaxy, as noted in the introduction. The top of the mountain is a ritual landscape. At this point, a new memory that is also an old one takes root.

Social practice begins to take precedence here, even if the text alludes to Lwin having learned to see reality from many viewpoints while staying centered in his personal perspective. It is also the point in the text where the narrative voice decisively adopts the point of view of Lwin as a subject of consciousness. This continues throughout the last chapter. Indeed, at this point in the textual order, a free indirect style takes over the narrative, marking the withdrawal of the author as utterer while effacing all traces of his discourse and ceding center stage to Lwin, in much the same way that Banfield has analyzed narrative style and direct and indirect speech.[33]

In this last—the thirteenth—chapter, Lwin becomes an organizer. The story continues to operate at a faster pace. There seems to be a temporal ellipsis, an omission of a time span that is not only perceptible but measurable as well. The narrative voice informs the reader that "para entonces comenzaban a florecer cabellos blancos en su cabeza" (231; "that's when his hair began to turn to grey" [213]).[34] What is outstanding here, as previously indicated in this chapter, is that Lwin appears as the sole community mastermind. He had reached his own conclusions on how to organize his people politically as a consequence of his meditation on the mountain. This event fulfilled his destiny. He was not imitating Ladino political organizers, nor was he influenced by Western-centric thinkers.

As he becomes a noted leader, Lwin is offered the office of mayor, but he turns it down (241; 222). He is not interested in temporal power and ego recognition—which he perceives to be cultural alienation—but rather in the kind of ancestral Maya knowledge that activates the human spirit and understands the web of life. Time again moves swiftly: Lwin is old and has many grandchildren (243; 223). He then has a dream about the future, one in which his town is blooming in prosperity, and his community is living in total integrity with itself, fulfilling its destiny as it reconnects with its patrimonial cultural sources. More than a cosmic or mystical dream, this is a textual reaffirmation of transcultural elements to underpin the recognition of Indigenous modernities. Lwin then gets sick. A wolf appears near the village (244; 224). Lwin, feverish, begins to hallucinate about his teacher beating him up when he was a child at the Ladino school (245; 225), an echo of the traumatic experience that defined his existence and marked the textual flow. The narrative voice informs the reader, "La comunidad entera estaba reunida en la casa grande, era como su propia casa" (245; "the entire community was gathered in the large house, as though it were their own house" [225]).[35] The narrative voice claims that he was the man who had "señalado el camino, el que había cambiado su destino" (245–46; "shown them the way to success, and had changed their destiny" [226]).

Then, an image of an old wolf is represented as walking westward, signaling the Maya quest for transcendence in the face of death.

At the end of the text, closure between the first and second narrative is brought by the last words Lwin speaks as he dies a natural death in old age. After his successful run as a political organizer, his parting words in chapter 13 are, "Que . . . no . . . haya . . . un . . . grupo . . . ni . . . dos . . . que . . . se . . . quede . . . atrás . . . de . . . los . . . demás" (246; "Let . . . there . . . not . . . be . . . any . . . group . . . that gets . . . left . . . behind" [226]). These words are a direct quotation from the *Popol Wuj*. However, they were also the slogan deployed by the Committee for Peasant Unity (CUC) during the early 1980s. This organization was the primary instrument of massive resistance founded mostly by Mayas. The CUC exposed the disjunctions between Western and non-Western practices by contesting the authority ascribed to Western parameters of modernity, including revolutionary struggle. The CUC slogan was taken from the *Popol Wuj*. Using the slogan enabled them to join the Maya past and present—that is, the Classic period represented in the *Popol Wuj*, and present-day Maya oppression. This phenomenon takes place at the closure of the novel, while also reappropriating the CUC as an emblematic all-Maya organization, and the *Popol Wuj* as a validating contemporary text. Both together signal the foundational way for Mayas' decolonizing mobilizations. This imagery also roots this experience in multiple transcultural features that are heavily anchored in a thorough understanding of ancestral knowledge. This has become integral to contemporary Maya culture dynamically spread out within the altered ecospace of Iximuleu. If on the surface the text would appear more traditional, in reality it operates like contemporary Maya conceptual art such as contemporary Maya artists Angel Poyón's globalized hats or Edgar Calel's thirteen wires to denote the Maya cycle, combining the past with the present within a globalized aesthetic context.

COMING TO TERMS WITH VISIBILITY AND A DECOLONIAL TURN

Gaspar Pedro González had not yet published his first novel when the massacres of Maya villages by the Guatemalan army began in the early 1980s. Shocked, he began to collect newspaper clippings and all the information that could reach his hands.[36] His concern also had to do with close collaborators being kidnapped. González's own Huehuetenango office space was raided, so he had to move to Chimaltenango, closer to the capital. Another time, driving near Nahualá early in the morning, he saw a line of corpses, most likely guerrillas, each shot in the back. It had just happened, and the police had not yet arrived. He was so shocked that he needed help to get back behind the wheel, after some bystanders told him he better get out of there immediately.[37] These experiences became the source of his second novel, *El retorno de los mayas* (1998; *The Return of the Maya, 1998*). Before completing it, though, many more notable events would occur—namely, in the extended process of peace negotiations initiated by President Vinicio Cerezo Arévalo in Esquipulas, Guatemala, in 1988, which lasted until a peace treaty was signed on December 28, 1996, under the presidency of Alvaro Arzú. Prior to the signing of the peace treaty, United Nations representatives had visited the refugee camps in Mexico and recorded the names and personal traits of all official refugees before they were repatriated. González managed to visit one such camp under these circumstances and interviewed a number of Q'anjob'al Mayas.

Return of the Maya was written in Castilian. While this may generate controversy, it is a deliberate discursive event on the part of the author. Language is, after all, the bearer of culture and subjectivity, articulating power in a Foucauldian sense, one operating through the construction of new objects of knowledge by way of recalcitrance in order to name what has been previously invisible in languages deprived of an intransigent exercise of freedom. The choice of Castilian expresses a need to articulate a communicable sense with Western readers. It is an incision within the cumulus of discursivities—all in Castilian—on the topic of Maya refugees in the context of the Guatemala Peace Accords. Whether Mayas, or those sympathetic to their cause, like it or not, Castillian dominates the discursive field of that entity named Guatemala. It is the language of crucial institutions of political or cultural power, and González wants to have access with this text to their administrative and political reach, and impact them with his conception of historical becoming. Adding his own voice enables González to mark this body of language with a will to question Ladino truth. González evidences this stand in the text ("Ya me cansé de que otros, los charlatanes, hablen por mí" [2]; "I am tired of others, the charlatans, speaking for me" [2]).[38] He also restores to Castilian discursivity the living presence of a writing that, while Castilian, is also Maya. As such, it is an event scarring this historical situation, and also a felt need to abolish the sovereignty of Ladino signifiers, by virtue of the peculiarity of those personal pronouns constructing his own subjectivity.[39] This comes into being in language alone, in *q'anej*, Maya words. Yet through the narrator's enunciations it is clear that González felt that this linguistic turn was necessary to confront/inform Ladino readers to grasp the difference between their social imaginaries and his own ("esta palabra aunque no es la mía, sin embargo la tomo para decir lo que siento y lo que pienso" [3]; "please allow me to speak, though this language isn't mine" [2]), obviating temporarily the symbolic, constitutive function of Q'anjob'al ("un día lo diré en mis propias palabras mayas, *q'anej*, cuando en este país las hayan valorado" [3]; "one day I'll say it in my own Mayan words, when they are valued in this country" [2]). As in the previous novel, the English translation undermines some of the Castilian narrative emphases, adding the pleading "please allow me to speak," which is not present in the Castilian version and ratifies the speaker's subaltern's status, instead of signaling a transgression of his subalternized status by addressing Ladinos in Castilian as equals. Notwithstanding these translation flaws, as in de Lión's *Time Commences in Xibalbá* in the previous chapter, we see González's Castilian permeated by Q'anjob'al signs, signifiers, and referents of all sorts, a decolonial gesture of appropriation of the master's language.

Indeed, following the logic stated above, *Return of the Maya* is narrated by a nameless individual defined only as a *meb'ixh* (orphan), a Q'anjob'al child who goes into exile in Mexico but returns to his homeland as an adult many years later. His father and brother were killed by the military. His mother sought to save both him and a younger sister by fleeing to the Mexican border, but she died during the journey. Throughout the text the *meb'ixh* expresses frustration at not being able to learn his grandfather's Maya name, which was also his own—another reason he calls himself an orphan. He is not only an orphan in a literal sense but also an orphan of his own language, his own culture, and his own lineage.

Michael T. Millar sees this novel as representing "a much more extensive examination of the legacy of political and military violence in Guatemala" (75). Though tempted to associate this text with testimonios, most likely because of the rhetoric of the second part and the beginning of the third, Millar explains that this is a "literary construct based on the stories of seven different young people with whom he [i.e., González] worked during his time volunteering in the Mexican refugee camps in the 1980s" (77). He still feels, however, the need to argue that the main character articulates "a more collective sense" in this experience by virtue of the nature of this compilation, as if this has not been the way authors have compiled novelistic characters since the beginning of time, while also adding that the text "rejects individualism" and seeks "a more transcendent Indigenous identity." Whereas the latter is indeed correct, this would not necessarily weave the textual narrative within the testimonio tradition.

The text itself is divided in three sections, addressing the three *meb'ixh*'s crucial lived experiences: the flight from the Guatemalan army into Mexico, life as a refugee in a camp, and the return to his homeland as an adult.

The first section, referred to as "Bab'el Tuqan" in the text, is titled "El éxodo de Yichkan" ("Exodus from Yichkan") in both Castilian and English. The name alludes to the jungle region in the north of the department of Quiché, bordering on the Mexican state of Chiapas, near the Chixoy River, one of the tributaries of the great Usumacinta River—the Amazon of Mesoamerica—where all the commerce from the highlands to the lowlands traveled during the Maya Classic period, where the Guerrilla Army of the Poor (EGP, in its Castilian acronym) operated in the 1970s and early 1980s, and where many Maya immigrants—who had originally abandoned their communities due to lack of land and settled in the Ixcán (Yichkan) region—were then forced to flee the invading Guatemalan army which implemented a genocide through the exercise of necropower—in the sense of Cameroon's philosopher Achille Mbembe's notion—and created a death-world in Western Guatemala.[40] Surviving Mayas were forced to live in refugee camps on the Mexican side of the border.[41]

Our *meb'ixh*, speaking in the first person, informs the reader from the beginning, "Yo vengo de allá. De un allá lejano y sin nombre" (1; "I come from there. From a faraway place with no name" [1]). He then adds, "Yo tampoco tengo nombre: ni apellidos, ni papeles, ni identidad, ni patria, ni tierra, ni pueblo, ni familia, ni padres, ni hermanos" (1; "I have no name either; no last name, no papers, no identity, no country, no people, no family, no parents, brothers or sisters" [1]). As readers, we are facing nothingness; a relative nonexistence. And yet, within this apparent nonexistence, there is a speaking subject, letting readers know that they all fell by the wayside as he abandoned "este lugar llamado Yichkan" (1; "this place called Yichkan" [1]). However, we soon turn to "great time" as in the previous novel, a textual interplay of the double gaze—the classical past and the present as simultaneous horizons of beingness—to stress the continuity of Maya culture, when the *meb'ixh* states that "vengo rastreando las huellas petrificadas de mis ancestros los mayas . . . descubriendo las huellas de sus pies en el polvo del tiempo, en la cara de la piedra, en la cara del barro" (1; "I walk along, dragging the petrified tracks of my ancestors, the Maya . . . discovering their footprints in the dust of time, on the face of the rock, on the surface of the clay" [1]).

After establishing the temporal double gaze that validates Maya culture, as well as an affirmation that, no matter what, there will always be a Maya grandeur, the narrator then elaborates a rhetorical monologue noted by previous critics. In the fragment in question, he plays with the articulation of lists about topics associated with historical Maya achievements that he will *not* be talking about. In this logic, the narrator disrupts this alluded presence of grandeur with a substitutive one, that of genocide against Mayas:

> Debo hablar de lo que he visto, de lo que he vivido y de lo que me han hecho para que quede constancia, para que quede memoria de ello. Debo narrarles los testimonios de las obras de los hombres para exterminar una raza, una cultura y un pueblo, mi pueblo. (2)

> I must speak of what I have seen, what I have heard and what they have done to me, so that a record will be left behind and its memory continue. I must testify to the attempts of some to exterminate a race, a culture and a people—my people. (2)

He then offers his linguistic consideration about *q'anej*, previously cited, adding to the notion of Maya words the challenge that he will use his own language when Ladinos have also learned it, when they have learned to listen to Indigenous subjects like him, and when language prevails over arms. That seeming explanation for the non-usage of Q'anjob'al in this text is arguably an indication of González's movement of interests from the local to the public and national. It is almost as if Q'anjob'al is to be deployed only in a homely context from which it acquires energy and purpose, whereas the public need to address genocidal grievances forces him into a sphere where he is compelled to express himself in Castilian.

Establishing the grounds on which his monologue is rooted, the *meb'ixh* then begins to tell his story. We learn that his is a story of thirty years. His language clearly strains the existing tension and dispute between written Castilian and the *meb'ixh*'s Q'anjob'al voice attacking those Castilian utterances in an even more pronounced way than de Lión did. It is as if having willed this struggle among linguistic points of view, González now wants to put Castilian in evidence for its shortcomings: "Ahora, un *k'atun* después, han transcurrido veinte *hab'il* (años). Los cargadores del *q'inal* (tiempo), se encargaron de transportar sobre sus espaldas este trecho pasado" (3, original italics; "Now, one *k'atun* later, more than twenty *hab'il*, years, have gone by. The *Iqom Hab'il*, the Year Bearers, carried on their backs this long, heavy stretch of time" [3]). They are not accidental catachreses (a term that, after all, means "abuses") but a deliberate intention to signal a lexical gap within Castilian. After all, *k'atun* has no translation (it is a twenty-year period), though the text says "veinte años después" on page 5 ("twenty years later on" on page 4 in the English version).[42] An uninformed reader would never guess the relationship between one and the other. The text also claims that *hab'il* means "years," but there is no explanation as to whether they are solar or lunar years (they are solar, less common for Mayas, whose daily practices are ruled by lunar years, by the Cholq'ij calendar year of 260 days). Indeed, on page 7 the narrator declares, "pero son otros *hab'il* los nuestros," ("but ours are different kinds of year" [6]) and adds that they are counted by the "*txolq'in,*" Q'anjob'al for Cholq'ij, making them lunar years in this case. Likewise, the reader is also told that *q'inal* means "time," but not that it literally means "sun," a connotation also associated with gratification and health, nor that *q'inal* is merely emblematic, as days have different designations anyway, such as "*saqmay*" ("days when you can plant corn"), "*si wil*" ("the day you first plant corn"), "*imox*" ("the day of celebrating the land"), etc. We have here a case of deliberate inexactness to both mock and maintain social pressure on Ladino monolingual readers, while also informing them of the crimes that their people have committed against Mayas. Just lines after the previous one cited, we are also told that Yichkan is named "Ixcán" in its "forma castellanizada" (3; "Ixcán in Castilian" [3]); and, to underscore Ladino ignorance, the meaning is spelled out in the following page:

> Yichkan, punto de convergencia de dos dimensiones de la naturaleza: *yich*, "base, raíz, a los pies de"; *kan*, "cielo, firmamento, espacio infinito." Esta palabra compuesta q'anjob'al quiere decir donde se inicia el firmamento o la raíz del cielo. . . . En el fondo se levanta la inmensa cortina azul, el *kan*, el firmamento en cuya base (*yich*) se extiende la alfombra verde de la vegetación. (4)

> Yichkan is where two dimensions of nature converge: *yich*, "base, root, at the foot of"; *kan*, "heaven, sky, firmament, infinite space." It is a compound Q'anjob'al word that means "where the sky begins" or "the root of heaven". . . In the background an immense blue curtain rises, the *kan*, the firmament at whose base lies a green carpet of vegetation. (3-4; the English version omits the Q'anjob'al term *yich* between "base" and "lies")

Ladinos exploit this land, but they have no idea why it is named the way it is, any more than Americans know what "Mississippi" or "Ohio" truly means. The abuse of metaphorical transfers here is clearly deliberate, wrenching meaning out of the Indigenous language that dominant Ladinos ignore. This gesture establishes a linguistic boundary signaling Ladinos' lack of knowledge by comparison with Mayas. Ladinos are here the ones who have no proper terms available. After all, the *meb'ixh* is a poor Q'anjob'al, certainly not a lettered Maya. His parents were poor enough to be landless and thus forced to migrate to the Yichkan, the destination of the poorest of the poor among Mayas. And yet he adds to the copiousness of language by accomplishing the difficult task of providing a name for those (modern) insolated expanses for which Ladinos merely mispronounce a Maya name whose meaning they ignore, while speaking an imposed language (Castilian) they do not control or even fully understand.[43] The *meb'ixh* does claim symbolic authority here, despite the fact that the cultural battle for linguistic forms takes place in an unevenly structured linguistic world, in which subalternized and racialized subjects like the *meb'ixh* lack any true social influence in their occupied country. It is an outstanding display of wit, a truly imaginative rhetorical invention what we see in this section of the text.

As if all of this were not enough, immediately afterward the *meb'ixh* explains that his story begins in *Yich syelal*, the origin of pain (4 in both versions). As mentioned previously, we know that *yich* means "base" or "root," and the narrator leaves the reader assuming that *syelal* refers to pain, without any further explanation, thus extending the empire of Maya names as a validating cultural code.

The chain of Q'anjob'al signifiers continues throughout the entire text. This arrangement also suggests liberating rhetorical positions beyond territorially grounded notions of Maya and belonging, as a consequence of the original migration to Yichkan. In turn, the previous migration will be followed by newer ones to the refugee camps. Through all these displacements, we have a manifestation of the infinitely ramifying character of Maya discursivity breaking out of its so-called traditional boundaries. The deterritorialization of Q'anjob'al stresses decolonial positionalities, as well, by signaling that language's momentum by virtue of its self-reflexivity. Its very rhetoric articulates the presuppositions on which it grounds itself and deploys its power by subverting a Ladinoized Castilian emblematic of a differentiated society, yet a language framed in the text without narrative substance of its own.[44] We cannot trace, however, this thorough chain of signs traversing the entire novel without risking having to write an entire book to contain its vastness.

Regarding the actual narrative instance—that is, the conjunction between the narrative voice and story—the *meb'ixh* recalls that his childhood memories were triggered by an *iqb'alej*, a rainbow, as the family traveled to Guatemala City to participate in a demonstration while his mother sang to him "*Kitzini tzinini, tzinini tzinin.*" No translation is provided for this (it is onomatopoetic of marimba playing). The soldiers charged the demonstration. His mother fell with him on her back. They were both beaten up, and he lost the red hat his mother had woven for him (10; 9). Sometime later—the *meb'ixh* does not recall how long because he still did not know how to count the *xajaw* (moons)—armed men came to his hut looking for his father. They did not find him, but they killed the *meb'ixh*'s twelve-year-old brother, evidencing how Mayas are excluded from the protection of the law while remaining subject to it, as Agamben describes this situation in *Homo Sacer*. It was the first time the *meb'ixh'* saw the *ajkamom*, the owners of death (11; 10). After the funeral, the father stopped sleeping with them to avoid being captured, but the *ajkamom* came one night and waited for him. When the father arrived at the family hut in the early morning, they captured him and beat him up (13; 12). The description is poignant and saturated with affective traits:

> Yo tapé mis oídos y cerré mis ojos para ya no seguir oyendo y viendo las veces que le daban con la culata y la bayoneta a mi padre. Ya me quité de la rendija en donde podía ver algo. Me hacía mucho daño. Sentía que cada golpe, eran corrientes eléctricas que terminaban por las puntas de los dedos de mis manos y pies. Se encogía mi cuerpo al sentir los golpes y ver la sangre que corría por la cara de mi padre. (13)

> I covered my ears and closed my eyes so I wouldn't hear or see how many times they struck my father with the butts of their rifles or their bayonets. I drew back from the crack from where I could see, because it hurt me too much. I felt as if each blow was an electric shock flowing to the tip of my fingers and toes. My body recoiled with each blow as I saw blood flowing down my father's face. (12)

As in the previous novel, we have a representation of suffering corporeal creatures imbued with subliminal affective intensities. González forces us to share the narrator's trauma to facilitate an entry to those meanings underlying this critical experience. They will point in the direction of a withdrawing of being, while at the same time the subject displays resilience. A concern with death and with the movement of presencing becomes from this point on the situation that defines the character's adversity without yielding to melancholia. It marks future survival, living on while surviving the death of others, continuing to live within the paradox that the juxtaposition of both experiences implies.

After this we have a follow-up description that is strikingly similar to that of the girl and her dog in chapter 3 of *La otra cara*. It is repeated here as a sort of fetishized narrative of dispossession:

> Vi que su figura triste desaparecía por el final del caminito que se iba a la milpa. . . . Desaparecía una y otra vez por las pequeñas colinas. La figura borrosa de mi padre se iba haciendo cada vez más chiquito [*sic*] (13–14).
>
> I saw his sad silhouette disappearing at the end of the path that led into the corn field. . . . Again and again he would disappear over the little hills. The blurred figure of my father was getting smaller and smaller. (13)

The juxtaposition of both images not only complements the sense of losing the father but also articulates a rhetorical cry to frame this event within an affective experience. The text seems to indicate corporeal states recording presubjective, visceral forces at work. These intensities would seem to desire to cloud reason deliberately while simultaneously appealing to automatic responses on the part of the reader's organism, as if presuming that language would efface the cognitive characteristics of the higher-order mental processes, while validating in the same gesture the *meb'ixh*'s survival purposes.

Continuing with the story, we know that the dead body of the *meb'ixh*'s father was later found dangling from a tree, eaten by birds of prey (14; 13). Every time word of the *ajxolaqte'* (those who lived in the wilderness [i.e., guerrilla fighters]) made an appearance, the army would return and massacre more villagers (15; 14). Consequently, the elders held a meeting and decided to flee, though this had to be kept from local authorities. The *meb'ixh*'s mother tells him to go say good-bye to his *k'exel* (namesake—in this case, his grandfather), who is buried in the cemetery (17; 16). He accompanies his mother, notices that she starts crying, and then addresses the dead grandparents with a Q'anjob'al formula employed only when someone is leaving forever (19; 18). After a long prayer, his mother asks for their blessing (21; 20). They leave that same night.

Another touch of affect emerges with the farewell to their dog, which had to stay behind (22; 21). Once more as in the previous novel, the trope of the dog stands as a depository of non-verbal despair. The narrator adds that the family had to throw stones at the dog so it would not follow them. As they leave, they realize someone must have talked, because soldiers appear, and all the dogs begin to bark. The soldiers light the old huts, burning the entire village, including those individuals who did not leave (23; 22). This description is personalized by the *meb'ixh* when he recalls what he left behind: his toys inside his only piece of furniture, an old willow basket, objects that trigger the one basic emotion of joy he has known. With a reflex-like desire to recuperate them, he would have run back to their rescue were it not for his mother's intervention, which evidences in the episode a nonintentionalist, corporeal account of the emotions arousing the subject.

The reader is informed that about sixty people had fled in the night, this number defined as *oxk'al* (three times twenty) (24; 23). The text then elaborates a narrative ellipsis to record a performance of ethical worth by way of the *meb'ixh*'s contradictory explanation of Maya spirituality. It is contradictory because on page 25 he claims that because of his experience, he lost this knowledge (24). And yet, on the following six pages, he proceeds to explain it, and he even compares the names employed by Q'eq'chi's (30; 29) to those in Q'anjob'al, before returning to the escape narrative. The performance does, however, emphasize a felt need for ethnic and cultural respect going beyond the display of the character's actual knowledge of Maya spirituality. The ellipsis represents a more developed alternative and superior ethical sensibility translating into an appeal for respect. Only then does the *meb'ixh* continue with the narration of their escape.

The contrast is then marked between the wealth of knowledge and spirituality that Maya culture represents, and the narratological effects of the refugees' ruined condition and lack of vigor as they flee into the middle of a jungle with no open trails. The escape is described as phantasmatic; "parecíamos fantasmas con nuestros bultos cargados en medio de la noche" (31; "we looked like ghosts carrying our burden in the dead of night" [29]). This effect is both an end and a continuity, a lingering sensation that this sense of beingness will never come to an end. It is like being dead before dying while, paradoxically, surviving death. Their being ghosts themselves unsettles the propriety that delimits the community's accepted behavior. They become, in Avery Gordon's words, a "symptom" (63) of what is missing for them. Yet by the very act of survival, they keep representing, again in Gordon's words, "a future possibility, a hope" (64).

The escape itself is harrowing. Babies have to be gagged so they will not cry and thus betray their position to the soldiers (31). Small children like the *meb'ixh* cannot walk as fast as the adults, yet they are pressured to hurry so as to put distance between them and the pursuing army, while being blamed for slowing the group's pace. As a result, they learn to "cry in silence" (33; 31). The *meb'ixh* is exhausted and falls behind, along with an old woman who cannot continue. She orders him to go on without her, after blessing him and giving the child an amulet. His mother, in the meantime, has noticed the *meb'ixh*'s absence and forced the refugees to stop so her son could be rescued. They find him caught in a bush full of thorns, about to fall into a ravine. He has lost all his belongings. Finally they stop out of sheer exhaustion and agree to hide in a ravine to rest. The narrative then continues with their travails during the following days "como una permanente maldición" (38; "like a permanent curse" [37]), as if they were in a condition of being "left over," struggling between material permanence and material transience. The *meb'ixh* is confused, because, as a child, he does not understand from whom they are fleeing or even why they are fleeing. All he has to sense the gravity of the situation is his mother's expression as the embodiment of their fate (39; 38), a trait scattered throughout the text that evokes Massumi's definition of affect as a nonsignifying, nonconscious "intensity."[45] The narrative voice states:

> En los momentos más críticos, yo percibía que eran como nubes negras que ensombrecían de pronto el rostro de ella; palidecía, se le iba la sangre de la cara, la respiración era más agitada y respiraba profundamente, sus manos entre las que iban las mías por lo general, comenzaban a sudar sin que ella se percatara; se ponían frías y temblorosas, dejaba de hablar, excepto un susurro que yo percibía, casi inteligible. De sus pálidos labios salían palabras secas, agudas, sueltas. (39)

> During the most critical moments, I perceived black clouds that suddenly darkened her face; then she turned pale; the blood left her face; her breathing became deeper and more agitated. Her hands, which usually were clasping mine, would begin to sweat without her being aware of it. Then they would go cold and begin to tremble. She would stop talking, except for an almost unintelligible whisper I could barely hear and which was [*sic*]. From her dry lips came dry, sharp, disjointed words. (37–38)

In this sense it is important to remember what Leys summarizes from Massumi, Thrift, and Shouse: that affect should not be confused with personal feelings, because, while feelings are personal and biographical, emotions are social. An affect is "a non-conscious experience of intensity; it is a moment of unformed and unstructured potential." She continues with her summary, writing that "affect is the body's way of preparing itself for action in a given circumstance," adding that "the body has a grammar of its own that cannot be fully captured in language."[46] We could very well place the quoted passage within this scheme.

The escape continues for many days, with air bombardments, mines, and animal attacks (40; 38). The next transcendental event in this first part is his mother's death. This happens after days of trekking in the rain, and after spending over a day hidden in a cave because of a major storm (57–60; 54–57). Most of the refugees have developed a severe cough. They thought the rain had not been an ordinary one, *ojob'*, but one accompanied by a bad spirit, *q'aqachnuq'* (60; 57). The *meb'ixh*'s mother was already very weak. She no longer carried his sister, and stayed at the very back of the line, coughing desperately (61; 58). All of a sudden, as the *meb'ixh* watches, she stumbles, tripping on her *corte* (Maya skirt), and collapses. He runs to her and then starts screaming to stop the line. She regains consciousness, only to tell the *meb'ixh* to take care of his sister, that she is leaving this world because she cannot take any more (61; 58). Her last words are "*¡chilk'al hab'aaa!*" ("take care"). Yet she still hangs on, coughing and breathing with difficulty, while he offers her water. Seeing her gaze, the *meb'ixh* understands that she wants him to hold her hand. He does so, intuiting that she does not want to die, until she does: "Un buen rato después, se fue así tan callado, tan simple, y de manera imperceptible, como quien no quiere decir adiós. Se fue sola y se perdió entre la llovizna de la distancia" (62; "A while later, she went, so quietly, so simply, and so imperceptibly, like someone who doesn't want to say good-bye. She went alone, and was lost in the distant mist" [59]). He then understands the full implications of being an orphan, talks to her despite her being dead, and tries to make her body more comfortable by pulling stones from under her back and putting rags under her head, although she was already "*max paxi*" (63; "going away" [60]).

In this episode we have a full display of affect, even if the adult narrative voice also appeals to cognition. The *meb'ixh*'s actions in this sequence evidence autonomic responses occurring below the threshold of consciousness (talking to the dead body, accommodating her head and body, warming her cold feet with his hands, assuming she's smiling at him), while the narrative voice of the adult *meb'ixh* offers an appraisal of the affective situation by reflecting on the memory of her death. He tells us that, at this point, he understood that being an orphan is not just a physical or biological state but also a spiritual one, a state in which anyone could give him orders and in which he was "a la disposición de todos y a toda hora . . . ocupa el escalón más bajo del grupo de los desposeídos" (65; "at the mercy of everyone and at all times . . . occupying the lowest rung of the ladder of the dispossessed" [62]), because he lacked the protection of any adult. He also recognizes that, while he was tending her body, the others watched him with pity but were impatient to get back on the road, because they had already seen many corpses, and their feelings were "insensibles" (63; "numb" [60]). He also explains that *max paxi* does not mean only "no going back." Rather, such a simple understanding is a catachresis, as *paxi* really implies that something has no actual return; it is a departure with no coming back, contrary to leaving with the possibility of a future return, which is *hoqin paxoq* (63; 60). There is thus evidence of a gap between the subject's affect and his cognition, in much the same way that Leys theorizes the separation between the two, where cognition comes as a later process to emotions.[47]

His mother's death indeed impacts the *meb'ixh* emotionally. The narrative voice informs the reader that in the temporal present of the story, he is walking back to the place where she died, looking for the location of the event (64; 61). The narrative voice then returns to the action and behavior of the moment that determined the *meb'ixh*'s affective disposition. He describes that, as the last individuals remaining at the *meb'ixh*'s side pushed him to move on and rejoin the walking refugees, he looked back to where she had been buried, tried to memorize the location of the exact place with his sight so that he could return on a future day, to light a candle and talk to her more slowly. The *meb'ixh* then said good-bye with his hands, as a "great sigh" emerged from his heart, while he cried in silence before rejoining the marchers (65; 62). All the actions in this sequence operate independently of the main character's consciousness or mind control.

Before the refugees reach their destination, more dramatic events take place. Helicopters drop bombs on them (67; 63). Then one of the young men steps on a mine very close to the *meb'ixh* and his sister, and the explosion affects them as well (74; 71): he is only bruised and breaks his water gourd, but she is knocked unconscious and suffers head wounds. They are also accosted by a group of guerrillas who try to recruit the young men by force (76; 72). His sister worsens, and he hallucinates while suffering a nervous breakdown (79–80; 75–76). The *meb'ixh* is subsequently tied up but forced to keep moving in that condition. Finally, they get within sight of the border (87; 83). Nonetheless, helicopters spot them before they actually cross, shoot at them, and disembark soldiers to engage in pursuit. They succeed in crossing but lose over twenty people, including their guides and leaders, who deliberately moved in a different direction to attract the soldiers' fire, thus sacrificing themselves to protect the community. Once on the other side, the survivors say a prayer in the memory of their rescuers and keep moving (89; 85–86).

The second part, titled "Skab'tuqan" ("The Torment of Exile"), summarizes the *meb'ixh*'s memory of the many years spent on the Mexican side of the border. He informs the reader that he visited many refugee camps and talked to many people, thus compiling an angry enunciation of the dehumanizing conditions of exile, articulated as if it were a series of Foucauldian limit-experiences. Yet the absence of plot transforms the denunciation into a nonpersonalized monologue, too general and too descriptive to engage the reader beyond the compilation of the evident horror. These fragments primarily appear at first glance to evidence the narrative voice's lack of focus on the *meb'ixh*'s actual everyday doings. It works much like Gordon describes an analogous situation in Argentina, as "the debris of a system barely thinkable and yet abounding in excessive significations" (67).

The narrative voice limits itself to enumerating the lack of jobs, the presence of infiltrators, and the mixture of Maya languages as a consequence of there being refugees from many ethnic groups. This makes communication difficult among them and leads to a loss of tradition and an inevitable embracing of Western cultural forms. The *meb'ixh*'s then mentions that he lost touch with his sister after he had left her—not without feeling guilty—with Lolen, the lady who was to take care of her. He himself left with another couple for work in a place named San Isidro (97–98; 93). When he returned, neither Lolen nor his sister was in the original location, so he began looking for her. Given his state of malnutrition, he had difficulty working the land. Ultimately, missionary doctors took him under their wing (114; 109). He later learned to read and write (116; 110). Then he met an orphan girl. One afternoon, after walking to a lake, they shared an orange and held hands while male dogs mounted a bitch; for the first time he discovered both his capacity for feeling love for another person and the dizzying energy of sexual attraction, though neither of them exchanged a single word (118–19; 113). Nor does the narrative voice inform the reader of any continuity of their relationship beyond this brief encounter.

This scene, though, refocuses the subject within the perspective of affect; it also evidences how ethnicity marks sexuality. The couple's comportment is clearly an ethnosexual moment, as Joane Nagel would state it (x), one in which ethnic boundaries are also clearly sexual boundaries: bare physical contact, no words exchanged. This behavior may also be generational, but it does reflect tensions associated with forced physical and cultural displacement as well. Still, it is the sole moment of regeneration of the subject in the second part.

Indeed, the lack of focus on the *meb'ixh*'s personal experience and feelings as a subject creates in the reader, at first glance, a sense of loss of narrative interest in the second part of the text. During the long monological discursivity, readers lose the narrative focus found in González's first novel—or in the first part of this one—as the text elides subjectivity while sliding into what would appear to be an endless denunciation of the refugees' miseries, an unrestrained explosion of rage. The *meb'ixh*'s mouth is unable to persuade, as a consequence of his trauma. His loss of voice leave him mired "in a world where dispossession and unreality rule," (104) as Gordon would have it. He has not "disappeared" in the political sense of the word, but his behavior does correspond to that of a ghostly figure who did.

In the third part, "Ox Tuqan" ("The Return"), the reader learns that the *meb'ixh* is back in the Yichkan on December 29, 1996, the day when the peace treaty was signed in Guatemala. Attempting to reorder his memories of the previous twenty years, the reader is exposed, more than to narrative action or personal reflections, to a hortatory speech denouncing Ladinos' hypocrisy. The main character does establish a link between the civil war and the Spanish invasion as expressions of the same process of racialized genocide (127; 121), within the hortatory framework previously indicated. This is followed by a fantasy whereby "The General" (undoubtedly an allusion to General Ríos Montt, who presided over the genocidal process during 1982–1984 and was condemned for genocide in 2013, though the verdict was overturned by a higher court for political reasons, under great pressure from extreme right-wing military officers and the country's economic elite) looks at himself one morning in the mirror, discovers his Indigenous traits and the ethnic contours of his face, and, horrified, orders the beginning of the ethnocide (129–31; 123–25). After another dose of the hortatory speech previously indicated, the main character evokes his dead family members, claiming to be able to talk to their spirits (147–48; 141).

Within this third section emerges the last part, titled "Jelq'ab," or "Tejiendo las manos" ("Joining Hands"), where we finally return to the subject's doings as an actant, with a new touch of both narrativity and affect. The *meb'ixh* first returns with a group of repatriated refugees to the country through Guatemala City's airport, where all of them are enthusiastically welcomed ("hubo aplausos a nuestra llegada, hubo cantos, música, cohetes, abrazos y lágrimas. . . . Nos dieron la bienvenida a nuestra tierra, a nuestro pueblo" [153]; "there was applause as we arrived, songs, music, Fireworks, hugs and tears" [146]). Then he heads back to the Yichkan, where he joins a collective farm given to returning refugees, finding the refugees in the process of preparing the first communal harvest, called *jelq'ab'* in Q'anjob'al Maya (154; 147). Their job done, the members of the collective exchange stories about their past experiences, while the *meb'ixh* just listens silently, until he notices a young woman "que tampoco habla ni ríe como los demás" (154; "does speak or laugh like the others" [147]). When he walked toward her, she asked him if he had anything to tell about his own life. He replied that it was not unlike the others'. She then commented that he must be Q'anjob'al, and he acknowledged this, yet admitted that he had lost his language after his mother died. She had a very similar story. He asked for her name. She said it is María Aguirre, which was not her real name, but rather the one given to her in her Mexican legal documents. When she asked him in turn, the *meb'ixh* replied that he was just called Juan, but his real name was the same as his grandfather's. He did not yet know it, however. As this exchange continued, in a nonconscious affective process of great intensity, the *meb'ixh* intuited that they were related, and he finally asked her if by chance the woman who raised her was named Lolen (156; 149). She immediately froze, then dropped the corn on the cob that she was eating, as she realized that the *meb'ixh* was her brother. They embraced in what appeared to be almost an unconscious motor movement: "Llorábamos abrazados con lágrimas de felicidad. No nos dimos cuenta en qué momento nos rodeó el grupo que también derramaba lágrimas que regaron la solidaridad en aquella comunidad" (157; "We were embracing, crying tears of happiness, oblivious to the group which surrounded us, also shedding tears that nourished the solidarity of that community" [150]). The group's reaction was not only a demonstration of political and human solidarity but also evidenced the close links existing between emotions and cognition, articulated through the affections of the body. Almost immediately, a conscious awareness of the situation that was taking place sparked a recognition of the magnitude of the event to which they were bearing witness, which in turn generated bodily movement conveying the sense of this particular affect. It was also a display of raw emotions embodied as a Foucauldian limit-experience.

Afterward, the brother and sister held long conversations. They decided to travel together to the location of their original Yichkan community, to explore the possibility of discovering the origin of their beingness and subjectivities, if they were able to locate their grandfather's grave and find what their mother left in it when he was buried. Nevertheless, Yichkan was by this time utterly different from their childhood memories. There was a vast number of newly arrived immigrants, and many more new towns. Even the landscape was different. They asked everywhere for their place of origin, but no answers could be found. Finally, the *meb'ixh* seems to recognize one day "la colina lejana por donde comienza el camino del día" (159; "the faraway hill where the day begins its journey" [152]) in a town named Nueva Esperanza. It resembled the place where, as a child, he would always welcome the new day. However, instead of a village with a few scattered huts with palm roofs, they found a town with corrugated tin roofs (159; 152). He was baffled but followed an intuition to search for the cemetery. It was a new one, to their great disappointment. However, the owner of a little country store where they bought something to drink told them that before he arrived, the town used to be named something else. "Pananlaq," said María, and he recognized the name (161; 154). The store owner informed them that there used to be an older cemetery indeed, but, as the town grew, it was moved to the new place (162; 154–55). The older cemetery was then transformed into a landing strip for small planes and helicopters.

Again, affect here is a factor in determining the reader's empathy with the brother and sister as they were forced to come to terms with the inevitable loss of roots and identity. This was the moment they confirmed that the regime of social and political practice into which they came into being had been hopelessly transformed, begetting a new order in which their identitary concerns and spiritual values now seemed to be out of place. A deep sense of mourning thus ensued.

The *meb'ixh* resigned himself to this new situation, and he decided to create a new ethics of the self by work in his pluri-ethnic community of Nuevo Yichkan (162; 155). He still wished to unpack the political and ethical implications of his resistance, though, by planning to build a new community under the verifying gaze of international observers, where, the many different ethnicities and Indigenous groups constituting it notwithstanding, he would work within the cultural framework and identity of Maya peoples.

What is there to make of this second textual narrative of Gaspar Pedro González? Were we traditional, old-fashioned critics focusing on aesthetics, we could indeed, in paternalistic fashion, see flaws in the novelistic form, plot development, and in the construction of its characters. Yet our task is to make critical sense of the discursivity that we have encountered in this uniquely singular text with a clear, angry, decolonial perspective that is framed, nonetheless, within a legitimate strangeness. How can this text, therefore, make us think otherwise?

As we have noted, the subject of the text as such disappears from the moment he succeeds in crossing the border from Yichkan to Mexico, at the end of the first part. As such, the *meb'ixh* remains missing in action until his return to the country. The space he inhabited also remains a blind field. As readers, we learn nothing of the structure, organization, or details of everyday life in the refugee camps—what the routine was like, or the kind of work they performed. It is all a ghostly matter that looks like nothing, a nothingness that is, to return to Avery Gordon, just "a structure of feeling" (198). Seething feelings, boiling emotions that discombobulate the subject. The only exception in the second part is the brief interlude of the discovery of love and sexual desire late in that unit. Still, the *meb'ixh* will not be fully reconstituted until the last section of the third part, when he rediscovers his sister in the Yichkan and they launch their futile journey to discover their roots. In this sense, it seems evident that by being violently and traumatically torn from his parents, his community, and his spiritual and cultural environment—in addition to the continuous terror and violence suffered during the escape, which went far beyond the worst nightmares of most adults—the *meb'ixh* undergoes a dehumanizing set of experiences that tear him away from himself. The experience of the camps becomes a sort of inertia, which the *meb'ixh* is unable to convert into narrative meaning, leaving a nonconscious structure of feeling bearing only unbearable sorrow and numb, raw anger. The hortatory speech thus nullifies the main character as both an actant and a subject, while staging the effects of a variant of posttraumatic stress disorder in which the subject is nonfunctioning. The *meb'ixh* manifests symptoms ranging from difficulty in concentrating to depression and a sense of hopelessness about the future. Memories of the traumatic events certainly cause daily intrusive flashbacks of fear, insecurity, and bitterness, so deeply disturbing, so overwhelming, that the *meb'ixh* narrating his experience in the first person is unable to articulate coherently what he is suffering or has undergone. His experience is, then, a limit-transcending, challenging event that takes away his ability to narrate. He does recognize all the while the racialized, dominant sociohistorical structure that generated his suffering, something he knows intrinsically that has to be challenged. His only possible response is, then, his hortatory speech. He cannot bring together, under his traumatic conditions, the contradictoriness of both his trauma and his knowledge of what historically caused it, much along the lines of how Timothy O'Leary problematizes Foucault's concept of limit-experience.[48]

The subject's discursive solution is, therefore, to substitute that chain of narrative utterances that would have shown readers what he actually did while in exile. He is unable to enunciate conscious discourse about the experience. The *meb'ixh* has instead repressed the memories and passionate feelings that lie at the heart of his trauma, given the extreme forms of objectivation and coercion suffered. These are replaced by a substitutive hortatory speech that, though rhetorically challenging for any reader, in effect emblematizes the schizoid effects of his condition, or else stands in as a simulacrum of this same condition, venting forcefully the anger felt. It is, to paraphrase O'Leary creatively and in a different context, a "foundational gesture" (8) by which an excluded culture eliminates that which has always positioned it as on the outside, given Ladinos' execrable ways of making Maya subjects invisible.

The original experience in which Ladino culture actually created those limits that excluded Mayas has resulted, in turn, in an extreme experience that transgresses the limits of that excluding culture as well. In that context, it is only when the *meb'ixh* finds an empathetic other standing in for his mother's affect—whether it is the girl by the lake or his sister after the return to Yichkan and their reencounter—that he is again able to feel the care of the self and talk as a subject about his personal experience in narrative discursivity. The soothing effect of feminine affect and nurture succeeds in enabling the *meb'ixh* to cope with his psychosocial distress, a gesture represented textually by the successful return of the narrating "I."

O'Leary's delving into the meaning of experience, limit-experience, and "experience-book," and the tension between the senses of experience, though circumscribed to Foucault's own work in his article, is useful when we reconsider the traumatic effect of racism pushed to genocidal extremes through Guatemalan Ladino systems of thought, state institutions, legal apparatuses, and, needless to say, military measures. O' Leary states that "it involves the way in which a given object is *seen* and *conceptualised* in a given culture" (9).[49] It is something felt, a mode of perception that must be interrogated; it is the way a given phenomenon is perceived and lived by the subalternized, racialized subject. Out of this practice a new sensibility is born, new behavioral patterns are created, and many new ways of engaging with the limit-experiences suffered by this particular type of a subject are organized around new perceptions.

In chapter 1, I outlined the extreme violence that enveloped Guatemala's Ladino racism and the way Maya subjects were seen and conceptualized as inhuman objects to be used and discarded, to the point that, to this day, in late 2017, the Ladino elite and their military cohorts continue to develop those forms of knowledge that deny the institutional practice of genocide which overwhelmed the country in the 1980s, despite the abundance of testimonial, juridical, and scientific proof. They are indeed contemporary forms of subjugation of life to necropolitics, in Mbembe's terms, generating death-worlds that confer upon racialized populations the status of living dead. It is then comprehensible that González would frame his discursivity immersed in trauma, in the negation of subjectivity, and thus represent a subject drowned by bitter anger. After all, the first aspect of any experience is, according to O'Leary, "the forms of perception or sensibility which it makes possible—or even necessary" (9). In this process, the experience of Ladino discursivity gives way to a new experience uttered in this case, also in Castilian. Yet it is a non-Ladino Castilian, emerging within a Q'anjob'al root discursivity ceaselessly infiltrating the *kaxlan tzij* (literally, "foreign word," but it is how Castilian is called in many Maya languages) spoken by the *kaxlan winaq* ("foreign peoples"—that is, Ladinos, usurpers of Iximuleu), deployed to stage the mode of relation to self that the *meb'ixh* as racialized subject embodies throughout his limit-experience. As we already know, the *meb'ixh* goes from a certainty about his Q'anjob'al cultural world, through a limit-experience in which he is torn away from himself, thus ensuring that he will not remain as he was before. He then undergoes a perilous encounter with reality that leaves him with a fragmentary, alienated self, its pain represented by the hortatory discursivity. Nonetheless, he succeeds afterwards in constituting a new truth to power.

In turn, his nameless voice offers his readers a new way for Maya literature to act as an experience-transformer. González's text carries out a diagnosis of the Guatemalan present by evidencing the fractures existing between Ladino and Maya realities that, fictively rooted in the 1978–1996 period, continue to this day. His representation allows readers to engage with the need for a transformative intercultural experience by the very nature of his language. We see in the next chapter, in which we problematize the textual narratives of Víctor Montejo, another mode of how decolonial texts induce truth effects that productively engage with their own reality, in the context of a different historical moment that also illuminates the present moment in Iximuleu.

4

Víctor Montejo: The Framer of a New Imaginary

In the previous chapter I analyze the first two novels published by Maya Q'anjob'al novelist Gaspar Pedro González, *Sb'eyb'al jun naq maya' q'anjob'al /La otra cara* (1992; *A Mayan Life*, 1995) and *El retorno de los mayas* (1998; *Return of the Maya*, 1998). In this chapter I proceed to elaborate an analysis of Víctor Montejo's most significant novel, *Las aventuras de Mister Puttison entre los mayas* (1998; *The Adventures of Mr. Puttison among the Maya*, 2002), a text that offers a uniquely historical approach to representations of Guatemalan Mayaness. First, however, I examine one of his earlier works, *Komam Q'anil: Ya'K'uh Winaj/Q'anil: El hombre rayo*, reconfigured in a 1999 bilingual Popb'al Ti'/Castilian 1999 edition; his 1991 collection of short stories titled *The Bird Who Cleans the World and Other Mayan Fables*; and his singular testimonio of 1992, *Brevísima relación testimonial de la continua destrucción del Mayab' (Guatemala)*.[1] At the end, I make a brief allusion to Montejo's newest novel, *Pixan, el cargador del espíritu* (2014; *Pixan, the Keeper [or Carrier] of the Spirit*).

Montejo's life at times seems itself a fictional adventure rather than a conventional biography. A Jakaltek Maya born in the town of Jacaltenango (named Xajla' in its native language) in 1951, he is a native speaker of Maya Popb'al Ti'. He first studied to become a primary-school teacher at the Instituto Indígena deVarones Santiago in Antigua, from 1970 to 1972. Later, he would miraculously survive an army massacre in the early 1980s, as he narrates in his second published book, *Testimony: Death of a Guatemalan Village* (1987). By 1980 Montejo had been an elementary-school teacher for ten years in a small village he names "Tzalalá" in *Testimony* to avoid giving away its real name in times of war. It was located in northwest Huehuetenango. In July 1982 the Guatemalan army forced male members of the village to organize themselves into Civil Patrols, against the will of the community (12). They were local men armed with rudimentary weapons—slingshots, stones, and sticks, that were no match for the opposing forces' rifles; organized against the will of the community, these Civil Patrols allegedly served to protect local villages from guerrilla attacks (12). Participation in the Civil Patrol was not optional. In truth, this tactic was meant both to divide local citizenry from guerrillas, given that the latter operated in areas where the population was sympathetic to their cause and/or aided them with food and shelter, and to serve as human shields for the embattled army units. Civil Patrols were not trained in any way. They were simply ordered to do this or that by lower-ranking military officers in charge. This led to a tragic mistake. On September 9, 1982, the local Civil Patrols mistook "an army detachment dressed in olive fatigues for guerrillas" (13) and shot at them. The army's reprisal was brutal. The soldiers occupied the village, massacred most of the people, and took Víctor as prisoner to the Huehuetenango army base, where he was interrogated, tortured, and expected to be executed. As Montejo himself narrates in *Testimony*—a gripping text that provides a qualitative glimpse into the fear that permeated Guatemalan society during its civil war and the brutality and sadism of the country's military—he embarked on a desperate campaign to convince the colonel in charge of the army base that the entire incident was a tragic mistake, and that he was not a guerrilla, as claimed by the army detachment that destroyed the village. Ultimately, the colonel believed Montejo and released him, though Montejo was expected to remain under house arrest.

Clear about the negative prospects for saving his life were he to be rearrested, however, Montejo fled to Chiapas, Mexico, where he ended up in a UN-monitored refugee camp. Luckily for him, a few months afterward, Guatemalan American writer Víctor Perera (1934–2003) and US actress Jane Alexander visited the camp and became acquainted with his story. Impressed, they returned to the United States to launch a campaign to have him and his family admitted into the country. Their persistence succeeded, but the publicity that his case warranted led to his being placed again on a death list in Guatemala and to the continual harassment of his family. Other US citizens succeeded in helping his wife and three small children leave their native country, and the family regrouped in Lewisburg, Pennsylvania, as Perera and Alexander managed to obtain a scholarship for Montejo to complete his BA at Bucknell University. They also set him up with Oregon author Wallace Kaufmann of Signal Books, who sponsored his first fictional text, *Komam Q'anil: Ya'K'uh Winaj/Q'anil: El hombre rayo*, published in 1984 with an English translation by Virginia M. Scott, under the title *El Kanil, Man of Lightning: A Legend of Jacaltenango*.

Montejo went on to obtain an MA in anthropology at the State University of New York–Albany, in 1988, and a PhD in the same field at the University of Connecticut in 1993 (As mentioned in the chapter 1, during the American Anthropological Association conference in Chicago in 1990, a group of Maya scholars, led by Montejo, performed a religious ritual at the Newberry Library, where the original manuscript of the *Popol Wuj* is housed, advocating to "bring it back" to its original community). After completing studies for and earning his PhD, Montejo became a professor at the University of Montana (1995–1996) before landing a job at the Department of Native American Studies at the University of California–Davis, where he became the first-ever Maya chair of a department in a US research university. Montejo returned to Guatemala to fill a cabinet position in 2004 and formally retired from UC–Davis in 2011. He is presently living back in his native Xajla'/Jacaltenango.

Montejo is undoubtedly one of the most prolific writers in the Latin American Indigenous orbit. He has published novels, short stories, poetry, testimonios, and academic books, in three languages—English, Castilian, and Popb'al Ti'. His long list of publications includes—in addition to the books previously cited—*Q'anil, Testimonio,* and the novel whose analysis is the central aspect of this chapter, *Oral Tradition: An Anthropological Study of a Jacaltec Folktale* (1989), *Sculpted Stones/Piedras labradas* (poetry, 1996, translated to English by Víctor Perera), *Voices from Exile: Violence and Survival in Modern Maya History* (1999), *El Popol Wuj: Libro sagrado de los mayas (versión para niños y jóvenes* [1999]), and *Maya Intellectual Renaissance: Critical Essays on Identity, Representation, and Leadership* (2005). In addition to producing this impressive list of works, Montejo was a Fulbright scholar at the Universidad del Valle de Guatemala in 2003. He also served a four-year term as a congressman in the Guatemalan National Congress, during which time he created and passed the law commemorating a National Day of Indigenous People of Guatemala and also proposed the initiative titled *Ley de Consulta a Pueblos Indigenas* (Consultation of Indigenous Peoples' Law). From this post he was named Minister of Peace, and he established the National Program for Reparation to the Victims of the Armed Conflict in Guatemala. Montejo resigned his ministerial position in mid-2005 due to disagreements with the government's orientation. He then became president of the Congressional Commission of Indigenous People.

THE ETHICS OF HEROISM

In *Q'anil* (1984), his first publication, dedicated to his deceased brother, Montejo narrates in novella format the heroic, mythical story of Xhuwan Q'anil. The protagonist is forced to abandon his parents and his land, and to sacrifice his life in order to save his people. This is a text that stands as an emblematic double operation. On the one hand, it narrates the foundational myth of the Jakalteko people. On the other, Xhuwan Q'anil's doings and sacrifice are configured as a contemporary trope of the asymmetrical relation of power still existing in contemporary Guatemala between Mayas and "white people." For Xhuwan Q'anil, chosen by the gods to fight, his selection becomes an ethical responsibility that places him in opposition to distinguished members of his community, including the local sorcerers.

Montejo includes a prologue and a general introduction in the 1999 bilingual Popb'al Ti'/Castilian edition of *Q'anil*. In the prologue he explains that Q'anil is one of the four "*cargadores*" (3; "carriers of earth and sky," also translated at times as "keepers") of the Jakalteko year. He is also the guardian of war; and Montejo points out that Q'anil is a more benevolent figure in this role than analogous ones in other Iximuleu Maya ethnic groups, such as the K'iche', for whom the more bloodthirsty Tojil was the patron god, a war and sacrificial deity. Montejo believes that Q'anil is a pre-Hispanic Jakalteko myth to which anecdotal elements of the Spanish invasion and even folkloric aspects of the Iberian Christian–Moorish wars, may have been added (3). The bottom line, he claims, is that Jakaltekos were called at one point in time to fight a war beyond their habitus, their geographical ethnoscape in the Cuchumatán Mountains, to defend not only themselves but other Maya groups with whom they formed an alliance as well. In the legend itself, they went very far, "to the other side of the ocean" (3; my translation).

In the general introduction, Montejo makes a strong argument in defense of the oral tradition, claiming that it is not just a folkloric expression of an illiterate past. He understands it as a continuous way of configuring and reconfiguring representational morphemes that de facto frame identitary constituent segments. These are the mechanisms through which the very fluid notion of identity reconfigures itself, continually forming new tropes corresponding to a collective subjectivization that encodes spaces of possibilities perceptually considered as one's "own." They also carry within them historical markers of each Maya town that enable them to "articulate a creative and philosophical thought" (5; my translation). Montejo adds that it is likely that many of these narratives, presently oral, were written in hieroglyphs in pre-Hispanic times. He cites Guatemalan scholar Agustín Estrada Monroy as stating that in the lost *Título de Jacaltenango*, originally written in Náhuatl, Xhuwan Q'anil is mentioned as one of the founders of the town (9). Montejo adds that in Spanish conquistador Gonzalo de Alvarado's equally lost relation of the subjugation of the Cuchumatán Mountains, a great leader named Q'anil Akab' is mentioned as fighting together with Kaib'il B'alam, the historic Mam leader, according to Spanish *criollo* historian Fuentes y Guzmán's *Recordación Florida* (1690, 10; Flowery recollection). He goes on to mention how in the *Anales de los Kaqchikeles* there is the story that, while this group was enslaved by Alvarado, an *hombre rayo* (man of lightning) is mentioned as offering to free the Kaqchikeles, thus corroborating the belief in the existence of such a figure in pre-Hispanic Maya culture. In addition, Montejo recounts how lightning breaks the stone of K'unha Ch'en (the sacred House of Stone) in order to allow the corn seeds to emerge. This legend also explains the corn's colors. The seeds burnt by lightning became black. The corn seeds burnt only partially became yellow. Those seeds that remained untouched remained white.[2] Finally, he explains that the story itself begins with a *pórtico* (portico, or porch), "a form of respect demanded by tradition when telling the names and deeds of Maya ancestors" (19; my translation), before telling the legend itself.

Víctor Montejo has, by himself, succeeded in placing *Q'anil*'s Jakalteko legend alongside such classic Maya texts as the *Popol Wuj* and the *Books of Chilam Balam*, which is no small achievement. *El Q'anil* certainly offers a greater understanding of the Maya heritage, culture, history, love for community, and struggle through oppression against both domestic and foreign threats. In the epic itself, the narrator recounts the history of the Jakaltek Maya. The text explains how their lands were given to them by the first father, B'alunh Q'ana', and the first mother, Imox, both of whom are the mythical founders of Xajla'. The names of B'alunh Q'ana' and Imox are also the names of two of the days in the Jakalteko Maya calendar (31; 105, n12). Known as Jich Mam and Jich Mi', the founders "poured their blood into our veins / and made us strong and courageous" (7). However, the "natural gods" became haughty and destroyed their city, apparently through a volcanic eruption, while the sorcerers hid underground "like old wounded toads" (9). This forced the "heroic race" (9) to disperse itself in search of new lands after crying for their loss. They wandered for years in the wilderness until, eventually, they came to Ajul, near the present-day village of Xajla'. The sorcerers claimed that this was not the right place, so the leaders kept moving on, but Jich Mam sent his magical wand flying, and upon landing, it inserted itself in the fertile plain between Ajul and Meste.

A new city was built on this site, where "we had everything and lacked nothing" (11), until an unnamed enemy threatened the peace and prosperity of a neighboring kingdom. The enemies fought from the sea, using powerful, heretofore unknown weapons that could kill many people and destroy entire towns (51). Jich Mam then selected the best men to become warriors and go into battle, but the sorcerers mocked them, claiming that they would be unable to defeat the enemy, because they could not transform themselves into animals as the sorcerers said they themselves were able to (55). Jich Mam was cynical about the sorcerers' alleged abilities but allowed them to go participate in the battle as well. As they prepared themselves, Xhuwan volunteered to serve as a bearer for the group, though he was very small in stature. Xhuwan worried, nonetheless, that the arrogant sorcerers would be defeated, so, through prayer and penitence, he requested the power to use lightning from the *k'uh* (61), the protectors of the town. He was told, however, that as a human, he would be unable to handle this power and would destroy the world. So he was sent to see Kajeh, in the west, where he was again turned down (63). Then he sought help from the northern *k'uh*, but they just mocked him. In desperation, he turned to Q'anil, in the south. Q'anil was puzzled as to why he wanted power, so Xhuwan explained the sorcerers' arrogance and his conviction that they would all be killed. He claimed he was willing to die as long as he could save his people:

> "Therefore, Father Q'anil," Xhuwan declared,
> "I want to offer my life for those people.
> It matters not that my blood be spilled
> and that I never return to this land,
> as long as they achieve peace and are saved." (18)

Q'anil then asked him if, in return for his power, he was also willing to abandon everything he had and never return to his people after engaging in the coming war, and Xhuwan said yes. He was then granted Q'anil's power (65). The next day he showed up in town and modestly performed his role as a porter for the arrogant sorcerers. He marched off with them and shared his gift with the other porter, Xhuwan Mentes, who also would become a man of lightning. They practiced their powers and eventually got to see the beginning of the battle. The sorcerers were immediately defeated. The two boys then claimed to the local ruler, an ally of their kingdom, that they would defeat the enemy. Xhuwan Mentes first launched his lightning against the sea to make the enemy boats visible, as they had been hidden by the ocean mist, and then Xhuwan Q'anil destroyed them. The few survivors immediately surrendered. The local ruler wanted to celebrate their achievement, but the modest boys claimed that they had only fulfilled their mission and wanted to return as soon as possible to their hometown without any fanfare, choosing humility and modesty over personal fame and glory. Unable to return to Xajla', Xhuwan Q'anil and Xhuwan Mentes retired to the El Q'Anil volcano, becoming *k'uh* themselves. From atop El Q'anil, they protected the town as immortal heroes. The sorcerers were forced to confess what had truly happened, and the families of Xhuwan Q'anil and Xhuwan Mentes were then honored for their sons' heroism.

As Edward F. Fischer points out in the review of the English version of *El Q'anil*, Montejo put this text together from many oral and some anthropological, sources (711). He compares Montejo's work to "the *Kalevala*, the epic Finnish tale compiled and composed by folklorist Elias Lönnrot in the 1830s," adding that "it is a work of literature as much as of scholarship, and Montejo is to be commended for ignoring the borders that act to inhibit creative expression in academic disciplines" (711).

More importantly, *El Q'anil* is an exemplary ethical comportment that not only addresses Maya values, differentiating them from occidental moralism, but also singles out the Jakalteko people as a singular, if smaller, ethnic group within the Guatemalan pan-Maya purview. We have here, on the one hand, a form of premodern ethics, which consist of obligations to the community. But we also have, by contrasting the behavioral patterns of Xhuwan Q'anil and Xhuwan Mentes to those of the pompous, self-centered sorcerers who actually intended to deceive others, a transformation of the self to instantiate heroic values that become emulative for a conquered, racialized, and subalternized community, thus pointing a way out of the latter condition. Xhuwan Q'anil's transformation is not only a process of self-creation but also one of self-sacrifice. It is an elective-death decision that focuses not on the subject's competence and understanding of his situation, but rather on his willingness to sacrifice himself so that his people may live. Xhuwan Q'anil is willing both to comply with the warrior's heroic code and define himself as an ethical agent eager to work so as to become even more transformative of himself to fully achieve his ethical goals and strategic vision, regardless of its limit-experience implications. Thus, the narrative shifts from external constraints to internal subject-development, in a process that emphasizes the importance of relationships and outcomes.

In this sense, we should understand, in a very generic sense, Indigenous ethical frameworks operating in circular fashion. They are all processes in which each of the community's subjects would appear as if located at the center of a circle. This positionality may correspond to any member of a given community. But as they look at the outer layers of where they are standing, they would always envision a three-ring circle around themselves. They would be standing in the innermost one. The middle circle would include ethnic identitary issues, engagement, and communal cultural safety. The outer circle in turn would hold the values of cultural sensitivity and communal consultation. From the center to the outer ring, they would visualize four axes cutting across all three of the circles, articulated by social responsibilities, partnership, social roles, and participation. They would all be pointing in the direction of rights, protection, justice and equality, as well as cultural and social responsibility. We can understand Xhuwan Q'anil's ethical undertaking within this utterly Indigenous circular model framework. Likewise, many of Montejo's later writings, especially his novel *The Adventures of Mr. Puttison among the Maya*.

Given what is stated in the previous paragraph, there is no possibility that an individual could sidestep all the matters of communal experience and obligation to transform himself or herself into a Western-like moral subject exercising a sort of Kantian practice by implementing Kant's "regulative segments," the capacity to abstract, the need for an exercise of scepticism, a functional understanding of the capacities of thought, the submersion of experience in thought, and the distinction between real and possible, to limit ourselves to this Enlightenment model of the occidental subject.[3] Montejo thus effectively constructs an Indigenous ethic-philosophical knowledge within which he frames not only the foundational nature of Jakaltekos and, by extension, Mayas, but also the heroic behavioral codes tapped in limit situations, of which Iximuleu's civil war was certainly one. This extant behavioral model thus justifies the exercise of war, political militancy, and similar normativities. However, it comes not from a Marxist or liberation theology perspective, but rather from within an ingrained Indigenous cosmovision articulated on sound and coherent, as well as ancient, ethical components that plead for historically and culturally contingent conditions of real and local Indigenous experiences. We find that this initial effort by Montejo constitutes a marker, a trademark of his continuous narrative textualities, a succession of practices or forms of experience that are all underpinned by an ethical strain in an effort to consolidate an uncompromising reconstruction of Maya values functioning as ontologically coextensive with the Maya cosmovision, and with the practices they are surmised to structure. We pursue an analogous line of critique in the remainder of this chapter.[4]

ANIMAL SUBJECTS INTERACTING WITH HUMAN ONES

The Bird Who Cleans the World and Other Mayan Fables is, in the author's words, "a testimony to the values of respect, unity and understanding that existed between the people and their natural and supernatural environment" (15–16). It is also a validation of "animal subjects" and their interaction with human subjects in a holistic eco-space where everything is alive: people and animals, plants and springs, clouds and caves, light and wind, hills and valleys, stones and rivers, pots and griddles, crosses and roads, to rephrase Carlos Lenkersdorf's quotation cited in the introduction of this book. Montejo's fables have important doses of both humor and animal protagonists. These animal characters are also other-than-human persons, social beings participating in world-making relations among themselves and with humans, in much the same way Marisol de la Cadena describes her notion of cosmopolitics that closes the divide between nature and culture in her analysis of Runakuna world-making practices, where Earth Beings are more-than-natural entities that challenge modernity ontologically. As de la Cadena states:

> "religion" is also not religion, but interactions with other-than-human entities that are neither natural nor supernatural, but beings that are with runakuna in socio-natural collectives that do not abide by the divisions between God, nature, and humanity. (206)

De la Cadena thus opens up a dialogue between epistemic "worlding" and a state authority representing modern politics (266). This same issue is present in Montejo's fables from a Jakalteko perspective.

Montejo tells his readers in the author's preface that his mother scolded him by claiming, "The young people of today do not believe in their Mayan heritage. That is why they cannot understand and value them" (11). This is an allusion to a Westernization process that began advancing in the Guatemalan highlands in the early 1970s. Against this tide, Montejo wants to keep the Maya "heritage alive" (15). His fables emerge from an oral tradition dating back thousands of years that normatizes moral values in much the same way that descriptive or comparative ethics operate, without actually prescribing human comportment. We can understand the moral reasoning that lies behind the Jakalteko cosmovision, structuring the community's ethics. One of the best examples appears in the author's preface itself. Montejo tells his readers that when he was a child his mother would recount the story of a wild dove pleading for cotton cloth to protect her leg from the cold. When they asked her what the problem was, the dove would respond with the following:

> Mis, mis, k'uxumtoq tx'ow;
> tx'ow, tx'ow, holom b'itz'ab';
> b'itz'ab' mach xhchanik'oq kaq'e;
> kaq'e, kaq'e, ch'iniq'oq asun;
> asun, asun, ch'ok yinh sat tz'ayik;
> tz'ayik, tz'ayik, xhmak'nitanhoq chew;
> chew, chew, xhq'ahnitoq woqan. (13)
>
> (Cat, cat, that eats and eats mice;
> mice, mice, that gnaw, chewing holes in walls;
> walls, walls, that stop the wind;
> wind, wind, that carries the clouds;
> clouds, clouds, that shadow the sun;
> sun, sun, that kills the cold;
> and cold, cold, that hurts my leg. [14])

We can see here that, to explain why her leg is cold, the dove articulates a holistic understanding of her environment. She is cold within a relational process representing an Indigenous epistemic regime that does not distribute differences along the nature–culture divide, creating a complex entity where everyone and everything—cats, mice, walls, wind, clouds, sun, and dove—all function as full-fledged subjects belonging to a system in which everything is interconnected. As a consequence, their actions affect all stakeholders, who are thus bound as a community by virtue of how their singular actions have an impact on all other members of the same community. They all have, as a result, both an interest and concerns, in articulating this organization's apprehending multiplicities. This simple ethical model articulated by Montejo's mother allows for multiple, nonhierarchical entry and exit points (the dove could use other examples in complaining about the cold in her leg or begin in any other point of the many possible causal relations) while establishing transspecies connections.

Montejo adds that in the past, birds were the "living colors of the world," and the buzzard was especially appreciated, because he always cleaned the villages' surroundings (16). However, when the Guatemalan army invaded his region in 1982, besides massacring countless villagers, they used buzzards for target practice, thus breaking one more connection in the Mayas' holistic understanding of how the environment, the world itself, is shared by all subjectivities, regardless of the nature of their species. He says, "Respect for nature has diminished to the point that modern people destroy their environment systematically out of thoughtlessness or selfishness. People can destroy themselves by not recognizing the value of all living creatures on earth with whom they should coexist" (16). He then affirms that, while Mayas "continue to be active producers of knowledge" (18), their elders have been faulted for perpetrating "absurd ideas that are symbols of their 'backwardness'" (18). Ultimately, Montejo claims that, implicitly, his work is, rather than an expression of the past, "a symbol of resistance" (18). He thus reinscribes Maya cosmovision within a countermodernity opposing itself to the West's teleology, one capable of surpassing the nature–culture divide. We see this more clearly, perhaps, in the analysis of *The Adventures of Mr. Puttison among the Maya* later in this chapter.

The aspects pointed out in the previous paragraph are underscored by the fact that, as Allan Burns points out in the introduction to the volume, "the animal stories in Maya culture . . . are more substantial than the childlike animals of . . . other traditions. These Maya animals reveal profound character and personality traits, severe actions, and sometimes unpleasant ideas" (22). He adds that people like Montejo's mother were "the shapers of Maya history and cultural theory" (24), and that most stories in the volume are narrated in the dialogic form of conversations. "Characters do not so much engage in action as talk to each other. Their schemes, successes, and failures emerge from the talk they have with one another" (25), with very little emphasis on action or setting. Burns's remarks do emphasize the primacy of spoken interaction between subjects—whether human, animal, or divine—which is a distinctive trait of many Indigenous cultures. This implies that intersubjectivity takes the shape of what Hirschkop labels "ubiquitous dialogism" in reference to Bakhtin (67), one in which the dialogical nature of utterances reveals the ethical patterns operating within a given conception of the world. The dialogical nature of discursivity and the utterance generates the contexts of speech that differentiate the Indigenous world from Western-centered configurations, as actual intersubjectivity is given shape and articulated within Montejo's representations. After all, in Hirschkop's understanding, "The shape of the utterance depends on the social sphere in which it is located within its characteristic world-view, topos, style, and vocabulary" (209–10).

Montejo's collection contains thirty-two fables. The title story begins with a flood that "covered the whole world" (29). As the water receded, Usmiq, the buzzard, was sent to find out just how much the water had actually ebbed. Usmiq found a large number of dead and rotting animals, and, starved, he began to eat them. When he flew back, he stank of the dead creatures he had eaten on the reappearing dry land. His job then became to "clean the world of stench and rottenness," carrying off whatever might contaminate the land (30). The story thus evidences the buzzard's essential role in the well-being of the world, transforming an animal regarded as lowly in the Western world, a trope of lack of cleanliness in modern urban environments, into an ethical agent, one that, in being chosen as the subject in charge of cleaning the earth's environment, extends through this designation the traditional boundaries of ethics to include the nonhuman world.

In a different tone, "How the Serpent Was Born" becomes a cautionary tale about not dishonoring your mother. When the main character's mother was coming for a visit, he told his wife to hide their food and not feed her. After she left, they brought their pot of food back out, and a coiled rattlesnake appeared inside the pot. The story ends triumphantly with the downfall of the wicked son who scorned his mother. We have to note that more important than the role of the son, wife, or mother is the role of the snake as an executor of moral justice. The snake scares the couple, but it is at the same time a symbol of justice. The snake plays out its double role in the Indigenous world, one where it is associated with violence and revenge but is simultaneously revered, because it is considered sacred. Either way, in Montejo's fable the snake confronts the couple's lack of morality, thus incarnating the role of enforcer of a rough type of justice, a messenger of cosmic deities punishing those breaking laws or violating taboos. In Mesoamerican cultures, snakes are indeed associated with divinity, rebirth, and spiritual power and are often looked upon with both fear and awe.

It would be impossible to thoroughly analyze all thirty-two fables in this book. However, we can indeed claim that all of them, whether a fragment of the *Popol Wuj* as retold in "The First Monkeys" or the delightfully complex "The Little Boy Who Talked with Birds," deal with the ethical implications of respecting all living beings from within the situational perspective of the individual character, regardless of whether she or he is a person, an animal, or a thing. Relations are not established among only preexisting subjects or objects. Other relational modes exist. Much as de la Cadena, Escobar, and others working on the issue of cosmopolitics claim, in Montejo's fables the world results from relations, not from the action of subjects upon objects. Entities surface from interactions, marking both identity and difference, and introducing an ethical comprehension of territories and territoriality in terms of "rooted networks," where nature exists not as an object but, rather, as beings acting out or emerging out of dialogic relations among themselves, as well as with humans. De la Cadena indicates how representation is a Western epistemic mode, granting the power to speak in the name of what is represented.[5] She adds that "representation, as epistemic mode, implies an initial relation of separation between subject and object, between signifier and signified, which can then be either connected or disconnected in the process of scrutiny."[6] However, Australian anthropologist Helen Verran, working with Aborigines in her home country, argues that not all epistemic modes deploy these kinds of relations. When the worlds being talked about are enacted rather than represented, there is no distinction between a subject that observes and an object that is being observed, an argument confirmed as well by John Law and Ruth Benschop.[7] The enacting mode thus becomes epistemically primary, as Verran argues.[8] In a different text, Verran uses the phrase "epistemic disconcertment" to name the emotional discomfort experienced by Western-centric subjects when undergoing the emotional discomfort of having the certainty of their ontologies questioned by Indigenous positionalities.[9] Using this same logic, the works in question do not belong to its author as a private property; rather, they form part of the collective to which the works as a whole belong. We have an excellent portrayal of this non-Western ontology in Montejo's delightful fables.

A *TESTIMONIO* UNLIKE ANY OTHER TESTIMONIO

Ethical issues also appear in the most atypical testimonio ever written, *Brevísima relación testimonial de la destrucción del Mayab'* (1992; Brief Testimonial Relation of the Destruction of the Mayab). The text is deliberately placed in a liminal position between fiction and testimonio from the very start, as we are told that the joint authors are Víctor Montejo and Q'anil Akab'. But we know from the analysis of *Q'anil* that Q'anil Akab' was in fact the great leader mentioned as fighting with Kaib'il B'alam, according to Fuentes y Guzmán's *Recordación Florida*. Thus, we have a performative gesture registered from the very start, an efficacious figure to mark the political context in which the testimonio itself emerges, which operates as a complicitous gesture with Mayas familiar with this story, even if we are told in the introductory note that Q'anil Akab' is also a pseudonym of one of the refugees Montejo met in the Guadalupe Victoria Camp in Chiapas at the end of 1982, and again in 1989, when he began to write this book.

The testimonio begins with an introductory note signed by both "Víctor Montejo and Q'anil Akab'," claiming that since the Spanish invasion in 1524, Mayas have been writing denunciations of what we now call human rights violations and inhumane treatment, quoting the *Anales de los Kaqchikeles*.[10] "They" also speak for the first time in the name of the entire Mayab', the historical Maya region that includes, besides Iximuleu, southern Mexico, the Yucatán Peninsula, and Belize, as well as western Honduras. Immediately after this, "they" inform us of having visited Maya refugee camps in the Guatemalan–Mexican border, the pseudonyms of the informants, and the decision to write this book.

Immediately after the introductory note, we have a prologue. It consists of a letter written to King Juan Carlos I of Spain, in a deliberate intertextual relation with seventeenth-century Quechua chronicler Guamán Poma de Ayala, author of *El primer nueva corónica y buen gobierno* (1615; *The First New Chronicle and Good Government*, 2009).[11] The letter retains the rhetorical gestures of those original documents actively encoded within the production of this particular testimonio as an imitative conspiratorial wink with a critical difference:

> Muy alto y muy poderoso señor:
>
> En el año . Baktun, _ katunes y .. tunes del calendario Maya, y año gregoriano 1992, por gracia de la divina providencia, España mantiene con orgullo el más noble linaje de sus reyes, que por siglos han sido padres, guías y pastores a los pueblos de su dominio. Por otra parte, y aunque los reyes españoles gobernaron a sus pueblos con rectitud real, no cabe duda que en el pasado existieron problemas y agravios en sus dominio, mayormente en las Indias Occidentales, por parte de lo que se hicieron señores y dueños de las riquezas y de las tierras que arrebataron a los habitantes originales de este continente. En su oportuno momento (1550), el reverendísimo obispo de Chiapas, Fray Bartolomé de las Casas hizo una *Brevísima relación de la destrucción de las Indias*, informe que

> entonces envió a Su alteza, el Príncipe don Felipe (II), quien era el encargado de los negocios en las Indias. . . . Por desgracia, esa relación de despojo y desigualdad social, establecida desde los primeros días de la conquista, persisten hasta nuestros días.
>
> Ante este continuo sufrimiento del pueblo Maya, los que aquí ofrecemos nuestros testimonios . . . que después de 500 años de dominación extranjera seguimos orgullosos de nuestra herencia Maya, queremos recordar a Su Majestad que la cizaña que los españoles sembraron hace 500 años sigue creciendo y destruyendo las bases históricas, socio-políticas y culturales de nuestros pueblos. (7)
>
> (Your Royal Highness:
>
> In the year . ba ktun, _ katunes and .. tunes of the Maya calendar, 1992 per the Gregorian calendar, by the grace of divine providence, Spain proudly maintains the noblest lineage of kings, which for centuries have been fathers, guides, and pastors for the populations under their control. Nevertheless, and although the Spanish kings governed their populations with true integrity, there is no question that problems and injustices existing in the past, mainly in the West Indies, were perpetrated by those who became lords and owners of the riches and lands stolen from the original habitants of this continent. In an opportune moment (1550), the highly revered Bishop of Chiapas, Fray Bartolomé de las Casas, penned his Short Account of the Destruction of the Indies, a report that he then sent to his highness Prince Felipe (II), who was in charge of business in the Indies. Unfortunately, this story of plunder and social inequality, set into motion during the very first days of the conquest, continues today.
>
> Given this constant suffering of the Maya community, those of us who offer our testimonies here . . . who after 500 years of foreign domination continue to be proud of our Maya heritage, wish to remind Your Majesty that the discord sown by the Spaniards 500 years ago continues to grow and destroy the historical, sociopolitical and cultural foundations of our communities.)[12]

The prologue is followed by a poem about the prophecies of Maya priests from the *Books of Chilam Balam*, prophecies gathered by Franciscan friar Bernardino de Sahagún, and dreams and prophecies of Iximuleu Mayas in the 1980s.[13] The document in question plays a triple function: (1) it establishes an intertextual analogy with the role played by Fray Bartolomé de las Casas in relation to King Philip II (while also understanding that his own document will not actually reach King Juan Carlos I, any more than Guamán's reached King Philip III); (2) it establishes a paradigmatic continuity with the original destruction and genocide of the Spanish invasion; and, (3) it resituates the context in which the massacres against Maya peoples took place in the 1980s. It is based on these three elements that the testimonio becomes a foundational reconstitution of Maya identity, a position articulated on the basis of an ethical positionality as well.[14] The body of the text is composed of six "lamentations," as opposed to chapters, followed by an epilogue. The first lamentation begins with an *advenimiento* (coming) of violence in the Cuchumatán Mountains, which, unlike traditional testimonios, begins with omens, visions, and dreams that bad things are about to happen (15). They include packs of coyotes that arrive all of a sudden and howl outside the communities, followed by the arrival of mountain cats, owls, and other animals. Even dogs go outside at night and howl or run in deranged fashion on the village streets. Some people claim that they saw the devil throwing stones or whistling at passersby. Women and children stop going to the riverbanks, because they saw naked men with long noses and showing signs of torture, climbing trees while making dramatic gestures. Others see in dreams headless crosses (i.e., crosses where the crucified form of Jesus has been beheaded), or fireballs crossing the sky (16).

This first lamentation thus makes a critical statement. Unlike mainstream testimonios attempting to convey a "truth-effect" to an allegedly sympathetic Western reader enjoying guaranteed freedoms or a hegemonic position while performing a form of affective, empathetic reading, Montejo's text risks losing this particular kind of reader's solidarity, or his or her political identification with the massacre victims, by exercising Indigenous agency in such a way that he deliberately flaunts fantasy-like imaginative deliria whose meaning is hard to authenticate, as a contrary way of reconfiguring discursively traumatized Indigenous subjectivities by way of a structure of feeling that conveys haunted images of irrational fear and suffering.

When we take a second look, we can clearly see that the first lamentation indeed poses a deliberate transgressive resistance to Western credibility. Having said this, we should never forget that, in a general sense, Indigenous cosmovisions also, and always, resist Western teleologies. In this particular case, the first lamentation evidences both a resistance to Westernness and a resistance to a testimonial standard that was also configured by Western hegemony. In this allegedly implausible fashion, the text itself interrogates the tired structure, whereby in mainstream testimonios, as in ethnology, Indigenous subjects remain paradoxically objects. That is, poststructuralism notwithstanding, Indigenous subjects more often than not continue to be represented in testimonios as "native informants," whose utterances are mediated to the Western reader, if not in the representation of the subaltern voice itself, certainly through paratexts, those liminal devices and conventions, both within and outside the book, that form part of the complex mediation among book, author, publisher, and reader, according to French critic Gérard Genette, and which effectively normatize the material for Western readers.[15] The latter will a posteriori offer auratic recognition to those "well-behaved" individuals bearing witness within the protocols preestablished by Western academics who de facto "translate" subalterns' subjective explanations to the Western world, which continues at large to consider Indigenous cosmovisions as a form of incomprehensible, and/or nonrational, discursivity of peripheral value which are certainly inferior to Western metaphysics.

We have to recognize that the hegemony of the mainstream Western academic establishment remains intact in the neoliberal age. It gives only token credence to subaltern discursivities, mainly to those located in conflictive areas according to the West's interests. In the middle of the second decade of the twenty-first century, this would be primarily the Middle East and North Africa. Yet, as self-chosen arbitrators, Western academic mediators more often than not continue to impose their views on Indigenous peoples, instead of accepting their truth-manifestations on their own terms. Perceptive about these aporias and chiastic contradictions, Montejo chooses to play with the form, by resisting the rational "metaphysics of sovereignty" imposed on subalternized subjects and then reconfiguring Indigenous subjectivities from within this racialized contradiction.[16] He therefore deploys an array of floating signifiers constituting a communal performance and a reappropriation of collective cultural signs, which fundamentally refuse to dissociate Indigenous utterances from their cultural environment. They are displayed as a balanced assemblage conditioned only by Indigenous agency, while resisting rational interpretations. These signs bog down the latter in a sea of subjective contradictions that trap any semblance of "truth" within semantic ambiguities. Montejo's testimonio thus becomes a document that effectively hides the other's secrets while simultaneously revealing Western violence as exercised through the agency of the Guatemalan military. He effaces the fantasy that stages a comprehensible scenario behind the shifting meaning of the words themselves. After all, the ability of testimonios to give heteroglossic representations of a people and to assert their identities, experiences, and histories as if they were black-and-white issues remains of primary importance if they are to become visible and, as Spivak stated, "crawl into the place of the 'human'" (*Death of a Discipline*, 23).[17] In Montejo's testimonio, a dialogue evolves (or, worst-case scenario, a *différend*, in a Lyotardian sense; that is, a disagreement in which no consensus can be reached) between discursivity and the implicit reader, one leading to a crucial relationship between ethics and politics.[18] Testimonio implies, for him, accepting the word of the racialized other at face value, rooted in a particular discursive site (in relation to its translocality)—that is, accepting the word of racialized others both as their discursive property in the process of naming themselves (which allows those "othered" subjects to be the rightful "owners" of their subjectivity) and as an enunciative strategy for the sake of gaining agency (as a linkage to their subjectivity). We have, thus, a sort of Levinasian ethics, implying a fundamental openness to the other.

Montejo understands very well that testimonio is the one genre not produced by Western reason and knowledge, but as a hybrid response to the "coloniality of power."[19] It is hybrid because it is not "authentically" a native discursivity; most *testimoniantes* (providers of testimonios) are often illiterate, lack formal education, and would be unable to "arrange" a book within traditional Western parameters. But they usually partake of an extremely rich oral tradition.[20] Indeed, testimonio is, more often, the voice of nonwriters (occasionally, yet not always, illiterate) positioned in the interstice of modernity and coloniality, which their people have yet to overcome. This is also why they need the mediating role of an editor or compiler, usually a Western academic. The mediation between the *testimoniante* and the Western audience, problematic in itself because of the introduction of Western protocols of reading, is what converts the testimonio into a hybrid response to the coloniality of power. The hybridity is the end result of mixing the non-Western/anti-Western subaltern voice with the mediation exercised by the Western academic as manifest proof of knowledge–power relations.[21] However, in this case, we have as mediator a non-Western academic trained in the West—a Jakalteko Maya professor. He thus subverts the encoded fantasy of "comprehending" a testimonio. Montejo stresses the resistance to meanings (packs of coyotes howling outside the communities; the arrival of mountain cats, owls, and other animals; demented dogs on the village streets; the devil throwing stones or whistling at passersby; women and children seeing naked men with long noses and with signs of torture climbing trees, etc.), by virtue of the impossibility of translating and transculturating subaltern enunciations into anything other than imprecise metaphorizations. These shifting meanings deter any categorical assertion about establishing a truth. Their indeterminacy provides the grounds for legitimizing "listening" to subaltern subjects. That is, they facilitate the recognition of the validity of given discourses that operate as expressions of agency, as tropes for the construction of embryonic identities, even if they do not fit within the Western conception of rationality, which we now know is ambiguous and indeterminate as well.[22] In this sense, we have to return to Mexican colonialist José Rabasa's text *Without History* cited in the introduction. He states that when Indigenous subjects "choose to remain outside the state and history" (4), their own strategies "cannot be comprehended . . . by the state" (5)—that is, by the implicit Western reader of a testimonio.

The text moves on to a more conventional format in the subsequent lamentations. They are not only rich with details and significations but also saturated with perlocutionary effects and utterances that recontextualize the lived experiences of Indigenous subjects. They offer their testimony through speech acts that, operating virtually as performative rites, always represent unanticipated turns. They invariably break the expected contexts from which they emerge. We have the testimonio of an ex-soldier who is also an ex-member of military intelligence in the second lamentation. The third lamentation is the discourse of an ex-member of the Civil Patrols. The fourth lamentation consists of the story of a Maya peasant who escaped from a military base. The fifth revisits still another escapee from an army base. Finally, the sixth lamentation is a collection of children's testimonios. The text also includes children's drawings of the violence and massacres, quotations from las Casas's *Brevísima relación de la destrucción de las Indias* that separate each of the lamentations, pictures of some of the informants with their faces covered, and photographs of letters written by refugees about their situation.

Nearly twenty years after the signing of the Guatemalan Peace Accords in 1996, we cannot forget the contingent nature of testimonios as a genre. Nevertheless, Montejo's remains fresh, vivid, and impressionable, unlike many others that read as relics of an age gone by. Published eight years after Menchú's, it was indeed a qualitatively significant effort to both expand the epistemological and the ethical possibilities of a genre, at a moment when the Guatemalan war was still raging, and when many Maya intellectuals that have since come forward had not yet pronounced themselves on these particular issues. It was also, and unquestioningly, a strategic gesture. It took advantage of the quincentenary of Columbus's landing in the Americas to make the Maya genocide visible within the US academic horizon.[23] The text thus stands as the performance of a textual game, a testimonio that is not really one, that is structured with various intertextual layers as if it were a novel. Their stories accumulate rhetorical power by creating exemplary lives sustained by an ethical comportment, in which we can still trace utopian plots, mixing what happened with what should have happened. It is in those liminal spaces that Montejo's testimonial account explores a narrative doubling, a resistance to follow a single syntactic track while drawing a strategic map. The ethical performativity of hero-narrators articulates models of exemplary lives, because the hero-narrators display the work of the self on the self. This is a new ethical strategic possibility both in testimonios and within Indigenous discursivities. Those pseudologies are the phantasmatic projection of a new behavioral model for racialized subaltern subjects that denotes an art of living, an ethical stance on Montejo's part.[24] They are, he implies, the authors of a heroic comportment that validates them as ethical subjects launching interpellative speech acts. Montejo's words do not just disclose an unbearable, abject truth; they also create an event, produce an effect of belief. In this sense Montejo's ethics come closer to Argentinian theologian Enrique Dussel's. In both cases ethics begins with the perspective of the abject, racialized subaltern subject. It is he who enables not only the judgment of differences from within this perspective but also the dissolution of Eurocentrism, as this positionality articulates the need to transform the mechanisms of power in Western societies. In this logic, the latter stands, among other things, for the exclusion of non-European subjugated knowledges. Montejo's articulation is an exemplary experience of deconstruction, even when it becomes, in typical Derridean fashion, an exemplary experience of the impossible as well.[25]

The previous analysis evidences how Montejo's testimonio breaks the vulgar idealization of old-fashioned identity politics that, in the 1990s, trapped most exponents of subaltern studies in the United States. Bogged down in this predicament,[26] followers of this theoretical turn often mythified the subaltern subject as if it were a totemic identitary figure, dispossessing them in turn of their very complex and contradictory subjectivities that actually grounded them historically. I agreed with Rey Chow when she originally stated that we had to attack the idealism found at the basis of identity politics (xxi), thus breaking the crass simplicity located in its conceptual definition. As Bolivian scholar Javier Sanjinés states, "When the dominated rise in violent insurrection, they do not create a rational confrontation of points of view, but the untidy and grotesque affirmation of violence" (4–5). He created the notion of *viscerality*, which he employed as a bodily metaphor to explain "how Indigenous subalternity has resisted giving up its identity to rationalist Western discourse" (5). We could very well state that reading Montejo's testimonio is also a way of understanding viscerality. It is an exploration of the different uses of memory and narration to convey the surviving of human rights abuses, while also experiencing emotions such as anger, frustration, or dreams of revenge, which these abuses inevitably generate among those victims.

MARKING THE ORIGINS OF US ANTHROPOLOGY AS AN INVASIVE FOREIGN BODY

Las aventuras de Mr. Puttison entre los mayas is an acerbic satire of the presence of American anthropologist Oliver La Farge among the Jakalteko community during the 1930s.[27] In the text, when the anthropologist arrives for the first time in March 1930 (1), the village of Yulwitz, represented as a sort of "world without others" up to that point, mistakes him for a priest. This ironic confusion not only reflects the fact that coloniality does exist as a pretextual "regime of truth," the basis of the enduring continuity and causality of the village, but is also a symbolic allusion to a previous colonial oppression, effected largely in the name of the Roman Catholic Church.[28] At the beginning of the text, it is replaced with the anthropological American order, demarcating the Christian designs of Catholic Spain and neo-imperial US secular civilizing ones as two different forms of power/knowledge. It also implies the insertion of the modern Western element that violates the closed community and sets in motion a problematization of its values—that is, a transcultural, hybridizing mechanism within the realm of values, as we see in my analysis.

The unwelcome arrival of a foreigner is signaled by the fact that the narrative voice states that "el acceso a Yulwitz era muy difícil, por lo que ningún turista se había aventurado antes por estas tierras y *profanado con su presencia* a la pacífica comunidad" (1; "The access to Yulwitz was very difficult, which is why no tourist had ventured to these lands before, *defiling with his presence* this peaceful community"; my translation, my italics). We are also told that the sporadic visit of foreign subjects dated, according to the village elders, from "los tiempos de la invasión y de la colonia cuando los primeros misioneros e invasores invadieron con la espada y la cruz estas tierras mayas" (1; "the times of the invasion and the colony, when the first missionaries and invaders invaded with the sword and the cross these Maya lands"; my translation). The repetition of "invasores invadieron" ("invaders invaded") resonates at first sight as a stylistic mistake, a grammatical breach, a lack of editing prior to publishing the manuscript; the signs are contaminated by their repetition. However, the double emphasis on invasion can be read not as a mistake, but rather as a deliberate cacographic malapropism signaling a will to stress a rupture in the form of a repetition. The juncture of both words implies an unstable and traumatic point of departure for the alleged peacefulness of this village, grounding its local history in the violence, destruction, and genocide of the Spaniards' originary invasion. The repetition calls attention to a falsity; this community was *not* always peaceful. The repetition is but a mask, the mask of a semantic mistake beneath which lies the unspeakable, traumatic horror of a genocidal invasion that turned this community upside down, thus deterritorializing any solid sense of peacefulness and de facto questioning the hyperbolic rhetoric of a utopian, pastoral well-beingness as characteristic of this community, prior to the arrival of Mr. Puttison. After all, we are told immediately afterward that

> desde entonces y hasta la fecha, las autoridades ladinas exigen que el pueblo sea sumiso, obediente y servicial . . . a los oficiales del jefe político que obligaban a la gente trabajar forzosamente por medio de los "mandamientos" y la "libreta de vialidad," de manera que el que no trabajaba gratuitamente para el gobierno era castigado por medio de la *Ley Contra la Vagancia*. (1)

> (since then and up to now, the Ladino authorities demand that the village remain submissive, obedient, and helpful . . . to the officers of the political chief that compelled the village people to work by force through the "commandments" and "highway administration notebook," so any person who did not work freely for the government was punished through the application of the Vagrancy Law.)

Peace is but a mask under these oppressive circumstances, one signaled ironically by the narrative voices' rhetoric of pastoral well-beingness and communal utopianism.

The novel traces Mr. Puttison's residence in Yulwitz, from his first arrival, until his final, tragic departure. The text itself is divided into twelve chapters, a number that does not seem to play any calendric connotation, unlike what we saw with *A Mayan Life* in chapter 3. However, it should be noted that the name of the gringo character does come loaded with a bilingual reference that plays with its syntax. It is a signifier that draws attention to itself, catching the reader's attention by its apparent strangeness at first, a polysemic reference gathering bilingual meaning that at first appears opaque, until its Castilian/English sense emerges. "Son" stands by itself in English, even if it remains veiled to the Castilian or Popb'al Ti' reader. The opposite happens with "Putti." While the meaning remains unclear to a monolingual English reader, a Castilian reader immediately smiles upon discovering its hidden meaning, *puta*, or "whore," "bitch." Putti-son means "son of a bitch." In a nutshell, this is the story we are going to read, and when we first approach the text and decode the meaning of the name that appears in the novel's title, we know from the very start that we are going to read the story of an American (a "Mister," an often misleading euphemism used throughout Latin America to name American heterosexist male citizens with feigned respect) who happens to be, most likely, a despicable or contemptible person. What we find out through our reading is the nature of the acts that earned for him such a name, whether it is a true or false transgression, whether the main character's name is or is not tied to imperialism, to racism, to colonialism. The act of naming reaches here a great efficacy, one appearing simplistic at first, if not sophomoric, yet one that, through the miracle of linguistic alchemy, becomes a loaded sign, a portent of the lived history of an Indigenous village where the notion of well-beingness is hollowed out through the simple invocation of the main character's name.

Mr. Puttison appears at first as a jovial gringo who easily wins the trust of the young men in the village of Yulwitz, which, like González's village in *La otra cara* (see chapter 3 of this book), is located in the Cuchumatán Mountains in Western Guatemala, close to the Mexican border. The first chapter describes Mr. Puttison's arrival to Yulwitz in comical terms. We are told by the narrative voice that Tumaxh Aq'eh notices him and runs to the village to inform everyone that a priest is coming. Xhuxh Antil, the mayor, asks him how he knows that it is a priest, and Aq'eh replies:

> —Yo digo que es padre, porque tiene una estatura descomunal. Su cabello es rubio, sus ojos son verdes o azules; y ahora que viene caminando bajo el sol parece que la sangre se le fuera a reventar debajo de su piel de ratón tierno. (2)
>
> (I say he's a priest, because he is amazingly tall. His hair is blond, his eyes are green or blue, and now that he's coming here, walking under the sun, he looks as if his blood could burst out of his baby mouse skin.)

This description convinces Xhuxh Antil that a "gringo" (2) priest is coming to town. He then calls Koxkoreto, the catechist, to ring the church bell and announce the arrival of the priest. All the devoted women run out to kiss the man's hands, the children surround him, and the younger women offer him fruits. Koxkoreto remembers the arrival of previous priests, and, through his remembrances, we as readers learn of the colonial power exercised by priests in the past, events marked by a need to clean the village, offer the missionary a mule or horse and food, and welcome him with music and firecrackers, much like the entrance of kings to European towns in the Middle Ages. Koxkoreto nevertheless remains suspicious, and after bending down in great reverence until his nose nearly touches the visitor's knees (6), he asks him his name. The visitor says he is named Dudley Puttison. Unable to pronounce his name, Koxkoreto gives away from the start the double entendre in the main character's name:

> —Ah, ¡Dud-ley . . . Dudley!, pronunció con alegría Koxkoreto.
> —Padre Dudley Puto . . . Putoson? (7)

> ("Ah, Dud-ley . . . Dudley!" Koxkoreto articulated happily. "Father Dudley Bitch . . . Bitchson?" [my translation])

Needless to say, the disintegration of the main character's name, liberating the true meaning of his last name as he simultaneously foretells what the eventual outcome of their encounter may indeed turn out to be, cannot be understood in English, as my translation clearly indicates. It is a play on words limited to readers who understand Castilian (and Popb'al Ti' readers would be included among them, as insults in Castilian permeate Indigenous languages, retaining their loaded significations in their original form). Thus, the implicated person himself, Mr. Puttison, does not "get it" and limits himself to correcting the pronunciation of his last name, while adding in friendly fashion that he prefers to be called "Dud." Of course, we also know that a "dud" is a thing that fails to work properly or is otherwise unsatisfactory or worthless, something not working or meeting standards, faulty. Therefore, from whichever side we look at his name, the text is yelling to the reader that this is a chronicle of a tragedy foretold, and the only remaining issue is what the nature of this misfortune and bad end will be. Indeed, shortly after the party, the first lie is discovered by the community. Mr. Puttison is not a priest and therefore thinks he cannot sleep in the sacristy. But he did understand that he was confused for one by the village, and he reveled in the confusion until the issue of sleeping arose. Ultimately, he spends the first night in the sacristy. He refuses to eat the black beans he is offered though, because instead of appreciating the community's gesture of welcoming all foreigners in celebratory fashion and feeding them, he fears the community may want to poison him for impersonating a priest. Dud Puttison has cast aside the Spanish colonial value system symbolized by religion and the pomp and circumstance belying the power of the Catholic Church as outlined by Koxkoreto. Mr. Puttison's presence signals a beginning, a semantics of origin, but one initiating itself with the wrong value: an identitary lie. The narrative voice thus indicates Koxkoreto's rebelliousness by marking an ethical breach on the part of Mr. Puttison. He is left-handed, we are told. He literally uses the fingers of the "wrong" hand, the sinister one, to poke the black beans, the native food he refuses to taste. *Sinister* here becomes a signifier of something harmful or evil that is happening or will happen. At the same time, the narrative tone remains parodic. It is, as Gayatri Chakravorty Spivak says in relation to a different literary text, Coetzee's *Disgrace*, a figure "asking for dis-figuration, as figures must. And it is the representation of the 'I' as figured object." (322).[29] The rhetorical signals representing this provocation are indeed political. The "new" colonial agent displays a different behavior from the old ones. Yet his primary failure is fundamentally ethical. He is a usurper. He cannot interact with the racial other, a probable account that will mark the outcome of this novel, and one differentiating both expressions of imperialism, the Spaniard in the Renaissance, and the United States in the twentieth century. Whereas village members had learned to exercise a cautious form of agency in the previous regime, this possibility is annulled by the American's unwillingness to engage in otherness from the very start.

The latter point is reinforced in chapter 2, dealing with, and titled, "Las leyes comunales" ("Communal Laws"). The following morning the wives of the *principales* bring Mr. Puttison breakfast, and he can only complain about being bitten by fleas. Eventually, however, he is forced to admit that he is not a priest. Xhuxh Antil and Koxkoreto are called, and he confesses to them that he is only a "tourist, seeking the most beautiful spots of Mesoamerica to admire Maya grandeur" (17; my translation). They immediately interpellate him as to why he lied the night before, and he claims that the marimba music made him crazy. Thus, he piles one lie on top of another. Xhuxh Antil recognizes this, announcing that "this lying foreigner tried to deceive us" (18; my translation). They thus call for a *lahti'*, a communal meeting, to decide what to do with him. He is summoned to the meeting, asked to identify himself and to explain his intentions (22). He reiterates that he wants to stay to explore the beautiful sites of the region. He is then informed that only *yulwitzeños* (23) are allowed to live there, because the land is communal property. They fear that strangers would want to possess land, and this could break what has enabled them to live in peace for centuries. Mr. Puttison claims he is not interested in their land or in their women. He wants only to study their ancient culture. Because of this gesture, he is allowed to stay.

Dud Puttison then meets with don Lamun and don Lopin, two old *principales*, to discuss the origins of the town. At one point, Koxkoreto mentions that a priest hid the golden and silver chalices that were kept in the temple, and immediately Puttison "paró las orejas" (30; "paid close attention"; my translation) and asked what had become of them. He asks if any chalices are left in the church and gets upset when told that none are, adding, "Oh shit" (31). All others laugh, because they think he has said "xchet," which means "thick-lopped" or "pig's snout" in Popb'al Ti'. This is the first, but not the last, time when the narrative voice takes advantage of similar sounds in both languages to mock his speech and act as part of its rhetorical web. The irony is not colonialized resentment, but rather dialogical games played to bring into evidence the historical strength of a communal moral judgment, communal moral laws, over the lack of ethics of a single individual who does not appear to be bound to any community whatsoever. This is a long and vast chain of signifiers, intertwined with the ensuing dialogues that fill the chapters of the novel, mostly alluded to or suggested. They go far beyond what I can state at this point in the analysis, but I will revisit their implications when examining further chapters. The second chapter ends with Puttison sleeping for the last time in the sacristy, taking notes about village life, and feeling proud that he has established good relations with the village's authorities, thus opening Yulwitz to his inquiries.

In the following chapter, Mr. Puttison moves to the house of Pel Echem, the richest man in Yulwitz, because Echem is the only one with an extra room in his house. We then have a series of episodes in which Mr. Puttison befriends Echem's dog and also discloses his camera and a tape recorder to Lopin, Lamun, Pel Echem, and Koxkoreto, who are all sharing a glass of wine with their gringo visitor in his new room. After Lopin's voice is recorded and played back to him, Lamun says, "One never knows what foreigners may do with what they take with them. Besides having your voice stolen, it is also losing control of yourself" (45; my translation). Not only do recordings become somebody else's property, but the meaning of what was said can be misinterpreted or changed. Finally, a dog with rabies attacks Echem's dog. Puttison accidentally kills the latter with his machete while trying to protect the dog from the attack. He then goes out with Echem's shotgun and kills the dog with rabies, thus gaining communal recognition. Still, the mistake in killing Echem's dog instead of the one with rabies is telling of his lack of adaptation to his environment, his detachment from the community as a whole, his singular individualness.

After the last episode, the conversations between Puttison and his four Indigenous friends multiply in the text, becoming the salient trait of its plot development. At first, they follow the format whereby Puttison asks questions that could be viewed as of an anthropological nature, such as the use of local plants, local customs, and historical events, whereby the four Indigenous men respond. However, they do not "just" respond in the sense of providing an answer to Puttison's question. They respond in a way that justifies the choice for having made a given decision, one not only regarding their administrative skills based on communal interests but also their local knowledge of their environment, their flora, their fauna, and their place as a village with only so many resources at the time, within a broader regional context. We are thus exposed to bewildering complex responses to Puttison's simple questions. In these responses, evidence is offered of that fact that changes do take place, but based only on their concrete living conditions, in response to which they align new frames of reference within their Indigenous matrix. A concrete example of this is their explanations of why they have to burn a corner of their pine forest. Puttison condemns their burning of pine trees as a sad and destructive event. He is informed by Xhuxh Antil and Koxkoreto that only two trees are cut each year, and that a small corner of the forest is then burned, with the fire kept under careful control. This happens for three reasons: (1) to produce a yearly reserve of *ocote* (a heavily resinous piece of pine used until very recently instead of matches) to light their daily fires; (2) to enable women to collect firewood from the fallen trees without sliding and tumbling down, especially if they are pregnant; and (3) to get rid of hay and wild plants growing among the pines (57–58). Finally, he is told that, were the village to own more land, this would indeed become unnecessary.

This device is also reflected in the maneuvers of language itself. An example of this opposition emerges when discussing names, an action noted in Montejo's previous chapter. After Mr. Puttison insists that he be called "Dudley" instead of "Mister," Xhuxh Antil replies.

> "Okay, Mister," said Xhuxh Antil. "You must also learn to say the names of your friends in the Popb'al Ti' language. Always call me 'Antil' instead of 'Andrés.' I like that name a lot, but it is the name of

a type of toad that during the rainy season climbs into the trees to croak." (66; my translation)[30]

Mr. Puttison misses the irony and limits himself to replying, "Interesting." For Antil, his Castilian name is a verbal aggression, the verdict of a fundamental asymmetry in their relation of power that operates as an injurious, perlocutionary performative utterance that is instantiated by the particular linguistic act of naming. Mr. Puttison is oblivious to the insult because, having the power to mark Antil's consciousness with that hurt, he is himself unaware of his "naturalized" imperial stand. In another instance, Mr. Puttison, curious about the semiotics of identity, asks how his own name would be pronounced in their language.

> "Don Lamun says that your name would be pronounced *T'ut'* in our language."
>
> Mr. Puttison stood up angrily and screamed:
>
> "Oh, please, don't give me another name! My name's Dud."
>
> "Yes, mister, but the letter D doesn't exist in our language. The closest is *T'ut'*, but it is also something else." Everybody laughed.
>
> "What is *T'ut'*, then?"
>
> Xhuxh Antil came forward to explain with a picaresque smile.
>
> "*T'ut'* is the noise made when you fart." (66; my translation)[31]

In the second set of exchanges, Mr. Puttison gets offended because he finally detects a stigmatization in the act of being named that, for the first time, generates in him an awareness of being othered in a reductionist way, of losing his privileged insularity. He then insists on being called Mr. Puttison, a name that marks (cultural imperialist) authority, instead of *T'ut'*, a designation he perceives as an insult instead of an invitation to laughter. The villagers' joviality signals their ethical stance of making room for the other's subjective existence within their boundaries. Mr. Puttison, meanwhile, remains fully unaware of how the insult functions in relation to subaltern identity, and he is unwilling to dehegemonize his position to learn how to occupy the subject position of the other, as Spivak conceptualizes this notion.

As we can see in this quoted fragment, subject position is assigned in both instances of translation, but the exchange is really about respect for otherness. Still, the configuration of Maya ethics is not expressed through abstract conceptualization and logical exposition. It is, rather, represented literarily as sudden flashes of knowledge bursting through conventional storytelling and signaling radical heterogeneity. This is a performative counterpoint to Western reason that marks its lacunae. And, once again, the implicit unnamed reference in this counterstatement to occidentalist logic would be the *Popol Wuj*, a text favoring exemplary ethics. *Las aventuras de Mr. Puttison entre los mayas* would reappropriate and redefine the *Popol Wuj* as a philosophical matrix for postoccidentalist thinking.

It is on the return from the visit to the grinding of sugarcane in the oxen-driven mill that Koxkoreto shows Puttison the Swi' Kamom cave, where the objects of the *paywinaj* (ancient men) are hidden: "Mr. Puttison felt a visible satisfaction, as he got redder than ever when Koxkoreto mentioned the mysterious cave" (75; my translation).[32] Mr. Puttison insists on going in, despite warnings that no one had done so, and is bitten by a rattlesnake (in this case, it is important to remember the lesson of the rattlesnake in the story "How the Serpent Was Born" in *The Bird Who Cleans the World*). He nevertheless comes out carrying a human skull. Xhuxh Antil and Koxkoreto give him first aid and tell him to return the skull to its place, that one should never disturb the dead, but Puttison ignores their advice. Still, after he is carried back to the village, their old healer, Kux Ahawis, is called to cure Puttison, who is already suffering from a high fever (80).

During the night, Puttison remembers what he saw in the cave. The narrative voice, however, informs the reader that, according to the village people's beliefs, those riches belonged to Witz, the "owner of the mountain" (82). All mountain owners were wealthy, like Ladinos, and if anybody made a pact with them, it meant that they had automatically sold their soul to the "owner of the mountain." That explained why no one in Yulwitz paid attention to the treasure located inside the cave. Mr. Puttison, however, considering himself a modern, educated American man, believes this was merely superstitious behavior on their part. That same night, someone knocks on his door. He shines his flashlight, but no one is there. The sound repeats itself, but no one appears. Finally, he falls asleep. He then dreams of a woman dressed in an ancient *huipil*. She walks around his bed, telling him that they had stayed in the house where they hid from the Spaniards' gunfire, and no one had bothered them until he arrived and woke them up disrespectfully (83). She asks him to return her brother to his place. Koxkoreto later tells him he had dreamt of one of the *paywinaj* (85), and Pel Echem insists that he return the skull. In this chapter, Kux Ahawis comes again to examine Puttison's recovery, and the gringo praises him for his great knowledge of Maya medicine. Ahawis replies that a person should never brag about his or her abilities, as they come from the Supreme Being, and they are given "to do good works and serve the people" (88; my translation). After he leaves, Puttison is told how Ahawis became a healer and that he never charges for his services.

The narrativization of this long episode in chapter 5 is critical for the understanding of the novel as a whole. On the one hand, we clearly see how knowledge of the past is paramount to making sense of the present and, by extension, configuring a potential future. The historical and cosmological presence of the *paywinaj* in their continuing presentness forges an ethical sense that guides the community as a whole. The long passage described above foregrounds the continuing import of their reference system and history, in marked contrast to Puttison, bitten by a rattlesnake as a consequence of his egotistical actions. Unlike the community members, he lives in a world of agonistic political discourse in which opinions, rhetoric, and the ability to lie are signs of individual freedom. The trope of the healer as a selfless individual "chosen" by a higher authority to perform his duties versus Puttison's cynical fantasy of the cave's treasures that manifests his tendentious inclination to believe what one wants to believe without regard to contrary evidence—that is, the mysterious knocks and the contents of his dream signaling an invisible spirituality as cosmological rector of human behavior, establish the two parameters from which to achieve opposing configurations of modernity. The text stands as articulating the ethical comprehension of the villagers' intention. Its rhetoricity clearly juxtaposes both systems of belief and finds Puttison's wanting. The narrative sanctions the villagers' behavior as positive. It is the result of conscious self-scrutiny and consensus building. Puttison, in turn, is represented as evidencing the limits of an individualized, selfish practice, as someone clearly trying to distance any understanding of the role of lying from moral judgments, and as transgressing without being fully conscious of his acts. The absence of any transcendent referent, or even of any meta-normative behavioral pattern, makes the effect of Puttison's operation basely egotistical and fundamentally irreparable, while cleverly staging the performative function of the lie, though he has already been preemptively punished by the snakebite. As a result, the oscillation of textual judgment stands between a rich, powerful foreigner, who, though winning materially, is evidenced as being ethically weak, and a poor, local community, who, in losing materially, ultimately wins the moral battle as a result of their ethical strength anchored in a vision that respects the wisdom of the *paywinaj,* whose living memory expresses the fundamental values underlying Maya culture. This is reaffirmed in the following chapter, aptly titled "The Spirits of the Ancestors."

In this sixth chapter, Puttison has another nightmare. He is carrying valuable objects through a dark forest, when four thieves with machetes intercept him (99). He fights them off and kills two (100). He throws the first corpse in a ravine, but when he tries to throw the second one, his hands and legs cling to the dead thief's neck and waist. Though he struggles the entire night to throw him off, he is unable to do so. Finally, at daybreak, a villager discovers him and accuses him of murder (101). The villager then performs a ritual to free Puttison of the corpse and tells him to throw it in a cave. But when he is about to do it, the police arrive (as he is later told by Xhuxh Antil, there are no police in Yulwitz), arrest him, and order his execution to set an example (103). At the same time that the guns pointing at him go off in the dream, a gourd filled with the sugarcane molasses he had left fermenting under his bed explodes, and he screams, waking up Pel Echem and his wife.

Except for my understanding of the detail of the gourd, the *paywinaj* never appear in this chapter. Why, then, the title of chapter 6? We can conclude only that not only is the gourd, or calabash, a trope for the *paywinaj*, one of its most sacred symbolic objects, but the entire nightmare segment is induced by them, as we already know from the previous dream in chapter 5.[33] Dreams articulate for most Indigenous cultures the silent, invisible wisdoms that constitute their memory as a people and give them a sense of beingness. They express the moment when some singular act forces itself into existence, even if this may be experienced very subjectively and appear as "magical" to the Western, "rational" mind. A dream is something "in the air" and about to happen. Dreams often give Indigenous peoples, for the most part, the actual experience of an event, rather than appearing, as many dreams do, as just a series of discrete, unrelated moments. They connote a transformation that takes them back to ancestral times. This linking of dreams to ancient cultural origins means that dreaming is not really about a single individualized subject having a dream in Freudian fashion, as something merely subjective originating in the individual human psyche. Rather, dreams are a reference to the presence of the past within their present in coetaneous fashion. Dreaming is a way of beingness that is always informed by a spiritual presence, by a "cosmic timing," a place where all life exists within a state that blends past, present, and future simultaneously. Dreams operate more like synchronicities, as what physicist Carl Johan Calleman has described as "the 'timing' of the cosmos" (32). We should also remember the opening episodes of the different sections of Luis de Lión's *Time Commences at Xibalbá* described in chapter 2, and Lwin's shamanic trance in Gaspar Pedro González's *La otra cara*, described at the end of chapter 3, in this same light. At the same time, dreams are always associated with lessons to be learned or moral tales to be encoded ethically. Ultimately dreams also underlie the power of Indigenous spirituality, as in this particular text, influencing the apparently irreverent and materialistic take on the world displayed by Puttison's acts.

In chapter 7, Puttison pushes the visits and conversations with his four friends, Xhuxh Antil, Koxkoreto, don Lamun, and don Lopin, without forgetting to ask if any other caves with treasures, such as Swi' Kamom, exist in the area (118). He always waits for all four to have drunk enough *cusha* (a locally made alcoholic beverage) that they will open up to him. During this particular visit with don Lopin in chapter 6, Xhuxh Antil confesses that yes, there is Smuxuk Witz, a cave that no one has ever been able to go down into. Puttison persists, asking Antil if he would show him one day where this particular cave is (119). The narrative voice mocks him at the end of the chapter, though, when he confuses a young woman named Kat Tulis, who is bathing in the pond, with the *llorona* (the Weeping Woman) and pours *cusha* on her head (122–23).[34] He gets a mouthful from the woman as a result.

From the subsequent dialogues between Mr. Puttison and members of the community emerges a series of rhetorical movements allowing Montejo to play Western and Maya values against each other. For example, in the chapter that follows, Mr. Puttison goes out hunting with Pel Echem and discovers that Echem is afraid because he believes that dwarves haunt him (133). Mr. Puttison insists that he is confusing skunks with dwarves, and he provokes Echem by saying that he had heard that his father was no coward and often hunted alone at night (135). Pleased by Mr. Puttison's words, Echem tells the story of how his father ran into the guardian of the forests, who forbade him to hunt any more deer, a story whose tone feels derived from the *Popol Wuj*. Once again, Puttison finds the story "wonderful" (139) as folklore. But he does not draw from it any lessons about ethical behavior. On the contrary, for Echem, the object of the narrative and, implicitly, of the foundational nature of the *Popol Wuj* and its variant manifestations on other Maya communities, is ethical: the story represents the transfiguration of the guardian as symbolizing the normative principle that collective well-being stands above the selfish desires of an individual. Thus, his wife, Usep Pel, supports the narrative. Puttison, however, is disinterested in the ethical implications of the story and, bored, leaves for his room (139).

In chapter 9, all the able men are forced to do their thirty-day service of *vialidad*, free service to the state to build roads as indicated at the beginning of the analysis of this novel. To avoid being arrested by the country's dictatorship as "vagrants," they have to walk three days to Huehuetenango, the capital of their department. Though Xhuxh Antil is spared this service because of his being mayor, he decides to accompany the men as a gesture of communal solidarity, and he visits Puttison to let him know he will be gone for a week (146). The American then insists he accompany him for one last walk and, while doing so, show him where the cave of Smuxuk Witz is located. They head there and Puttison goes down into the cave with the ropes that Pel Echem prepared for him (148). Puttison spends some time inside the cave while Xhuxh Antil waits outside, and finally comes back out, just saying, "Maravilloso, maravilloso" (149).

When they return to the village, there is a farewell party for those leaving for their *vialidad* service. Puttison buys some *cusha* for the party (152) and then starts dancing himself, while throwing pennies to those watching him. Children and others wrestle in the mud to catch the pennies while Puttison yells loudly, "This is the friendship that Dudley Puttison offers you!" (153; my translation). Puttison then decides to temporarily leave the village, walking with the group of men toward Huehuetenango (154).

In chapter 10, the men are still gone, and so is Puttison. As a result, women have to do the work in the fields. When Usep Pel goes to her husband's field one day at noon, the "evil hour," she finds a big snake undulating and sidewinding around the corn plants (157). She immediately thinks this a bad omen, echoing once more Montejo's fable on the role of the snake in *The Bird Who Cleans the World*. She wraps some of her hair on a cob, throws it at the snake, and flees. Lamun dies a while later, falling into a ravine, and they think this may have been the event indicated by the bad omen. In chapter 11 the men return from their *vialidad* service, mostly sick and worn out. Some unspecified time later, Puttison comes back as well, accompanied by two other gringos, Dave and Arthur (172). He informs Xhuxh Antil that they will not stay long.

That evening Puttison gathers with his old friends to talk, asking them about the *vialidad* service. Besides the usual account of Ladino abuses, we learn that they were working by the Santa María volcano, but the Ladinos resented that they were opening its entrails and provoked continuous collapses of rocks on the work they were doing.[35] Pel Echem claimed they would dig tunnels all day, and the next day the tunnels would collapse. Everything would look as if no work had taken place the day before (175). Though this is a secondary sequence within the narrative, it is important to point it out as another example of non-Western ontologically and epistemically potent imaginaries in which natural entities act out as subjects, thus connecting particular people with specific ecospaces, closing the divide between nature and culture. At this point I simply mark it as part of a needed recognition of the myriad liminal assemblages with which Indigenous peoples constitute not just their world but also ours. The interferences between different modes of making these worlds have helped to denaturalize the assumptions built into multinatural perspectivism as a form of representation. These interferences offer a sort of narrative pause, making it easier to explore the varying methods for constituting subjectivity, the different ways in which the spatiality of our societies is produced, and, paraphrasing Law and Benschop, the diversity that is possible in the relationship between spatialities and narrative when the distinction between nature and culture cannot be articulated to define areas that are internal to non-Western cosmologies (174). An analogous element is introduced in this same sequence, about the sorcerers' inability to destroy the Ladino straw boss, El Cuervo, because as a Ladino, it was not known what his *nagual* or "*yijomal spixan*" was, and therefore they could not locate it so as to control him (177).[36]

A week later Puttison informs Xhuxh Antil and Koxkoreto that he plans to leave the following day and will not return (180). He requests that he and his two friends be taken one last time to Smuxuk Witz. Koxkoreto says it is not good to go there unless it is to light candles and *pom* to honor their ancestors.[37] Xhuxh Antil, however, agrees to take him, as long as he brings candles to perform the ritual (181). The next day they go to the cave. While Xhuxh Antil performs the ritual, Puttison and Arthur go down with ropes, flashlights, and burlap sacks. Once they return, with the sacks loaded and weighing very much, they keep Xhuxh Antil somewhat apart (183). He gets offended, and Puttison offers him some coins, while they distribute the cargo three ways, and then head toward the Mexican border (184). In the last lines of the chapter, the narrative voice denounces the situation that Xhuxh Antil himself has not yet registered: "As three souls carried away by the devil, the three thieves began to run like crazy, trying to abandon that place as soon as possible" (184; my translation).[38]

The true identity of Puttison—the implied play on his name at the beginning of this analysis, the direct relationship to the nature he represents—is thus exposed textually. With the performativity of Puttison's farewell gesture, readers clearly see how the US anthropological order, inaugurated symbolically through the trope of the main character, rears its ugly head. It is represented as just another form of colonial oppression, one as rapacious and as interested in the exploitation of precious metals and ancient goods as the Spanish regime was. This is indeed, to a certain extent, the leading thematic configuration traced in this text. Within these parameters, readers also understand the usage of the sign "defiling" at the beginning, in relation to what will become Puttison's future actions in the fabulation, his last gesture in Yulwitz. The narrative voice, of course, already knows the outcome of the story.

The fall guy in this tale is Xhuxh Antil. At the end of chapter 11, he is in shock. Simultaneously angry and incredulous, he cannot quite digest the event that has just taken place. His first reaction, though, is his one unethical act in the narrative. He pretends that he was gathering firewood; he was planning to return to the village as if nothing had happened. This gesture is his one significant violation of the communal sense of politics, whose ultimate goal consists of protecting the well-being of all its members. Unfortunately for him, though, his plans go awry. In the last chapter, he is confronted by the angry villagers while heading back with his load of firewood. Tumax Pech, described as "rebellious" (186), a symbolic surplus, an important sign encoding a hypothetic post-textual future, saw what took place as he was returning from working in his field. He blames Antil and indicates that he is carrying the coins Puttison gave him in his satchel, which are immediately found. Antil, as a result, has to not only confront the angry mob but also suffer the ultimate humiliation of being discharged from his position as mayor (189). With the money Puttison gave him, says Kat Tulis, the woman over whom Puttison emptied his *cusha* bottle at the end of chapter 7, the community should buy the candles needed to pray to the ancestors and apologize for the profanation that has just taken place (190).

Antil's naivete appears both as descriptive (he was indeed gullible in trusting Puttison) and as evaluative (he was indeed a fool and also lacked agency in his relationship with Puttison, behaving as allegedly did all "pre-political" Indigenous subjects metonymically represented by this textual character, in the Western Ladino/gringo perception of the Guatemala of the early 1930s). Indirectly, this is also a critique of a character that otherwise behaves ethically throughout the previous sequence of events. Except for the very end, he did follow the norms of his community. The narrative voice, however, is already somewhat external to this same community and no longer subscribes to the values it embodies. Yulwitz is presented as a stable and presentable topos, but it also represents a double bind, a split between internal harmony and subalternized marginalization. The narrative voice commemorates the stability of Yulwitz due to its "old ways," when religious tradition and internal hierarchies still prevailed, while also undoing, in subtle, allusive fashion, the racialized subalternity associated with such a state of affairs.

The humor within the text is the irony that traces a deconstructive process disarticulating delicately the idealized well-beingness of such a village, in which events such as Puttison's profanation were inevitable, tragedies just waiting to happen. It is not an argument per se. But this trace hints at something not represented in the text itself, suggesting a stain already clouding the pastoral idealization of Yulwitz. The last lines of the novel, its very closure, inform the reader that Xhuxh Antil's gaze contemplated the sunset as increasing darkness covered the town, "in an atmosphere mixed with remembrances, amities, and mysteries" (193; my translation).[39] Whereas Xhuxh Antil, the symptomatic connection with the dying patriarchal system, may remain as a stain in the community's visceral field of vision, his gaze is the one, post-fall-from-grace, also divining their troubled future. Or is this analogy the product of the narrative voice?

The latter possibility most likely gives the reader an appropriate and corrective model of an understanding of the true state of the village circa 1930. Whereas affect goes in the direction of the fallen mayor, and ideological condemnation clings to Puttison like mud stains—he is a vulgar thief, after all—the true lesson of this text is traced by the narrative voice. The village is an island in the past, surviving in a field where such behavioral patterns no longer have a place. While emphasizing Indigenous knowledge systems and forms of knowledge production, the narrative voice deliberately circumscribes the sequence of events represented to the early 1930s as a way to mark a past very different from where Guatemala's Mayas are at the moment of their end-of-the-century renaissance—that is, after the country's civil war, the period lived by Montejo as a protagonist, and theorized as well in his book *Maya Intellectual Renaissance*, the moment when this novel was written and published.

The text develops a perspective that emphasizes diversity and contrast between Western and Indigenous knowledge production. It also downplays the emancipation of the racialized other, though we could read as a *mise en abyme* of the latter the revolt that deposed Xhuxh Antil, complicit however naively with the doings of American imperialist exploiters. The choice of a member of a younger generation, Pel Nolaxh, to succeed him (189), the emergence of women such as Kat Tulis as leaders of this revolt, and the reaffirmation to understand the teachings of the elders, all implying that no individual should operate without communal consensus (190), are also signs of the future. They flag a new phenomenon. Not only a changing of the guard from a generational perspective and the entrance of women to leadership roles, but also the emergence of collective agency. These issues are all connected to the predicament taking place, and all working synecdochically together as agents of change. While the cleansing ritual begins the following day, Kat Tulis and the other women leading this process say,

"Let's all walk together without anyone falling behind the group" (190), a clear paraphrase of the historic Committee for Peasant Unity (CUC) slogan of the late 1970s: "Let there not be any group that gets left behind," a slogan taken from the *Popol Wuj* that also closes González's *A Mayan Life*, as pointed out in the previous chapter.

The narrative voice therefore implies a combination of preservation of the old ways, while also celebrating the need for social change. It subtly mocks Xhuxh Antil as a trusting, naive person perfectly positioned for a fall, while categorically rejecting his "innocence." It also lambastes Puttison in name and actions for being a sign of the new imperialism to come, a representation somewhat contaminated with a dose of bad faith. Still, the narrative voice sounds reasonable, taking a moderate approach. We do not have a visceral, dualistic, judgmental, hysterical, or simplistic discourse. But it is historical. This voice does not fear the destruction of old ideas, while also signaling the urgency to properly evaluate them before discarding any. It also stresses the responsibility to create new ones. The narrative voice articulates a critical reflection on disenchantment with Eurocentric modernity, while also performing a subtle transformation of communal relations. It is a disquisition that remains scrupulous and vigilant enough not to overstate them, though. This can happen, of course, only because the representation, though historical, is also experiential for the author. Therefore, every aspect of the conflict depicted resonates.

Xhuxh Antil's gaze is indeed loaded in the end, given what had just happened. But his point of view is not just individual. Antil is connecting with something greater than himself. He is linked with the co-inhabitants of a spatially delimited affective world, in which he is now a pariah. Nevertheless, Antil's ego is not bent on exculpating himself, or in redeeming his name, as we would see in a more traditional Western story. In the narrative past of this particular fabulation, Antil had constituted himself as an ethical being and a social actor. This implies, at the juncture where the novel ends, that he knows he is accountable to his community and has therefore made peace with his disgrace. Ethics, he knows, do not belong to an individual subject but are the purview of the community as a whole. Whereas he was found wanting, the community's collective effort has yielded ethical results in dismissing him.

However, the book also ends with an indication that a sort of interregnum has begun. Things will no longer be able to be the same in Yulwitz. Guatemala's civil war is still decades ahead of that moment in the early 1930s, when Xhuxh Antil contemplates with a mournful gaze the Mexican mountains where Puttison and his partners in crime have disappeared. The narrative voice implies that he is meditating on the recent events that have taken place. Readers can, however, guess that the experience has forced Antil, and the entire community, to rethink their place in their world, the constitution of their ethnicity, their beingness as racialized and subalternized subjects, what constitutes kinship, gender relations.

A reader of this text has thus been exposed to a way of life that no longer exists. He/she is being asked to imagine what will come. Yet, historically, we know what comes. Montejo told us in his first book, *Testimony, Death of a Guatemalan Village*. Yulwitz is that same village of Tzalalá, half a century before. We can now attach both ends of that historical continuum to see where Puttison's action ultimately leads, and, after the destruction has taken place in *Testimony*, explore the ideas of *Maya Renaissance* to see how communities such as Yulwitz may in time reconstitute themselves within decolonial parameters.

In this same logic, Montejo's *Testimony: Death of a Guatemalan Village* can be seen as an emblematic Indigenous auto-representation. Reread thirty years after its conception, this text shows a discursive effort that originally claimed to be rooted in a collective belongingness to a community, thus subordinating the attainment of individual goals to the common good, actually representing a subject that struggles to gain agency by distancing himself somewhat from his community. In my reading, it is this process of the writing subject that comes to constitute an Indigenous auto-representation, regardless of issues of individual belongingness, tensions between individual and collective goals, or ethical issues or power relations that have to be navigated carefully.

Testimony is as close as Indigenous written production has come to auto-representations in Latin America. This is because the so-called testimonial "I" projects itself metonymically to a collective "us" that still points in the direction of community, though with the contradictions indicated in the previous paragraph. This enunciating position empowers the individual subject despite his felt obligation to speak in the name of a community of which he forms a part. It evidences Montejo's transition from a marginal witness to a fully developed subject exercising agency in his interactions with subjective antagonists. His two implicit story lines—the one constructing the narrator as a subject and the one about his village and community—are interdependent and signal the complexity and conflict in the struggle to constitute an authentic Indigenous self, while also mediating politically and juridically in the name of a victimized community. Thus, the writing itself displays the anxieties confronting the individual voice with the testimonial protocols requiring subjective self-effacement.

By enabling his agency to emerge from within the text itself, Montejo speaks back to the codification of genres which attempt to circumscribe his writing freedom and that of subalternized and racialized lettered subjects. It is this will that ultimately leads to his latest novel, *Pixan, el cargador del espíritu*, written exclusively in Castilian. It is without question his most satirical text ever. This book is extremely critical of Maya subjects who participated in various Non-Governmental Organizations (NGOs). I stated in chapter 1 that the 1990s was also the decade of Maya NGOs. A number of independent NGOs appeared between the late 1980s and the early 1990s. Most were financed by European agencies, whether dependent on political parties, the governments of European nations, or international organizations. Some were formed since the late 1980s as contributions to the Central American peace effort. Others resulted from the signing of the Peace Accords in 1996. Most were formed to aid the Iximuleu Maya population, perceived internationally as the major war victims, given the outrage generated by the genocide perpetrated by the Guatemalan army. As a result, a high number of Maya cadres, whether trained in the country's universities or abroad, ended up participating—when not actually running—many of these NGOs.

In this novel, Montejo focuses on a character, Juan Kiej. Like other Mayas in analogous circumstances, he has become "Ladinoized" as a consequence of the sudden experience of being *nouveau riche* by his management of an NGO, of which he is president. In the text the organization in question is named Consejo Posmoderno de Desarrollo Rural, with an acronym of COPODER. In English, this would be the Postmodern Council of Rural Development, but the acronym's play with words only works in Castilian. COPODER literally means "sharing power," as with a national government. Thus, one of the elements underlining the satire rests in the understandings that members of this NGO saw themselves as sharing power with the Guatemalan government and abusing the excesses that political power entails, while forgetting their Maya roots and the communities they were supposed to serve. They are thus defined textually as *sal-wes*, or "mayas falsos" (13), and the discursive voice adds for emphasis that their critics named them *madinos*, which stood for "Maya-Ladinos" (13).

Power has gone to their heads. Kiej is called by the members of the governing board of COPODER "el señor presidente" (Mr. President), an allusion to Miguel Angel Asturias's novel of the same title about dictatorship in Guatemala. The all-male members of the top leadership have used donors' money to buy new cars. They also spend most evenings in a house of prostitution displaying abject heterosexist behavior. Needless to say, this has led to an identitary crisis. As the text states at one point, “Había que decidir si seguían representando a los indígenas, aunque ellos mismos no estaban seguros de su propia identidad” (84; “they had to decide whether they would continue representing Indigenous peoples, though they were no longer sure of their own identity”; my translation).

Montejo focuses his critical gaze on various double binds, staging the polyphony of voices of the members of the governing board, which besides Kiej also includes fake spiritual guide Hipólito Suk Tunuk, Kiej’s leading accomplice, and those of the true defenders of Maya spirituality and culture such as the *ah’beh* (healer) Modesto Sanik, and Casimiro Tukul, as well as Kiej’s own daughter Yulisa, a university student. While being opposed to each other, these voices nevertheless form a cohesive unity. The text depicts the speed in which Maya leaders can now travel from one corner of the country to the other. Yet, as Montejo’s reflections show, this factor only increases a sense of isolation for alienated Maya subjects. The workings of satire compromises whatever autonomy these *arriviste* individuals think they have gained in the Ladino world. As Juan Kiej’s subjectivity begins to cave in from within, melancholia takes over.

Needless to say, it is Kiej’s own alienation that leads to his downfall. First, he becomes sexually impotent and needs the help of famous healer Casimiro Tukul to regain his prowess. Then, he cuts down the tree that protects his village of origin. Since this stands explicitly for the Tree of Life as Luperto Sanik states in the text (210), this action would have killed his *yijomal spixan* (82), the animal keeper [or carrier] of the spirit, much like the nagual or nawal that has been previously explained, though in Popb’al Ti’ language. Luckily for him, Modesto Sanik rescued and then healed the ugly bird that plays this role for Kiej.

The topic of an increase of isolation through the forgetfulness of Maya spirituality and duty to community lays Montejo’s finger on the wounds of the potential destruction of Maya cultural achievements inherent in a form of political participation that operates within the boundaries of neoliberal globalization. This behavior activates and aggravates thought about contemporary Indigenous issues. Satire establishes a critical distance between the narrative voice and the subjects depicted in the text, a textual strategy which also separates the reader from the trauma that this representation has possibly inflicted to Montejo himself. We should not forget that Montejo was a governmental figure in the first decade of this century, a trajectory that ended with his burning all his bridges with the country’s political establishment.

Implicit in this positionality is Montejo's empathy with the victims of Guatemala's genocide. If this text represents indirectly a work of mourning, it mourns simultaneously for the ensuing corruption of the emerging Maya leadership whose opportunism makes them incapable of learning something from that recent historical period, as well as from their cultural or personal formation as Maya subjects. The narrative voice thus quivers with anger over a catastrophe that has already occurred, but from which no history lessons seem to have been learned. Here, the imaginative work of comical satire underlies the real work of mourning. In consequence, this becomes an utterly grim depiction of Maya leadership. It is this bleakness that constitutes the true content of his satirical way of writing. The characters' fat bodies, their vulgar language, their food and drink habits (Kiej is addicted to Coca-Cola, for example), their everyday behavior—everything that has to do with postwar Maya leadership—emerges as an integral part of a form of economic development that does not correspond to progress but to an emerging form of alienating horror. This vision in turn establishes a distancing from reassuring postwar efforts to make sense of a traumatic past. Instead, Montejo grapples with a senselessness that thematizes the absence of the "real" in the lives of Kiej and his associates.

The "real," however, is present in the text in the ethical doings of Tukul and Sanik. Kiej's *yijomal spixan* is restored to health by Sanik, who visualizes his job as "la expresión de su amor y compasión que se extendía a todos los seres naturales de la tierra" (105; the expression of his love and compassion that extended to all natural beings on Earth). Unfortunately, the ugly bird that Sanik is healing escapes, and Kiej is forced to seek once more the wisdom of Casimiro Tukul to be cured of his recurring headaches and *chij-at* (sexual impotence). Tukul informs Kiej that he suffers from *hustisya* (118), a sickness that is a sort of supernatural punishment resulting from abusing nature. Kiej thinks only of commercializing the medicinal plants that Tukul gives him. Still, his *yijomal spixan* returns to Sanik (129). Ultimately, it is only when Kiej recognizes that he has abandoned his Maya ways, pays for all the damage he has inflicted on his community, and plants a new tree in the place where the old one he had cut down used to be, that he is able to recover from his ailments.

Montejo deals in his last novel with a modern malaise by returning to the *Popol Wuj* and the roots of Maya spirituality. Like in Gaspar Pedro González, we have here a double dimensionality. Not the Maya classical past per se, but Maya spirituality as a definer of ontological beingness, in opposition to the neoliberal globalized present and the religion of capitalism that threatens Maya leaders almost as much as the recent genocide did. Both are deployed in the novel as simultaneous horizons of beingness. Thus, Montejo's satire becomes an exemplary discourse. His text deals with the excesses and temptations of contemporary capitalism by an appeal to non-Western Maya spirituality. This approach presupposes distance and the ability to face the meaninglessness of Western globalization without the comfort of rational and aesthetic devices that could impose an accessible structure onto the radical contingency of traumatic events. Similarly to González, Montejo returns to the core of Maya metaphysical principles to grasp the roots of modern Western-centered alienation and to better understand the contemporary ramifications of both genocide and colonialism. Montejo's work shows how the roots of colonial and genocidal violence lie in behavioral patterns that originated in the colonized past, but also have a place in the material temptations nurturing the spiritual vacuum of the present. This implies that, in his last novel, Montejo must give an account of the inferiority complex that racialization, subalternization, and Eurocentric violence has generated over time as a stressful traumatic resentment that still lives inside many Maya subjects. This forms part of their daily lives and can easily transform Maya leaders into the new oppressors if they "forget" the lessons of history and their true beingness. The body language of Kiej and his associates manifests these traumatic habits signifying aggression, a disease that can be overcome only by appealing to the ramifications that reach deep into the Maya past.

It is precisely these epistemological conundrums that are fascinating about Montejo's oeuvre. Reading Montejo's satire, we can understand it as a form of vital self-criticism. Montejo was himself a governmental functionary for close to a decade after all. At the same time, the knowledge represented in his text enables an exposure to the Maya other, to an unethical becoming that also haunts postwar Mayas. *Pixan* ultimately argues that those who fortify themselves against the onslaught of otherness, in actual fact, destroy not only those whom they consider others, but also themselves.

Conclusion

This volume examines Guatemalan Maya narratives through the lens of their own particular knowledges, yet from a generic decolonial theoretical perspective, that stresses the reflective assessments—in this particular case—of contemporary Maya contexts and epistemologies. Whereas I believe in the emerging distinctiveness of Global Indigenous and Native American literary categories of analysis—an argument already signaled in my introduction—the critical apparatuses employed to analyze the fictions in question in the present volume do not all fully apply some of their theoretical presuppositions. It may indeed be possible to construct methodologies and theoretical apparatuses to study hemispheric Indigenous literatures. Yet the task of these conclusions are, rather, an explanation of the hybrid decolonial literary apparatus chosen for the analyses of Iximuleu's Maya texts in question.

My original goal with the first in a series of volumes on Latin American Indigenous narratives was to make a contribution to the growing field of contemporary Maya literature and, more broadly, to the growing field of contemporary Indigenous literatures of the Americas. In this latter logic, I aim to explain both the aspects that imbricated them, but also to critically tackle those which also divided theorists from the North and the South, while deepening the hemispheric expansion of the emerging field of Native American and Indigenous studies.

This search did not happen in a vacuum. In contemporary cultural scholarship, we experienced in the United States and other areas of the world a reorientation of knowledge away from Eurocentric thinking, and—at least since the emergence of both postcolonial and subaltern studies in the late twentieth century—a movement towards new epistemologies that explored subalternized and racialized subjective outlooks, while disavowing previous Western hegemonic epistemic affirmations. In the Americas, both of these categories pointed in the direction of Indigenous and

Afro-descendant experiences, evidencing the advance of decolonial points of view in the hemisphere. The analyses of the texts in the present volume thus explore the representations of varying Iximuleu Maya epistemic and ontological perspectives generated by the writers studied from their given experiences and positionalities. This constitutes a small yet significant aspect of hemispheric Indigenous cultural and literary production.

In the introduction to their book *The Creolization of Theory* (2011)—a trope in the title that works much like Jack Halberstam's scavenger methodology, implying an interdisciplinary theoretical mélange and multiple close readings to craft an understanding of the object of study (and perhaps both tropes being the unacknowledged inheritors of Lévi-Strauss's category of *bricolage*, meaning the skill of using whatever was at hand and recombining them to create something new)—editors Françoise Lionnet and Shu-mei Shih spoke of an "Eurocentric self quivering at the moment of encounter with an abstract otherness" (8), which their text named as "women, blacks, and other minorities" on the same page. This led to a statement that

> the two recurring phrases in Derridean postructuralism regarding otherness, "always already" (toujours déjà) and "to come" (à venir), denote the places where otherness is banished: to the always already existing structure, either yoked to a past from which there is no escape or linked to an uncertain future existing only as a promise. (9)

On the one hand then, Eurocentric subjects could not of course articulate the undoing of colonialized structures that effectively liberated subalternized and racialized subjects. Yet the latter also needed elements of Western thinkers of difference (Foucault, Derrida, Deleuze, by way of example) to craft their lines of attack within validated protocols of critical theory to achieve their objectives of undoing the colonial structures of knowledge, as well as to hone their own critical categories. In other words, to fully comprehend the epistemological quagmire that exists between the knowledge systems of colonizer and colonized, and thus avoid recolonizing their own positionalities. Yet those same subalternized and racialized positionalities had specificities as well, given the differences produced by colonialism and the multiple structuring postulates of racialization and subalternization. As Walter Mignolo states on his article titled "I Am Where I Think," edited as well in Lionnet and Shih's text, the task of subalternized and racialized subjects othered by Eurocentric colonialism and thinking, is "to engage in barbarian theorizing and knowledge construction" (168). They encourage scholars, in consequence, to acknowledge the connections binding together subjectivity, geography, and epistemic affirmations.

Yet all those "barbarians," in this particular case, Iximuleu Maya communities and subjects as well as myself, are not one. As Mi'kmaq scholar Marie Battiste claims, most Indigenous epistemologies derive from their immediate ecology and their interaction with the spiritual world (499), but contain linguistic categories, rules, and relationships unique to each knowledge system (501). Thus, our witnessing disagreements between ontological positionings among the hundreds of Indigenous communities living very different experiences as heterogeneous inhabitants of Abya Yala, located in dissimilar expansions and contractions of multifaceted ecospaces, while also coexisting with variable topographic features generating dissimilar relationships to their biotic environment. All these issues, to say it in as simple a fashion possible, impacted every single community's modes of life. However, some contemporary debates are also the consequence of trying to explain decolonial categories of knowledge in Western imperial languages, such as English or Spanish. This is why Temagami First Nations scholar Dale Turner states:

> This tension arises because . . . an indigenous intellectual culture needs to address what it means to claim that indigenous peoples have unique ways of understanding the world, and that those differences matter. (95)

Turner recognizes the lack of clarity in naming Indigenous knowledges (98), due to the multiplicity of languages. Concomitantly, he says that epistemological problems inherent in publishing Indigenous ontologies derive from their being rooted mostly in oral traditions and expressed in Indigenous languages that have only just recently been written down (100).

Indeed, if Indigenous systems of knowledge from Abya Yala represent a point of enunciation from which Indigenous subjects utter their beliefs, we should always remember that they are naming their knowledges and beliefs in hundreds of different languages, with innumerable linguistic and conceptual implications. Thus, Battiste reminds us that Algonkian languages preserve those relationships, and she underscores the central role of language in preserving each peoples' concepts of epistemology. Paradoxically, these become more culturally distinct the more these native languages and belief systems remain dynamic and functional. At the same time, the ability to grasp systems of knowledge not written, spoken, or practiced ritualistically and performatively in Western languages by subjects who are trying to decolonialize their own societies and systems of thought from Western colonial intrusion remains highly complex, if not impossible. The risk of renormatizing non-Western languages and interlocutors through Western parameters and common usage of Eurocentric conceptual thinking, continues to be a major conundrum.

As scholars, we always equate a foreign language with interpretation. That is, with assigning meanings to knowledge framed in a different linguistic code. But how valid can this practice be when the original language, and the conceptual categories and notions framed in it, are inaccessible? Especially, when even the original language requires a series of rituals and rites of passage as a selected few gain access to the often secret knowledge involved in integrating natural and built features corresponding to, reproducing, or representing an actual view of the cosmos, either whole or in part. In addition, unlike Eurocentric thinking, where philosophy and theology are separate categories, most Indigenous societies do not separate the sacred and mundane worlds. The spiritual dimension of Indigenous knowledge is key, while differing from Christian spirituality. Thus, rather than attempt to normatize conceptual terms, we should accept their plurality, and listen to how the many variable communities conceive of and envisage their respective knowledges as "coherent logics for ordering and knowing the world" (170), in the words of Cherokee sociologist Eva Marie Garroutte, and recognize them as legitimate sources of knowledge.

In this last sense, it is not gratuitous that Mesoamerican Indigenous cultures used the term "cosmovision" when speaking in Spanish as we explain in the Introduction, irrespective of the terms crafted in their languages, which vary from one Maya language to another, not to speak of all the other Mesoamerican languages. There are six major linguistic families in the region, as well as a few smaller families and isolates, totaling a minimum of close to one hundred languages, without including dialectical variants, which could easily triple that number. Cosmovision, we stated, relates to cultural astronomy, located at the core of Mesoamerican knowledges. Since ancient times and into the present, Mesoamerican peoples reflected on social, political, and religious issues at play in a relationship with nature and the cosmos (2014). Archeologist Anne S. Dowd added that the core of the cosmovision is the idea of reproducing, or representing an actual view of the cosmos on Earth.[1] According to Eleanor Wake, this is why in 1699, when the Indigenous leaders of San Antonio Zoyatzingo defined the boundaries of their land, they said that it began "toward the east, where the sun rises," ending where the sun met with Mercury upon setting. Wake explains that at least eight Nahuatl títulos from central Mexico have celestially defined territory (203), using not just the sun and moon to measure, but also the North Star, Alpha Crucis on the south, Sirius or Antares on the southeast, Spica on the southwest, and of course Mercury, which doubles for the evening star for thirty-eight days of the year in this area.

It is in this logic that leading contemporary Maya intellectuals such as Leopoldo Méndez return, when using Spanish, to the notion of cosmo-knowledge. Speaking among his peers, Méndez uses *Ruxe'el Maya' Nojib'äl*, a Kaqchikel phrase literally meaning "the root of Maya thought," though most Kaqchikels may say *Qab'anob'al* or *qab'antajik*, meaning "our customs." Méndez's use of "root" is emblematic of the tree of life. Mesoamericans believe those roots extend from our planet to the center of the galaxy. In K'iche' the formal knowledge would be *Uxe'eel Mayaab' No'jib'al*, connoting the same meaning, even if the common street naming of it would be *qanojib'al*, or *qana'oj*, meaning "our thinking." Some may simply say *qeta'mab'al*, "our knowledge" to invoke the logic of their community. Thus, when a Kaqchikel scholar Ajpub' García Ixmata' was asked by the Rafael Landívar University—Guatemala's Catholic university—to put together a team and write a book explaining Maya epistemology, they titled it *Ruxe'el Mayab' k'aslemäl*, literally "the root and spirit of life and knowledge in the Mayab"," with the term *ruxe'el* again connoting a cosmic link, to which he added the emphasis of spirituality on the title. "Cosmovision" is understood as articulating the roots of the tree of life bounding our planet with the galaxy. Mayas believe that it is the presence of this Tree of Life what enables the continuity of spirituality. In consequence, the Maya cross, in which all four sides are of equal size, represents the four pillars of the universe, and the four stations of the sun during the day and the year. They indicate that humans live in the center of a fourfold universe. The median of the cross represents the axis mundi or Tree of Life, emblematic of the central cosmic axis of a galaxy symbolized by thirteen layers of the overworld—what Westerners would call the atmosphere, the stratosphere, and so forth—with the feathered serpent at the highest layer, enveloping the Tree of Life. Mesoamericans saw the circling Dippers as the pole of this tree, pointing to the celestial center, the axis of the four directions and their four trees, bringing the cosmos into a coherent vertical hierarchy.

Global Indigenous scholars continue the task of rediscovering lost knowledges and learning the languages in which they are named. As Battiste reminds us, no uniform or universal Indigenous perspective on Indigenous knowledge exists (501). What connects them, she emphasizes, is diversity. Even if there are unifying strands as Tewa scholar Gregory Cajete has argued, diversity prevails given the specific ecology of every single group. "Indigenous people are people of place," he states, "and the nature of place is embedded in their language" (946). Cajete adds that "Native American science may be said to be based upon perceptual phenomenology" (45), whose roots he locates in cosmology (46).

I cannot in consequence emphasize one sole pan-hemispheric "Indigenous critical theory" that would conflate and flatten out a vast sea of cosmopolitical heterogeneities. To do so would simply display flawed thinking. Thus, in both the example depicted above and in the analysis of Maya narratives displayed in this volume, I refer exclusively to the specific knowledges of the communities of the writers in question, which may or may not, be similar to other Mesoamerican Indigenous epistemologies—perhaps in some specific issues even to hemispheric Indigenous knowledges. Yet I refused to conflate and totalize them. Had I done so, I would have essentialized preconceived assumptions over a junction of dissimilar yearnings and tensions between polity, identity and practice that exceed any single identitarian stance. On top of that, it would have been an academic display of power exercised from an external positionality to extremely diverse Indigenous subject positions. Had I acted in this fashion, I would have indeed performed what Mapuche scholar Luis Cárcamo-Huechante described as a new colonizing attitude behind which he perceived a taxonomical drive on the part of many US scholars.[2]

The logic pointed out in previous paragraphs demanded a thorough and critical examination of discursive practices to tease out concrete and significant evidences from the many positionalities at play in the texts examined, while refusing to simplistically craft fit-all labels that could prejudice my readings. By way of example, we know from South African professor David Theo Goldberg's *The Racial State* that the definition of race in modern states emerged conceptually from the Valladolid debates between theologian Juan Ginés de Sepúlveda and Dominican Bishop of Chiapas Bartolomé de las Casas in 1550–1551, where the nature of "Indianness" specifies the role that the invaded population played in the colonial model just emerging at that very moment (4). We know as well Peruvian sociologist Aníbal Quijano's assertion that the modern idea of race did not exist prior to the invasion of the Americas, and that this category produced new social identities such as Indians, Afro-descendants, and Mestizos (534). Yet in both cases we have only generic assertions that have been often treated as abstractions whose alleged truth rests on the scholarly authority of the scholars in question. It took a book like Nancy van Deusen's *Global Indios: The Indigenous Struggle for Justice in Sixteenth-Century Castile* (2015) to clearly see, thanks to her meticulous and painstaking study of Indigenous slaves' bills of sale, the ways in which "Indio" and "slave" identities were specifically constructed in sixteenth-century Seville, and to her utmost precision in reading over one hundred lawsuits that Indio slaves brought to the Spanish courts of Castile between 1530 and 1585 in an effort to regain their freedom, to flesh out the evidence that proved the truthfulness of the previously cited abstractions by Goldberg and Quijano.[3]

My aim was analogous to van Deusen's. I did not claim a priori that all Maya narratives were decolonial by nature. Rather, I performed close readings of the texts in question to examine their particular claims, so as to discover how each one of them framed their issues in a unique way within the context of their particular epistemologies. Only then did I evaluate the general socio-political and cosmopolitical implications that could be construed from their literariness. Needless to say, I was more than willing to explore the emancipatory possibilities of these texts, and to pursue my own conclusions regardless of whether they transgressed or not the boundaries of traditional cultural studies' research and scholarship, in ways analogous to Leslie Brown's and Susan Strega's *Research as Resistance: Critical, Indigenous, and Anti-oppressive Approaches.*

To perform my close readings, there were at least two more critical issues to confront and resolve. First and foremost, I had to decide how to "read" the texts in question: in other words, what methodologies and theoretical apparatuses to choose for the study of Iximuleu Maya narratives. Needless to say, I was familiar with various Native American and Indigenous specific methodologies for the study of the given critic's literatures. As previously indicated in the Introduction, Maya Q'anjob'al novelist Gaspar Pedro González used the category of *K'otz'ib'*, "our" literature in his language. I also stated in the same opening, Mexican scholar Luz María Lepe Lira's affirmation that some Mexican Indigenous writers such as Binnizá poet Victor de la Cruz, had previously elaborated genre categories for their respective literary production, or that Maya Yukateko playwright Feliciano Sánchez Chan had stated that genres and critical categories should be named in their own language and within categories created from within Indigenous knowledges. In Peru, Quechua writer and critic Pablo Landeo Muñoz developed critically the Andean category of *willakuy* as a discursive form different from the Western short story because of its performative nature (267–68), one that required a dialogic interchange between a *willakuq* (narrator) and an *uyariq* or *uyarikug* (a listener who also performed verbally, modifying the original narration). My introduction also addressed some Native American literary critics' preoccupations, from

Creek scholar Craig S. Womack's concern for how Indians view Indians, to Cherokee scholar Jace Weaver's coining the category of *communitism*. I also made a reference to Tonga scholar Timote Vaioleti and his methodology of *talanoa*, and Māori scholar Leonie Pihama developing *kaupapa*, Māori research.

Other Native American literary scholars not mentioned in the introduction point in the direction of discursive strategies anchored in specific Native American communities as well. Osage scholar Chadwick Allen's *Trans-Indigenous: Methodologies for Global Native Literary Studies* (2012), may be the sole exception, as it compares Native American and Māori texts written in English. He claims not to be displacing specific traditions and contexts, but wants to complement them by expanding to broader Indigenous fields of inquiry (xiv) within the Anglocentric world. Allen thus aims to explore Indigenous literary texts written in English that transit beyond what he perceives as limiting mechanistic scenarios whereby a book from Tradition A may be explored solely within the parameters of that tradition. Like Steven Leuthold's underlying premises in *Indigenous Aesthetics* (1998), I believe that literary expression is interconnected with cosmologies, and that Maya aesthetic experiences shaped their collective identities. It is, after all, impossible to separate Indigenous self-representations from coloniality and struggles over sovereignty and agency. They all form part of a model of artistic agency that belongs to the public domain. Yet I also found that Leuthold did not pay sufficient attention to particulars. He did not dwell on the different nature of the communities from which the filmmakers he analyzed came from, thus conflating dissimilar Native American experiences as if it were all one. This distinction is critical. Styles and approaches are impacted by the specific nature of a given community and their conditions of existence in a given moment. There was also the problem of "aesthetics" itself, a category historically anchored in the Eurocentric philosophical tradition, independent of the fact that all Indigenous groups have standards of artistic excellence, even if they generated "a provocative strangeness," in the words of Chadwick Allen, when performing their aspirations through various dissident or transgressive means.[4]

In light of this logic, my task was to perform my literary analyses through the application of Maya methodologies. Yet the problem I immediately had to contend with was that, to this day, said categories do not exist. None enabled me to explore the performances of Maya speech acts that shaped and generated emergent forms of subjectivities, cultures, and, ultimately, decolonial attitudes. Given this statement of fact, my sole alternative to perform in-depth critical readings was by mongrelizing hybrid decolonial, literary and Native American methodologies to move textual analyses forward. In this spirit I examined what these narratives had to say, but especially, how they performed linguistically those discursivities, what their signifiers enunciated, while never forgetting to take into account the specific epistemologies within which they were written. There is, after all, a relationship between producing meanings about the world and the ontological nature of tools of doing research, as Strega reminds us (200). At times we have to make uneasy tactical alliances with a few salient poststructural theorists who themselves championed subjugated knowledges and critiqued Western teleology. Their analytical tools were readjusted and accommodated to my needs, while I remained attentive to epistemological conflicts and knew on what kinds of assumptions, what kinds of ontological practices they rested. I always kept in my mind Linda Tuhiwai Smith's cautionary tone in assessing the political implications of my research. I never forgot for whom I was performing it, while remaining alert to my own positionality both in US academia and in the Mesoamerican social structure.

I was happy to discover that my own critical approach was not much different from the way most of these texts were written. That is, by reenacting their cosmic visions while interpellating Western parameters, they de facto structured literary processes that always implied an a priori in-depth knowledge of dominant Western paradigms. Their respective discursivities structured critiques of these from the very first. Undoubtedly both approaches, whether performed from a creative or from a critical angle, implied different ways of transforming the writers' and the critics' relations to the world and our involvement with it from Indigenous perspectives, while unavoidably intertwining epistemologically, to some degree, cognitive systems that originated both in the colonizing and in the colonized worlds. New interactions and cultural dynamics resulted from this dialogical wrestling of knowledges. Without denying potential contradictions, these processes furthered a transition away from hegemonically sealed Western-centered teleologies. In this logic, my approach formed questions in relationship to what I encountered in my readings, while emphasizing Maya sources whenever possible and privileging them for epistemological and political reasons. This procedure enabled me to develop a reciprocal, relational, and intersectional critical methodology attentive to the legacies of colonialism and Eurocentric thinking. I did my best to turn deep-seated conceptions upside down, while offering alternative discursive interpretations that drew attention to political issues whose symbolic guidelines articulated a systemic critique of colonialism and coloniality.

I conclude by stating that Indigenous literatures already represent serious undertakings at this early stage of their emergence and production. After all, they are extremely young endeavors. Their voyage is merely but half a century old, if with millenarian antecedents. Yet in such a brief period of time, these literatures have already yielded a rich and powerful body of work that is becoming indicative of their enormous possibilities and of the vast wealth of knowledge located in their cultures.

This literary production is most certainly a liminal undertaking between Indigenous worlds and Western modernity even when they craft the colonial underpinnings of Eurocentric practices deployed by colonizing and colonializing forces to undermine Indigenous communities. It could not be otherwise. The processes required for writers to become such inevitably forced them to transition through Spanish literacy prior to a reengagement with written forms in their own languages, if not also the prior elaboration of standardized alphabets and dictionaries. These mechanisms automatically implied that the writers were forced to immerse themselves in Western literary culture, with all their ontological booby traps, prior to exploring the world that defined them and for whose members they wanted to write.

The Iximuleu Maya narratives studied in this volume proved to be decolonial texts, if by "decolonial" we understand uneven and non-systematic processes of furthering resistance to Westernness and globalized intrusions in a belated effort to rescue their cosmovisions. Many heterogeneous modes for these phenomena appear in the texts studied, each entangled with diverse symbolic forms of resistance to Western-centered intrusions and/or impositions, even when these were performed by Mestizo subjects. They have in common the trauma of colonialism and omnipresent violence. Some were regional, but most were certainly local in their singular ways of crafting discursively the abjection suffered by Maya subjects as they struggled against colonial configurations that degraded their communal and corporeal reality in variants of cognitive dissonance with Ladinos' despotic power and social control. The characters depicted in these texts all struggle to improve the overall conditions of their poverty-stricken communities. To succeed, most have to come to terms with a definition of "community" that implies a relationship with their respective ecological environment, a turn that leads them to a more conscious understanding of its cosmic implications. In those texts in which this issue is manifest, this process enables the characters to fathom a continual regeneration of the cosmos, one where differences are always welcome and incorporated. Humanity is displayed as subordinated to a cosmic equilibrium. In working out their reciprocity with the supernatural world, they represent a cosmocentric one that does not differentiate between humanity and nature. It is portrayed as a dynamic flow of reality for which the rivers on Earth and the cosmic river (the Milky Way) are apt metaphors, an organically interdependent beingness, one in which all things in the physical world have their own life and cosmic energy. As Mayas often say, everything has *winaqil* or is *winaq*. That is, everything has life, an image, a heart, a spirit, traits shared not only among humans, but with animals, plants, stones, and natural manifestations such as mountains or lakes, stars, and everything in the cosmos.

NOTES

INTRODUCTION

1. Cherokee scholar Christopher B. Teuton claims in "Indigenous Orality and Oral Literatures" that "the conception of 'orality' and 'oral literature' arises out of a colonial context" (170). Teuton recognizes that its usage to name Indigenous discursive practices has become standardized even among Indigenous communities. He ends his article by stating that " 'orality' is becoming understood as one form of textuality that exists in relation to others—visual, material, gestural, kinesthetic, digital—in increasingly wide networks of Indigenous knowledge. In this way, when Indigenous ways of knowing are privileged, Indigenous communication becomes formally and contextually expansive" (173).
2. Though written in their native languages, these works are always translated to Castilian and published bilingually, in Hispanic America.
3. In this text I use the name Castilian (*castellano*) over Spanish (*español*) to denominate the language spoken in the two autonomous communities—Castile and León, and Castile-La Mancha—which historically dominated the Iberian Peninsula and imposed their Spanish language on other nationalities constitutive of Spain. Since Spain's return to democracy in 1978, the languages of those autonomous communities (Catalonia, the Basque Country, Galicia, etc.) have been made legal. Thus, their citizens should not be identified with the usage of the language of Castile, any more than Indigenous peoples should be associated with the language of their invaders.
4. Elizabeth Hill Boone and Walter Mignolo argue that pre-Columbian Mesoamerican cultures had systems of writing that did not strive to represent speech. See *Writing Without Words*. Mignolo has pointed out since *The Darker Side of the Renaissance* that European forms of literacy, and their presumption of the supposed priority of alphabetic writing over other forms, facilitated the New World colonization by enabling the accusation that sophisticated

Indigenous civilizations were illiterate, backwards, or savage, by virtue of not employing alphabetic writing.

5. See Tuck and Yang, "Decolonization Is not a Metaphor."
6. See Hale's "Cultural Agency and Political Struggle in the Era of the *Indio Permitido*." Hale states in note 2 that Rivera Cusicanqui developed the category in a workshop at the University of Texas at Austin in 2001 but had not published the term.
7. Opaque as this may seem for some readers working outside of the purview of the Anglo-American cultural-studies framework, it is a necessary task, so as to place where these volumes are going.
8. See Cofiño and Chirix, *Emma Chirix conversa con Ana Cofiño*, p. 37.
9. Wallerstein, "Remembering Andre Gunder Frank While Thinking about the Future," p. 54.
10. Though Mignolo articulated these modes of thinking in his seminal book *The Darker Side of the Renaissance*, he kept working on this category and later published the article "The Geopolitics of Knowledge and the Colonial Difference."
11. Escobar labeled this process the "modernity/coloniality research program" in his article "Worlds and Knowledges Otherwise." He located its origins in Latin America: "I would argue that this body of work, still relatively unknown in the English speaking world for reasons that go beyond language and that speak to the heart of the program, constitutes a novel perspective from Latin America but not only for Latin America but for the world of the social and human sciences as a whole" (179). The English version of his article, published in 2003, appeared in *Cultural Studies* in 2007, with some variations from the original.
12. See Hale and Stephen's text *Otros saberes*.
13. Walsh, " 'Other' Knowledges, 'Other' Critiques: Reflections on the Politics and Practices of Philosophy and Decoloniality in the 'Other' America."
14. For Marisol de la Cadena, see "El Movimiento Indígena-Popular en los Andes y la Pluralización de la Política: Una Hipótesis de Trabajo." For Arturo Escobar, see his original formulation in " 'Mundos y conocimientos de otro modo': El programa de investigación de modernidad/colonialidad latinoamericano," already explained in note 11.
15. See Zapata Silva, *Intelectuales indígenas en Ecuador, Bolivia y Chile* (2013).
16. The comparative approach initiated by Florencia Mallon and others with the conference Narrating Native Histories at the University of Wisconsin-Madison in April 2005, is critically important. It is an initiative that should be both praised and imitated.
17. Castro-Gómez and Grosfoguel were close followers of Mignolo. They formed part of the Latin American Modernity/Coloniality network, which orbited around Argentinian philosopher Enrique Dussel, Peruvian sociologist Aníbal Quijano, and Mignolo, the three outstanding figures working on coloniality.

The M/C network stopped being active by 2010. Castro-Gómez is a Colombian philosopher. Grosfoguel is a professor of Chicano/Latino Studies at UC Berkeley's Department of Ethnic Studies.

18. In Castro-Gómez and Grosfoguel's defense it could be argued that some of the edited articles do analyze grassroots movements and cite Indigenous intellectuals. Still, this kind of oversight also happened during the controversy surrounding Maya Nobel laureate Rigoberta Menchú. The debate about testimonio in US academia in the mid-1990s was one between progressive and conservative US academics in light of the neoliberal turn, rather than one displaying concern for the genocidal tidal wave impacting Mayas in Guatemala. All the same, when progressive scholars were interpellated by conservative forces gaining strength in the United States, the object of their attack (evidenced in this case by David Stoll's infamous 1998 book) was Menchú, the foreign, subalternized woman of color who, in Stoll's eyes, offended by her very status, and against whom he performed a racialized, sexualized, spatialized, symbolic lynching. Only secondarily did Stoll and conservative academics target those testimonio academics who had first instigated their concerns.
19. A geographical and cultural region in the western part of the state of Veracruz bordering on the states of Tamaulipas, Veracruz, Puebla, Hidalgo, San Luis Potosí, Querétaro, and Guanajuato; the pre-Hispanic Huastec people lived in this region.
20. Excerpt from introductory chapter in *Reading and Writing Nahuas: Mexican Indigenous Intellectuals from the Colonial Period through Today* (2014). McDonough adds that "the great sixteenth-century Franciscan grammarian and lexicographer Alonso de Molina glossed the Nahuatl term *tlamatini* (sing.) as "sabio" (wise person) and *tlamatiliztli* as "sabiduría, o embuacamiento" (knowledge or trickery). Both have as their root the verb *mati* or "saber algo" (to know [something]). For example *ixtlamatini/meh* can be broken down in the following manner: *tla* (nonspecific nonhuman object prefix [thing/s or "stuff"] + *mati* [to know] + *ni/nimeh* [singular/plural present agentive suffix]); *tlamatiliztli* is an "action noun": roughly, "the act or action of knowing."
21. By way of comparison, even in Aotearoa (New Zealand), which is almost the best possible place and space for indigeneities, Māoris complain about analogous treatment and relate to the experience of Latin America's Indigenous peoples.
22. See Mallon, ed., *Decolonizing Native Histories*, p. 17.
23. "First Peoples" is another self-chosen designation by some Indigenous groups. The United Nations and the International Labour Organization have outlined a few traits to define Indigenous groups: They are descended from the precolonial/preinvasion inhabitants of their region; they maintain a close tie to their land in both their cultural and economic practices; they suffer from

economic and political marginalization as a minority group; and they define themselves as an Indigenous group. This designation is not be confused with "First Nations," who comprise more than 630 recognized Aboriginal peoples in Canada who are neither Inuit nor Métis.

24. McDonough, *Reading and Writing Nahuas*, p. 7.
25. Kirk Zebolsky was a Native literature student of Womack at the University of Nebraska at Omaha.
26. The real issue, to use a cliché, is semantic. As Mi'kmaq scholar Marie Battiste claims, most Indigenous epistemologies derived from their immediate ecology and their interaction with the spiritual world (499), but they contain linguistic categories, rules, and relationships unique to each knowledge system (501).
27. These arguments were stated in Castilian in the article "Literaturas de Abya Yala," published in the *LASA Forum* in 2011. My colleagues Luis Cárcamo-Huechante and Emilio del Valle Escalante and I co-wrote the article. I want to recognize that this particular aspect of our collective argument was made by Professor Cárcamo-Huechante.
28. The 2013 revised edition of Tuhiwai Smith's monograph has added two significant chapters.
29. The word, "race" appears to be derived from the Arabic word *ras*, "سأر," indicating the head of any given selected species, which could also be animals or plants. Thus its link to another Arabic term, *genat*, "تانيج," meaning clan, stock, or people. As John Hartigan argues in a forthcoming book, *Care of the Species: Cultivating Biodiversity in Mexico and Spain*, this explains the use of the term *race* with plants and, especially, the designation of races of corn in Mexico.
30. Recall Pablo Neruda's "Alturas de Macchu Picchu" from his *Canto General* (1950) to verify the monumental part that Indigenous imaginaries play in modern Latin America, albeit at a symbolic level.
31. In Castilian, Sí, los peones empiezan el jornal como fantasmas en la neblina del amanecer. Al medio día la cólera del sol los tuesta, pero no interrumpen el corte de pencas con su machete corvo. Después de quitarles las espinas, las tiran para completar el atado de cincuenta hojas, que luego cargan hasta la vera del camino. Sus harapos son sudor y polvo, sangran en los pies, manos y espalda; y a veces levantan un calabazo para beber su amargura. (318)
32. See Stuart, "Maya Decipherment: A Weblog on the Ancient Maya Script."
33. Ibid.
34. I defined the notion of "narrative textuality" in *Taking Their Word*. Narrative textualities are posited as encompassing all genres and forming a communicative occurrence that presents a temporal, sequential order and stresses the potential eventfulness of duration (xiv).
35. See Carolina Escobar Sarti's article "Ruk'u'x."

36. See the end of chapter 3 in *La vanguardia plebeya del Titikaka: Gamaliel Churata y otras beligerancias estéticas en los Andes*, where Monasterios analyzes a poem in Aymara by Manuel Kamacho Allqa.
37. It should be noted that the Indigenous holocaust in the Caribbean had already taken place by the date Cortés landed in Mexico. The virtual extinction of Indigenous peoples in the Caribbean has made it impossible to think of a reemergence of Indigenous literatures in their own language in this region.
38. In the Mayas' cyclical notion of time, the k'atun, which is already present in the earliest forms of the Maya calendar dating back three thousand years, is a period of twenty years. A prophecy is attached to each of the twenty-year K'atun cycles. There are thirteen K'atuns, and they repeat themselves in cyclical fashion.
39. This kind of critique is already occurring to a certain degree with Te Ara Tika, Māori research in Aotearoa, principally at both the Te Ahurutanga and the Te Kotahi Research Institutes of Waikato University, as well as at the Center for Māori Studies of the University of Auckland, and other analogous projects in the Pacific.
40. See *Without History: Subaltern Studies, the Zapata Insurgency, and the Specter of History*.
41. See Best and Marcus, "Surface Reading: An Introduction," p. 9, defining surface as meaning "what is evident, perceptible, apprehensible in texts; what is neither hidden nor hiding."
42. See Kristeva, *Revolution in Poetic Language*, pp. 59–60.
43. See Sommer, "Rigoberta's Secrets."
44. In Guatemala alone there already exists literature written in seven Indigenous languages derivative of classical Maya. There are four more in Mexico. This means that in languages evolving from classical Maya alone, we already have contemporary texts written in eleven languages.
45. Rappaport and Pacho refer here to Chow's *Primitive Passions*.
46. Recorded in *Decolonizing Native Histories*.
47. See Cárcamo-Huechante, del Valle Escalante, and Arias, "Literaturas de Abya Yala," note 1.
48. See Rabasa, "Intencionalidad, invención y reducción al absurdo en la invención de América."

CHAPTER 1

1. As outlined in the introduction, *Ladino* is the word used in Guatemala to define a Mestizo: a person or culture of mixed Indigenous and Spanish traits, usually having a Western outlook and set of beliefs. The word *Ladinization*

was coined by US anthropologist Richard N. Adams to propose a theory stating that over time Mayas would lose their intrinsic cultural traits and adopt a Ladino perspective. In her dissertation's first chapter, Amy Olen illustrates how in this process, three basic Indigenous identities could be observed: (1) "authentic" Indigenous peoples, defined by Adams as "traditional Indians" retaining "unadulterated" cultural practices; (2) "modified Indians," who had hybridized cultural traits of both cultures; and, finally, (3) "ladinized Indians," who already had conformed to the cultural practices of Ladinos and discarded their own Indigenous cultural practices.

2. At present there are at least two Kaqchikel dictionaries, including one on the Web, the *English–Kaqchikel Dictionary* online: http://en.glosbe.com/en/cak/.
3. See Morales Santos, "Luis de Lión y Nuevo Signo."
4. Literally, the General Headquarters of Fine Arts. Bearing this awkward title copied from Spain's bureaucracy, this institution fulfilled the role of the Ministry of Culture prior to the Ministry's actual foundation in 1986. See Morales Santos, "Luis de Lión y Nuevo Signo."
5. See also Morales Santos, "Luis de Lión y Nuevo Signo."
6. Luis Alfredo Arango was born in Totonicapán, a well-known K'iche' town in western Guatemala. However, his family was part of the Ladino circle of Totonicapán, holding important positions in the town's public administration; and, while not wealthy, they certainly enjoyed many more privileges than most Indigenous peoples in this town. Arango also migrated to Guatemala City and became a teacher. His first teaching experience was in San José Nacahuil, an Indigenous town twenty kilometers (twelve miles) from the city. That experience changed his life. Nacahuil was exemplary of the miserable conditions of the Guatemalan Indigenous people. An extremely sensitive and ethical person, Arango became an ardent supporter of Maya causes at this point in his life. See Dante Liano, *Visión crítica de la literatura guatemalteca*, pp. 235–36.
7. See Arias, "Racialized Subalternity as Emancipatory Decolonial Project," p. 87.
8. See Quijano's "Coloniality and Modernity/Rationality."
9. See de Sousa Santos, "The World Social Forum: A User's Manual."
10. In a recent article titled "Tras las huellas del futuro: Los procesos de reconfiguración de los países de Centroamérica en el nuevo siglo" (Behind the footsteps to the future: processes of reconfiguration of Central American countries in the new century; my translation) delivered on October 26, 2006, at the Central American Congress of Sociology, Ceto argues,

    El tema que hoy nos reúne en este espacio, rebelión y genocidio, de alguna manera, resume una de las características más importantes de la historia de Guatemala que inicia a partir de la invasión castellano española en 1,524. Es una historia llena de motines, levantamientos y rebeliones indígenas contra la esclavitud, el despojo, la represión, el exterminio y el genocidio.

(The topic that brings us together in this space, rebellion and genocide, in a way sums up one of the most important characteristics of Guatemalan history that begins with the Castilian-Spanish invasion in 1524. It is a history full of mutinies, riots and Indigenous rebellions against slavery, plundering, repression, extermination, and genocide).

11. See "Local Histories and Global Designs: An Interview with Walter Mignolo," p. 9.
12. Javier Sanjinés employed viscerality in *Mestizaje Upside-Down* as a bodily metaphor "that helps explain how Indigenous subalternity has resisted giving up its identity to rationalist Western discourse" (5).
13. Although Mayas and other Indigenous groups recognize their origins—including their literary origins—in this paradigmatic text, Ladinos often regarded it more as a kind of Mongolian spot, inevitably marking an Indigenous inheritance that they would prefer to hide and deny. Dr. Erwin Bälz (1849–1913) was a German internist, anthropologist, and personal physician of the Japanese imperial family. In 1885 he published a paper in a German anthropological journal calling attention to an unrecorded feature among Japanese babies. They were often born with a dark blue stain on the lower back that gradually fades and disappears after about a year. He called the stain *Mongolische Flecken*, Mongolian spots, and associated the stain with all peoples he thought were of Mongolian origin. This label adhered to Indigenous peoples who were born with a purplish spot in the small of the back. In Guatemala this led to a widespread fear of being born with this mark. The Mongolian spot has remained an invisible scar, a phantasm of an ethnic inferiority complex on the part of Ladinos, pointing to their difficulty in constituting themselves as a hegemonic class.
14. For more on mestizaje, see Marilyn Miller's *Rise and Fall of the Cosmic Race*.
15. See my article "Changing Indian Identity: Guatemala's Violent Transition to Modernity," p. 233.
16. Catholic Action was the name of many groups of lay Catholics who in the nineteenth century tried to encourage a Catholic influence on society and emergent industrialism in historically Catholic countries that fell under anticlerical regimes such as Spain, Italy, Bavaria, France, and Belgium. Exported to the so-called Third World after World War II, these groups eventually converged with those practicing liberation theology when attention turned to social and economic issues of development and international relations, and

the obligation of rich countries to assist poor ones. In Guatemala it was originally founded in 1948 as an anti-Communist organization to oppose the democratic governments of the 1944–1954 period.

17. "Green Revolution" is the euphemism for a series of developmentalist projects, beginning in the late 1940s but hitting Guatemala only in the late 1960s, which increased agriculture production. The initiatives, led by Norman Borlaug, the "Father of the Green Revolution," were credited with saving over a billion people from starvation. They consisted of developing high-yield varieties of cereal grains, expanding irrigation infrastructures, modernizing management techniques, and distributing hybridized seeds, synthetic fertilizers, and pesticides to farmers. Unfortunately, they also led to an exhaustion of arable lands due to the abuse of fertilizers and to an overdependence by subsistence farmers on bank loans to pay for both fertilizers and machinery. The term "Green Revolution" is attributed to the United States Agency for International Development (USAID) director William Gaud, who first used it in 1968.
18. From the early 1940s there was a close proximity between ideologues of the Mexican Revolution and opponents of the Guatemalan dictator General Jorge Ubico (1931–1944). Many of these Guatemalans, most of whom exercised administrative and/or bureaucratic positions in the Arévalo presidency (1945–1951), went on to found the communist Guatemalan Workers' Party (PGT) in the late 1940s.
19. One of the more radical priests of the 1960s, Thomas Melville, tried to create the first-ever Catholic guerrillas in Huehuetenango, the northwestern corner of the country.
20. The best-known books that came out of this debate are *La patria del criollo* by Martínez Peláez and *Guatemala: Una interpretación histórico-social* by Carlos Guzmán Böckler and Jean-Loup Herbert, but it also produced seminal articles such as "El nacionalismo indígena: Una ideología burguesa" by Mario Solórzano Foppa.
21. Xelajuj Noj' comes from *Xe'* (below), *lajuj* (ten), *No'j* (spiritual guides). Ten mountains surround the valley where Xela is located. Thus the name: below the ten spiritual guides.
22. All details appear in Arias, "Changing Indian Identity: Guatemala's Violent Transition to Modernity," p. 248.
23. This is a reference to Ángel Rama's text, where he argues that a small group of letrados (men of letters) exerted power and intellectual hegemony in Latin America's major cities from the consolidation of colonial times to the 1960s. At first they were of Spanish origin, later, Mestizos or descendants of European immigrants. Customarily, they were members of the elite, mostly male, and defined the intellectual projects of nationhood and modernity.

24. Personal communication with Pablo Ceto, Mexico City, Avenida Universidad 1900, spring 1981.
25. Guevara had been named the godfather of the son Ricardo Ramírez had with Aura Marina Arreola, during the baby's Catholic baptism in Cuba. Personal communication with Aura Marina Arriola, Mexico City, Sanborn's de San Ángel, January 1983.
26. Personal communication with Mario Payeras, Mexico City, Sanborn's Colonia del Valle, March 1984.
27. Personal communication with Mario Payeras, Mexico City, Rancho El Encanto No. 29, April 1984.
28. See Hale's "Between Che Guevara and the Pachamama."
29. See Sieder et al., eds., "Who Governs? Guatemala Five Years after the Peace Accords," p. 21.
30. See Hale's *Más Que Un Indio.*
31. See Chase-Dunn et al., *Global Democracy and the World Social Forums* for an explanation of this paradigm. Other authors involved with World Systems theories that have problematized this issue include Immanuel Wallerstein and Giovanni Arrighi.
32. See de la Cadena, "El Movimiento Indígena-Popular en los Andes y la Pluralización de la Política," p. 38.
33. See http://ukuxbe.org/Mision.html. Mayab' Tinamit means "Maya Homeland" in most Maya languages.
34. See http://ukuxbe.org/Index.html for information on the U'k ux B'e Maya Association. Interestingly, one of its leaders and founders is Domingo Hernández Ixcoy, himself a founder of CUC, the preeminent organization of maya populares. Despite his political and personal background, Hernández Ixcoy would now be heading one of the premier organizations that we could label in contemporary terms *maya culturales.* This stands as evidence of the contemporary fluidity between both strands.
35. See Gutiérrez and Gómez's prologue to Raúl Zibechi's book *Dispersar el poder.*
36. Quetzaltenango, or Xelajú, is Guatemala's second-largest city. *Juegos Florales* translate as "floral games," a bizarre name for a literary contest, yet one inherited from colonial times, associated with the many creative crafts implemented during the times of the annual fair celebrating the patron saint of the town.
37. See del Valle Escalante, "El viaje a los orígenes y la poética decolonial Maya en *Madre, nosotros también somos historia* de Francisco Morales Santos."
38. Morales Santos, *Madre, nosotros también somos historia/Nan, Ri Oj Xuquje Oj Ojer Tzij K'wi Chi Taq B'ix*, published by the Fondo de Cultura Económica in the Luis Cardoza y Aragón Intercultural Collection.
39. See "Luis de Lión y Nuevo Signo."

40. See Fischer and Brown, eds., "Introduction" to *Maya Cultural Activism in Guatemala.*
41. See Edward F. Fischer's "Induced Cultural Change" in *Maya Cultural Activism in Guatemala*, p. 66.
42. Ibid.
43. The PLFM cites among its achievements the formation and training of 106 technicians in linguistics, who belong to the Akateka, Awakateka, Ch′orti′, Chuj, Ixil, Popti′, Kaqchikel, K′iche′, Mam, Q′anjob′al, Poqomam, Poqomchi′, Q′eqchi′, and Tz′utujil ethnic groups and languages. It has also produced interactive material to learn K′iche′, Kaqchikel, Mam, and Q′eqchi′, opened a linguistics, education, and Maya culture library that is open to the public, and has created reading and writing centers in Kaqchikel, Mopan, Tz′utujil, K′iche′, Mam, and Q′eqchi′, which serve more than a thousand children yearly. See http://www.plfm.org/.
44. See "The Current Situation in Research on Mayan Languages: Bibliography of Linguistic Studies of Mayan Languages in Guatemala 1990–2006, with Special Reference to OKMA," compiled by Roberto Zavala (CIESAS-Sureste) and Thomas C. Smith Stark (COLMEX), with the collaboration of Romelia Mó Isém, p. 4.
45. PLFM opened with two purposes: (1) to teach the Castilian language, and (2) to teach, investigate, and preserve Maya languages and culture. As the oldest Castilian-language school in Antigua, a feature that enables it to survive economically, PLFM also teaches Maya languages. Native Maya professionals have run it since the 1980s, when Martín Chacach served as the director. It is presently affiliated with the Consejo Nacional de Educación Maya (CNEM; National Council of Maya Education), a national organization promoting Maya education.
46. See "Acerca de CIRMA," http://www.cirma.org.gt/index.php?showPage=2&cache=1.
47. Fischer lists all the organizations involved. See p. 98.
48. See Adrián Recinos's *Crónicas Indígenas* (*Indigenous Chronicles* [1984]).
49. See Arias, *Taking Their Word*, p. 54.
50. See analyses by Francisco Javier Guerrero and Claudio Lomnitz.
51. See Narciso Cojtí's November 2006 *History of ALMG*, http://www.almg.org.gt/historia.html.
52. See Candelaria Dominga López Ixcoy's prologue to *Ri Ukemiik ri Tz'ib'anik pa K'ichee' ch'ab'al/Manual de redacción k'ichee'*, p. 9.
53. See "Evaluation of Asociaciòn Oxlajuuj Keej Maya Ajtziib: OKMA Linguistic Research," http://www.norad.no/en/tools-and-publications/publications/publication?key=109824.

54. Zavala, Smith Stark, and Mó Isém claim in their document that in accordance with the norms that have prevailed since the start of the twentieth century, the fundamental documentation of a language must include its grammar, a dictionary, and a collection of texts that have been analyzed. See p. 4.
55. Personal communication with Humberto Ak'abal, Momostenango, Guatemala, June 29, 2013.
56. Ibid.
57. Personal communication with Francisco Morales Santos, e-mail, June 11, 2013.
58. Personal communication with Humberto Ak'abal, Momostenango, Guatemala, June 29, 2013.
59. Ibid.
60. Personal communication, Guatemala City, June 27, 2013.
61. Personal communication, Guatemala City, July 1, 2013.
62. Ibid.
63. See Arias, *The Rigoberta Menchú Controversy.*
64. See Arias, "Constructing Ethnic Bodies and Identities in Miguel Ángel Asturias and Rigoberta Menchú."
65. See chapter 8 of Arias, *Taking Their Word.*
66. See http://www.cholsamaj.org/antecedentes.php.
67. See catalogue, http://www.cholsamaj.org/busca.php.
68. See Fernando Peñalosa's "La literatura maya: Tres perspectivas: el editor."
69. See *Seeking Community in a Global City: Guatemalans and Salvadorans in Los Angeles.*
70. See http://www.kstrom.net/isk/maya/mayastor.html.
71. See *Istmo* no. 4, July–December 2002.
72. For Colop's ideas and standing, see chapter 6 in *Indigenous Movements and Their Critics: Pan-Maya Activism in Guatemala* by Kay B. Warren. The August 7, 1996, panel included Morales and Colop—and myself. Although I also presented on Asturias on that occasion, I witnessed Colop's talk, Morales's reply, the audience heckling Morales and supporting Colop—and Morales stepping off the podium angrily and abandoning the room to a crescendo of boos from the audience.
73. See Arias, *Taking Their Word*, pp. 74–75.
74. See *Maya Nationalisms and Postcolonial Challenges in Guatemala*, chapter 5.
75. See Yashar, "Contesting Citizenship," pp. 33–34.
76. See "Humberto Ak'abal rechaza Premio Nacional de Literatura" by Marta Sandoval.
77. Ibid.
78. Ibid.

79. Personal communication, Momostenango, Guatemala, June 29, 2013.
80. Ibid.
81. I employ hybridity in relation to race, as it has developed in 1990s transnational theories traced by Joshua Lund in *The Impure Imagination: Toward a Critical Hybridity in Latin American Writing*.
82. *B'atz'* also means "monkey" in Maya K'iche'. Monkeys are the artists and creators in Maya lore, as explained in the *Popol Wuj*. *Monkey* is known as *chuwen* in Yukateko Maya. Interestingly, in the Maya calendar the monkey's energy is named *aq'ab'al*, essentially the same word as the poet Humberto Ak'abal's last name.
83. See "Premio de Literatura Indígena B'ATZ' para Leoncio Pablo García Talé y Miguel Angel Oxlaj Cúmez," *Istmo*, http://istmo.denison.edu/n15/noticias/premio1.html.
84. In Mexico there is, since 1993, a biennial award, Premio Netzahualcoyotl, given for the best manuscript written in any Indigenous language spoken in Mexico.
85. See Maurice Echeverría's blog titled *lpv*, "Literatura maya actual: Inventario mínimo."
86. Ibid.

CHAPTER 2

1. As Gayatri Spivak has argued recently, the boundaries of nation-states "are increasingly inconvenient," yet we have no choice but to consider them, since "the limits and openings of particular civil society are state-fixed" (*An Aesthetic Education*, 100). Such is the case for Mayas in Guatemala, one of the most racist nations in the world.
2. By "coloniality of power," I mean the imposition of a racial/ethnic classification onto a population, which establishes a hierarchy of inequality among European and non-European identities. Also included in this is the domination of the former over the latter, for which mechanisms of social domination are established and designed to preserve this historical foundation and social classification. As stated in the introduction, the concept was invented by Aníbal Quijano in 1992 and later developed by Walter Mignolo, Arturo Escobar, Javier Sanjinés, and other theorists of decoloniality.
3. "Luis de Lión: 'Yo siempre tuve un cielo'" by Gustavo Adolfo Montenegro, article published in the Sunday supplement of *Prensa Libre* on May 8, 2004. See http://servicios.prensalibre.com/pl/domingo/archivo/domingo/2004/mayo04/090504/central.html.

4. Ibid.
5. See "Un libro que se niega a morir y a nacer." This text is also quoted by Rita M. Palacios in her analysis of de Lión's novel (85), though she attributes it to "La insignia," the name of the column, rather than the newspaper, *Siglo veintiuno*. The column has since been reprinted as the prologue to Morales's novel *Obraje* (2010).
6. See note 14 in Arias, "Kotz'ib': The Emergence of a New Maya Literature."
7. See Fanon, *The Wretched of the Earth.*
8. Amy T. Olen handled all English translations of Luis de Lión's stories. The book has yet to be published in English. The line quotation here says, "Este es el pueblo de los juanes" in the original Castilian.
9. Mestizos are historically known in Guatemala as *ladinos*; however, contemporary Mayas are making the distinction between the terms: for them, a Ladino is a racist subject, whereas a Mestizo is a nonracist subject of mixed Indigenous/European descent, who may even manifest an alliance with or recognition of Indigenous perspectives over his/her own. See Cofiño and Chirix, *Emma Chirix conversa con Ana Cofiño*, p. 37.
10. See the first pages of Baudrillard, *Simulations*.
11. In the United States, *encomienda* is a land grant. However, the term stands for a system started in 1503 that gave certain Spaniards an estate or tract of land in the Americas in addition to those Indigenous inhabitants who were living on that land; thus, it refers to a tract of land and its inhabitants. The owner of the land tract stood to benefit from the slave labor of the Indigenous inhabitants, allegedly in exchange for being taught the Catholic doctrine. The *encomienda* became a backdoor method to justify slavery in the Americas after King Charles V of Spain issued *las Leyes Nuevas*, the New Laws, on November 20, 1542, to prevent the exploitation of the Indigenous peoples of the Americas by the *encomenderos* as a result of the campaign of Fray Bartolomé de las Casas against the *encomienda*.
12. In the original Castilian, "sudando, pujando, apoyándose en un bordón de madera" and "nada más unos pedazos de cuero le cubrían las partes."
13. In the original Castilian, "un hombre sin nada en medio del cielo y la tierra, porque ni el pedacito de mi hoy en que estaban mis pies era mío, mucho menos el tiempo que ocupaba mi sombra."
14. Criollos are descendants of the Spaniards born in Guatemala. Though extremely few criollos survived the Liberal Revolution of the 1870s, their worldview and teleology remain dominant in present-day Guatemala. This includes a Western-centered notion that "whites" are considered superior and civilized, while Indigenous subjects continue to be regarded as barbarian and irrational. For more on Guatemala's criollos, see Marta Casaús, *Guatemala: Linaje y racismo*.

15. In the original Castilian, "ya era mucho que el tatita de nosotros no gozara su alfombra, que el otro le dejara las sobras."
16. In the original Castilian, "mi nana, mi tata y mi chucho bajamos a La Antigua para acompañar un rato al nuestro."
17. *Ixcos*, a Maya term, denotes the four stakes or posts placed on the ground to mark the piece of land a peasant is supposed to clean on a plantation.
18. See Trigo, *Memorias migrantes*.
19. In the original Castilian, "éramos una plebe de patojos tixudos, piojentos, media Castilla."
20. Spaniards forbade Maya religious practices in the sixteenth century. These practices were legalized only after the 1996 peace treaty. In de Lión's time these practices, thus, were still illegal and consequently secretive—that is, hidden from public view to avoid repression.
21. Myth has it that the Mongolian origin of Indigenous peoples of the Americas can be detected by a "Mongolian stain," a physical mark that all indigenous children have at birth and that disappears after a few weeks.
22. In narrative theory, *actant* is a term from the actantial model of semiotic analysis of narratives. A. J. Greimas (1917–1992), professor of semiotics, is widely credited with producing the actantial model in 1966. Julia Kristeva also attempted to understand the dynamic development of the situations in narratives with Greimas's actant model. She thought the subject and the object could change positions mutually, and the Supporter and the Opposition also change positions accordingly. See *Structural Semantics: An Attempt at a Method* by Greimas and *Le Texte du Roman* by Kristeva.
23. I remember that throughout the 1950s, the featured strip on the front page of the Saturday comics section of the country's most important paper, *El imparcial*, was *Tarzan*. (There were no Sunday papers at the time.)
24. In the original, "que tenía a su servicio un chorro de psicólogos para implantar el terror."
25. In the original, "que don Juan mantenía en el altar y que le daba a beber a toda la gente que le consultaba."
26. In the original, "cuando yo la vi, pensé en el niño que días antes había sido velado en la estación del tren y había sido enterrado envuelto en unos periódicos."
27. See Bataille, *The Accursed Share*, pp. 25–26.
28. These lines are part of "The New Colossus," a sonnet by American poet Emma Lazarus (1849–1887), written in 1883. In 1903 it was engraved on a bronze plaque that stands inside the lower level of the pedestal of the Statue of Liberty.
29. In the original Castilian, "—Recordá que en este país de indios, vos llevás sangre alemana. No importa que sea poca—le decía su padre."

30. A *nagual* or nawal, as previously indicated, is in its simplest understanding, the power to magically transform oneself into an animal form. The general concept of nagualism is pan-Mesoamerican, though it has different names in the many languages of the region. Nagualism is linked to pre-Columbian religious practices, where all humans have an animal counterpart to which their life force is connected. Normally, a healer whispers into the ears of the newly born person, telling him or her who his or her nagual is, according to the calendar.
31. See Arias, *Taking Their Word*, p. 47.
32. Francisco Morales Santos provided this information via e-mail dated June 9, 2011.
33. Ladinos have a mixed European and Indigenous identity with a Western worldview; Guatemala's rulers have all been Ladino since independence from Spain in 1821.
34. See Coe, *The Maya Scribe and His World.*
35. See Carlos M. López, *Los "Popol Wuj" y sus epistemologías.*
36. Ibid., chapter 1.
37. See van Akkeren's *Xib'a'b'a y el nacimiento del nuevo sol.*
38. See Tedlock, *Popol Vuh: The Definitive Edition of the Mayan Book of the Dawn of Life and the Glories of Gods and Kings.*
39. Sam Colop speculates that it remained, or remains, in the hands of the "principals," or traditional leaders, of Chimaltenango, but in extremely bad shape, if it has not crumbled altogether (15).
40. See Morales, "Un libro que se niega a morir y a nacer."
41. See Morales Santos, "Luis de Lión, poeta de la cotidianidad y de la tierra," p. 32. Rita M. Palacios quotes this same document on page 85 of her dissertation.
42. Laura Martin cites in her article a personal communication from de Lión's son, Xbalanque de Lión, dated from 2005, stating that "de Lión entered into a private competition with other writer friends whereby each would produce a novel written according to certain specifications. According to his son, de Lion's contribution was to be circular, a novel you could begin to read at any point" (49). I would argue that, notwithstanding this testimony, de Lión was fully aware of the circularity of time in the Maya calendar and chose this form because it fit his design.
43. As both Poe and Martin have pointed out, in Latin America *concha* (shell) is a vulgar term for female genitalia. See Poe (89) and Martin (51).
44. Laura Martin notes the irony of the name Concepción (conception) for both the Virgin and Concha: "Neither one can conceive, one because she is made of wood and one because she is infertile" (51).
45. *Indigenismo* was a literary current in Latin America in the 1930s whereby mostly urban writers celebrated Indigenous cultures and berated their exploitation,

advocating their conversion into "modern" (i.e., "Western") subjects, thus depriving them of their culture. In his own note 15, del Valle Escalante states that de Lión explicitly told Mario Roberto Morales of his opposition to the political stance of Asturias and spoke against *mestizaje* ("Maya Nationalism and Political Decolonization in Guatemala: Luis de Lión and *El tiempo principia en Xibalbá*," 212).

46. The narrative voice informs us that it is not a hurricane, but it does echo those possibilities, alluding not only to the *Popol Wuj*, where Juraqan (Hurricane) is one of the deities of Heart Sky, but also to Asturias's *Strong Wind* (1950), the first title of his Banana Trilogy, as well as to the wind that wipes Macondo off the face of the earth at the end of Gabriel García Márquez's *One Hundred Years of Solitude* (1967).
47. See Maldonado-Torres, "On the Coloniality of Being."
48. A boy then discovers that the couple does not sleep together, because from the first time her husband refused to touch her or have any sexual contact.
49. If she was born on the same day and at the same time as Pascual, she was also born on the Day of the Dead. Thus, all the symbolic twins in the text are "deceased."
50. The Virgin of Concepción is the patron saint of de Lión's hometown, San Juan del Obispo.
51. Even this scene evokes the *Popol Wuj*. The way in which Pascual cut the child's finger off is reminiscent of how a bat named Kama sotz' cuts off the head of Junajpu. The twins were in Xib'alb'a, spending the night in the House of Bats. They squeezed themselves into their own blowguns to defend themselves from the circling bats. Junajpu stuck his head out of his blowgun to see if the dawn had arrived, and Kama sotz' immediately snatched off his head and carried it to the ball court to be hung up and used as the ball by the gods in their next ball game. This points in the direction of the unnamed town actually being Xib'alb'a, and this would make Pascual and Juan the equivalent of the two principal lords, Jun Kame (One Death) and Wuqub' Kame (Seven Death).
52. Suffice in this respect to quote the many testimonies offered by Ixil women—and part of the public record—during the trial for genocide of Guatemala's ex-head of government, General Efraín Ríos Montt, in 2013.
53. A similar scene of an Indigenous subject falling in love with a blonde virgin is the topic of the film *The Other Conquest* (2000). Del Valle Escalante reminds us that Serge Gruzinski has traced the imposition of Catholic religious icons by Spaniards in the sixteenth century to legitimize the Spanish imperial enterprise.
54. Gustavo Lins Ribeiro argues that it is also necessary to explore a parallel category that he labels "nationality of power" in interim fashion. This would

account for the structuring effects of national elites when articulating social relations reflecting the coloniality of power within a given nation-state, where they most often find their natural ground and stability, their space of emplacement.

CHAPTER 3

1. The heavy Eurocentric influence on Guatemala is also manifest in its nineteenth-century French influence. Guatemala names its political divisions "departments," a concept that originated in Napoleonic France.
2. This biographical information was shared with me over lunch on July 23, 2008, at the Pan American Hotel in Guatemala City. However, it also appears in the Sitler interview; see note 4.
3. Personal communication, Guatemala City, July 27, 2009. This information is also in the Sitler interview; see note 4.
4. Interview with Professor Robert Sitler when González visited Sitler's institution. Sitler works at Stetson University, translated one of González's books to English, and has written on the meaning of a change of eras in 2012.
5. Ibid.
6. The following quotation explains the complex difficulties involved in achieving this purpose:

   Empezamos a tocar puertas en varias instituciones y no recibí ninguna respuesta hasta que llegué al Ministerio de Cultura. Allí había un señor que está bien identificado con la cultura maya. Estaba de Vice Ministro en esa época y tuve una entrevista con él. Me dijo, "Bueno, déjeme una copia de su trabajo y voy a enviarla a nuestro consejo editorial." Había en el consejo cinco escritores ladinos, personas no indígenas. Yo tenía pocas esperanzas. En tres semanas, el señor me dijo, "Tenemos buenas noticias." Pero muy pronto ese señor dejó su puesto y yo no sabía quién iba a sustituirlo. Nadie sabía dónde estaba el manuscrito. Pasaron tres o cuatro meses sin que yo tuviera noticias de mi trabajo. A fin de cuentas tuve que comenzar todo de nuevo y el nuevo jefe finalmente aprobó el proyecto.

   [We began knocking on doors in various institutions and I didn't get any response until I got to the Ministry of Culture. There was a gentleman there who identified with Maya culture. He was a Vice Minister at the time, and I had an interview with him. He said, "Well, leave me a copy of your work and I'll send it to our editorial board." There were five Ladino writers on the board, non-Indigenous peoples. I had little hope. Three weeks later, the gentleman told me, "We have good news." But soon this gentleman left his post and I had no idea who'd come in his place. No one knew where the manuscript was. Three or four months passed and I had no news of my work. In the end, I had to start all over again, and the new boss finally approved the project; my translation].

The original Castilian quotation is from the Sitler interview.

7. The fragment of the interview quoted is a part of the one conducted by Professor Robert Sitler mentioned in the previous note. However, it was first quoted by Rita Palacios in her 2009 dissertation.
8. Sitler interview.
9. Ibid.
10. Ibid.
11. See Wellmeier's article in Warner and Wittner's *Gatherings in Diaspora*, p. 118.
12. Sitler interview.
13. Ibid.
14. I owe my student Nanci Buiza gratitude for introducing me to Charles Altieri's work in the spring of 2013. Prior to her intervention, I was unaware of his oeuvre.
15. See "Kotz'ib': The Emergence of a New Maya Literature."
16. See Boes, "Modernist Studies and the *Bildungsroman*."
17. Jolomk'u is named "head of the sun" because it alludes to the emergence of the sun over the top of the mountain as it rises. González's childhood home faced this mountain. See Montenegro, "Soy un pez sacado del agua."
18. In this sense, it is important to remember that the Maya calendar is a system of calendars used in pre-Columbian Mesoamerica. At least sixty variants have been recorded. It is based on a system commonly used throughout the region, dating back to at least the fifth century BCE. It also shares aspects with calendars employed by other Mesoamerican cultures, such as the Zapotec and Olmec, and contemporary or later ones, such as the Mixtecs and Aztecs.
19. The Committee for Peasant Unity (CUC, Castilian acronym) was the major peasant mass organization just prior to the civil war. By 1980 most members of CUC had joined the Guerrilla Army of the Poor (EGP), and the CUC virtually disappeared. However, it came back after the signing of the Peace Accords in 1996, and it exists as a powerful organization to this day.
20. In their narrative, it is the Ladino politicized intellectuals who recruit reluctant Mayas into rebellion against the state.
21. Personal communication, Guatemala City, August 4, 2007.
22. The English translation in this line fails to underline the importance attributed to the name in Castilian.

23. Metaphorical and catachrestic, as the sign "mil/thousand" may be, in Maya time we are talking of twenty thousand years, whereas in the English version, of one million years, placing the counting in different variables of comprehension.
24. See "La parole soufflé" in Derrida, *Writing and Difference*, p. 178.
25. For Gloria Chacón, see book manuscript "Unsettling the Canon: the Rise of Maya and Zapotec Writers," still unpublished. For Kab'awil, Damián Upún Sipac's, *Maya' Ajilab'äl Q'ij: La cuenta maya de los días.*
26. See Leys, "The Turn to Affect."
27. See my analyses of Wyld Ospina, (1891–1956), Herrera (1895–1968), and Samayoa Chinchilla (1898–1973) in *Ideologías, literatura y sociedad.*
28. Chapter 4 covers Lotaxh's life in Jolomk'u while Mekel is working on the plantation (58; 57). It also includes, toward its end, a typical Sunday on the coast, where Mekel observes how his plantation-worker colleagues get drunk in a cantina (69; 67). Following this, the narrative voice follows the child of Petlon, the cook at the hacienda. He dies of dysentery (77; 73), as do his siblings immediately afterward. This traumatic experience prompts Mekel to attend the funeral and then give up his job on the coast, returning to Jolumk'u (81; 77).

    Chapter 5 shows us Mekel taking care of his corn-planted fields and teaching a very young Lwin how to do so. He also gets a dog named Tz'ib'in (Spots) (84; 80; the Maya name does not appear in the English version) that will live until Lwin is eight years old. Lwin participates in the collective corn harvest of his father's land at Sti'ch'en (85; 81), the lower part of Jolomk'u, at the confluence of two small rivers. We learn about a young couple in love, prefiguring Lwin's own courting of Malin in chapter 9. At the end of the day, the harvest ceremony takes place. Afterward, Lwin wants to meet Mam Tioxh, the creator of things, so he is taken to see his grandfather, also named Lwin (93), so the latter can explain to him what Tioxh stands for and how he is present in everything.

    In chapter 6 we are told how, in the village, his elders taught Lwin ethical behavior (95). Then the rural police appear in the village, allegedly to discover clandestine *kuxha* makers, but in reality to steal what they can (96; 92). They enter the family ranch, where only Lotaxh and Lwin are present, speaking to them in Castilian, which neither understands; and they destroy all the cooking utensils in their search for *kuxha* (97; 93). Cleverly, Lotaxh had put a lot of pine needles in the fire, so the policemen would be drowned by the excessive smoke and leave their home relatively quickly. Lwin learns to fear Ladinos and has nightmares about them. Lwin is also taught what the word *indio* means (100–101).
29. See Susan Rubin Suleiman's "Judith Herman and Contemporary Trauma Theory."

30. See Visser, "Trauma Theory and Postcolonial Literary Studies."
31. See Arias, "Indigenous Women at War: Discourses on Revolutionary Combat."
32. Brutal as it may seem, this practice was routine in Guatemala until the signing of the Peace Treaty in 1996.
33. See Banfield, "Narrative Style and the Grammar of Direct and Indirect Speech."
34. Once again, this is a bad translation. The English version implies that Lwin's hair began to turn grey *because* he began his organizing task, by virtue of the clause "that's when." This is not the case in the original version, or in the Castilian one, where it simply denotes a passage of time: Lwin is older, simply because the years have passed.
35. This is another bad translation to English. In the original and Castilian versions, the narrative voice claims that Lwin's big house was like their own house for all community members, alluding to the many meetings and time they had all spent there. The English version, through the usage of the clause "as though it were," makes it sound as if this is exceptional and uniquely attributed to Lwin's sickness.
36. Personal communication, Guatemala City, June 27, 2013.
37. Ibid.
38. The English translation was published in 1998.
39. See Foucault's *The Archaeology of Knowledge & The Discourse on Language*, in which he addresses decisions to erase logophobia. Regarding personal pronouns, we turn to Derrida's argument on page 224 of "Structure, Sign and Play in the Discourse of the Human Sciences," possibly the most famous chapter in *Writing and Difference*.
40. See Mbembe's essay "Necropolitics."
41. González told me that he had never been to the Ixcan when he wrote the novel and relied on research and testimonies from Mayas who had lived in what used to be until very recently "frontier territory" at the edge of the jungle. Personal communication, Guatemala City, June 27, 2013.
42. From this point on in the analysis, the second number to cite a reference will always correspond to the 1998 English version.
43. Ruud van Akkeren has proven how until the arrival of the Spaniards, but especially during the late Classical period, the Yichkan area was one of the most inhabited among Mayas, and a commercial hub for trade between highlands and lowlands. See *Xib'alb'a y el nacimiento del nuevo sol*.
44. Rhetoricality is what John Bender and David E. Wellberry see at work in our contemporary world. For them, this condition "manifests the groundless, infinitely ramifying character of discourse in the modern world. For this reason, it allows for no explanatory metadiscourse that is not already itself rhetorical" (25). See Bender and Wellberry, eds., *The Ends of Rhetoric*.

45. See Massumi, *Parables for the Virtual.*
46. See Leys, "The Turn to Affect."
47. Ibid.
48. See O'Leary, "Foucault, Experience, Literature." The previous citation is taken from page 7.
49. O'Leary, of course, is talking here about Foucault's *History of Madness*, and his allusions are addressing Foucault's perception of the Western experience of madness during the Renaissance and during what Foucault labels "the classical age."

CHAPTER 4

1. Some linguists claim that Jakalteko language is named "Popti'," but Montejo insists that it is named "Popb'al Ti'." I respect his wishes in this chapter.
2. In this respect, it is interesting to note that a newspaper article from Saturday, August 24, 2013, published in *El periódico de Guatemala* claims that a genetic study conducted on the Q'anil volcano proves that the geoplasm of teosinte (*Zea mays*) of the subspecies "parviglumis," originally grown around the volcano five thousand to seven thousand years ago and known scientifically as *teosinte parviglumis*, is the direct antecedent of modern-day corn. *Q'anil* in Popb'al Ti' means "seed." UN (Food and Agriculture Organization (FAO) experts have not yet corroborated this argument, but, as of this date, they do not discard it either. See http://elperiodico.com.gt/es/20130824/pais/233340.
3. This argument appears in the first chapter of Marc Djaballah's *Kant, Foucault, and Forms of Experience.*
4. My student Judith Thorn was the first person to point out the ethical issues in Montejo's *Q'anil* to me in the early 1990s. She went on to publish a book based on her master's thesis at San Francisco State University, *The Lived Horizon of My Being*, in which she examines this angle from a Bakhtinian perspective and, more particularly, from Bakhtin's earlier, neo-Kantian texts, *Art and Answerability* and *Toward a Philosophy of the Act.*
5. See "Indigenous Cosmopolitics: Dialogues about the Reconstitution of Worlds."
6. Ibid., p. 5.
7. See "Resisting Pictures: Representation, Distribution and Ontological Politics."
8. See "Re-Imagining Land Ownership in Australia." Helen Verran, as well as John Law and Ruth Benschop, are all quoted by de la Cadena in "Indigenous Cosmopolitics." Verran was also a participant in the seminar in question. Analogous arguments are also made from a religious perspective in John

Grim, "Knowing and Being Known by Animals: Indigenous Perspectives on Personhood" and in Paul Waldau and Kimberly Patton's *A Communication of Subjects: Animals in Religion, Science, and Ethics*. See also Marie Battiste and James (Sa'ke'j) Youngblood Henderson, *Protecting Indigenous Knowledge and Heritage: A Global Challenge*, pp. 41–42.

9. "Engagements Between Disparate Knowledge Traditions: Toward Doing Difference Generatively and in Good Faith."
10. *Annals of the Cakchiquels* (in Castilian: *Anales de los Cakchiqueles*, also known by the alternative Castilian titles, *Anales de los Xahil*, *Memorial de Tecpán-Atitlán*, or *Memorial de Sololá*), is a manuscript written in Kaqchikel by Francisco Hernández Arana Xajilá in 1571. It was completed by his grandson, Francisco Rojas, in 1604. The manuscript, which describes Kaqchikel legends, also has historical and mythological components. It is regarded as one of the more important historical documents on Postclassic Maya civilization in the highlands of Guatemala.
11. Guamán wrote "*Corónica*" instead of "*Crónica*" by mistake. His book is the most important critique of Spanish colonial rule produced by an Indigenous subject in the entire colonial period. It was written between 1600 and 1615 and addressed to King Philip III of Spain. The book points out the injustices of colonial rule and reaffirms that the Spaniards were foreign settlers in Peru.
12. Translated by Amy T. Olen.
13. The *Books of Chilam Balam* are Yukatek Maya texts from the seventeenth and eighteenth centuries, named after the Yucatán towns where they were originally kept. They preserve important Indigenous Maya knowledge. Written in the Yukatek Maya language and using the Latin alphabet, the manuscripts are attributed to a legendary author called Chilam Balam. A *chilam* is a priest who gives prophecies, and *balam* is a common surname meaning "jaguar." Some of the texts contain prophecies about the coming of the Spaniards to Yucatán while mentioning a Chilam Balam as their author. Language and content both indicate that parts of the books date back to the Spanish invasion of Yucatán (1527–1546). Bernardino de Sahagún (1499–1590) was a Franciscan friar, missionary priest, and foundational ethnographer who participated in the Catholic evangelization of Mexico, who wrote *Historia general de las cosas de la Nueva España* (1585; *General History of the Things of New Spain*, 2002), a bilingual Castilian/Nahuatl text.
14. See Arias, *Gestos ceremoniales: Narrativa centroamericana 1960–1990*, p. 281.
15. See Genette's *Paratexts*.
16. Derrida refers to "a certain onto-theological metaphysics of *sovereignty* (autonomy and omnipotence of the subject—individual or state—freedom, ecological will, conscious intentionality, or if you will, the ego, the ego ideal,

and the superego, etc.)" in his essay "Psychoanalysis Searches," which appears in *Without Alibi*, to justify resistance to these kinds of structures.

17. This is also a reason why some lazy readers prefer testimonios to the complexity of novels. They are easier to read and digest.
18. Spivak has mentioned this as a crucial element for both Derrida and for herself. The latest reference regarding this matter appears on p. 30 of *Death of a Discipline*.
19. As already stated in the introduction to this book as well as in chapter 2, Aníbal Quijano created the concept in Castilian in his essay "Colonialidad del poder, cultura y conocimiento en América Latina" (1997). Walter Mignolo reconceptualized it in *Local Histories/Global Designs* (2000). I subsequently quote Javier Sanjinés's description because of its brevity and succinctness.
20. It is when we understand this that we can begin to differentiate testimonio from testimony, in a juridical sense, a critical difference that is not made by critics who still confuse both because they are thinking from within the Western perspective of a universalist modern paradigm.
21. As far as coloniality of power is concerned, Javier Sanjinés summarizes Mignolo's and Quijano's position as "a pattern whose specific axes are: (a) the existence and continual production of identities based on the notion of race; (b) the hierarchized relation of inequality between 'European' and 'non-European' identities, and the domination of the former over the latter; and (c) the construction of mechanisms of social domination designed to preserve this historical foundation of social classification." See *Mestizaje Upside-Down*, 191n1.
22. I made a point almost identical to this one in the last section of my article "Authoring Ethnicized Subjects: Rigoberta Menchú and the Performative Production of the Subaltern Self."
23. The book was published by the Guatemala Scholars Network, a group of US scholars in solidarity with the Maya peoples and with the struggle against the military genocide taking place in the country.
24. *Pseudology* is a term employed by Derrida to explain a misunderstanding that could very well be a mistake, a falsehood, a cunning way of avoiding a lie, a deception, or a poetic invention. See his essay "History of the Lie: Prolegomena" in *Without Alibi*.
25. See, in this respect, Shyh-jen Fuh's arguments in "Derrida and the Problem of Ethics."
26. That is, the paradox of wanting to end racism by overemphasizing its most stereotyped traces.
27. Víctor Montejo, personal communication. La Farge worked with Frans Blom in Mexico in the mid-1920s, helping in the rediscovery of the ruins of La Venta,

one of the major Olmec centers. He then went to Guatemala and wrote the first and only monograph on Jacaltenango, titled *The Year Bearer's People* (co-written with Douglas Byers), published in 1931. The La Farge papers are presently at the Harry Ransom Center of the University of Texas at Austin. Also a novelist, La Farge wrote *Sparks Fly Upward* (1931) about his experiences in Guatemala.

28. We are told on the first page that the Catholic priest, a missionary, visits the village every two years to celebrate Mass and remind villagers of their Christian duties.
29. See Spivak, *An Aesthetic Education in the Era of Globalization*.
30. In Castilian, "—Muy bien Mister, dijo Xuxh Antil. —Usted debe también aprender a decir los nombres de sus amigos en idioma Popb'al Ti'. Llámeme siempre 'Antil,' en vez de 'Andrés.' A mí me gusta mucho ese nombre, aunque así se llama también una clase de ranas que durante la estación lluviosa se trepan a los árboles a cantar."
31. In the Castilian version, "—Don Lamun dice que su nombre en nuestra lengua se pronuncia como *T'ut'*. Mr. Puttison se paró de su asiento inconforme y gritó: —Oh, por favor, no me busquen otro nombre. Mi nombre es Dud. —Sí, míster, pero la D no existe en nuestra lengua. Lo más parecido es *T'ut'*, pero es otra cosa. Todos se rieron. —¿Qué es *T'ut'* entonces? Xhuxh Antil se adelantó a explicar, con una sonrisa picaresca. —*T'ut'* es el ruido que produce el aire al soltar un pedo disimulado."
32. In the original Castilian, "Mr. Puttison experimentó una visible satisfacción, pues se puso más colorado que nunca cuando Koxkoreto le mencionó la cueva misteriosa."
33. Gourds have also been used as musical instruments among Indigenous cultures of the Americas for thousands of years.
34. *La llorona*, or the Weeping Woman, is a Mesoamerican legend of a ghostly woman who wanders along canals and rivers crying for her missing children. *La llorona* is both faceless and ageless, a compendium of many symbols and pre-Hispanic deities. She's both a condemned woman and, at the same time, a goddess bearing an ominous message. In *La visión de los vencidos* (*The Broken Spears: The Aztec Account of the Conquest of Mexico*, 2006), Miguel León-Portilla cites the forebodings that the Mexica people received before the arrival of the Spaniards. One of these omens makes reference to a woman, *la Cihuacoatl*, or serpent-woman, who wandered about Tenochtitlán wailing and lamenting: "My dearly beloved children; your departure is near; we're about to become estranged! Oh, my children! Where shall I take you?"
35. Santa María is a large active volcano in the western highlands of Guatemala, close to the city of Quetzaltenango, or Xelajuj Noj. Prior to the Spanish invasion it was called Gagxanul, or Q'aq' Ixkanul in K'iche'. Its eruption in 1902 was

one of the four largest eruptions of the twentieth century. Santa María is part of the Sierra Madre range of volcanoes, which extends along the western edge of Guatemala.

36. *Nagual* is the human ability to transform him/herself into an animal as previously indicated on note 30 of chapter 2. However, the animal is not just any animal. This is determined according to the day, time, and place, where the person was born—factors circumscribed by the Maya calendar.
37. *Pom*, also known as *copal*, is an aromatic tree resin used by Mesoamerican cultures as incense for ceremonial and spiritual purposes. The word *copal* originated in the Náhuatl word *copalli*, meaning "incense." Mayas know it as *pom*, a Mixe-Zoquean word.
38. In the original Castilian, "Como tres almas que lleva el diablo, los tres ladrones comenzaron a correr como locos, tratando de abandonar aquel lugar lo más pronto posible."
39. In Castilian, "en un ambiente mezclado de remembranzas, armonías y misterios."

CONCLUSIONS

1. "Maya Architectural Hierophanies."
2. Oral discussion. Mellon-Sawyer Seminar. Lozano Long Institute of Latin American Studies, University of Texas at Austin. September 19, 2014.
3. Because plaintiffs had to prove their "Indianness" in a Spanish juridical context, van Deusen was able to detail the "serial dislocation" (72) that these subjects went through, from their being first uprooted violently from their places of origin and assigned generic geographical references such as "Peru," or "Guatemala" (73), to their being shipped as slaves to various points in the continent that further displaced them from their respective identities, before they were finally sent across the Atlantic in trips which stripped them of all remaining "spatial or temporal references" to their original identity and sense of belongingness (65). Once in Seville, they were sold as "Indio" slaves based on racial markers constructed by the Spanish, which took in account empirical traits such as language, head shape, or color (169,171). Thus, based on a series of detailed case studies, van Deusen is able to concretely evidence many specific details of those lived historical processes by which "Indios" were indeed constructed as such in the sixteenth century, while also confirming how severely disjointed this process was.
4. Allen uses this phrase in his article "Engaging the Politics and Pleasures of Indigenous Aesthetics."

BIBLIOGRAPHY

Agamben, Giorgio. *Homo Sacer: Sovereign Power and Bare Life*. Translated by Daniel Heller-Roazen. Stanford, CA: Stanford University Press, 1998.

Aguirre Beltrán, Gonzalo. *Obra antropológica VI. El proceso de aculturación y el cambio sociocultural de México.* México D.F.: Fondo de Cultura Económica, 1992.

Ak'abal, Humberto. *Ajyuq' /El animalero*. Guatemala: Cholsamaj, 1995.

Akkeren, Ruud van. *Visión indígena de la conquista*. Introduction by Luis Pedro Taracena. Guatemala: Serviprensa, 2007.

———. *Xib'alb'a y el nacimiento del nuevo sol: Una visión posclásica del colapso maya.* Guatemala: Piedra Santa, 2012.

Allen, Chadwick. "Engaging the Politics and Pleasures of Indigenous Aesthetics." *Western American Literature* 41, no. 2 (Summer 2006): 146–75.

———. *Trans-Indigenous: Methodologies for Global Native Literary Studies*. Minneapolis, MN: University of Minnesota Press, 2012.

Altieri, Charles. *The Particulars of Rapture: An Aesthetics of the Affects*. Ithaca, NY: Cornell University Press, 2003.

Anonymous. "Premio de Literatura Indígena B'ATZ' para Leoncio Pablo García Talé y Miguel Angel Oxlaj Cúmez." *Istmo* 15 (July–Dic 2007). http://istmo.denison.edu/n15/ noticias/premio1.html. Accessed May 3, 2013.

Arana Xajilá, Francisco Hernández, and Francisco Díaz Gebuta Quej. *The Annals of the Cakchiquels*. Translated by Daniel G. Brinton. Philadelphia: Library of Aboriginal American Literature 1, no. 6 (1969): vii, 9–234.

———. *Memorial de Sololá, Anales de los cakchiqueles*. Edited by Adrián Recinos. Translated by Dionisio José Chonay. México D.F.: Fondo de Cultura Económica, 1950.

Arias, Arturo. "Authoring Ethnicized Subjects: Rigoberta Menchú and the Performative Production of the Subaltern Self." *PMLA* 116, no. 1 (January 2001): 75–88.

———. "Changing Indian Identity: Guatemala's Violent Transition to Modernity." In *Guatemalan Indians and the state, 1540 to 1988*, edited by Carol A. Smith and Marilyn M. Moors, 230–57. Austin: University of Texas Press, 1990.

———. "Constructing Ethnic Bodies and Identities in Miguel Angel Asturias and Rigoberta Menchú." *Postmodern Culture* 17, no. 1 (September 2006). http://muse.jhu.edu/ journals/pmc/v017/17.1arias.html.

———. *Gestos ceremoniales: Narrativa centroamericana 1960–1990.* Guatemala: Artemis-Edinter, 1998.

———. *Ideologías, literatura y sociedad durante la revolución guatemalteca 1944–1954.* La Habana: Casa de las Américas, 1979.

———. "Indigenous Women at War: Discourses on Revolutionary Combat." *A contracorriente* 10, no. 3 (2013): 108–40.

———. "Kotz'ib': The Emergence of a New Maya Literature." *The Latin American Indian Literatures Journal* I, no. 24 (2008): 7–28.

———. "Racialized Subalternity as Emancipatory Decolonial Project: *Time Commences in Xibalbá* by Luis de Lión." In Luis de Lión. *Time Commences in Xibalbá*, translated by Nathan C. Henne, 85–115. Tucson: University of Arizona Press, 2012.

———. *The Rigoberta Menchú Controversy.* Minneapolis: University of Minnesota Press, 2001.

———. *Taking Their Word: Literature and the Signs of Central America.* Minneapolis: University of Minnesota Press, 2007.

Arrighi, Giovanni, and Beverly J. Silver. *Chaos and Governance in the Modern World System (Contradictions of Modernity).* Minneapolis: University of Minnesota Press, 1999.

Asturias, Miguel Ángel. *El problema social del indio y otros textos, recogidos y presentados por Claude Couffon.* Edited by Claude Couffon. Paris: Centre de recherches de l'institut d'études hispaniques, 1971.

———. *El Señor Presidente. Edición crítica.* Edited by Gerald Martin. Madrid: Archivos, 2000.

———. *Hombres de maíz. Edición crítica.* Edited by Gerald Martin. Madrid: Archivos, 1992.

———. *Men of Maize.* Translated by Gerald Martin. Pittsburgh, PA: University of Pittsburgh Press, 1993.

Bakhtin, Mikhail. *Art and Answerability.* Edited by Michael Holquist and Vadim Liapunov. Translated by Vadim Liapunov and Kenneth Brostrom. Austin: University of Texas Press, 1990.

———. *The Dialogic Imagination: Four Essays by M.M. Bakhtin.* Translated by Caryl Emerson and Michael Holquist. Austin: University of Texas Press, 1981.

———. *Speech Genres and Other Late Essays.* Austin: University of Texas Press, 1986.

———. *Toward a Philosophy of the Act.* Edited by Vadim Liapunov and Michael Holquist. Translated by Vadim Liapunov. Austin: University of Texas Press, 1993.

Banfield, Ann. "Narrative Style and the Grammar of Direct and Indirect Speech." *Foundations of Language* 10 (1973): 1–39.

Bataille, Georges. *The Accursed Share*. Vol. 1: Consumption. Translated by Robert Hurley. New York: Zone Books, 1991.

Battiste, Marie. "Research Ethics for Protecting Indigenous Knowledge and Heritage Institutional and Researcher Responsibilities." In *Handbook of Critical and Indigenous Methodologies*, edited by Norman K. Denzin, Yvonna S. Lincoln, and Linda Tuhiwai Smith, 497–509. Los Angeles, CA: SAGE, 2008.

Battiste, Marie, and James (Sa'ke'j) Youngblood Henderson. *Protecting Indigenous Knowledge and Heritage: A Global Challenge*. Saskatoon, SK: Purich Publishing, 2000.

Baudrillard, Jean. *Simulations*. Translated by Phil Beitchman, Paul Foss, and Paul Patton. Foreign Agents Series, Semiotext(e). New York: Columbia University Press, 1983.

Bender John, and David E. Wellberry, eds. *The Ends of Rhetoric: History, Theory, Practice*. Stanford, CA: Stanford University Press, 1990.

Best, Stephen, and Sharon Marcus. "Surface Reading: An Introduction." *Representations* 108, no. 1 (Fall 2009): 1–21.

Boes, Tobias. "Modernist Studies and the *Bildungsroman*: A Historical Survey of Critical Trends." *Literature Compass* 3, no. 2 (2006): 230–43.

Boone, Elizabeth Hill, and Walter D. Mignolo, eds. *Writing Without Words: Alternative Literacies in Mesoamerica and the Andes*. Durham, NC: Duke University Press, 1994.

Bourdieu, Pierre. *The Logic of Practice*. Stanford, CA: Stanford University Press, 1990.

Brown, Leslie, and Susan Strega, eds. *Research as Resistance: Critical, Indigenous, and Anti- oppressive Approaches*. Toronto, ON: Canadian Scholars' Press, 2005.

Butler, Judith. *Excitable Speech: A Politics of the Performative*. New York: Routledge, 1997.

Cacho, Lisa Marie. *Social Death: Racialized Rightlessness and the Criminalization of the Unprotected*. New York: New York University Press, 2012.

Cajete, Gregory. "Philosophy of Native Science." In *American Indian Thought*, edited by Anne Waters, 45–57. Malden, MA: Blackwell, 2004.

Calleman, Carl Johan. *The Purposeful Universe: How Quantum Theory and Mayan Cosmology Explain the Origin and Evolution of Life*. Rochester, VT: Bear & Company, 2009.

Cárcamo-Huechante, Luis. "Introduction: Some Critical Challenges for Emerging Indigenous Studies." *LASA Forum* 43, no. 1 (February 2012): 5–6.

Cárcamo-Huechante, Luis E., Emilio Del Valle Escalante, y Arturo Arias. "Literaturas de Abya Yala." *LASA Forum* 43, no. 1 (October 2011): 7–10.

Carmack, Robert M. *Quichean Civilization: The Ethnohistoric, Ethnographic, and Archaeological Sources*. Berkeley: University of California Press, 1973.

———. (ed.) *El Título de Totonicapán*. México, D.F.: UNAM, 1983.

Casas, Bartolomé de las. *Brevísima relación de la destrucción de las Indias*. Barcelona: Linkgua Ediciones, 2009.

Casaús, Marta. *Guatemala: Linaje y racismo*. Guatemala, F&G, 2010.

Castro-Gómez, Santiago, and Ramón Grosfoguel, eds. *El giro decolonial: Reflexiones para una diversidad epistémica más allá del capitalismo global*. Bogotá: Siglo del Hombre Editores, 2007.

Chacón, Gloria. "Unsettling the Canon: the Rise of Maya and Zapotec Writers." Unpublished manuscript. 2016.

Chase-Dunn, Christopher, Jackie Smith, et al. *Global Democracy and the World Social Forums*. Boulder, CO: Paradigm Publishers, 2007.

Chinchilla, Norma, and Nora Hamilton. *Seeking Community in a Global City: Guatemalans and Salvadorans in Los Angeles*. Philadelphia, PA: Temple University Press, 2001.

Chow, Rey. *Ethics after Idealism: Theory—Culture—Ethnicity—Reading*. Bloomington: Indiana University Press, 1998.

———. *Primitive Passions: Visuality, Sexuality, Ethnography, and Contemporary Chinese Cinema*. New York: Columbia University Press, 1995.

———. *Writing Diaspora: Tactics of Intervention in Contemporary Cultural Studies*. Bloomington: Indiana University Press, 1993.

Coe, Michael D. *The Maya Scribe and His World*. New York: Grolier Club, 1973.

Cofiño, Ana, and Emma Chirix. *Emma Chirix conversa con Ana Cofiño*. Translated by Silvia Trujillo y Gemma Gil. Guatemala: Librovisor (Colección Pensamiento) 2, no. 3, 2008.

Colop, Sam, ed. and trans. *Popol Wuj: versión poética K'iche'*. Guatemala: Proyecto de Educación Maya Bilingüe Intercultural, Editorial Cholsamaj, 1999.

Comisión de Esclarecimiento Histórico. *Guatemala: Memory of Silence/Tz'inil Na'Tab'al: Report of the Commission for Historical Clarification*. Guatemala: United Nations, 1999.

Corntassel, Jeff. "Partnership in Action? Indigenous Political Mobilization and Co-optation During the First UN Indigenous Decade (1995–2004)." *Human Rights Quarterly* 29, no. 1 (February 2007): 137–66.

Courtine, Jean-Jacques. "Global Anxiety: A Contemporary History of the Fear of Fear." Unpublished document. 2013.

Cu Choc, Maya. "Poemaya." In *Novísimos*, edited by Marco Antonio Flores, 69–102. Guatemala: Editorial Cultura, 1996.

———. *Recorrido. Poemas*. Guatemala: Editorial Saquil Tzij, 2005.

———. *La Rueda*. Guatemala: Editorial Cultura, 2001.

De la Cadena, Marisol. *Earth Beings: Ecologies of Practice Across Andean Worlds*. Durham, NC: Duke University Press, 2015.

———. "Indigenous Cosmopolitics: Dialogues about the Reconstitution of Worlds," unpublished manuscript. John E. Sawyer Seminar on the Comparative Study of Cultures. University of California–Davis, academic year 2012–2013.

———. "El Movimiento Indígena-Popular en los Andes y la Pluralización de la Política: Una Hipótesis de Trabajo." *LASA Forum* 38, no. 4 (Fall 2007): 36–38.

De la Campa, Román. *Latin Americanism*. Minneapolis: University of Minnesota Press, 1999.

De Lión, Luis. *La puerta del cielo*. Guatemala: Ministerio de Cultura, Colección narrativa, Serie Miguel Ángel Asturias 20, 2011.

———. *El tiempo principia en Xibalbá*. Guatemala: Artemis Edinter, 1996.

———. *Time Commences in Xibalbá*. Translated by Nathan C. Henne. Tucson: University of Arizona Press, 2012.

———. *Su segunda muerte*. Guatemala: Nuevo Signo Editores, 1970.

———. *Los zopilotes*. Guatemala: Editorial Landívar, 1966. Published under the name José Luis León Díaz.

De Sousa Santos, Boaventura. "Beyond Abyssal Thinking: From Global Lines to Ecologies of Knowledges." Paper presented at the University of Victoria, December 1, 2006. http://www.law.uvic.ca/demcon/victoria_colloquium/documents/desousasantos.pdf. Accessed Sept. 9, 2009.

———. "The World Social Forum: A User's Manual." Madison, 2004. http://www.ces.uc.pt/bss/documentos/fsm_eng.pdf. Accessed Sept. 9, 2009.

Del Sarto, Ana. "Introduction: Part II: Foundations." In *The Latin American Cultural Studies Reader*, edited by Ana del Sarto, Alicia Ríos, and Abril Trigo, 153–81. Durham, NC: Duke University Press, 2004.

Del Valle Escalante, Emilio. "Maya Nationalism and Political Decolonization in Guatemala: Luis de Lión and *El tiempo principia en Xibalbá*." *Latin American and Caribbean Ethnic Studies* 1, no. 2 (September 2006): 203–13.

———.*Maya Nationalisms and Postcolonial Challenges in Guatemala: Coloniality, Modernity, and Identity Politics*. Santa Fe, NM: School for Advanced Research, 2009.

———. "El viaje a los orígenes y la poética decolonial Maya en *Madre, nosotros también somos historia* de Francisco Morales Santos." *Revista de Crítica Literaria Latinoamericana* 37, no. 74 (January 2011): 351–72.

Delgado, Elena, and Rolando J. Romero. "Local Histories and Global Designs: An Interview with Walter Mignolo." *Discourse* 22, no. 3 (Fall 2000): 7–33.

Derrida, Jacques. *Aporias: Dying - Awaiting (one Another At) the "limits of Truth."* Translated by Thomas Dutoit. Stanford, CA: Stanford University Press, 1993.

———. *Of Grammatology*. Translated by Gayatri Chakravorty Spivak. Baltimore: Johns Hopkins University Press, 1976.

———. *Margins of Philosophy*. Translated by Alan Bass. Chicago: University of Chicago Press, 1982.

———. *Specters of Marx: The State of the Debt, The Work of Mourning & the New International*. Edited by Bernd Magnus and Stephen Cullenberg. London: Routledge, 1994.

———. *Without Alibi*. Edited and translated by Peggy Kamuf. Stanford, CA: Stanford University Press, 2002.

———. *Writing and Difference*. Translated by Alan Bass. London: Routledge, 1978.

Dirlik, Arif. "Race Talk, Race and Contemporary Racism." *PMLA* 123, no. 5 (October 2008): 1363–79.

Djaballah, Marc. *Kant, Foucault, and Forms of Experience (Studies in Philosophy)*. New York: Routledge, 2008.

Dowd, Anne S. "Maya Architectural Hierophanies." In *Cosmology, Calendars, and Horizon-Bases Astronomy in Ancient Mesoamerica*, edited by Anne S. Dowd and Susan Milbrath, 37–75. Boulder: University Press of Colorado, 2005.

Dussel, Enrique. *Etica de la Liberación en la Edad de la Globalización y de la Exclusión*. Madrid: Trotta, 1998.

Echeverría Maurice. "Literatura maya actual: inventario mínimo." *Lpv* (2005): http://laspaginasvulgares.blogspot.com/2009/02/literatura-maya-actual-inventario_2472.html. Accessed Nov. 10, 2013.

England, Nora C. "Mayan Efforts Toward Language Preservation." In *Endangered Languages: Language Loss and Community Response*, edited by Lenore A. Grenoble, Lindsay J. Whaley, 99–116. Cambridge, UK: Cambridge University Press, 1998.

Escobar, Arturo. "'Mundos y conocimientos de otro modo': El programa de investigación de modernidad/colonialidad latinoamericano." *Tabula Rasa* 1 (Enero–Diciembre 2003): 51–86.

———. "Worlds and Knowledges Otherwise: The Latin American Modernity/Coloniality Research Program." *Cultural Studies* 21, nos. 2–3 (March–May 2007): 179–210.

Escobar Sarti, Carolina. "Ruk'u'x." *Prensa Libre*. http://www.prensalibre.com.gt/opinion/Ruk-u-x_0_1255674673.html. Accessed Nov. 27, 2014.

Estrada Monroy, Agustín. "Título de Jacaltenango." *Anales de la Academia de Geografía e Historia de Guatemala* 59–61 (January/December 1985): 291–296.

Fanon, Frantz. *The Wretched of the Earth*. Translated by Constance Farrington. New York: Grove Press, 1963.

Farriss, Nancy M. "Remembering the Future, Anticipating the Past: History, Time, and Cosmology among the Maya of Yucatan." *Comparative Studies in Society and History* 29, no. 3 (July 1987): 566–93.

Fischer, Edward F. "Review Essays Representing the Maya." *Ethnohistory* 50, no. 4 (2003): 707–12.

Fischer, Edward F., and McKenna Brown, R., eds. *Maya Cultural Activism in Guatemala*. Austin: University of Texas Press, 1996.

Foucault, Michel. *The Archaeology of Knowledge & The Discourse on Language*. Translated by A.M. Sheridan Smith. New York: Pantheon/Random House, 1982.

———. *Discipline and Punish: The Birth of the Prison*. Translated by Allan Sheridan. London: Penguin, 1978.

———. *The History of Sexuality*. Vol. 1: *An Introduction*. Translated by Robert Hurley. New York: Pantheon, 1978.

———. *Interviews and Other Writings 1977–1984*. Translated by A. Sheridan and edited by L. D. Kritzman. New York: Routledge, 1990.

———. *Language, Counter-Memory, Practice: Selected Essays and Interviews*. Edited by D.F. Bouchard. Ithaca: Cornell University Press, 1977.

———. "Practicing Criticism." In *Politics, Philosophy, Culture: Interviews and Other Writings, 1977–1984*, edited by Lawrence D. Kritzman, 152–56. London: Routledge, 1990.

———. *Society Must Be Defended: Lectures at the Collège de France, 1975-76*. Edited by M. Bertani and A. Fontana. Translated by D. Macey. London: Penguin, 2004.

———. "So Is It Important to Think?" In *Power: Essential Works of Foucault 1954–1984*, Vol. 3, edited by James D. Faubion, and translated by R. Hurley, et al., 454–58. London: Penguin, 2002.

———. "Two Lectures." In *Power/Knowledge: Selected Interviews and Other Writings 1972-1977*, edited by Colin Gordon, 78–108. New York: Pantheon, 1980.

Freyd, Jennifer J. *Betrayal Trauma: The Logic of Forgetting Childhood Abuse*. Cambridge, MA: Harvard University Press, 1996.

Fuentes y Guzmán, Francisco Antonio de. *Recordación florida: discurso historial, demostración material, militar y política del reyno de Guatemala: libros primero, segundo y tercero de la primera parte de la obra*. Guatemala: Biblioteca de cultura popular "20 de octubre" 9, no. 15 (1967): 163.

Fuh, Shyh-jen. "Derrida and the Problem of Ethics." *Concentric: Studies in English Literature and Linguistics* 29, no.1 (January 2003): 1–22.

Gabriel Xiquín, Calixta. *Hueso de la tierra*. Guatemala: Libros San Christobal, 1996.

———. *Tejiendo los sucesos en el tiempo/Weaving Events in Time*. Translated by Susan G. Rascón and Suzanne M. Strugalla. Rancho Palos Verdes: Yax Te' Foundation, 2002.

García, Pablo. *B'ixonik tzij ke uk'ulaj kaminaqib/Canto palabra de una pareja de muertos*. Guatemala: F&G Editores, 2009.

García Ixmata', Ajpub'. *Ruxe'el Mayab' k'aslemäl/ Raíz y espíritu del conocimiento maya*. Guatemala: Universidad Landívar, 2009.

Garroutte, Eva Marie. "Defining 'Radical Indigenism' and Creating an American Indian Scholarship." In *Culture, Power, and History: Studies in Critical Sociology*, edited by Stephen Pfohl, Aimee Van Wagenen, et al., 169–98. Chicago: Haymarket, 2009.

Genette, Gérard. *Paratexts: Thresholds of Interpretation*. New York: Cambridge University Press, 1997.

Goldberg, David Theo. *The Racial State*. Oxford: Blackwell, 2002.

Gómez Navarrete, Javier. *Cecilio Chi', Nen óol k'ajlay/Cecilio Chi', novela histórica*. México D.F.: SEP, 2006.

González, Gaspar Pedro. *The Dry Season: Q'anjobal Maya Poems*. Translated by R. McKenna Brown. Cleveland, OH: Cleveland State University Poetry Center, 2001.

———. Interview with Robert Sitler. "Entrevista con Gaspar Pedro González." http://www.stetson.edu/~rsitler/CV/GasparInt.doc. Accessed April 30, 2013.

———. *Kotz'ib': Nuestra literatura maya*. Ranchos Palos Verdes, CA: Fundación Yax Te', 1997.

———. *A Mayan Life*. Translated by Elaine Elliott. Rancho Palos Verdes, CA: Yax Te' Foundation, 1995.

———. *La otra cara*. Guatemala: CEDIGUAT, 1992.

———. *El 13 b'aktun: La nueva era, 2,012, el fin del ciclo desde la óptica maya contemporánea*. Guatemala: [publisher not identified], 2006.

———. *13 B'aktun: Mayan Visions of 2012 and Beyond*. Translated by Robert Sitler. Berkeley, CA: North Atlantic Books, 2010.

———. *El retorno de los mayas*. Guatemala: Fundación Myrna Mack, 1998.

———. *Return of the Maya*. Translated by Susan Giersbach Rascon and Fernando Penalosa. Ranchos Palos Verdes, CA: Yax Te' Foundation, 1998.

———. *Sb'eyb'al jun naq maya' q'anjob'al*. Ranchos Palos Verdes, CA: Fundación Yax Te', 1996.

———. *Sq'Anej Maya'/ Palabras Mayas*. Rancho Palos Verdes, CA: Yax Te' Foundation, 1998.

Gordon, Avery F. *Ghostly Matters: Haunting and the Sociological Imagination*. Minneapolis: University of Minnesota Press, 1997.

Greimas, Algirdas Julien. *Structural Semantics: An Attempt at a Method*. Translated by Daniele McDowell, Ronald Schleifer, and Alan Velie. Lincoln: University of Nebraska Press, 1983.

Grim, John. "Knowing and Being Known by Animals: Indigenous Perspectives on Personhood." In *A Communication of Subjects: Animals in Religion, Science, and Ethics*, edited by Paul Waldau and Kimberly Patton, 373–90. New York: Columbia University Press, 2006.

Grosz, Elizabeth. *Volatile Bodies: Toward a Corporeal Feminism (Theories of Representation and Difference)*. Crows Nest, AU: Allen & Unwin, 1994.

Guerrero, Francisco Javier. *Indígenas y campesinos: siete temas a debate con Arturo Warman*. México D.F.: INAH-CONACULTA, 2012.

Gutiérrez, Aguilar Raquel, and Luis A. Gómez. "Prólogo." In *Dispersar el poder: Los movimientos como poderes antiestatales*, edited by Raúl Zibechi. Buenos Aires: Tinta Limón Ediciones, 2006.

Guzmán Böckler, Carlos, and Jean-Loup Herbert. *Guatemala: Una interpretación histórico-social*. México, D.F.: Siglo XXI Editores, 1970.

Halberstam, Judtih (Jack). *Female Masculinity*. Durham, NC: Duke University Press, 1998.

Hale, Charles R. "Between Che Guevara and the Pachamama: Mestizos, Indians and identity politics in the anti-quincentenary campaign." *Critique of Anthropology* 14, no. 1 (1994): 9–39.

———. *Más Que Un Indio (More Than an Indian): Racial Ambivalence And The Paradox Of Neoliberal Multiculturalism in Guatemala*. Santa Fe, NM: School of American Research, 2006.

Hale, Charles R., and Rosamel Millamán. "Cultural Agency and Political Struggle in the Era of the *Indio Permitido*." In *Cultural Agency in the Americas*, edited by Doris Sommer, 281–304. Durham, NC: Duke University Press, 2006.

Hale, Charles R., and Lynn Stephen, eds. *Otros saberes: collaborative research on indigenous and Afro-descendant cultural politics*. Santa Fe, NM: SAR Press, 2013.

Hayles, N. Katherine. *How We Became Posthuman: Virtual Bodies in Cybernetics, Literature, and Informatics*. Chicago: University of Chicago Press, 1999.

Hernández, Natalio. *El despertar de nuestras lenguas/Queman tlachixque totlahtolhuan*. Estudio introductorio y epílogo de Miguel León Portilla. México D.F.: Diana/Fondo de Culturas Indígenas, 2002.

Hirschkop, Ken. *Mikhail Bakhtin: An Aesthetic for Democracy*. Oxford: Oxford University Press, 1999.

Houston, Stephen, Oswaldo Chinchilla Mazariegos, and David Stuart, eds. *The Decipherment of Ancient Maya Writing*. Norman: University of Oklahoma Press, 2001.

Joyce, James. *Ulysses*. Introduction by Cedric Watts. London: Wordsworth Editions, 2010.

Kauanui, J. Kēhaulani. *Hawaiian Blood: Colonialism and the Politics of Sovereignty and Indigeneity*. Durham, NC: Duke University Press, 2008.

Klopotek, Brian. "Dangerous Decolonizing Indians and Blacks and the Legacy of *Jim Crow*." In *Decolonizing Native Histories: Collaboration, Knowledge, and Language in the Americas*, edited by Florencia Mallon, 179–95. Durham, NC: Duke University Press, 2012.

Kristeva, Julia. *Revolution in Poetic Language*. Translated by Margaret Waller. New York: Columbia University Press, 1984.

———. *Le Texte du Roman: Approche sémiologique d'une structure discursive transformationnelle*. The Hague: Mouton de Gruyter, 1970.

Landeo Muñoz, Pablo. *Categorías andinas para una aproximación al* ***willakuy***. Lima: Fondo Editorial de la Asamblea Nacional de Rectores, 2014.

Law, John, and Ruth Benschop. "Resisting Pictures: Representation, Distribution and Ontological Politics." In *Ideas of Difference: Social Spaces and the Labour of Division, Sociological Review Monograph*, edited by Kevin Hetherington and Rolland Munro, 158–82. Oxford: Blackwell, 1997.

León-Portilla, Miguel. *The Broken Spears: The Aztec Account of the Conquest of Mexico*. Foreword by J. Jorge Klor de Alva. Translated by Lysander Kemp. Boston: Beacon Press, 2006.

———. *La visión de los vencidos: Relaciones indígenas de la Conquista*. Translated from Náhuatl to Castilian by Angel María Garibay K. México D.F.: UNAM, Biblioteca del estudiante universitario, 1959.

Lepe Lira, Luz María. *Lluvia y viento, puentes de sonido: Literatura indígena y crítica literaria*. Monterrey, NL: Universidad Autónoma de Nuevo León, 2010.

Leuthold, Steven. *Indigenous Aesthetics: Native Art, Media and Identity*. Austin: University of Texas Press, 1998.

Lévi-Strauss, Claude. *The Savage Mind*. Chicago: University of Chicago Press, 1966.

Leys, Ruth. "The Turn to Affect: A Critique." *Critical Inquiry* 37, no. 3 (Spring 2011): 434–72.

Liano, Dante. *Visión crítica de la literatura guatemalteca*. Guatemala: Ed. Universitaria, 1997.

Lionnet Françoise, and Shu-mei Shih, eds. *The Creolization of Theory*. Durham, NC: Duke University Press, 2011.

López, Carlos M. *Los "Popol Wuj" y sus epistemologías: las diferencias, el conocimiento y los ciclos del infinito*. Quito: Abya-Yala, 1999.

López Ixcoy, Candelaria Dominga. *Ri Ukemiik ri Tz'ib'anik pa K'ichee' ch'ab'al/ Manual de redacción k'ichee'*. Guatemala: Cholsamaj, 1994.

Lomnitz, Claudio. *Deep Mexico, Silent Mexico: An Anthropology of Nationalism*. Minneapolis: University of Minnesota Press, 2001.

Lugones, Maria. "Heterosexualism and the Colonial/Modern Gender System." *Hypatia* 22, no. 1 (Winter 2007): 186–209.

Lukács, Georg. *History and Class Consciousness: Studies in Marxist Dialectics*. Translated by Rodney Livingstone. London: Merlin Press, 1971.

Lund, Joshua. *The Impure Imagination: Toward a Critical Hybridity in Latin American Writing*. Minneapolis: University of Minnesota Press, 2006.

Lyotard, Jean-François. *The Differend*. Translated by George Van Den Abbeele. Minneapolis: University of Minnesota Press, 1988.

Maldonado-Torres, Nelson. "On the Coloniality of Being: Contributions to the development of a concept." *Cultural Studies* 21, nos. 2, 3 (2007): 240–70.

———. "Sobre la colonialidad del ser: Contribuciones al desarrollo de un concepto." In *El giro decolonial: Reflexiones para una diversidad epistémica más allá del capitalismo global*, edited by Santiago Castro-Gómez y Ramón Grosfoguel, 127–67. Bogotá: Siglo del Hombre Editores, 2007.

Mallon, Florencia, ed. *Decolonizing Native Histories: Collaboration, Knowledge, and Language in the Americas*. Durham, NC: Duke University Press, 2012.

Martin, Laura. "Traditional Mayan Rhetorical Forms and Symbols: From the *Popol Vuh* to *El tiempo principia en Xibalbá*." *Latin American Indian Literatures Journal* 23, no. 1 (Spring 2007): 43–65.

Martínez Peláez, Severo. *La patria del criollo. Ensayo de interpretación de la realidad colonial guatemalteca*. San José, CR: EDUCA, 1973.

Martínez Salazar, Egla. *Global Coloniality of Power in Guatemala: Racism, Genocide, Citizenship*. Baltimore, MD: Lexington Books, 2012.

Marx, Karl, and Friedrich Engels. *The Communist Manifesto*. Translated by Allen Lutins with assistance from Jim Tarzia. Project Gutenberg EBook. Release Date: January 25, 2005 [EBook #61]. http://www.gutenberg.org/cache/epub/61/pg61.html. Accessed March 13, 2013.

Massumi, Brian. *Parables for the Virtual: Movement, Affect, Sensation*. Durham, NC: Duke University Press, 2002.

Mbembe, Achille. "Necroolitics." Translated by Libby Meintjes. *Public Culture* 15, no. 1 (Winter 2003): 11–40.

McDonough, Kelly. *Reading and Writing Nahuas: Mexican Indigenous Intellectuals from the Colonial Period through Today*. Tucson: University of Arizona Press, 2014.

Méndez, Leopoldo. *Cosmovisión Mayab': Dos, tres palabras sobre sus principios*. Guatemala: Asociación Maya Uk'ux B'e, 2009.

Mignolo, Walter D. *The Darker Side of the Renaissance: Literacy, Territoriality, & Colonization*. Ann Arbor: University of Michigan Press, 1995.

———. *The Darker Side of Western Modernity: Global Futures, Decolonial Options*. Durham, NC: Duke University Press, 2011.

———. "The Geopolitics of Knowledge and the Colonial Difference." *The South Atlantic Quarterly* 101, no. 1 (2002): 57–96.

———. "I Am Where I Think: Remapping the Order of Knowing." In *The Creolization of Theory*, edited by Françoise Lionnet and Shu-mei Shih, 159–92. Durham, NC: Duke University Press, 2011.

———. *Local Histories/Global Designs: Coloniality, Subaltern Knowledges, and Border Thinking*. Princeton: Princeton University Press, 2000.

Mignolo, Walter D., and Madina Tlostanova. "The Logic of Coloniality and the Limits of Poscoloniality." In *The Postcolonial and the Global*, edited by Revathi

Krishnaswamy and John C. Hawley. Minneapolis: University of Minnesota Press, 2008.

Millar, Michael T. *Spaces Of Representation: The Struggle For Social Justice In Postwar Guatemala*. New York: Peter Lang, 2005.

Miller, Marilyn Grace. *Rise and Fall of the Cosmic Race: The Cult of Mestizaje in Latin America*. Austin: University of Texas Press, 2004.

Monasterios, Elizabeth. *La vanguardia plebeya del Titikaka. Gamaliel Churata y otras beligerancias estéticas en los Andes*. La Paz: Plural Editores, 2016.

Montejo, Victor. *The Adventures of Mister Puttison among the Maya*. Rancho Palos Verdes, CA: Fundación Yax Te', 2002.

———. *Las aventuras de Mister Puttison entre los mayas*. Rancho Palos Verdes, CA: Fundación Yax Te', 1998.

———. *The Bird Who Cleans the World and Other Mayan Fables*. Willimantic, CT: Curbstone, 1991.

———. *El Kanil, Man of Lightning: A Legend of Jacaltenango*. Translated by Virginia M. Scott. Carrboro, NC: Signal Books, 1984.

———. *Maya Intellectual Renaissance: Critical Essays on Identity, Representation, and Leadership*. Austin: University of Texas Press, 2005.

———. *Oral Tradition: An Anthropology Study of Jacaltec Folktale*. Albany, NY: State University of New York Press, 1989.

———. *Pixan, el cargador del espíritu*. Guatemala: Piedra Santa, 2014.

———. *El Popol Wuj: Libro sagrado de los mayas (versión para niños y jóvenes)*. Illustrated by Luis Garay. Toronto, ON: Groundwood Books/Douglas & McIntyre, 1999.

———. *El Q'anil: Man of Lightning*. Tucson: University of Arizona Press, 2001.

———. *Q'anil: El hombre rayo/Koman Q'anil: Ya'k'uh winaj*. Rancho Palos Verdes, CA: Fundación Yax Te', 1999.

———. *Sculpted Stones/Piedras labradas*. Translated by Victor Perera. Willimantic, CT: Curbstone, 1995.

———. *Testimony: Death of a Mayan Village*. Willimantic, CT: Curbstone, 1987.

———. *Voices from Exile: Violence and Survival in Modern Maya History*. Norman: University of Oklahoma Press, 1999.

Montejo, Víctor D., and Q'anil Akab'. *Brevísima Relación Testimonial de la Continua Destrucción del Mayab' (Guatemala)*. Providence, RI: Guatemala Scholars Network, 1992.

Montenegro, Gustavo Adolfo. "Luis de Lión: 'Yo siempre tuve un cielo.'" *Prensa Libre*. Guatemala City May 8, 2004. http://servicios.prensalibre.com/%20pl/domingo/archivo/domingo/2004/mayo08/090504/central.html. Accessed November 7, 2011.

———. "Soy un pez sacado del agua: Escritor Gaspar Pedro González." *Prensa Libre*. Guatemala City May 26, 2013: 12–13.

Morales, Mario Roberto. "Un libro que se niega a morir y a nacer." *Siglo Veintiuno*. October 29, 2002. http://www.lainsignia.org/2002/octubre/cul_104.htm. Accessed Oct. 14, 2013.

———. *Obraje*. México D.F.: Praxis, 2010.

Morales Santos, Francisco. "Luis de Lión, poeta de la cotidianidad y de la tierra." In *Conversatorio: homenaje imaginario a la obra literaria de Luis de Lión*, 29–32. Antigua Guatemala: Galería Imaginaria, 1991.

———. "Luis de Lión y Nuevo Signo." Unpublished. 2013.

———. *Madre, nosotros también somos historia/Nan, Ri Oj Xuquje Oj Ojer Tzij K'wi Chi Taq B'ix*. Guatemala: Fondo de Cultura Económica, 2001.

Moura-Koçoglu, Michaela. *Narrating Indigenous Modernities: Transcultural Dimensions in Contemporary Māori Literature*. Amsterdam: Rodopi, 2011.

Muyolema, Armando. "De la 'cuestión indígena' a lo 'indígena' como cuestionamiento: Hacia una crítica del latinoamericanismo, el indigenismo y el mestiz(o)aje." In *Convergencia de tiempos: estudios subalternos/contextos latinoamericanos*, edited by Ileana Rodríguez, 327–63. Amsterdam: Rodopi, 2001.

Nagel, Joane. *Race, Ethnicity, and Sexuality: Intimate Intersections, Forbidden Frontiers*. New York: Oxford University Press, 2003.

Nandy, Ashis. "History's Forgotten Doubles." *History and Theory* 34, no. 2, Theme Issue 34: World Historians and Their Critics (May 1995): 44–66.

Nayar, Pramod K. *Literary Theory Today*. New Delhi: Prestige/Asia Book Club, 2002.

Neruda, Pablo. *Canto General*. México D.F.: Talleres Gráficos de la Nación, 1950.

O'Leary, Timothy. "Foucault, Experience, Literature." *Foucault Studies* 5 (January 2008): 5–25.

Olen, Amy. "Guatemalan Discourse and Identity: Imaginaries of Indigeneity and Luis de Lión's Decolonial Shift." PhD. dissertation. University of Texas at Austin, 2015.

———. "Hacia una lectura decolonial de *El tiempo principia en Xibalbá* de Luis de Lión." Graduate paper. University of Texas at Austin, 2011.

Owen, David. *Maturity and Modernity: Nietzsche, Weber, Foucault and the Ambivalence of Reason*. London: Routledge, 1994.

Oxlaj Cúmez, Miguel Ángel. *Ru taqikil ri Sarima'/ La misión del Sarima'*. Guatemala: F&G Editores, 2009.

Palacios, Rita M. "Indigenousness and the Reconstruction of the Other in Guatemalan Indigenous Literature." PhD. dissertation, University of Toronto. https://tspace.library .utoronto.ca/bitstream/1807/19072/1/Palacios_Rita_M_200911_PhD_thesis.pdf, 2009. Accessed April 14, 2014.

Palerm, Ángel, Enrique Valencia, Margarita Nolasco, et al. *De eso que llaman antropología mexicana*. México D.F.: Escuela Nacional de Antropología e Historia, 1970.

Paz Cárcamo, Guillermo. *La máscara de Tekum/Ri uk'oj Tekum*. Guatemala: Cholsamaj, 2006.

Peñalosa, Fernando. *Introduction to the Sociology of Language*. Rowley, MA: Newbury House Publishers, 1981.

———. "La literatura maya. Tres perspectivas: el editor." *Istmo* 4 (July–December 2002): http://istmo.denison.edu/n04/foro/maya.html.

———. *The Mayan folktale: An introduction*. Ranchos Palos Verdes, CA: Yax Te' P, 1996.

———. *Tales and Legends of the Q'anbjob'al Maya*. Ranchos Palos Verdes, CA: Yax Te' P, 1995.

Perry, Keisha-Khan Y., and Joanne Rappaport. "Chapter 2: Making a Case for Collaborative Research with Black and Indigenous Social Movements in Latin America." In *Otros saberes: collaborative research on indigenous and Afro-descendant cultural politics*, edited by Charles R. Hale and Lynn Stephen, 30–48. Santa Fe, NM: SAR Press, 2013.

Pihama, Leonie. "Keynote: A Conversation About Kaupapa Māori Theory and Research." In *Kei Tua O Te Pae Hui Proceedings: the Challenges of Kaupapa Māori Research in the 21st Century*, edited by Te Wāhanga Jessica Hutchings, Helen Potter, and Katrina Taupo. Wellington: New Zealand Council for Educational Research, 2011.

Poe, Karen. "Sexo, cuerpo e identidad en *El tiempo principia en Xibalbá* de Luis de Lión." *Reflexiones* 82, no. 2 (2003): 83–91.

Pratt, Mary Louise. "Modernity and Periphery: Toward a Global and Relational Analysis." In *Beyond Dichotomies: Histories, Identities, Cultures, and the Challenge of Globalization*, edited by Elisabeth Mudimbe-Boy, 21–47. Albany, NY: State University of New York Press, 2002.

Quijano, Aníbal. "Colonialidad y Modernidad/Racionalidad." *Perú Indígena* 13, no. 29 (1991): 11–20.

———. "Colonialidad del poder, cultura y conocimiento en América Latina." *Anuario Mariateguiano* 9 (1997):113–21.

———. "Colonialidad del poder: eurocentrismo y América Latina." In *La Colonialidad del saber: eurocentrismo y ciencias sociales. Perspectivas latinoamericanas*, edited by Edgardo Lander, 201–42. Buenos Aires: CLACSO/UNESCO, 2003.

———. "Coloniality and Modernity/Rationality." *Cultural Studies* 21, nos. 2–3 (March/May 2007): 168–78.

Rabasa, José. "Intencionalidad, invención y reducción al absurdo en la invención de América." *Nuevo Mundo Mundos Nuevos*. Workshops 2012: 2. Réinvention de l'histoire coloniale. http://nuevomundo.revues.org/63440?lang=en. Accessed March 28, 2013.

———. *Without History: Subaltern Studies, The Zapata Insurgency, and the Specter of History*. Pittsburgh: University of Pittsburgh Press, 2010.

Rama, Ángel. *La ciudad letrada*. Hanover, NH: Ediciones del Norte, 1984.

Ramírez, Ricardo. *Documento de Marzo 1967*. Guatemala: [publisher not identified, undated].

Ramos, Julio. "Hemispheric Domains: 1898 and the Origins of Latin Americanism." *Journal of Latin American Cultural Studies* 10, no.3 (2001): 237–51.

Rappaport, Joanne. "Alternative Knowledge Producers in Indigenous Latin America." *LASA Forum* 36, no.1 (Spring 2005): 11–13.

Rappaport, Joanne, and Abelardo Ramos Pacho. "Collaboration and Historical Writing: Challenges for the Indigenous Academic Dialogue." In *Decolonizing Native Histories: Collaboration, Knowledge, and Language in the Americas*, edited by Florencia Mallon, 122–43. Durham, NC: Duke University Press, 2012.

Recinos, Adrián. *Crónicas Indígenas*. Guatemala: Editorial Universitaria, 1984.

———, ed. *Memorial de Sololá, Anales de los Kaqchikeles; Título de los Señores de Totonicapán*. Guatemala: Piedra Santa, 1998.

Reinaga, Fausto. *Indianidad*. La Paz: Litografías e Imprentas Unidas S.A., 1978.

Ribeiro, Gustavo Lins. "World Anthropologies: Cosmopolitics for a New Global Scenario in Anthropology." *Critique of Anthropology* 26, no. 4 (December 2006): 363–86.

Rice, Prudence M. *Maya Calendar Origins: Monuments, Mythistory, and the Materialization of Time*. Austin: University of Texas Press, 2007.

Riet Delsing, Maria. *Articulating Rapa Nui: Polynesian Cultural Politics in a Latin American Nation-State*. Santa Cruz: University of California Press, 2009.

Rivera Cusicanqui, Silvia. *Ch'ixinakax Utxiwa: Una reflexión sobre prácticas y discursos descolonizadores*. Buenos Aires: Tinta Limón, 2010.

Rodríguez, Ileana. "Reading Subalterns Across Texts, Disciplines, and Theories: From Representation to Recognition." In *The Latin American Subaltern Studies Reader*, edited by Ileana Rodríguez, 1–32. Durham, NC: Duke University Press, 2001.

Roys, Ralph L., trans. *The Book of Chilam Balam of Chuyamel*. Norman: University of Oklahoma Press, 1967.

Rus, Jan, and Diane L. Rus. "The Taller Tzotzil of Chiapas, Mexico: A Native Language Publishing Project, 1985–2002." In *Decolonizing Native Histories: Collaboration, Knowledge, and Language in the Americas*, edited by Florencia Mallon, 144–74. Durham, NC: Duke University Press, 2012.

Sahagún, Fray Bernardino de. *The Florentine Codex: General History of the Things of New Spain*. Translated by Arthur J. O. Anderson and Charles E. Dibble. Salt Lake City: University of Utah Press, 2002.

———. *Historia general de las cosas de la Nueva España*. México D.F.: Editorial Pedro Robredo, 1938.

Saldívar, José. *Trans-Americanity: Subaltern Modernities, Global Coloniality, and the Cultures of Greater Mexico*. Durham NC: Duke University Press, 2012.

Sandoval, Marta. “Humberto Ak’abal rechaza Premio Nacional de Literatura.” *elPeriódico de Guatemala*. Thursday January 22, 2004, Cultural Section. http://www.literaturaguatemalteca.org/akabal2.htm. Accessed September 2, 2013.

Sanford, Victoria. “Breaking Down the Wall of Impunity in Guatemala.” *NISGUA*. Thursday, March 14, 2013. http://nisgua.blogspot.com/2013/03/breaking-down-wall-of-impunity-in.html. Accessed April 28, 2013.

Sanjinés, Javier C. *Mestizaje Upside Down: Aesthetic Politics in Modern Bolivia*. Pittsburgh, PA: University of Pittsburgh Press, 2004.

———. *Rescoldos del pasado: Conflictos culturales en sociedades post-coloniales*. La Paz: PIEB, 2009.

Sarmiento, Domingo Faustino. *Facundo: civilización y barbarie*. Madrid: Cátedra, 1990.

Schwab, Gabriele. *Imaginary Ethnographies: Literature, Culture, & Subjectivity*. New York: Columbia University Press, 2012.

Sembou, Evangelia. “Foucault’s Genealogy.” 10th Annual Meeting of the International Social Theory Consortium. University College Cork, Ireland. June 16–17, 2011. http://www.academia.edu/679231/_Foucaults_Genealogy_. Accessed May 15, 2013.

Sieder, Rachel, Megan Thomas, George Vickers, and Jack Spence, eds. *Who Governs? Guatemala Five Years After the Peace Accords*. Cambridge: Hemisphere Initiatives, 2001.

Silva, Noenoe. *Aloha Betrayed: Native Hawaiian Resistance to American Colonialism*, Durham NC: Duke University Press, 2004.

Tuhiwai Smith, Linda. *Decolonizing Methodologies: Research and Indigenous Peoples*. 2nd ed. London: Zed Books, 2012.

———. “On Tricky Ground: Researching the Native in the Age of Uncertainty.” In *The SAGE Handbook of Qualitative Research*, edited by Norman K. Denzin, Yvonna S. Lincoln, 85–107. Thousand Oaks, CA: Sage, 2005.

Solórzano Foppa, Mario. “El nacionalismo indígena: Una ideología burguesa.” *Polémica* 3 (January–February 1982): 44–47.

Sommer, Doris. “Rigoberta’s Secrets.” *Latin American Perspectives* 18, no. 3, Voices of the Voiceless in Testimonial Literature, Part I (Summer, 1991): 32–50.

Spillers, Hortense J. *Black, White, and in Color: Essays on American Literature and Culture*. Chicago: University of Chicago Press, 2003.

Spivak, Gayatri Chakravorty. *An Aesthetic Education in the Era of Globalization*. Cambridge, MA: Harvard University Press, 2012.

———. *Death of a Discipline*. New York: Columbia University Press, 2003.

Stoll, David. *Rigoberta Menchú and the Story of all Poor Guatemalans*. Boulder, CO: Westview, 1998.

Stuart, David. "Leaf Glyphs: Spellings with yo and YOP." *Maya Decipherment: A Weblog on the Ancient Maya Script*. March 6, 2013. http://decipherment.wordpress.com/2 013/03/06/leaf-glyphs-spellings-with-yo-and-yop/. Accessed March 13, 2013.

Suleiman, Susan Rubin. "Judith Herman and Contemporary Trauma Theory." *Women's Studies Quarterly* 36, no. 1/2 (Spring–Summer 2008): 276–81.

Taller Casa de la Unidad del Pueblo Ja C'amabal I'b. Mexico: [publisher not identified], 1989.

Tedlock, Dennis. *Popol Vuh: The Definitive Edition of The Mayan Book of The Dawn of Life and The Glories of Gods and Kings*. New York: Touchstone, 1985.

———. ed. *Rabinal Achi: A Mayan Drama of War and Sacrifice*. New York: Oxford University Press, 2003.

Teuton, Christopher B. "Indigenous Orality and Oral Literatures." *The Oxford Handbook of Indigenous American Literature*. Edited by James H. Cox and Daniel Heath Justice. Oxford, UK: Oxford University Press, 2014.

Thiong'o', Ngũgĩ wa. *Decolonising the Mind: The Politics of Language in African Literature*. Portsmouth, NH: Heinemann, 1986.

Thorn, Judith. *The Lived Horizon of my Being: The Substantiation of the Self & and the Discourse of Resistance in Rigoberta Menchú, MM Bakhtin, and Víctor Montejo*. Tempe: Arizona State University Press, 1996.

Trigo, Abril. *Memorias migrantes: Testimonios y ensayos sobre la diáspora uruguaya*. Rosario, Santa Fe: Beatriz Viterbo/Ediciones Trilce, 2003.

Tuck, Eve, and K. Wayne Yang. "Decolonization Is not a Metaphor." *Decolonization: Indigeneity, Education & Society* 1, no. 1 (2012): 1–40.

Turner, Dale. *This is Not a Peace Pipe: Towards a Critical Indigenous Philosophy*. Toronto, ON: University of Toronto Press, 2006.

Upún Sipac, Damián. *Maya' Ajilab'äl Q'ij: La cuenta maya de los días*. Guatemala: Cholsamaj, 1999.

Vaioleti, Timote. "Talanoa Research Methodology: A Developing Position on Pacific Research." *Waikato Journal of Education* 12 (2006): 21–34.

Van Akkeren, Ruud. *Xib'alb'a y el nacimiento del nuevo sol: Una visión posclásica del colapso maya*. Guatemala: Piedra Santa, 2012.

Van Deusen, Nancy E. *Global Indios: The Indigenous Struggle for Justice in Sixteenth-Century Castile*. Durham, NC: Duke University Press, 2015.

Verran, Helen. "Engagements Between Disparate Knowledge Traditions: Toward Doing Difference Generatively and in Good Faith." In *Contested Ecologies: Dialogues in the South on Nature and Knowledge*, edited by Lesley Green, 141–61. Cape Town: HSRC Press, 2013.

———. "Re-imagining land ownership in Australia." *Postcolonial Studies* 1, no.2 (1998): 237–54.

Visser, Irene. "Trauma Theory and Postcolonial Literary Studies." *Journal of Postcolonial Writing* 47, no. 3 (2011): 270–82.

Wake, Eleanor. *Framing the Sacred: The Indian Churches of Early Colonial Mexico.* Norman: University of Oklahoma Press, 2010.

Wallerstein, Immanuel. "Remembering Andre Gunder Frank While Thinking about the Future." *Monthly Review* 60, no. 2 (June 2008): 50–61.

———. *World-Systems Analysis: An Introduction.* Durham, NC: Duke University Press, 2004.

Walsh, Catherine. "'Other' Knowledges, 'Other' Critiques: Reflections on the Politics and Practices of Philosophy and Decoloniality in the 'Other' America." *Transmodernity* 1, no. 3 (2012): 12–27. http://escholarship.org/uc/item/6qd721cp#page-17. Accessed March 23, 2014.

Warren, Kay B. *Indigenous Movements and Their Critics: Pan-Maya Activism in Guatemala.* Princeton, NJ: Princeton University Press, 1998.

Weaver, Jace. *That the People Might Live: Native American Literatures and Native American Community.* New York: Oxford University Press, 1997.

Wellmeier, Nancy J. "Santa Eulalia's People in Exile: Maya Religion, Culture, and Identity in Los Angeles." In *Gatherings in Diaspora: Religious Communities and the New Immigration*, edited by R. Stephen Warner and Judith G. Wittner, 97–122. Philadelphia, PA: Temple University Press, 1998.

Wilderson III, Frank B. *Red, White, & Black: Cinema and the Structure of U.S. Antagonisms.* Durham NC: Duke University Press, 2010.

Womack, Craig S. *Red on Red: Native American Literary Separatism.* Minneapolis: University of Minnesota Press, 1999.

Yashar, Deborah J. *Contesting Citizenship in Latin America: The Rise of Indigenous Movements and the Postliberal Challenge.* New York: Cambridge University Press, 2005.

Zavala, Roberto (CIESAS-Sureste), and Thomas C. Smith Stark (COLMEX), with the collaboration of Romelia Mó Isém, "The current situation in research on Mayan languages: Bibliography of linguistic studies of Mayan languages in Guatemala 1990–2006, with special reference to OKMA." Guatemala: Royal Norwegian Embassy in Guatemala, 2007.

Zapata Silva, Claudia. *Intelectuales indígenas en Ecuador, Bolivia y Chile: Diferencia, colonialismo y anticolonialismo.* Quito: Abya-Yala, 2013.

INDEX

www.ingramcontent.com/pod-product-compliance
Lightning Source LLC
LaVergne TN
LVHW040159080826
844660LV00001B/39